Weyerhaeuser Environmental Books

William Cronon, Editor

Weyerhaeuser Environmental Books

Weyerhaeuser Environmental Books explore human relationships with natural environments in all their variety and complexity. They seek to cast new light on the ways that natural systems affect human communities, the ways that people affect the environments of which they are a part, and the ways that different cultural conceptions of nature profoundly shape our sense of the world around us.

VOLUMES IN THE SERIES

The Natural History of Puget Sound Country

Arthur R. Kruckeberg

Forest Dreams, Forest Nightmares:
The Paradox of Old Growth in the Inland West

Nancy Langston

NANCY LANGSTON

Forest Dreams, Forest Nightmares

The Paradox of Old Growth in the Inland West

UNIVERSITY OF WASHINGTON PRESS

SEATTLE & LONDON

Forest Dreams, Forest Nightmares: The Paradox of Old Growth in the Inland West has been published with the assistance of a grant from the Weyerhaeuser Environmental Books Endowment, established by the Weyerhaeuser Company Foundation, members of the Weyerhaeuser family, and Janet and John Creighton.

Printed and bound in the United States of America by
Thomson-Shore, Inc.
Typeset by Graphic Composition, Inc. Athens, Georgia
Design by Audrey Meyer

Library of Congress Cataloging-in-Publication Data
Langston, Nancy.
Forest dreams, forest nightmares : the paradox of old growth in the Inland West / Nancy Langston.
p. cm.
"Weyerhaeuser environmental books"—Prelim. p.
Includes bibliographical references (p.   ) and index.
ISBN 0-295-97456-7 (alk. paper) .
1. Forest policy—Blue Mountains (Or. and Wash.)—History.   2. Forest reserves—Blue Mountains (Or. and Wash.)—Management—History.
3. United States. Forest Service—History.   4. Forest ecology—Blue Mountains (Or. and Wash.)—History.   5. Blue Mountains (Or. and Wash.). I. Title.
SD565.L36   1995
333.75'09795'7—dc20   95-14973
CIP

The paper used in this publication meets the minimum requirements of American National Standard for Information Sciences—Permanence of Paper for Printed Library Materials, ANSI Z39.48-1984.∞

Contents

Illustrations

Foreword:
With the Best
of Intentions

WILLIAM CRONON

In *Forest Dreams, Forest Nightmares,* Nancy Langston tells the story of changing human land use and forestry practice in the Blue Mountains of eastern Oregon and Washington. Since the Blues are not well known outside the Pacific Northwest, and since the history of professional forestry is not ordinarily the stuff of popular nonfiction, many would-be readers may be tempted to pass up this volume. To do so, however, would be a great mistake, for this is a book that deserves to be read by any American who cares about the future of the natural environment. Langston combines the technical expertise of an ecologist with the archival skill of a historian and the literary talent of a fine writer. The result is an immensely readable book in which the Blue Mountains emerge as a most suggestive paradigm for the environmental problems that Americans have confronted in many other parts of their national landscape over the past century. *Forest Dreams, Forest Nightmares* represents a new generation of scholarship in American environmental history, and could hardly be more relevant to contemporary debates about the environmental future not just of the Pacific Northwest but of the nation as a whole.

Stripped to its most basic argument, Langston's story is both simple and tragic. Americans came to the Blue Mountains with very clear visions of the resources and natural wealth they would find there. As has happened so often in our national history, early settlers exploited the land in a variety of ways depending on how they chose to earn their livelihoods, and each different group and activity provoked different changes in the landscape. By the time

professional foresters arrived in the Blues at the start of the twentieth century, they found a landscape that had already been dramatically transformed by longstanding human interventions stretching
back to before the arrival of white settlers. The foresters saw themselves as being quite different from the people who had preceded
them. Their job, they thought, was to bring the best, most enlight-
ened science to the task of managing the timber and grassland
resources of the mountains so as to achieve Gifford Pinchot's
much-vaunted goal of "the greatest good of the greatest number
for the longest time." Committed to a professional vision that es-
chewed self-interest and personal profit in an effort to serve the
nation as a whole, Forest Service employees began a decades-long
process of careful, scientifically informed management designed to
maximize the yield of the forest in ecologically sustainable ways
that would improve the forest's productivity and health. And yet,
as Langston demonstrates in poignant but devastating detail, the
result was an ecological disaster. By the 1990s, even the Forest Service was acknowledging that its own policies had helped produce
catastrophic results for the very forest they were intended to
protect.

Langston's goal in this book is not to engage in the all-too-
common practice of "bashing" the Forest Service or the people
who work for it. Quite the contrary. Trained as a forest ecologist
herself, she writes with great sympathy toward those who confronted an ecosystem they thought they understood in pursuit of
goals that seemed to them both ecologically and socially benign.
What fascinates her, and what makes her book so troubling, is that
actions taken with the best of intentions could yield results so trag-
ically unexpected. *Forest Dreams, Forest Nightmares* is quite simply
the most comprehensive and sophisticated study of ecological
management in a western national forest that has yet been written
by an environmental historian. And yet for all of its technical mas-
tery and fine-grained detail, the book never loses sight of its core
argument, which brilliantly explores the ways in which our expectations and ideas of the natural world shape the way we use and
manipulate it, often in ways that we ourselves understand imper-
fectly at best.

It is this core argument that makes Langston's book so relevant and so important to contemporary environmental debates in many other settings. The problems that foresters faced in the Blue Mountains flowed as much from their own scientific paradigms as from the ecological phenomena going on in the forest itself—phenomena that those paradigms sometimes rendered all too invisible. The moral of this story should be clear. Even well-intentioned management can have disastrous consequences if it is predicated on the wrong assumptions, and yet testing those assumptions is always much harder than people realize. To do so, we must realize that ecosystems are profoundly *historical*, meaning that they exist *in time* and are the products as much of their own past as of the timelessly abstract processes we think we see going on in them. Perhaps Langston's most important argument is that ecological management will be most robust in the face of unexpected change if it incorporates a much richer historical understanding of the system being managed. To see how foresters got into trouble in the Blues, we need to examine the changing ecological dynamics *in time* of the forests they were managing—and, no less, the changing cultural dynamics *in time* of the human ideas of nature that led the foresters themselves to act as they did. If the consequence of this book is to encourage resource managers and ecologists to work more closely with historians and other students of human culture to find better ways of using forests and other natural resources, then the nightmare of the Blue Mountains may in the end move us a little closer to the dream so many share of a more sustainable future for humanity and nature alike.

Acknowledgments

Without the enthusiastic and critical faith of Sievert Rohwer, professor of zoology and my graduate adviser at the University of Washington, this project would never have been started, much less finished. When I decided to make the switch from evolutionary ecologist to ecological historian and writer, Sievert's excitement about the idea helped me over the inevitable moments of uncertainty. He was the ideal audience, because he initially knew little about forests or history but was endlessly curious about both.

Bill Cronon, the editor for the Weyerhaeuser Series, vastly improved this book with his extensive and insightful comments. His vision of what the book could be helped transform it from a technical dissertation into a work that could appeal to an audience composed not just of foresters.

The Forest Service in the Blue Mountains was enthusiastic about this project and gave me every possible assistance. Torolf Torgersen, Arthur Tiedemann, Jon Skovlin, Steve Fletcher, and D. Dether—among many others—generously spent a great deal of time talking with me about Blues forests. Numerous staff members at the Malheur Supervisor's Office, the Wallowa Whitman Supervisor's Office, and the Umatilla Supervisor's Office helped me find historical files that had been buried in attic storage rooms.

Many residents of the Blues talked with me about the land, and their views made this a much more balanced work. Mark Henjum of Oregon Department of Fish and Wildlife discussed wildlife issues with me, and showed me Jerry Gildemeister's report on wildlife. Rick George of the Confederated Tribes of the Umatilla helped with Upper Grande Ronde watershed questions. The Donovans offered me a place to stay on their ranch near Enterprise, and talked with me about grazing and wilderness issues. In Walla Walla, Judy Johnson of the National Audubon Society gave me a place to stay whenever I came through, and both Judy and Kevin Scribner of the Blue Mountain Native Forest Alliance were enthusiastic critics as well as great advocates of this work. Their faith in the importance of a historical analysis helped keep my own faith intact.

Rita Dixon—once a fellow ecology intern at Manomet Observatory, then an ecologist with the Forest Service—first introduced me to the Blues eight years ago. Over the years, Rita has taken me to numerous fine places in the Blues, not least among them the marble baths at Hot Springs, the Eagle Cap wilderness, Hells Canyon, and the sage grouse leks. Talking with Rita about cavity nesters, forest ecology, and logging effects on wildlife helped inspire me to write this work.

Richard White, Gordon Orians, and James Karr, all of the University of Washington, were generous with their suggestions. Staff at the National Archives and the Pacific Northwest Branch of the National Archives were very helpful, and the librarians at the University of Washington forestry library tracked down numerous government reports for me.

Financial support came from the American Philosophical Society's Michaux Research Grant in Silvicultural History. I began the project while I was supported by a National Science Foundation predoctoral fellowship. The Eddy Fellowship also provided support while I was a postdoctoral fellow at the Burke Museum of the University of Washington. I am deeply grateful to the trustees at Dorland Mountain Arts Colony, who offered me a residency at a critical time in writing this work. Finally, I thank my mother, Joann Langston, for many things (including chasing down photos in the National Archives), but mostly for having faith in whatever strange new thing I decided to do, no matter how obscure or risky it seemed at the time.

Forest Dreams, Forest Nightmares

The Paradox of Old Growth in the Inland West

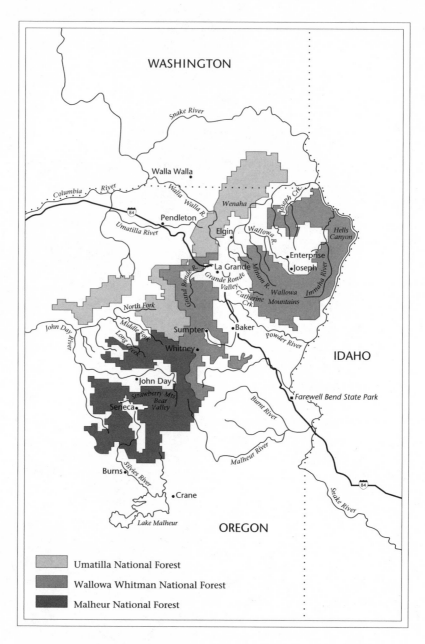

WASHINGTON

Snake River

Walla Walla

Columbia   River

Wenaha

Pendleton

Umatilla River

Elgin

Wallowa R.

Joseph Crk.

Innaha River

Hells Canyon

Enterprise

Joseph

La Grande

Grande Ronde Valley

Catherine Crk.

Wallowa Mountains

North Fork

Sumpter

Baker

Powder River

IDAHO

John Day River

Middle Fork

Long Creek

Whitney

John Day

Strawberry Mts.

Bear Valley

Seneca

Farewell Bend State Park

Burnt River

Malheur River

Burns

Silvies River

Crane

Snake River

Lake Malheur

OREGON

Umatilla National Forest

Wallowa Whitman National Forest

Malheur National Forest

The three national forests in the Blues: the Wallowa Whitman, the Malheur, and the Umatilla, showing towns, rivers, and mountains.

Introduction

When whites first came to the Blue Mountains of eastern Oregon and Washington in the early nineteenth century, they found a land of lovely open forests full of yellow-bellied ponderosa pines five feet across. These were stately giants the settlers could trot their ponies between, forests so promising that people thought they had stumbled into paradise. But they were nothing like the humid forests to which easterners were accustomed. Most of the forest communities across the inland West were semi-arid and fire-adapted, and whites had no idea what to make of the fires.

After a century of trying to manage the forests, what had seemed like paradise was irrevocably lost. The great ponderosa pines vanished, and in their place were thickets of fir trees. Although the ponderosas had resisted most insect attacks, the firs that replaced them were the favored food for numerous pests. As firs invaded the old pine forests, insect epidemics spread throughout the dry western forests. By 1991, on the five and a half million acres of Forest Service lands in the Blue Mountains, insects had attacked half the forest stands, and in some stands nearly 70 percent of the trees were infested.

Even worse, in the view of foresters and many locals, was the threat of catastrophic fires. Although light fires had burned through the open pines every ten years or so, few had exploded into infernos that killed entire stands of trees. But as firs grew underneath the pines and succumbed to insect damage, far more fuel became available to sustain major fires. By the beginning of the 1990s, one major fire after another was sweeping the inland West, until it seemed as if the forests might all go up in smoke.

The Forest Service understandably saw the situation as a major crisis in forest health. A few years earlier, loggers had harvested over 860 million board feet a year of timber from the Blues—nearly 600 million of this from the three national forests in the area, the Wallowa Whitman, the Malheur, and the Umatilla. To get some sense of the magnitude of these harvests, consider that a board foot—the standard measure for timber—is a piece of wood twelve inches square and one inch thick. The total harvests of Forest Service timber in President Clinton's 1994 forest plan for the entire Northwest were set at about one billion board feet a year—only 15 percent more than the Blues alone were producing a few years earlier. The Blues once had the largest stand of commercial forest between the Cascades and the Rockies, but by 1993 the harvests had slowed to a trickle. A lot of money, a lot of timber, and a lot of jobs were at stake. In an unusual admission of guilt and confusion, the Forest Service stated that this crisis was caused by its own forest management practices. Yet no one could agree exactly which practices had caused the problems, or why foresters followed those practices in the first place.

On one level, the landscape alterations were the result of a series of ecological changes. When the federal foresters suppressed fires in the open forests dominated by ponderosa pine, firs grew faster than pines in the resultant shade, and they soon came to dominate the forests. When droughts hit, the firs succumbed to insect epidemics. What these changes mean, however, is not a simple question. Declaring a crisis in forest health assumes a shared cultural ideal of what a healthy forest should be. The succession of ponderosa pine stands to fir-dominated stands, and the resultant insect infestations and catastrophic fires, do not mean that the forest itself is threatened: they only mean it is changing. If we were to stop trying to fix the forests today and step back and watch the results, spruce budworm and Douglas-fir tussock moth epidemics would kill numerous trees, and fires would kill many more. But such an outcome would not necessarily be a disaster; it might indeed be better than the results of intensive attempts to "fix" the forests. The result would be ideal conditions for the establishment of new ponderosa and larch stands interspersed with older mixed-conifer stands in areas where the fires had been less intense. What would be threatened by insect epidemics and catastrophic fires is not the forest, but our ability to extract certain resources. Thus the forest health crisis in the Blues is political more than ecological.

Changes in the land are never just ecological changes. People made the decisions that led to ecological changes, and their motives for making those decisions were complex. Many environmentalists claim that things went wrong in the inland West because of simple greed: the Forest Service worked hand in hand with the industry to cut trees as fast as they could, and this devastated the forests. Many other people claim just the opposite: the forests fell apart because the Forest Service bowed to the demands of sentimental preservationists and refused to manage intensively enough to save the forest from its natural enemies—fire, insects, and disease.

Neither of these versions tells the whole truth. Forest problems did not come about because of greed, incompetence, or poor science; better science would not have prevented the current crisis. Across the inland West, the troubled history of land management has its roots not in ignorance but in American visions of the proper human relationship to nature. Americans shaped the western landscapes according to a complex set of ideals about what the perfect forest ought to look like and what people's role in shaping that perfect forest ought to be. Landscape changes were the result of human attempts to manage, perfect, and simplify the forests: to transform what one forester called in 1915 "the general riot of natural forest"—by which he meant the old growth—into a regulated, productive, sustained-yield forest. In other words, this is not just an ecology story; it is a story about the complex metaphors people use to mediate their relationship to nature—and the ways those metaphors have led to millions of acres of dying trees.

Whites came to the Blues for many reasons, but foremost among them was the desire for land, and for a particular relationship with land. They wanted not just to admire nature, but to put natural resources to good use. Federal foresters, in particular, came with a vision of working with wild nature to make it perfect: efficient, orderly, and useful. To many people, this meant extracting whatever commodities they could from a place they saw as an earthly paradise. Most whites viewed resource extraction not as destruction, however, but as a long-term partnership. They wanted to be good land stewards, to make everything just right, to clean out every timber stand so it would be free of decay and full of elk, and to transform every marsh into an orderly and fertile field. Yet in trying to make the land green and productive, they ended up making it sterile. This is not a story with a villain (the greedy timberman) and a hero (the brave environmentalist). Instead, it is a tragedy in which decent people with the best of intentions destroyed what they cared for most.

On June 25, 1991, the *Seattle Post-Intelligencer* had a front-page story by Rob Taylor with the headline: "Man-made blight strips mountains; 'Catastrophe' feared east of Cascades." The story argued that the forests were dying because six million acres of insect-resistant ponderosa pine forests had changed to fir forests through Forest Service mismanagement. As an ecologist, I decided to quantify exactly how much the Forest Service had changed the landscape, but I soon realized that this would not be a simple task. There is no single moment in the past we can point to and say: "That's what the forests were really like before people started messing around with them." Yet an extraordinary policy directive has stated that the Forest Service must manage the Blue Mountains so that future forests resemble the forests that were here before whites arrived. No old growth, for example, can be cut from watersheds that have less old growth than was there a century ago, and all forests are supposed to be returned to their original state, or at least to within what the Forest Service calls the "natural range of variability." Yet landscapes always change, regardless of human influence, and the forests that existed just before the Forest Service began management were not any more "natural" than the current forests, even if we might now find them more desirable. Most ecologists working in the Blues realize that there was no single original forest, yet they are required to manage as if there were.

Much more frustrating than the difficulty of saying exactly how much the forests had changed was finding a persuasive reason *why* the forests had changed. How could insect-resistant forests have changed to susceptible forests without anybody noticing? Why were federal foresters unaware that the forests would change if they suppressed fire? Didn't they know anything about plant succession? The answers I first heard from foresters now working in the Blues were simple: nobody in the early years of the Forest Service worried about plant succession or fire ecology. Nobody dreamed these changes would happen; foresters were just ecological innocents out cutting trees. One day they woke up and noticed in a panic that their five million acres of lovely open pine stands had suddenly changed to tangled forests full of fire and bugs and dead firs. As explanations go, this was less than satisfying. Were early foresters really that simple-minded? I dug deeper, and realized almost immediately that the first foresters in the Blues were obsessed with ecology, fire, and change—particularly with preventing the succession of pine forests to fir forests. They were extremely self-conscious of their mission, and proud of their new scientific discipline. Nevertheless, for all their concerns about the possibility of pine forests changing to fir forests, they set into motion exactly the changes they were trying to guard against.

When you talk to Forest Service people working in the Blues today, you hear many stories about what went wrong. One set of ecologists sees the source of the problem as too much management. They argue that excessive harvests, soil compaction, selective logging that removed ponderosa pines and left only firs behind, combined with even-aged management—all this led to a simplified ecosystem that became increasingly susceptible to epidemics. Many other Forest Service employees believe exactly the opposite: they put the blame on past decades of light, selective cutting and argue that only intensive timber management can save the forests. These foresters argue that since ponderosa pine is shade intolerant, clearcutting, even-aged harvests, and intensive management are the only ways to ensure that fir stands do not replace pine stands. In their view, the best way to eliminate insects, disease, and fire from a stand is to manage it as intensively as possible.

These two perspectives on the history of forest health problems obviously lead to radically different management prescriptions. It is also probably obvious that these two versions of what went

wrong are, at least in part, shaped by the different ideologies of
their proponents. A traditional forester who sees the "natural" old-
growth forest as a place of decay and waste tends to believe that
the human role in forestry is to prevent waste and promote a clean,
productive, growing stand. Conversely, someone trained in an ecosystem perspective will see insects and disease as having value in a
forest, and will value old-growth stands more than single-species
stands under even-aged management.

Ideology is not everything, however, even though it certainly
shapes one's view of who is to blame about the past. The story is
more complicated than either perspective suggests. The training
of early foresters was heavily influenced by European silviculture,
which had as its ideal a waste-free, productive stand: nature per-
fected by human efficiency. Early Blue Mountains foresters all
agreed that their goal was to transform decadent old growth into
vigorous, regulated stands for sustained-yield forestry. Yet at first
they never tried to implement these ideals, largely because there
were no markets for the trees. It was neither economically nor technologically feasible to cut the Blue Mountains forests heavily
enough to bring about intensive sustained-yield forestry. Now,
however, intensive management is economically unjustifiable (a
majority of Blue Mountains forest sales were below cost in 1991),
and increasingly ideologically unjustifiable. But still intensive
management is proving extremely hard to displace. The point here
is not the strangeness of Forest Service management, but that these
practices do not make sense if you consider them in ecological,
economic, or ideological terms alone.

Early foresters tried to simplify the complexity of old-growth
forests, with the hope of making them produce more of the commodities people wanted, and fewer of the commodities people
didn't want. In the process of trying to manage extremely complex
landscapes, foresters set into motion a chain of events that increasingly swung out of their control. In part, this is certainly a caution-
ary tale. When I started this project, I was a scientist who believed
her mission was to save the wilderness—someone who felt that
science was indisputably on her side. But what I learned sobered
me. The federal foresters had come with attitudes much the same

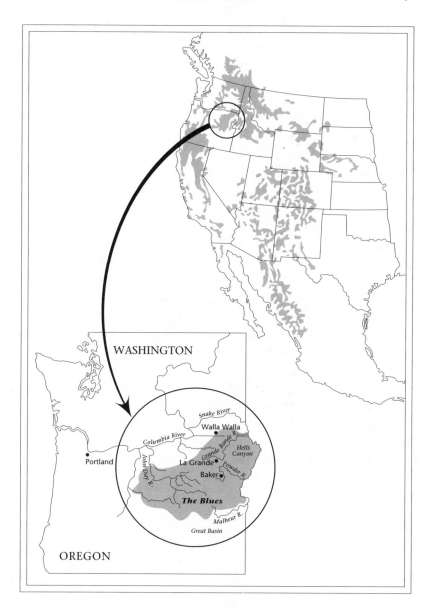

Map 1. The range of ponderosa pine in the inland West, and the Blue Mountains in particular. After Sudworth, *Forest Atlas* (1913), 16; and Thomas, *Wildlife Habitats in Managed Forests: The Blue Mountains of Oregon and Washington* (1979), 19.

as my own—with the certainty that they could use science to fix the forests, and that with the help of science, they could do no wrong. Foresters got into trouble not because they were greedy, but because they were absolutely certain it was their mission to save the forest from its enemies, which they defined as the logging industry, fire, and decay. Yet their enthusiasm and faith made it difficult for them to see what was going wrong.

What happened in the Blue Mountains happened across the American West, from Washington south to Arizona and from the Dakotas west to the Pacific: wherever there were dry forests dominated by pine (Map 1). The inland West has witnessed a massive set of errors, tragedies, and follies, yet these disasters have the potential to catalyze a revolution in the way we live and work on the land in the West. This is an exciting time in land management. As a nation—as foresters, land managers, tribal members, environmentalists, ecologists, farmers, ranchers, and loggers—we are trying to figure out new ways of working with the western lands. Yet before we can come up with sustainable ways of managing ecosystems, we need to understand how we ended up in the current mess. Without a historical and ecological perspective on what has happened to the landscape, there is little chance that current restoration efforts will avoid repeating past mistakes. To help us decide how many trees to cut, how many cows to graze—how to work with the land, instead of against it—we need a new set of stories about the relationship between wild forests and people.

Place and Ecology

In the winter of 1811, an exhausted group of thirty-two white men, three Indian men, one Indian woman, and two children, all led by an American named Wilson Price Hunt, crossed through a land of canyons and mountains east of the Snake River. They were racing the British to the Pacific, hoping to establish an American fur empire that would rival the British Hudson's Bay Company. Instead, they got thoroughly lost. Ignoring the advice of Shoshones who told them to turn back, Hunt's party spent a month struggling through snowdrifts into bewildering Hells Canyon, the deepest canyon in North America. They expected the river to lead to the Pacific, but it took them into a nightmarish maze where nothing was what they expected. Canyons led to cliff walls, not to the gentle valleys they hoped for. The snows got deeper and they got desperate. One man fell off a cliff to his death. Marie Dorion, the Indian wife of the interpreter, bore a child along the Powder River, and nine days later the infant died. Finally, close to starvation, Hunt's party stumbled on a lovely snow-free valley filled with beaver and friendly Shoshone Indians, who obligingly saved their lives. This valley they named the Grande Ronde, and then they started over the hazy, snow-covered mountains just beyond: the Blue Mountains.[1]

Two years later, Marie Dorion and her children spent an even worse winter in the Blues, after all the other members of her party were killed by hostile Indians when they were out checking beaver traps. Marie took refuge in a canyon near the headwaters of the Walla Walla River, keeping herself and her children alive for the winter on the smoked flesh of two horses. When she finally emerged with her story, the American fur traders began to get discouraged. They were no closer to their dreams of great wealth; all they had to show for their efforts were lost explorers and dead trappers. After a series of similar mishaps, the American attempt to establish a base for the fur trade ended in failure, and the British won control of the trade.

People now tend to read these misadventures as purely political stories, but they are also stories written upon the land. What effects did extracting resources have on the local ecology, and what effects did the local ecology have on the people who tried to extract resources? Different groups came to the Blues with differing ideas about what their relationship to the land should be, and these cultural ideas shaped how they saw the land and how they acted in the land. Some people fell off a cliff because they were convinced that all normal valleys ought to lead to outlets, not to cliff edges; others starved to death because they were convinced that a passable route had to exist to the Pacific. The history of outsiders in the Blues has been a history of people getting lost—lost in geographical space, lost in their attempts to quickly extract fortunes, and lost in their hopes of reshaping the landscape to fit an American ideal.

Whites who first arrived in the Blues found a land completely unlike the humid forests of home. Most of the forest communities across the inland West were semi-arid and fire-adapted, and whites rarely knew what to make of these fires. What seemed familiar at first glance proved not to be, and this was unsettling. People expected forests to be moist and fertile, but these forests seemed too dry, too open, and not very fertile. Fires burned much more often than people thought normal or desirable, and no one understood how forests could survive constant fires. Sagebrush typically indicated poor soil, but the soil under this sagebrush seemed better than much of the forest soil. Rivers normally drained to the sea, but many of these rivers drained into the Great Basin—a salty, barren, frightening place—and never flowed out. The canyons were far too steep; people could not believe what they saw. Trees grew on top of these steep canyons but not down by the water, where trees were supposed to grow. It seemed like someone had turned the world upside down.

Outsiders came to the Blues to mine, to trap, to cross the mountains in search of land for farming, but these men and women never thought of the area as a single region defined by a specific resource. They saw simply several mountain ranges (the Elkhorns, the Blue Mountains, the Strawberries, the Wallowas) with forests in the upper elevations, grasslands in the mid elevations, and sagebrush in the canyons. Nobody thought of the area as a region until the Bureau of Forestry reserve inspectors came from the East in 1900 to classify and protect forests under the new federal forest reserve system. The government inspectors had the task of defining the area as a place worthy of government preservation, a place they could securely set within political and economic boundaries. Their definition of the region depended not on the mountains but on the commodity they believed to be most valuable there: trees.

The Blues are still largely defined as a region by their trees. The term basically includes the range of ponderosa pine and Douglas-fir in northeastern Oregon and southeastern Washington. The Blue Mountains are a forested place marooned in the seemingly endless, barren, inhospitable lands of the arid interior Northwest. Trees are not all that is special about the Blues, but they are one of the region's critical resources, and this is a place with a history—like that of all the West—shaped by disputes over whose vision will determine how natural resources are used. The relationship between people and a place is never simple; people shape the land and the land shapes the people, and sometimes both are shaped by forces largely outside their control—forces that originate in another place entirely.

To outsiders, the Blues are a hinterland far from any place where political decisions are made. Yet when whites first came, the Blues were the nexus of a thriving trade between Plateau, Great Plains, and Pacific Coast Indian nations. For the next half century, they became the focus of international struggles over control of the beaver-trapping empire. After the beaver trade dwindled, the Blues became a critical foreground for American expansion west, as tens of thousands of Americans struggled through a formidable crossing of the mountains on the Oregon Trail. But now the Blues have receded to the margins of our culture's perceptions. Most Ameri-

cans have never heard of them; even some lifelong residents of the
Pacific Northwest stare in bewilderment when you mention them.
"Are they in Virginia?" is what most people ask, thinking of the
Blue Ridge Mountains. The region does not meld with popular conceptions of a wet and mild Northwest, nor does it fit into the
slightly more accurate perception of a barren interior, a dry desert
wasteland.

This obscurity is part of what is so interesting about the Blues.
For many whites, the Blues were just a place to extract commodities: the "industrial forests" was their nickname in the 1980s when
logging was at its peak. But for other people, both whites and Indians, the region's deceptive mazes and high, dry plateaus offered a
particular kind of freedom. They were a place to get lost in, a place
to be left alone in, and that was exactly what many people wanted.
Some Nez Percé, for example, spent winters between the knife-edge
cliffs of the Imnaha River and the Snake River, and unless people
knew the canyons well, they were not going to mess around in
Nez Percé territory. The deepest canyon in North America—Hells
Canyon—was hidden in here. On one ridge, there would be snow
and ice and Engelmann spruce, just like any other high forest in
the West; but if you stepped too quickly, you would plunge six
thousand feet to a desert gorge of cactus and temperatures well
over 100 degrees. Intruders into Nez Percé lands found themselves
lost in blind canyons, vulnerable and dependent on the good will
of the people who knew the land's secrets. Many whites also took
off for the canyons and the high plateaus, where they hoped to
be left alone to wander without the constraints of the dominant
American culture. Instead, they had to reckon with the land's constraints, and many people gave up trying after a few hard winters.

Eventually, however, white Americans thought they'd gotten
the Blues under control. They'd driven the Indians out of the canyons and settled them on tiny reservations; they'd put the forests
under efficient management; they'd uprooted the sagebrush by using chains; they'd reclaimed the marshy valleys, ditched them and
drained them and planted them with alfalfa. There were schools in
the towns and soon even sidewalks. By 1908 matters seemed tame
enough for nostalgia to set in, and the myth of the wild west blos-

somed in the Pendleton Roundup—an elaborate tourist ritual complete with painted Wild Indians pretending to kill white people.

This high, dry sweep of open land promised a great deal to the early white settlers and government managers—timber, minerals, grazing, space, privacy, a home, a new life, a new world. But something went wrong with those dreams. The harder that people tried to manage, the worse things got. The more that foresters tried to keep out fires, the fiercer they burned; the more they sprayed insects, the worse the next round of epidemics turned out to be. When foresters finally banished light fires from the ponderosa forests, those forests changed, and nobody liked the changes.

To understand what went wrong in the Blues, we need to consider the complexity of the dry forests, particularly how they differed from humid eastern forests. Water and fire—and the changes that water and fire brought—were at the heart of these differences. Much of what went wrong was a failure to pay attention to the land's signs. Trees made the Blues appear to be a fertile, promising, easy place, but those perceptions proved illusory. The forests' fertility was based on ash soils that were quite different from the eastern soils, and when managers tried to apply eastern forestry techniques, the ash soils were decimated. The constraints that aridity imposed were unfamiliar to people who knew only forests that grew in moister places.

The critical resource in the Blues was not trees or grass, or even soil, but water. Water—the lack of water, the distribution of water, the storage of water—affected every aspect of forest and grassland ecology. Because most precipitation was in the form of winter snows, the water that trees needed to grow came not from rains that fell during that period of growth, but from stored water.[2] Anything that decreased the ability of the forest soils to hold snowfall had magnified effects on the forests.

Annual precipitation varied across the Blues, with some areas receiving less than 10 inches a year, and others up to 62 inches.[3] More snow fell the higher one went; likewise, the north and east slopes tended to be much moister and cooler and hold snow longer, partly explaining why they supported denser forests. Nothing was mild or temperate or easy about this climate: temperatures on the Umatilla ranged from −30°F to 100°F. On the Malheur National Forest, farther south, it was even hotter and colder and drier: in the winter the temperature could drop to −56°F, and in the summer it sometimes reached 110 degrees in the shade.

Warm winds in the early spring were common. They often brought rain that melted the snow more quickly than the soils could handle, leading to floods in the spring and dried-up creeks in the summer. Floods were normal, not solely an effect of overgrazing or overlogging. But patterns of vegetation cover and some tree harvesting practices certainly affected the way water moved across the soil and into the soil. People easily caused changes that they neither expected nor wanted. Graze too many cattle in an area and the creek would dry up; cut too many trees in a watershed and the spring floods would get even worse.

Nothing was ever stable about the climate in the Blues. Droughts, disturbances, and wide fluctuations in temperature, rainfall, and snow accumulation were normal—not rare natural disasters that people could engineer away. The forests and grasslands that did well here were those that had adapted to this variability. Tree-ring studies show that droughts have occurred about every thirty-seven years during the last three centuries.[4] But managers have had trouble taking this into account, because from 1952 to 1980 the Blues had unusually high precipitation and unusually low variation, and the government based its expectations of normal rainfall on this period. Trying to manage the forests as if droughts were a rare condition meant that too many trees were cut, because foresters often greatly overestimated the rate at which trees could grow in the Blues.

The Forests of the Blues

Geological history explains much of what seemed so unusual about the Blue Mountains to the early foresters: the steep canyons, the trees where no one expected trees, the fragility of the soils. About 65 million years ago, repeated layers of lava flows and volcanic ash spread over the Blues; some 40 million years later, during the Miocene epoch, fluid basalts flowed up through holes in the lava. Layers of hard basalt on top of lava and soft volcanic ash created a landscape entirely different from the rolling hill and valley terrain of the East. Because less dense flows eroded much more rapidly than denser layers on top, rivers carved these lava layer cakes into knife-edge canyons running nearly straight up and down. These layers have made for a land that is slippery, prone to landslides, and often spectacular: a place of "great rivers coursing through deep, perpendicular, basaltic walled canyons below the undulating surface of a vast treeless plain," in the geographer Donald Meinig's words.[5]

None of this by itself would explain why huge trees grow in the middle of a barren steppe: water alone is not sufficient for the growth of ponderosa pines five feet across. Beginning about 6,500 years ago, Mount Mazama in southern Oregon exploded repeatedly, creating Crater Lake and blowing a layer of volcanic ash three to four feet deep across the Blues. These thick ash soils were the foundation for much of the area's forest productivity. This fertility, however, proved fragile: step too hard on ash soils and they compact into hardpan that will not grow a thing; cut too many trees on steep slopes and the soils wash away.[6]

Not all the Blues were forested when whites arrived. The steep south and west slopes were often barren or sparsely timbered, whereas the north slopes supported thick stands of trees. This pattern emerged because it was much hotter and dryer on the slope facing the sun. Fewer trees, herbs, and shrubs could stand the heat, and that in turn meant fewer roots to hold the soils in place each year when the spring thaw came. This created a self-perpetuating cycle: fewer roots allowed more soil to erode, so less vegetation could grow, which meant next year even more soil ran down to the rivers.

Nearly half the area of the Blues did not support trees at all, either because the soil had eroded too much for trees to grow or the site was too dry and hot. Repeated fires may also have converted some forest to grassland or sagebrush steppe. The shifting balance between forest, sagebrush, and grassland depended in large part on the site's climate regime, which varied dramatically across the Blues. In the northern end of the region, cool marine air swept up the Columbia Gorge from the Pacific Ocean, rising only 1,500 feet before it reached the Blues. These cool winds brought a fairly mild climate to the northern mountains, with minimum tempera- ture variation, maximum humidity, wet snow, and high rainfall. In sharp contrast, dry winds from the Great Basin parched the southern end of the Blues, leading to a continental climate with extreme temperature variations, little rain, and fairly low snowfall. Between the two extremes were areas with mixed climate, which favored diverse vegetation patterns. Cold air draining down hills in these mixed climate areas would create cooler pockets where lodgepole pine flourished in the midst of other trees. Frost heaving along the backbones of ridges led to shallow-soiled scablands where little could grow. In the cooler areas, sagebrush gave way to grasslands, since sagebrush competed poorly in areas with winter cloud cover.[7]

Part of what seemed strange to easterners, especially to those used to the vast stretches of climax forests in Maine and the Mid- west, was the diversity of vegetation types within the Blues (Map 2). When the government forest inspectors came to classify the Blues forests at the turn of the century, the variety of trees, habi- tats, and forest types astonished them. The inspectors walked through steep treeless grasslands covered with sagebrush and bunchgrass, and then crossed into juniper woodlands. These gave way to ponderosa forests with stately trees five feet wide, spaced in as open and pleasing a pattern as any that the inspectors knew from the landscaped parks in eastern cities. Along the creeks, strips of lush cottonwood forests shadowed the waters, and these cool riparian zones offered shelter from the brutal summer sun. When the inspectors crossed from the south face of a canyon to the north face, they moved out of the ponderosa forests into much denser forests dominated by Douglas-fir, grand fir, and larch—communi- ties they called the north-slope type or fir-larch forests. At first glance, these north-slope forests appeared uniform, but when the foresters looked more closely, they realized that there were many small patches of larch, fir, spruce, and pine jostled together. The inspectors climbed higher into the hills, finding themselves in thickets of lodgepole pine. Their way became nearly impassable, as

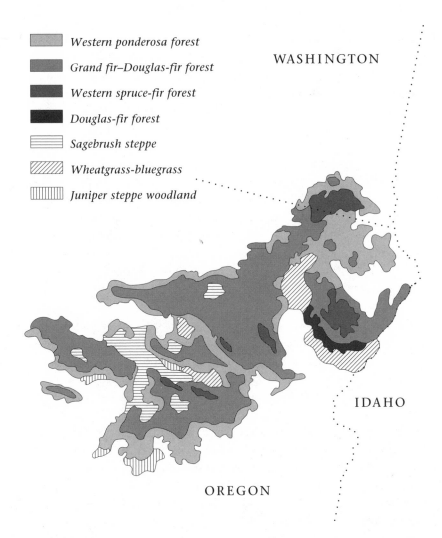

Western ponderosa forest

Grand fir–Douglas-fir forest

Western spruce-fir forest

Douglas-fir forest

Sagebrush steppe

Wheatgrass-bluegrass

Juniper steppe woodland

WASHINGTON

IDAHO

OREGON

Map 2. The diversity of forest and range ecosystems of the Blue Mountains in 1964, illustrating "potential natural vegetation," or the climax communities that would theoretically exist in the absence of disturbance. Mixed-conifer, Douglas-fir, and grand fir communities are all grouped together into one community here: "Grand fir–Douglas-fir forest." Much of this community would once have been dominated by ponderosa pine, rather than fir. After Küchler (1964), and Thomas, *Wildlife Habitats in Managed Forests: The Blue Mountains of Oregon and Washington* (1979), 20.

piles of dead wood and tangles of wind-thrown lodgepole blocked the route. If the men kept climbing, they would enter high, eerie forests filled with the stumps of subalpine fir and contorted, wind-twisted whitebark pines. Where fires had burned in small, hot patches, lush meadows interrupted the high forests, and finally the forests gave way to mats of wind-cropped fir and then rock and snow.[8]

Out of all these forests, it was the ponderosa pines that caught men's eyes. These were trees to warm a lumberman's heart: the largest ponderosa recorded on the Wallowa forest was 74 inches across at breast height, a granddaddy of a tree. Even the averages were impressive. Back in 1912, the average size ponderosa pine on the Wallowa was 33 inches across; eighty years later the average had shrunk to 19 inches—not because ponderosa had stopped growing, but because loggers had cut most of the oldest trees.[9]

Once ponderosas reached maturity, their bark changed from black to a warm yellow color, and they took on the smell of butterscotch. Early foresters and loggers called these big trees "yellow pines," and when loggers were in a good mood, they nicknamed them "yellow bellies." Ponderosas were sturdy, sun loving trees that seemed as if they could take anything. They had very long taproots, giving them the edge over Douglas-fir on the hot, dry south slopes; they could reach water deep in the soil and thrive where Douglas-fir could barely survive. Because their taproots solidly anchored them during high winds, often the only tree standing out on a bare south slope like some lonely sentinel would be a ponderosa pine. They could do without the protection of close companions. Thick furrowed bark made the older trees extremely fire resistant. Even the young trees were quite resistant to fires, because when they got to be about ten years old and two inches across, they put on a layer of dead bark that protected them from damage.[10] In sum, they were long-lived trees: they resisted drought, fire, winds, storms, and most insect attacks. All they needed were sun and space and time to grow.

Walking today in one of the few remaining forests of big ponderosa pines gives you a strong sense of déjà vu. "Where have I seen this before?" you wonder. You saw it in a thousand Westerns, where the cowboys rode their ponies between the trees, and a glimpse of granite peaks broke the upper right-hand corner of the frame. These forests feel like the real West, or at least like the real Western. Charming is a good word for them. The grass lies green and lush and lovely in the spaces between the trees, which are huge and many. People call these forests parklands: a perfect name for the open, easy feeling they evoke. There is just enough shade to keep the sun off your forehead, just enough breeze filtering through the trees to keep the flies away. The parklands appeal even to people who do not much like forests. They are forests on the edge of forestedness, forests that claim grandeur and awe among their forestlike attributes, without being claustrophobic. This is not a tangled, terrifying wilderness of nasty beasts and wicked wood-cutters; this is the land of butterscotch and ponies and Westerns.

From the time that whites first came to these forests in 1811, they were struck by nostalgia. Journals of explorers and travelers repeatedly tell of how the pinelands gave rise to sweet memories of an imagined childhood home. As Narcissa Whitman wrote in 1836 when she was making her way across the Blues to help estab-lish a mission among the Cayuse Indians: "The scenery reminded me of the hills in my native county. . . . Here I frequently met old acquaintances, in the trees & flowers & was not a little delighted. Indeed I do not know as I was ever so much affected with any scenery in my life. The singing of the birds, the echo of the voices of my fellow travelers, as they were scattered through the woods, all had a strong resemblance to bygone days."[11] Whites loved the ponderosa forests because they seemed like wilderness tamed and made easy—not by a gardener wielding a hoe and trowel, but by nature. Ironically, the pinelands were a managed landscape. But Indian burning, not just natural processes, had shaped these for-ests. Whites saw the frequent Indian-set fires as a threat to what they loved, rather than an essential part of what they loved, so they did their best to protect the forests from fire—a decision that led to changes nobody quite expected.

For all their charm and promise, the ponderosa forests deeply confused the foresters who came to protect them. By the turn of the century, after only a decade of intense industrial logging, the pinelands were inexplicably changing to much less desirable forests. As the forester H. D. Foster wrote in 1906: "Old cuttings have modified the forest. . . . On burned areas the new growth is apt to be either white fir or lodgepole pine. . . . The yellow pine type may change after logging to the mixed conifer type, the mixed conifer type after burning may change to the lodgepole pine type, while after clear-cutting the lodgepole pine type is prone to deteriorate to the white fir type."[12] This was a forest in motion, a changing forest, and the foresters knew they did not understand these changes. Why was one forest made up of pine, another forest of fir? They had no idea. In trying to save the forests, managers soon realized they needed to learn how those forests developed. To manipulate the forest so that its future proceeded in the directions they preferred, foresters needed to understand something about its history: how pine forests got there, and why there was pine and not fir in a particular place.

Part of what confused foresters was the belated recognition that all pine forests were not the same, and thus did not change in the same ways. Some of the parklike forests dominated by pine had only pine. On the drier sites, on the south slopes and ridges and down along the sides of steep canyons, grassland and brush graded into ponderosa forests that were "climax" to pine—communities of trees that experienced frequent light fires. Even when the disturbances of constant fires were kept out, the forests stayed pine, for it was too hot and dry for firs to grow up in the shade of the pines.

Many of the forests dominated by pine, however, had a few other conifers scattered throughout. These mixed-conifer forests looked almost exactly the same as the pure pine forests. They were open, and most of the trees were big ponderosa pines of various ages. The overstory in both types of forests mostly consisted of pine, but the mixed-conifer forests had also a seemingly insignificant number of Douglas-fir, grand fir, larch, Engelmann spruce, and lodgepole. The reproduction—the youngest trees that would form the basis of the next forest after the overstory trees died or were cut—was mostly ponderosa, but there was some Douglas-fir along with some grand fir. These mixed forests were still easy and open, as promising as the pure pine forests. Early foresters did not distinguish between the mixed-conifer forests and the pure pine forests; they called them both the yellow-pine type. Although the two forest types looked much the same, the mixed-conifer forests had a very different ecological history from that of the pure pine forests, and this meant they would respond to management in completely different ways. After less than a century of Forest Service management, the pure pine forests stayed pine, while the mixed-conifer forests changed to cluttered stands of firs with few pines.

To add to the early foresters' confusion, another forest greeted them when they arrived, one that clung to the north slopes—a much denser, darker, less profitable forest known as the north-slope or fir-larch type (Map 3). Douglas-fir and grand fir grew thickly here, with a scattering of larch, lodgepole, spruce, and ponderosa.[13] The tree species were the same as in the mixed-conifer forests, but the proportions were entirely different. Early foresters looked at these forests and were discouraged. There was nothing very profitable in sight; the pine was nice but sparse, and mills had little interest in the other trees. Foresters lumped the unprofitable species together under one name: the "inferiors." The north-slope forests were good for protecting watersheds, foresters figured, but not for much else.

Foresters had thought that if they could only get pine in place, it would be enough—they would have a stable forest. But stability clearly was not happening; some yellow-pine forests stayed pine, while other yellow-pine forests turned to the hopeless north-slope type. To understand these changes that so confounded the early foresters, we need to consider the trees that took over the pine forests, the so-called inferiors: Douglas-fir, grand fir, larch, and lodgepole pine.

In the wet forests on the west side of the Cascades, Douglas-fir gave rise to a lumber country unlike any the world has known. Near the Pacific, Douglas-fir grew furiously: fast enough for Weyerhaeuser to manage it on 45-year rotations and call those 45-year-old stands old growth. On the dry east side of the Cascades, however, a 45-year rotation would be akin to harvesting toothpicks; Douglas-fir could take 230 years in the Blues to reach the

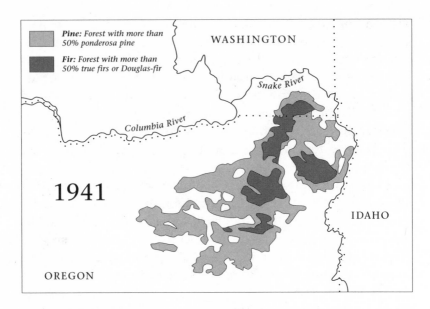

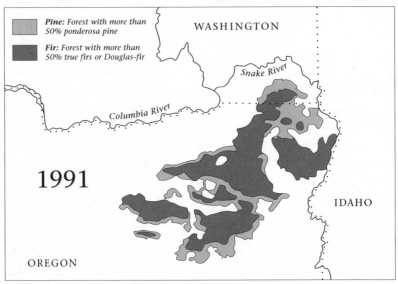

Map 3. Changes in forest composition between 1941 and 1991. The amount of forested land dominated by pine has substantially declined. Modified from Northwest Regional Council 1942, *Economic Atlas of the Pacific Northwest* (1942), 19; and Küchler (1964).

size a coastal tree achieved in 60 years. Slow growth meant that Douglas-fir was not a particularly valuable timber tree in the Blues, but that was how the tree adapted to life in a colder, drier, less productive environment. Douglas-fir traded off size and speed for the ability to survive in a harsh place.

The inland form of Douglas-fir present in the Blues (*Pseudotsuga menziesii*, var. *glauca*) was subtly different from the coastal form present in westside forests. The coastal form was partly fire dependent: it required a mineral seedbed for germination, and because it was not as shade tolerant as other coastal conifers, it tended to occupy fire-cleared sites. Therefore, managers argued that only clearcutting would ensure the regeneration of coastal Douglas-fir. By extension, foresters tended to assume that inland Douglas-fir needed the same silvicultural treatment. But the Douglas-fir present in the Blues was quite different from the westside Douglas-fir: it did not require a mineral seedbed for germination and so it did not depend on intensive fires for establishment. More important, because the young trees were more shade tolerant, Douglas-fir could regenerate in the moderate shade of mixed-conifer communities.[14] What all this meant was that it could grow up in the shade of pines if fire were kept out; it did not need clearcuts to thrive.

Larch was the third major player in these mixed-conifer forests. Many people thought larch was the perfect tree: fires, insects, and drought did not kill it. Unfortunately, there was never much of a market for its lumber. In its favorite sites, larch could reach massive sizes: trees five or six feet across used to be common.[15] The average was 30 to 40 inches across, far larger than most of the larches now present in the Blues. Seedlings grew quickly, and that was how larch made its way in the world: it came in after fire in pine stands on moist sites, and its seedlings outgrew associates, especially lodgepole.[16] But it was not a prolific seed producer, so it rarely grew in single species stands. Because it needed more moisture than ponderosa, larch occurred at slightly higher elevations than ponderosa and tended to congregate on the moister, north-facing slopes. Like ponderosa, larch needed sun and space, so stands of larch quickly gave way to grand fir or lodgepole.

The last two major species, grand fir and lodgepole, were trees

that confused and frustrated the foresters, who devoted their efforts to eliminating them, but with little success. Grand fir and
lodgepole seemed like sneaks: not only did they refuse to produce
decent timber, they rushed in and, in one forester's words,
"usurped the territory" of far more valuable timber trees.[17] They
refused to compete on the normal grounds of size, longevity,
strength. Instead they were short-lived trees that grew quickly,
stole resources from more stolid trees, and died not long after they
showed up.

Grand fir (also known as white fir) was the most persistently
annoying tree to lumbermen. Not only was it fairly useless for lumber, but it rotted quickly, fell over in strong winds, died at a young
age, and got attacked by seemingly every insect and disease in the
vicinity. Juvenile growth was fast; at 100 years, a grand fir might
reach 100 feet tall. But after another hundred years, insect damage,
root rot, fungal diseases, and heart rot slowed the tree down. "It is
but a 'weed tree,'" the Blues forester H. D. Foster wrote with con-
tempt in 1908, "and as such should be removed as much as possible in all logging operations in order to give way for better
species." Grand fir trees were lazy, decadent, rotten trees: "indeed
it is a waste of time to handle the tree," Foster concluded.[18] Grand
fir was bad enough as timber, but much worse was its tendency to
grow up under the shade of more valuable trees, stealing their water and nutrients and eventually taking over the stand. Grand fir
thrived in shade and moisture and coolness, and it found these in
two major places in the Blues: on north slopes and in the understories of older forests, down in the shade and moisture of the
forest floor.[19] Once a ponderosa-dominated forest got established
on a fairly moist, cool site, then grand fir could come up in pine's
shade, if there was nothing else to keep it out.

Across the Blues and throughout the West, foresters would suddenly find themselves in a dense thicket of lodgepole, all the same
size and all ready to burst into flame at the drop of a match.
Lodgepole was a classic fire-adapted tree, a fact that was at first
surprising because of its extremely thin bark. Even the lightest of
fires killed a lodgepole pine; yet after fire, lodgepole moved in before anything else. As one biologist put it, "lodgepole pines are

tricksters on the ecological playing field. They don't seem to compete on the same grounds as our other conifers—size, longevity,
shade tolerance, and fire resistance. They excel instead at profligate
and gimmicky seeding habits, short-distance speed, and tolerance
of poor soil."[20] Lodgepole's weedy seed habit allowed it to rush in
first after a destructive fire. A high seed year would come every one
to three years (instead of five to ten years, as for many conifers),
and lodgepoles could release seeds all year round instead of just
once a year. Trees as young as five years old—an age when other
conifers would be nowhere near sexual maturity—could produce
viable seeds. The seeds lasted practically forever, waiting for the
perfect combination of chance conditions to sprout and take over
the forests: 80-year-old cones had seeds that were still patiently
biding their time.[21] Some lodgepole trees were particularly fire-
adapted, with serotinous cones that opened only after being exposed to the heat generated by a fire, ensuring that the next stand
would consist of lodgepole.[22] Once lodgepole seeds germinated,
the saplings and seedlings grew much faster than other conifers,
thus swamping the other trees out, leading to the dense thickets of
single-aged lodgepole.

Although individual lodgepoles got killed almost instantly by
fires, those same fires set the stage for more lodgepole stands,
which in turn created the conditions perfect for intense fires,
which in turn led to more lodgepole. The current dominance of
lodgepole in many areas arises from turn-of-the-century intense
fires.[23] Since lodgepole lacks a taproot, it is very susceptible to
windthrow, especially after being attacked by mountain pine beetle
and Western pine beetle. These thickets of dead trees created the
ideal conditions for another round of intense fires, which could
establish a fire-lodgepole cycle that persisted for centuries. Early
foresters thought that if lodgepole got into a stand, it could take
over and become nearly impossible to eradicate, because it would
attract vicious fires long before other trees could grow up and push
out the lodgepole.

What, then, determined which tree grew where? Early foresters
thought competition for light and space explained succession—

the development of a forest on a site. Ponderosa needed strong sun to grow after its first few years, while Douglas-fir could tolerate far more shade in its youth and grand fir thrived in shade. Pine would therefore come in first in an open, sunny site, but it would create enough shade that its own young trees would not do very well. Douglas-fir, being more shade tolerant, would grow up in the pine's shade, but it could not tolerate its own denser shade. Since young grand fir could grow well in the shade beneath its parents, it would eventually become the climax species on sites moist and cool enough to support it.

Many pine forests followed this pattern—succeeding to forests dominated by Douglas-fir and grand fir—but other pine forests stayed pine. On south-facing sites where the sun shone steadily, most conifer seedlings dried out before they could gain a foothold. Only ponderosa pine seedlings, with their moisture-gleaning tap-roots, could manage the driest sites, and foresters thought that explained why some yellow-pine stands never changed to fir stands. Yet this still did not explain why pine had dominated mixed-conifer forests when whites arrived. Why had not Douglas-fir and its associates taken over the moister pinelands long before? And why did firs begin invading as soon as whites started working in the forests?

Foresters had trouble thinking about these questions, because to understand them people needed to give up their faith in the orderly development of stable forests. Their visions of natural order precluded disturbance, making it hard for them to see that frequent fires could have shaped the forests they loved. These plant communities were extraordinarily complex in ways the foresters could not recognize; they wanted badly to protect the pine forests, but what they did not realize was that the forests were not a static entity that could be protected. Because they did not know how pine forests developed, they made the obvious and reasonable assumption that to get more pine forests, what they needed were young pine trees.

Two major things seemed to endanger the pine forests: loggers and fire. Fire killed young trees, and since young trees were the future of the forest, fire was clearly the enemy. Loggers threatened pine forests by cutting them down, of course, but this was more complicated than it seemed, since cutting the old trees down was not a problem if more young pine trees grew up afterward. But instead of pine regenerating in the clearcuts, thickets of grand fir or lodgepole pine were growing instead. That was baffling, because ponderosa was a sun lover which should thrive in clearcuts. Foresters reasoned that the culprit might be fires sweeping through the cutover sites. Sparks from the logging railroads set alight piles of slash and dead wood left after cutting, and the resultant fires burned so hot that what grew up afterward were often thickets of lodgepole. The foresters decided that to protect the pine forests, they needed to keep out fire and encourage reproduction. Sensible as these two recommendations sounded, they were precisely the wrong things to do. Together, they would ensure the demise of the open pine forests. To understand why, we need to consider the roles fire played in the history of different forest communities.

Fire Ecology

Fire shaped the pine parklands, and without fires those forests changed to something utterly different. In the presettlement ponderosa forests—the pure pine communities as well as the mixed-conifer communities—light fires swept through about every eight to ten years.[24] These fires kept the stand open, killed off the youngest trees, reduced fuel loads, and released a surge of nitrogen into the soil that stimulated the growth of grasses and nitrogen-fixing shrubs such as ceanothus. The fires were frequent enough to keep the stands well thinned, but they were infrequent enough that a few young trees would survive to form the future stands. This, however, was not at all evident to early foresters. They saw the reproduction dying in the frequent fires, and they saw the effects of intense slash fires on soil and water, so they thought that suppressing fires was the only way to save the forests.

Although early foresters lumped all yellow-pine forests together, different plant communities responded individually to fire and disturbance. The pure pine communities grew on sites that were too hot and dry for firs to survive, so even when fire was excluded, the pines stayed dominant. But across the Blues, most of the pine forests were mixed-conifer communities that grew in places just moist enough for the survival of Douglas-fir and grand fir, at least in years with adequate rainfall.[25] Fire, more than anything else, determined the history of those forests. With frequent light fires, ponderosa pine dominated the forests; without fires, the forests became something quite different.

Early foresters recognized that fires were common in the open pine forests, but they were unable to imagine how trees could survive such frequent fires. Logically, frequent fires would kill young growth; therefore, after a century, forests would be made up entirely of old trees. While light fires might maintain nice open stand conditions for old trees, such fires seemed disastrous for future forests, and future forests were the Forest Service's responsibility. But in the mixed-conifer communities that greeted the early foresters, the trees were of many different ages, and ponderosa was somehow reproducing. This raised two questions that stymied early foresters: How could ponderosa pines survive fires that burned every ten years or so, and why did ponderosa pine do better than Douglas-fir and grand fir in those conditions?

Mature Douglas-fir could survive fires nearly as well as mature ponderosa pine, so it appeared that fire should not favor pine. Since young ponderosa trees were far more fire resistant than young Douglas-fir, however, pine could reproduce in fire regimes while Douglas-fir could not. Enclosing needles and thick bud scales shielded ponderosa pine's meristems—the growing buds—from fire, and young Douglas-fir trees lacked this protection. More important, ponderosa bark would put on a layer of protective dead cambium when the young tree was two inches in diameter, whereas Douglas-fir did not do this until it was four inches in diameter. In good conditions, ponderosa could reach two inches in six to twelve years, just under the average frequency of light fires. Since fires burned at different frequencies—sometimes every six years, sometimes every fifteen—most of the young trees that survived were ponderosa, but a few of the other conifers survived too when the interval between fires was long enough for them to reach their safe size.

The other question that perplexed early foresters was why some fires became intense, stand-replacing fires, and other fires stayed light. They recognized that fires in open forests dominated by ponderosa rarely became crown fires, but they were not entirely sure why. Light fires did not always stay light, of course: there were some major conflagrations even in south-facing pine sites. Yet usually ponderosa forests resisted intense fires because the trees were far apart, the pine bark was relatively unburnable, and there were few low branches, making it difficult for fires to make their way into the crown. Open ponderosa forests also tended to have light fuel loads, and this led to a self-perpetuating cycle that could stay stable for years. Frequent light fires kept the stands open, and this ensured that fuel loads would stay low, so that the next fires would be light. The converse was also true: fire exclusion created conditions that led to intense fires, which led to thickets of regeneration, which led to dense stands, which led to high fuel loads, which led to intense fires. The result was a cycle of high fires that might go on for centuries.[26]

Early foresters recognized that the thickets of young trees that fire suppression and logging created were not an ideal situation. Yet they argued that allowing fires to thin the stands would lead to problems, since thinning would lessen competition and competition was what led to manly, vigorous trees. An anti-fire Forest Service report from the 1930s argued that trees would be "hardier, taller, straighter and cleaner for having this heavy competition in their early lives. Dense young thickets of forest seedlings or saplings are what make our tall, straight, clean-limbed forest giants. Did anybody ever see a big, bushy-topped, limby tree that grew in the open, all by itself, that was worth a whoop as a sawlog?"[27] Stand development theory stated that in a forest some seedlings should grow faster, become dominant, suppress, and then eliminate their neighbors, thus allowing a few trees to grow rapidly into big trees. Competition was a natural and virtuous process, which ensured that only the best would survive. Overcrowded stands were a good thing, because they would lead to strong trees. But in reality, western conifers—ponderosa, western larch, Douglas-fir, and lodgepole in particular—do not obey stand development the-

ory. They do not self-suppress, and this is one reason why fire suppression was such a problem in mixed-conifer stands. In the absence of fire, no trees became dominant; the undergrowth became
a thicket of same-aged trees whose growth rates had slowed almost
to a halt.[28]

Foresters worried that frequent fires would destroy the forest,
not just by killing trees, but also by the indirect effects of burning:
erosion, understory destruction, and nutrient loss. Heavy fires certainly could cause a great deal of soil damage, yet not all fires behaved the same. When fires were frequent, they were usually very
light—consuming litter, herbaceous fuels, foliage, and small twigs
on living undergrowth. Yet they rarely consumed the upper duff
(the organic layer in the soil), nor did they kill foliage on understory trees or destroy the understory plants, as moderate and
severe fires in north-slope forests tended to do. Nearly all mature
understory shrubs survived light fires, and the majority of herb
species also survived, especially those with rhizomes and root
crowns underground.[29]

Even when they burned every decade, many of the forests
stayed productive. Yet early foresters feared that frequent burning
would eventually deplete the soil of nutrients, and eventually only
sagebrush would survive. In contrast, many people now argue that
because fires were frequent before settlement, they were natural
and therefore necessary; the forests must have somehow adapted
to frequent fires. Yet this is not necessarily true. Presettlement fires
were not wholly natural; Indians set a substantial (although unknown) fraction of them. Even if they were natural, they could still
have been harmful. Frequent natural fires might have slowly altered the soil so that not even pine could persist. Alternatively, fires
might have encouraged plants that replaced the nutrients that the
fires depleted.

There was no simple answer to the simple question: were fires
good for inland forests? The effects fires had depended a great deal
on the particular site, and how people judged these effects depended on what kinds of forests they preferred. Historic (as well as
current) concerns about fire focused on "long-term site productivity"—the ability of a forested site to keep growing trees. Recently,

many people have argued that burning should increase nutrient cycling, return nutrients to the soil, and therefore enhance site productivity. They reason that on dry sites, moisture appears to limit the decomposition of woody debris and plant material; thus fire might play a role in nutrient cycling similar to that played by moisture west of the Cascades. In the absence of fire, decomposition in dry sites would become very slow, and the system could become nutrient impoverished. Early foresters, and some current fire ecologists, have argued exactly the opposite: fires deplete soil nutrients.[30] Both arguments have validity; the results depend on the particular fire and the particular site.

In 1906, a forester named H. D. Foster came to study the new Wenaha reserve in the northern Blues (now the Umatilla National Forest). He wrote: "Surface fires which usually do not cover a large area are more or less frequent. These fires, which are often started by lightning, run over the ground, burning the litter and any dead timber standing and down."[31] Foster walked through a land of fires, his boots covered with ash, soot on his hands, and finally despaired of the effects those fires might have on future productivity. Fires did not harm mature trees, he noted, but they destroyed the forest floor, burning up the humus layer with its nutrients, and "leaving a shallow soil unprotected from erosion." But how would the Wenaha's soil and its nutrients have reacted to the fires that Foster witnessed? Was he correct in concluding that fires were ultimately the enemy of the inland forests?

Different nutrients would have reacted in different ways to fires that Foster saw, and their combined effects would have been even more complex, depending on the fire's temperature and on the past history of fires within those forests. Even at very low smoldering temperatures, burning would have volatilized nitrogen and sulfur oxides; the amount lost was directly proportional to the amount of organic material that the fire had consumed. Foster noted that "the soil is left dry and is destroyed in patches," and the forest floor on those patches would have lost nearly all its nitrogen and sulfur. For example, at very low temperatures (375° to 575°C), fire would oxidize more than half of the sulfur from ponderosa pine litter after just five minutes. Yet ammonium nitrates would have been increased by the burning, leading to lush growth of grasses the following spring. For two to five years after the fire, accelerated nitrogen mineralization would have increased the nitrogen available to plants as nitrates. But after five years, available nitrogen would have declined. Since levels of nitrogen and sulfur probably limited growth in most inland forests, long-term declines of either of these nutrients might have seriously affected the ability of the Wenaha to support trees.[32]

The light fires Foster saw would have increased some important nutrients in forms that plants could use for growth. Phosphorus and potassium would not have volatilized until temperatures reached 700°C, which meant that these nutrients were less sensitive to burning than nitrogen and sulfur. Cations such as calcium, magnesium, and sodium would have oxidized after each fire, forming the familiar gray and white ash that dirtied Foster's boots. As soon as water vapor and carbon dioxide were present, the oxides would convert to soluble compounds which could reach the plants. But if there had been a heavy rainfall after the fire, these nutrients might instead have leached into the soil or washed into streams. Some of the volatilized phosphorus could have been deposited with the ash and thereby reached the plants, but this would have depended on fire temperatures and subsequent rainfall.[33]

What these nutrient changes meant for the entire forest is unclear. Experimental ecologists measure the effects of burning on a single variable, holding other variables constant. This is a tricky way of interpreting the world, because outside the laboratory other variables rarely stay constant. For example, controlled experiments show that after a light fire, nitrogen levels ultimately decrease. But in the Wenaha reserve, the fires Foster observed might have had a very different effect on nitrogen levels. The temporary release of nitrogen probably stimulated the growth of nitrogen-fixing plants such as ceanothus, which would have persisted at higher levels for long after the nitrogen oxides had declined. The indirect result might have been a total increase in nitrogen within the local environment; but that would have depended on how many browsing herbivores ate the ceanothus, and that in turn would have depended on how many more palatable plants were available nearby.

Repeated fires lowered the acidity of the Wenaha soils, creating conditions that could either help or hinder growth, depending on the plant. Most conifer needles were quite acidic, and if litter accumulated on the forest floor, the soil could become increasingly acidic and conifer growth would slow considerably. In some mixed forests, hardwoods and shrubs pumped up bases from deep within the soil, preventing excessive acid accumulation. On most of the Wenaha Reserve, where there were few hardwoods and probably moderate numbers of understory shrubs in 1906, repeated light burning might have played a critical role in regulating soil acidity.

The season and temperature that a fire burned also determined its severity. Spring fires would have destroyed new growth. Foster noted, however, that surface fires burned during the summer and fall, not during the spring. Fall fires that occurred after most understory plants went dormant would have damaged them far less than spring fires. The season also affected fire duration, temperature, and acreage. After the fall rains had soaked soil and vegetation, fires burned much smaller areas at lower temperatures.

Light fires did some damage to soil, but stand-replacing fires and slash fires could destroy the soil structure, or remove the soil entirely. Severe fires, especially those on steep slopes, could kill tree roots, and since roots held the soil in place, fires would make the soil much more likely to slide away.[34] Foster and his colleagues were uncertain why some light fires exploded into intense fires, and they concluded that burning was simply too risky. Eventually the foresters managed to suppress most of the light fires, hoping that would eliminate all fires. This only complicated matters, however, since fire severity depended on the history of burning. With fire suppression, the buildup of fuels led to much higher fire temperatures. Severe fires had been rare in mixed-conifer forests, but they became increasingly common after several decades of fire suppression.

Fire suppression led to ecological changes that meant even very light fires had much more severe effects than they had when the

foresters first came. In open communities with a history of frequent light fires, plant roots had burrowed deep into the soil—in
part to escape the fires, in part because light fires led to a drier
microclimate on the forest floor, so roots could find water only by
going deep. After decades without fire, litter built up, cooling the
microclimates near the forest floor and increasing soil moisture.
Root structures changed to take advantage of the new soil moisture
profile, so far more roots were clustered close to the surface. In
those conditions, even a very light fire could singe the roots, destroying huge old ponderosa pines—trees that before would hardly
have noticed such a fire.[35] Foster and his colleagues never dreamed
of such complex, indirect, ecological changes; in effect, they were
groping blindly when they set out to protect the forest from fires.

After less than a century of fire suppression, Foster would not
have recognized the forests that resulted. Ponderosa pine still dom-
inates the pure pine communities, but those forests now have few
big pines, and their understories are crowded with small trees that
cannot get the space or nutrients they need to grow rapidly. The
other forests once dominated by ponderosa pine—the mixed-
conifer communities—are now entirely different forests. Because
they occurred on sites just moist enough for firs to survive, those
firs grew faster than the pines in the shade that resulted from fire
suppression. As it got shadier and shadier, the young pines did
worse and worse, and mixed-conifer forests eventually became
dominated by fir. Sixty years after fire suppression began in earnest,
the only ponderosas left were the big ones loggers had missed, and
the rest of the trees were crowded thickets of firs. Ponderosa used
to form half to nearly all of the overstory, and by 1991, pine was
only a fifth of the overstory. The understory used to be open and
grassy; in the 1990s, thickets of insect-attacked, stagnated true fir
and Douglas-fir trees formed the understory. Where pines used to
be dominant, firs could grow quickly in wet years and crowd out
the pines, but when droughts hit, the crowded firs slowed their
growth, becoming water and nutrient stressed and therefore susceptible to insect attacks. Both major insect defoliators in the
Blues—spruce budworm and Douglas-fir tussock moth—were far
more likely to attack fir than pine. But all firs were not equally at

risk. Defoliators much preferred to attack firs that grew on sites that ponderosa pine had historically dominated. Firs growing on the cooler, moister, north-facing slopes were far less susceptible.[36]

Across the Blues, millions of acres changed from pine to fir, and then from healthy fir to drought-stressed, insect-defoliated fir. On the Wallowa Whitman National Forest in 1906, 57 percent of the timber by volume was ponderosa pine, and in 1991 it was less than 20 percent. On the Umatilla National Forest, ponderosa was 34 percent of the tree volume in 1931, and only 16 percent in 1981. The percentage of open forest stands with a major component of ponderosa pine also dramatically changed. On the Wallowa Whitman in 1912, 71 percent of the stands were open and full of old pine; in 1991 only 10 percent fit this description. On the Malheur in 1938, 78 percent of the forests were open pine stands; by 1980 less than half those were still pine forests. On the Umatilla in 1905, 43 percent of the forest area was dominated by open pine stands; in 1991 only a seventh of those forests remained pine.[37]

Old growth faced the most drastic losses: probably less than a tenth of the presettlement old-growth forests remained by the early 1990s. Surviving old growth had become extremely fragmented; by 1993, 91 percent of the old-growth forests existed in patches of less than 100 acres. When the Forest Service first arrived, those mature forests stretched for hundreds of thousands of acres. For example, the Malheur National Forest once contained some of the finest stands of open ponderosa in the nation. In 1906, one report stated that an open, old-growth ponderosa-larch forest covered 800,000 acres south of the Strawberry Mountains. Fewer than 8,000 acres of these same old-growth ponderosa forests remained in 1993—less than 1 percent of what was present before the Forest Service began management. In 1912, the forester R. M. Evans wrote that on the Wallowa and Minam Forests, there were nearly 600,000 acres of uneven-aged forests containing more than 80 percent ponderosa. About half a million acres—or 85 percent—of these ponderosa-dominated forests were old growth. By 1991, only 18 percent of the forests on the Wallowa Whitman National Forest were mature or old-growth stands, and very little of that was ponderosa. The rest of the forests were dominated by young fir trees.[38]

Drastic as these recent human-caused changes have been, we
need to think about them in the perspective of ecological change
over millennia. Because the forests of the Blues now are so vast and
dense, it is easy to think of forests as part of the Blues' inherent
nature. Yet these are extraordinarily recent forests. Since the glaciers retreated from the Northwest 12,000 years ago, forests have
come and gone at least three times. On many sites, forests have
been present for only about 2,000 years. Compare this to some
central Asian ecosystems, where plants have been coevolving as
communities for over 60 million years. During the last great glacial
period, cold steppe dominated the land between the Cascades and
the Rockies. As the glaciers retreated, a period of gradual warming
and drying began, and the warming continued until about 4,500
years ago. Conifers briefly invaded when the glaciers first began
their retreat, but within 2,000 years those conifers had declined
and dry grasslands had taken their place. For the next two millennia, between 10,000 and 8,000 years ago, sagebrush and grass covered nearly all the places that are now ponderosa pine forests (and
many of the places that are now Douglas-fir forests). About 6,500
years ago, Mount Mazama exploded, depositing thick layers of volcanic ash over the region, and a few conifers began their advance
again. About 4,500 years ago, the climate began to cool, and this
cooling allowed forests to rapidly invade the grasslands. Fossils
show that the equivalents of our modern forests were finally apparent on most sites between 2,500 and 1,000 years ago. Yet even
then, the climate and the forests did not stabilize. About 1,000
years ago, the climate once again began to warm. A period of rapid
fluctuations ended about 300 years ago, at the end of the little ice
age, and since then the climate has largely been warming. Because
of human intervention, firs have invaded many pine sites during
a warming period; normally, they would have invaded only during
cooling periods, when the climate favored firs over pines. That,
of course, is partly why many fir-dominated forests have been so
susceptible to insect epidemics: they are teetering right on the edge
of their ability to persist.[39]

As climate shifts reveal, the plant communities of the Blues are
quite young; 2,500 years is not long for plants to coexist. Each

time the climate changed, the assemblages of plants that made up communities also shifted. Because individual tree species respond to climate changes in slightly different ways, plant communities would not have always moved together. Lodgepole pine, for example, would have responded more quickly to temperature changes than its associates; lodgepole seeds are more mobile, allowing trees to invade new sites before other conifers. This led to a continual reshuffling of the ecological cards in these plant communities. So, although communities did rapidly form intricate webs of interconnected functions, plants could also rapidly break up these associations and form new ones. What does this mean concerning the effects of human actions, which also broke up existing plant communities and formed new ones? Partly it means that the forests did not have an inherent stability which humans clumsily disrupted. It also means that trying to recreate an ideal forest community from the past would be hopeless. As the example with fire suppression and root patterns shows, after we interfere with a community, that community's history proceeds along paths quite different from those it would have taken without our interference. Each disturbance, whether human or natural, represents a branch in the path of forest history, and each action takes the forest in a slightly different direction. We cannot simply backtrack to a time before some particular decision we now regret, because so many additional changes have radiated out from that original action.

Patterns of disturbance shaped a diverse landscape in the Blues. Fires of different intensities, along with storms, windthrow, and insect attacks, created complex and shifting mosaics of forests across the landscape. For example, within the grand fir communities, hot fires let in pockets of sunlight where shade-intolerant trees such as ponderosa, larch, and lodgepole could get established in single-species stands. Some fires stayed light and almost harmless, but others flared into infernos that swept across the mountains, killing swatches of trees along the stream in one part of a watershed. The effects of those intense fires across the landscape were very different from what a hot fire would do today. Think of a watershed as your hand, and the streams feeding into a watershed as the fingers on your hand.[40] When H. D. Foster first walked the Wenaha in 1906, a catastrophic fire might have burned out all the cover along one of those streams, but there were four other streams with mature forests that buffered the disturbance to the entire watershed. Twenty years later along the burnt stream, cottonwoods and willows would have sprouted from the burned-out stumps, while ceanothus would have formed a thick low canopy that protected the soil from heavy rains. Across the creek, an old forest might have become so decadent that half the ponderosa trees were ravaged by pine beetle. But a mile away, another patch of pine matured, another stand of spruce grew, a thicket of lodgepole burst into flames and larch came in underneath. The trees shading another stream in the watershed might have been knocked over by a windstorm, but there were still three streams left with old forest, and one stream with a recovered vegetation cover. Again, complexity buffered the disturbance. As the vegetation cover along one stream fell apart, the forest along another stream recovered. The landscape was big enough and complex enough so that disturbances flowed across the landscape; fire, insects, plants, and forest types were all in motion.

Now, however, if a catastrophic fire were to wipe out one stream on the same forest, that might well be the only mature forest in the watershed. If the other four stream reaches had already been clearcut, there would be nothing left to buffer the fire's effects across the land, nowhere for the animals whose habitats were destroyed to go, no mature trees left to seed in the burnt site, and no pine forests nearby that could mature into old growth for another two hundred years. Whatever functions old-growth pine performed in the landscape would be missing for centuries. Presettlement landscapes had numerous redundant pieces and patches; when old growth got hit by fire, there was another patch of trees about to turn into old growth. Now most of the pieces are missing, and attempts to preserve the little bit that is left of old growth are constantly confounded by fire and insects and disturbances.

What has happened on federal lands has affected everything else—private land as well as the people who live on private land. The presence of the federal government is pervasive throughout

the Blues, as throughout most of the West. The government owns
more land than anyone else, and private and federal lands are inti-
mately linked. The national forests are broken into chunks; within
the federal boundaries lie numerous parcels of private land. This
broken pattern of landownership has complicated management
enormously, since both private landowners and federal managers
find that the others' actions constrain their own. But the links go
deeper than mere legal matters. One piece of land is never separate
from another, even if a string of barbed wire separates them. Water
connects all the lands in the Blues: a bit of dirt kicked free by a
falling pine finds its way into the stream and eventually gets deposited twenty miles away. A salmon that spawns in the clear headwaters of a wilderness area gets its gills clogged by that sediment,
far from where the tree first fell. And at the base of the mountains
forty miles downstream, the Confederated Tribes of the Umatilla
sue the Forest Service for ruining the traditional fish runs. Fences
and legal titles may keep some large vertebrates—people, cows, elk,
loggers—confined to one place, but their effects cannot be so easily confined.

Before the Forest Service

Many people assume that before whites showed up in the vast open lands of the inland Northwest, the area was a pristine wilderness. Federal foresters had much the same idea: they thought they had come to save wild nature. But the forests and grasslands were not natural, nor were they wild, if by natural and wild we mean free of human management. Indians had been changing those lands for millennia, reshaping them according to their needs and desires. The forests that so pleased the whites were in large part artificial creations.[1]

When the whites saw the open parklands full of yellow pine, they immediately lost their hearts to them. But they hated the fires that swept through the mountains, and usually saw the Indian burning practices as threatening the open forests they loved. They failed to realize that excluding fire would lead to the demise of what they liked most about the forest. To understand why the federal foresters felt they had to intervene to save the forests, we need to understand who preceded them in the Blues—Indians and whites—and how those people perceived the land.

Whites came to the Blue Mountains looking for paradise, and what they saw often deceived them into thinking they had found it. They brought their own cultural values and then imposed a web of expectations, needs, and assumptions onto the landscape that awaited them. Whites came in a slow trickle of fur traders that started in 1811, then in a stream of Oregon Trail emigrants and settlers, and finally in a flood of miners, ranchers, and loggers. How they changed the land depended on how they viewed it, and how they viewed it depended on two things: what kind of land they were familiar with, and what commodities they wanted from the land. They came with assumptions about the proper relationship between culture and nature, and these assumptions led them to misunderstand the land in different ways.

Although the first whites came in 1811, settlement did not begin in most parts of the Blues until the 1870s, and heavy logging began only after the transcontinental railroad reached Baker in 1884. Historians often argue that exploitation of the region was delayed because the area was so isolated.[2] But the Blues were anything but isolated for the tribes who lived, hunted, traded, and traveled there. The mountains and grasslands were a meeting ground for diverse cultures and the nexus of trading networks that connected the Plains, Plateau, and Pacific Coast tribes. Yet, because there was no easy access to American and European markets until the transcontinental railroad arrived, the region was indeed at the periphery of what the historians William Robbins and Donald Wolf called the "immense market-induced ecological exchanges" taking place in the post-Columbian world.[3]

The story of landscape change in the Blues is, in the simplest version, a story of the land's transformation into commodities that could be removed and taken elsewhere. Indians had certainly altered the landscape, but when whites showed up they set in motion changes that far outpaced any past ones. The critical difference was that the Blues finally became a source of resources— timber, gold, meat, and wool—to feed the engines of market capitalism. Yet before whites came, the region had been connected to outside markets. Local tribes had extensive ties to trading networks that spread west to the pacific Ocean and east to the Great Plains.[4] Indians did extract elements from the local ecosystem, and in the process they changed the local ecology to meet their needs. But their needs did not include removing large quantities of wood fiber for fuel, fertilizer, or construction. Indian land use was not necessarily sustainable, nor was it in any kind of inherent balance with the land's limits. Yet it was fundamentally different from the land use that whites instituted, for it did not include the wholesale extraction and export of resources.

The Forest Service arrived on a stage whose scene had been set by a century of conflict. During the nineteenth century, the Blues had witnessed massive transformations. An intense and often explosive meeting of cultures took place as Scottish explorers, American traders, French-Canadian trappers, Umatilla, Palouse, Blackfoot, Paiute, Cayuse, Shoshone, Nez Percé Indians, Belgian Jesuits, Protestant missionaries, and American emigrants all came with their own visions of ideal land. Each group affected the land in different ways, depending on their cultural expectations. At the heart of their conflicts were fundamental differences in how they envisioned the relationship between nature and culture: the proper role of humans in the landscape.

Indians

When whites first arrived in the Blues, they tended to see the place as an empty wilderness waiting for the hand of the white man to bring it to perfection. Some whites used this perceived wilderness to justify their own presence, but it was an illusion with little basis in reality. The Cayuse, Nez Percé, Paiute, Umatilla, and Shoshone tribes had heavily used the Blue Mountains for centuries and had altered the landscape accordingly. Native Americans had traveled, traded, hunted, fished, gathered roots and berries, maintained herds of horses, burned the hills to improve hunting and grazing, and fought wars in the Blues for centuries before whites showed up. Tribes differed in their use of resources and in their relationship to the forests and grasslands, yet all had a relationship to the land that was spiritual rather than exclusively commodity oriented. Indians altered the landscapes of the Blues, but they found bizarre the dominant American attitude—that wild nature needed to be improved and that people were the ones to improve it. Nature was not something out there; it was part of the blood and the bones and the breath. Nor was religion something opposed to nature, as it was for many—though certainly not all—of the whites who later came to the Blues.

Different tribes used the land in different ways, but they had one critical thing in common: they were nomadic rather than agricultural. Movement did not preclude emotional connections to particular places, for their wandering was not random, but it did allow the tribes to adapt to the central fact of the land—its aridity. Even while they altered the land to suit themselves, they were in turn shaped by the constraints of the land.

Tribes in the Blues split into two major groups: the northern tribes, members of the Sahaptin language group and Columbia Plateau culture; and the southern tribes, members of various Paiute groups that ranged down into the Great Basin. Shoshone groups— the Snakes or Bannocks—from the east also came into the Blues to raid, fish, and fight. No tribe had exclusive use of the Blues, and no group settled year-round in one place. The Nez Percé used the northern valleys along the Wallowa and Imnaha creeks for winter camps, and the Shoshone had winter camps along the southern valleys. The Shoshone, Nez Percé, and Cayuse gathered in groups of hundreds for summer trading in the Grande Ronde Valley, and the Blackfeet entered the Blue Mountains from the Plains on raiding forays.

All these tribes were nomads, but they differed in the frequency and patterns of their movements. Indian trails and camps formed a network upon the landscape. When whites began to move through the mountains, their survival often depended on these networks.[5] Whites generally saw the northern tribes as wealthier and more powerful because they lived in a more productive habitat, one that allowed larger concentrations of people, horses, large game mammals, and salmon.[6] To the biased eyes of the white explorers, the Paiutes in the drier southern Blues seemed to live a painful and bitter life on the edge of starvation. Peter Skene Ogden, an American fur trapper and explorer who worked for the British traders, found the Malheur River area arid and inhospitable. "A more gloomy barren looking country I never yet seen," he grumbled in his journal, and he liked the Paiutes little better than their land.[7] Although whites often considered the southern end of the Blues harsh and unpromising because the climate was arid, the area offered a kind of abundance in its forests, valleys, and waters. The Paiutes, for example, ate at least thirty-three different animals and nineteen plants, an adaptation to an uncertain and unstable climate. Using numerous species of plants and animals for food tended to lessen pressures on any single resource, while reducing vulnerability to drought.[8] Migration also helped prevent depletion of resources. When the missionaries convinced a few Indians to settle, overgrazing followed. James Clyman, an American fur trapper who guided a party of emigrants over the Blue Mountains in 1844, noted in his journal: "the wild Bunch grass of this country was intirely eat out near the Indian farms and does not seem to grow again."[9]

Indian Burning

Indians burned different kinds of forests for different reasons, and their fires had different ecological effects depending on the type of forest and the timing, intensity, and frequency of the fires. In denser stands of fir, light fires were set just after the rains began in the fall, when the risk of a fire escaping control was lowest. These light fires created small openings in the fir forests, increasing the amount of edge habitat. By allowing more light to reach the forest floor, and by releasing a short-term surge of nitrogen in a form available to plants, fires encouraged the growth of grasses, herbs, and shrubs such as huckleberry, blueberry, and grouseberry. These plants attracted browsing game animals such as deer and elk that tended to be rare in dense, unbroken stands of forest.

In the ponderosa pine forests, repeated light fires had very different effects: instead of encouraging shrubs, the fires kept the forests open, making hunting with horses much easier. Burning within the ponderosa forests favored herbs and forbs and discouraged woody undergrowth. These fires helped create the parklike setting that so pleased whites, and they did this by preventing succession to the more shade-tolerant Douglas-fir and grand fir.

Most years the fires were extensive enough that late summer was a difficult time to travel through the mountains. Hundreds of explorers' and settlers' diaries mention the smoke and fires, and to the settlers this kind of landscape change was hardly an improvement. When whites complained that Indians had no right to the land because they did not work it, they did not consider burning to be work, just as they did not consider hunting, fishing, or gathering as serious labor that gave one a right to the land. Burning seemed like careless destruction, not the labor of serious adults.

At times, light Indian-set fires escaped control, blowing up into stand-replacing fires. Washington Irving wrote that when Captain Bonneville tried to cross the Blue Mountains in late summer of 1834, he had enormous difficulty because "it was the season of setting fires to the prairie" and smoke and fire were everywhere. Bonneville's party ran into a "sea of fire" and wasted a great deal of time "blundering along in this region of mist and uncertainty," until finally they had to wait two weeks in the Grande Ronde Valley for the intense fires to subside.[10] These fires were probably unintended, and they had a host of unexpected results. They consumed substantial tracts of high elevation fir forest, and probably increased the number of lodgepole forests.

Indian-set fires could destroy riparian zones, the lush vegetation that protected creeks in the Blues. As one white settler complained in the 1870s, "There was, at this time, scarcely enough brush along Pataha Creek to make camp fires as the Indians were burning grass every year along the Pataha thus killing the tender willows."[11] According to what Bonneville told Irving, the 1834 fires burned so hot that they destroyed much of the riparian forests in the ravines. Reports by the trapper Peter Skene Ogden also suggest that Indian-set fires could destroy riparian habitat. In 1826, when he was leading a trapping party through the southern Blues, he referred to country "overrun by fire," and blamed the fires on the Indians. He wrote, "many small streams have been discovered in the mountains and were not long since well supplied with beaver but unfortunately the Natives have destroyed them all and probably by the aid of fire."[12] Ogden saw this burning as irrational, because it destroyed the commodity he thought most valuable: beaver.

Just as Indian burning practices led to the open pine forests that greeted the first whites, Indian fires also shaped the extensive grasslands and prairies. As Meriwether Lewis described in 1806, Indians burned off dry bunchgrass in late summer to ensure an abundance of new grass for their horse herds once the fall rains had come, and also to open up areas for gathering roots.[13] When the naturalist John Kirk Townsend crossed the Blues in September 1835, he noted that the Umatilla Indians had "fired the prairie" on the north side of the Umatilla River: "The very heavens themselves appear ignited, and the fragments of ashes and burning grass-blades, ascending and careering about through the glowing firmament, look like brilliant and glorious birds let loose to roam and revel amidst this splendid scene."[14] As this account suggested, grassland fires could sometimes become spectacular, high intensity conflagrations. Repeated fires of this intensity might certainly prevent the succession of grasslands to forests, and even remove forests where they had once existed.

Yet grasslands of the intermountain West were not entirely the result of Indian burning, as some historians have implied.[15] Grassland, forest, and sagebrush-steppe existed in a shifting balance across the dry Blues. When someone such as Townsend came to a place and saw grasslands, he assumed they had always been there. But the particular plant community that he found on a given site at a given moment depended on history: the changing climate and the patterns of disturbances such as lightning fires, Indian fires, and grazing by both native ungulates and introduced livestock. Some areas never supported trees, even during the moistest, coolest times, because the soil was too poor for tree growth, while other areas supported trees only during wet epochs. Human practices did not create these grasslands. But frequent fires kept trees off many sites that would otherwise have been able to support forests. In the century since fire suppression began, ponderosa and juniper have greatly encroached on the prairies even though the climate has become slightly drier and hotter, suggesting that fires had indeed destroyed forests and created grasslands in some places.

Because the major reason Indians burned grasslands was to provide better forage for their massive herds of horses, much Indian burning was probably a recent source of disturbance on the grasslands. Many travelers in the early nineteenth century enviously mentioned large bands of fine Indian horses.[16] These herds were enormous, with some estimates ranging upwards of half a million horses running in the Blues when white settlement began. At just one winter encampment along the Umatilla River in 1811, Wilson Price Hunt noted that there were two thousand horses for just thirty-four families.[17] Seasonal migrations helped prevent horse overgrazing; otherwise, the large herds would have rapidly depleted the fragile bunchgrasses. Nevertheless, thousands of horses grazing in one place for the winter probably did degrade the native bunchgrass communities, especially in drier places such as the Imnaha and Snake canyons where some bands of Nez Percé spent the winter. Heavy grazing during the first half of the nineteenth century might have altered the grassland communities—say, by favoring native annuals over native perennials—so that when whites brought cattle in and grazing pressure tripled after 1870s, the grasslands were less resistant to cattle than they might have been otherwise.[18]

Contact between Indians and whites changed the ways some tribes used the land, but those changes were not always losses, nor did they result in destruction of traditional relationships between people and nature. When some Nez Percé and Cayuse families adopted the cultivation methods urged on them by Protestant missionaries in the 1830s, they did so in a way that fit their own traditional migratory use of the land. For example, the Protestant missionary Marcus Whitman reported in 1843 that the Cayuse families farming at Waiilatpu (a mission near Walla Walla, on the north edge of the Blues) prepared the land for plants in early spring. Then in April they moved to the upland streams and meadows of the Blue Mountains to dig camas; in May they shifted to the Columbia River for the salmon run; in July they went to the Grande Ronde for more camas gathering and the annual trading rendezvous with the Shoshone; and in September they returned to the Walla Walla Valley and began to harvest what they had planted in the spring. After the end of the October harvest, they headed over the Rockies to buffalo country, and they returned to widely scattered tribal winter camps after the end of the hunt.[19] Yet fur trapping, grazing, commercial hunting, and particularly agricultural settlement did cause enormous changes to the tribes. The Protestant missionaries recognized this almost as soon as they arrived, and used it as a justification for the tribes to settle, give up their migratory ways, and adopt European attitudes toward the land.

Henry Spalding, one of the Protestant missionaries to the Nez Percé, argued that by the 1830s whites had already altered the ecology of the area enough to make it difficult for the Nez Percé and Cayuse to subsist on their accustomed diet of roots and game.[20] What he, and others, assumed was that these changes would mean the death of the tribes unless they adopted European ways. On the contrary, a culture is not destroyed when it changes. But often such changes to both land and people are seen as losses: if the land is no longer pristine and untouched, its wild nature has been irrevocably lost; and if tribes are no longer exactly the way they used to be, they are no longer Indians. Thus the status of both nature and Indians is ultimately diminished, and they are externalized into objects of nostalgia and regret. Once they have lost their purity, they are to be mourned and then dismissed.

Whites in the Blues

Whites who came to the Blues in the nineteenth century fall into two fairly distinct groups: those who extracted resources but had little intention of reshaping the land into an American home, and those who came looking for a place to create an American agrarian ideal. Fur traders, explorers, and miners were basically migrants with little intention of reworking the land to fit an ideal of American culture. Nor did they try to dispossess the Native Americans who lived there. Although they often formed strong emotional attachments to the land, they were wanderers whose true homes were elsewhere. Their efforts certainly changed the landscape— beaver were rare for a century after the trappers departed—but these changes were on a much smaller scale than those set in motion by settlers, and later by government managers. In contrast, settlers came to recreate an American ideal in a place that often proved resistant to such visions. The labor of farming formed an almost sacred relationship to the land. But this relationship was ironic at its heart, since farming was often profoundly destructive of what the farmers had originally loved about the land.

The whites who most admired the romantic scenery of the Blues were those who felt the least need to alter it: explorers and traders, rather than settlers. Settlers found that the effort of trying to create a home complicated their attitudes toward wild nature, since it was difficult to see nature as a pretty view when they were in the middle of it. Those who worked with the land formed a much more intimate relationship to the place, even as they tried to make it fit an agrarian—rather than a sublime—ideal. Yet even the men and women who were most eager to improve the land mourned what they lost in the process.

For most whites who came through the Blues, "wild nature" was whatever they did not yet control: the land, the flora, the fauna, and the Indians. The very presence of whites led to the loss of wild nature. In 1925, a Forest Service report mourned the loss of this wildness: "The scarsety of the Blue Grouse is nodoubt due to close grazing, settlement and cultivation . . . also the building of roads amd trails which has an attendncy to inhabit the country and take away the wild nature that this class of game birds require."[21] Wild nature, in this passage, meant the world without evidence of whites. In contrast, many whites saw Indians and their land use as part of nature, a habit of thought that persists today, when "natural" fire regimes are defined as those that existed before white settlement.[22] Wild nature was what disappeared when whites started to work the land. Some whites saw this loss as all to the good; some saw it as a pity; nearly all saw it as irrevocable and inevitable.

Beaver and the Fur Trade

The curious fashion of beaver hats transformed the Blues. The fur trade brought the inland Northwest into the global economy and ended its isolation from the European world. As Robbins and Wolf argued, "the worldwide expansion of market capitalism was the great driving force in transforming the human and natural world of the Pacific Northwest."[23] Beginning with the explorers and fur traders, whites brought with them new cultural visions of the relationship between land and humans, and these led to changes far more rapid than those that had preceded whites.

Once people saw nature primarily as a collection of resources destined for distant markets, competition over control of those resources soon led to policies that devastated the land. When fur companies believed they had a permanent hold on a region, they were fairly benign landlords, trapping on a sustained-yield basis—as the Hudson's Bay Company did in much of Canada when it had a monopoly on the fur trade. But when competition broke out between the Northwest Company and the Hudson's Bay Company over control of the lucrative Canadian beaver territory, both of them fiercely overtrapped. A few decades later in the Oregon Territory, the British and Americans struggled to control the inland Northwest's resources, and this too brought ecological havoc. The Hudson's Bay Company decided on a policy of rapid overtrapping south of the Columbia River in hopes of creating a fur desert—a buffer zone of "worthless" land that would keep Americans out. George Simpson of the Hudson's Bay Company wrote: "we have convincing proof that the country is a rich preserve of Beaver . . . which for political reasons we should endeavour to destroy as fast as possible."[24]

But while trappers were stripping the streams of beaver, they expressed complicated and often ambiguous attitudes toward what they saw as wild nature. Trappers arrived in the Blues just as a new vision was sweeping Europe and America—nature romanticized and idealized. By the early nineteenth century, poets and intellectuals had shorn wild nature of much of its earlier association with evil and ungodliness. The British Romantic poets—particularly Wordsworth, Byron, and Coleridge—had persuasively argued that nature's virtues existed in both the beauty of a fertile garden and the grandeur and power of the wild landscape. In the Romantic tradition, the experience of sublime nature revealed the intention and power of God. Rather than alienating one from God, wild nature could bring one closer. American transcendentalists, particularly Emerson, translated romanticism for Americans, arguing that nature reflected universal spiritual truths. The soul allowed one to

transcend the material world, but wild nature was not purely material; it offered the soul access to a spiritual realm.[25] Surprisingly,
perhaps, trappers came well versed in these ideals; when they tried
to describe their response to this western landscape, they quoted
Whitman, Emerson, Wordsworth, and Byron in their journals.

Romantic ideals of nature, however, offered the trappers little
help in interpreting the landscape that surrounded them. Trappers
first came to the Blue Mountains in 1811, in a party led by Wilson
Price Hunt and financed by the American John Astor—part of the
first American attempt to gain control of the fur trade.[26] Hunt's
journals, like those of many whites, were a record of continual confusion, signifying how strange and unfamiliar this new land was
for people used to the East. Hunt's journey was something of a
nightmare, since he ignored the advice of Shoshones and insisted
on crossing in the dead of winter. Although his party attempted to
follow the grid of trails laid down by Native Americans, they managed to become thoroughly lost, over and over again. They would
head up one valley expecting it to lead to the Columbia, but it
would end in a cliff wall. Ridge lines led to labyrinths of other
ridges instead of over the mountains, as normal ridges should. The
strangeness of the landscape bewildered and frightened them, and
finally made the men willing to trust neither their guides nor their
leader. This confusion is important to note, because it shows how
strange and unfamiliar this land was to the whites. The Blue Mountains were not just some place they had never been before; the
Blues formed a landscape completely different from anything
whites knew how to judge.

Wilderness, for these Astorians, was a place of fear, confusion,
and cold feet, and not a place of sublime raptures. Hunt's journals
lack any mention of picturesque views or the romantic thrills of
nature one finds in the memoirs and journals of the Scottish and
British explorers. These Americans were intent on profit. More important, they were lost and hungry, and at the time they had little
impulse to romanticize adventure. Three decades later, when
Washington Irving recounted Hunt's journey in *Astoria*, he decor-
ated his account with the romantic apparatus of adventure and

sublime scenery that are missing in Hunt's own journals. Irving may have seen this journey as a great American adventure in the new world, but Hunt saw it as a cold and wearying ordeal.

A second party of Astorians crossed the Blue Mountains far more easily the following summer. The leader, Robert Stuart, a twenty-seven-year-old Scottish explorer working for the Astorian Fur Company, paid far more attention than Hunt did to the aesthetics of landscapes. He categorized views as either picturesque or sublime, describing the Grande Ronde Valley as "a most enchanting tract . . . where the gloomy heavy timbered mountains subside into beautiful hills, chequered with delightful pasture grounds, which, when combined with the numerous rivelets murmuring over their gravely serpentine beds towards the glade below, afford a scene truly romantic, and such as is seldom to be met with in these regions of solitude and gloom." [27] Although Stuart was a fur trapper bent on making a fortune for himself and his company, he was fluent in the language and attitudes of romanticism. Even while he and his men stumbled through the snow, they looked on the land with eyes that could appreciate nature in romantic terms. Yet what they admired was scenery more than nature: a pretty view off in the distance and therefore not threatening.

The more difficult the traders found their passage through the Blues, the less they admired the scenery. In the midst of a wretched attempt to cross the Rockies, Stuart developed a fierce critique of romantic landscape aesthetics. One evening in his journal, after a particularly brutal day, he wrote: "the sensations excited on this occasion and by the view of an unknown & untravelled wilderness are not such as arise in the artificial solitude of parks and gardens." A romanticized wild nature was all very well when viewed from afar, "for there one is apt to indulge a flattering notion of self sufficiency, as well as a placid indulgence of voluntary delusions; whereas the phantoms which haunt a desert are want, misery, and danger, the evils of dereliction rush upon the mind; man is made unwillingly acquainted with his own weakness, and meditation shows him only how little he can sustain and little he can perform." [28] What frightened Stuart was how utterly powerless he was when nature was outside his control. Wild nature now offered him not a pleasant view but knowledge of the limits of individual control and a reminder of why Europeans had been so eager to tame the wilderness in the first place.

Stuart's men began to abandon their civilized behavior. As they slowly starved, they caught glimpses of game, but the animals seemed to mock their guns. The men decided on cannibalism, drawing lots and vowing to eat the loser. Stuart barely managed to prevent it. In a bitter response to American ideals of human nature, he wrote, "If the advocates for the rights of man come here, they can enjoy them, for this is the land of *liberty and equality*, where a man sees, and feels, that he is a man merely, and that he can no longer exist than while he can himself procure the means of support." [29]

Critiques such as Stuart's had little effect on the way Americans imagined and mythologized the wild West. Urban Americans saw the Blues, and the West at large, as a dazzling wilderness—a place for thrilling adventures in the midst of picturesque scenery. Their perceptions of the fur traders' romantic role in exploring and taming this wild West were largely shaped by one popular novelist: Washington Irving. In 1832, Captain Benjamin Bonneville arranged a leave from the Army and organized a 110-man expedition to explore the West. When Bonneville returned to the East after three years, he handed his notes over to Irving, suggesting that he flesh them out into "a stirring chronicle of adventure." [30] As Irving told it, Bonneville stumbled into Hells Canyon and the knife-edge canyons of the Imnaha River. Irving portrayed this voyage as a heroic epic, with Bonneville struggling along, finding himself stuck out on precipices, marveling at the sublime scenery, then getting rescued by Indians. In one passage, Irving wrote: "They remained for a long time contemplating, with perplexed and anxious eye, this wild congregation of mountain barriers, and seeking to discover some practicable passage. . . . They wrought their way with indescribable difficulty and peril, in a zigzag course, climbing from rock to rock, and helping their horses up after them." [31] The more savage and grand the scenery, the better it reflected Bonneville's bravery. The effect of Irving's account—wildly popular with an audience that had acquired a taste for depictions of the passing American wilderness—was perhaps unintentional. Whites avoided the Snake Canyon and the Nez Percé winter grounds of the northeastern Blues for forty years, largely because Irving had made the region sound so inhospitable.[32]

Fur traders came to the Blues only temporarily, yet many of them formed strong connections to the region. Their journals were marked by a sense of delight in the landscape, as well as by complaints about the frustrations and dangers of trapping. Like many who came for beaver, the Scotsman Alexander Ross was surprisingly attentive to scenery and well versed in landscape aesthetics. His memories of the land made it appear tranquil, even domestic. Thirty years after he left the Blues, when he was back in the relative civilization of Red River, Ontario (Hudson's Bay Company's Canadian headquarters), he wrote of the Umatilla Valley: "The wild fowls in flocks filled the air, and the salmon and sturgeon incessantly leaping ruffled the smoothness of the waters. The appearance of the country in a summer's evening was delightful beyond description."[33] He admired "the soft Blue Mountains whose summits are above the clouds and the wide extending plains with the majestic waters in endless sinuosities fertilizing with their tributary streams, a spacious land of green meadows."[34] The Astorians' sense of a terrifying wilderness was entirely absent from Ross's descriptions; nostalgia rather than hunger motivated these images of a fertile, picturesque paradise. Ross saw himself in exile from a lost Eden: "The roads are pointed out to all new-comers, the paths known, the Indians more or less civilized, so that the leaders of this day have little left them to do."[35] From the safety of memory and a comfortable armchair, Ross could envision wild nature as a nostalgic paradise, a place whose absence was regrettable yet irrevocable.

The fur traders came with much more complicated attitudes about wild nature than the simple association of beaver pelts with money. Good trappers knew a great deal about beaver habitat (otherwise, they would not have been effective). They could become infuriated when people harmed beaver habitat, as Peter Skene Ogden's comments about the Indian-set fires that destroyed streamside vegetation showed. But though these men did not perceive wild nature merely as a set of discrete commodities, their appreciation of nature failed to keep them from wiping out the beaver in an astonishingly short time.

Trappers such as Alexander Ross mourned the loss of wild nature even while they mourned the loss of their own livelihoods. But what they failed to imagine were the cascading effects that removing beaver would have on the ecosystem. Most people thought of nature as a collection of separate parts, like creatures in a zoo, and beaver as just one more animal. If one piece went extinct, well, there were thousands of other animals out there, so how much could it matter? Whites never expected that removing either Indian-set fires or beaver would have much effect, because they saw both fire and beaver as discrete pieces of the natural world, not members of interconnected communities.

But recent work by the ecologist Robert Naiman suggests just how complex were the effects of beaver on forests.[36] When Europeans arrived in North America, there were between 60 and 400 million beaver that ranged over about 6 million square miles of varied riparian habitats, from Arctic tundra down to the deserts of Northern Mexico. Beaver still occupied nearly every body of water when whites showed up in the Blue Mountains in 1811, but thirty years later the beaver had nearly vanished.

The riparian landscapes were products of the beaver's water flow management, just as the forest landscapes were products of Indians' fire management. Yet it is difficult now to imagine the extent to which beavers shaped their landscapes. All the streams that ecologists have ever studied have been streams that trappers had stripped of their prime shapers. All the models of nature that ecologists have ever used to formulate their ideas about how "normal" streams function are therefore not normal at all. They grow out of impoverished waters.

To understand the ecological effects of removing beaver from the Blues, we need to consider how they operated. They cut down trees and built dams—as many as fifteen to twenty-five per mile of creek in prime habitat—and all those dams had an enormous impact on the streams.[37] Dams slowed the water flow, and by creating wetlands, they buffered floods and helped prolong the late summer flow of streams—both critical factors in allowing dry forests to persist. The dams retained tremendous amounts of sediment and organic matter in the stream channel—one dam alone could gather 229,500 cubic feet (6,500 cubic meters) of sediment behind it—and this too had critical effects on the streams as well as the surrounding forests. The great heaps of sediment provided a massive reservoir of carbon—twenty times the carbon in free flowing stream sections. This accumulation served to buffer nutrient flows, because the sediment piles released carbon more slowly than surrounding areas.[38] Flooding the soil quadrupled the amount of nitrogen accessible to plants. Thus beaver activity enhanced nitrogen availability across the landscape, and because inland Northwest forests are nitrogen-limited, beavers probably indirectly increased forest productivity.

Beavers also shaped the direction of succession in riparian zones. When they chopped down vegetation, they were not indiscriminate clearcutters. They favored certain trees and shrubs and ignored others. Eventually the less-preferred trees would come to dominate the overstory, and the beavers would have to abandon that particular stream reach. If their numbers were great enough, they might virtually eliminate their preferred hardwood species, thus creating brightly lit patches in the riparian areas, where shrubs could grow thickly. The effect of all this cutting and moving about was an increase in diversity along the streams.

Beavers preferred smaller streams, because freshets—spring floods—would knock out their dams in larger streams. Yet their effects were not limited to the small streams they dammed. Beaver-cut wood from upstream dams swept into bigger streams, adding large woody debris that formed an integral part of salmon habitat. These logs in turn accumulated debris and sediment, which supplied carbon and nitrogen for the larger streams. Beaver alterations made watersheds more resistant to disturbance, as well as more resilient—quicker to recover from disturbance. Beaver modifications rippled across the landscape, and could last for the centuries it took an abandoned beaver pond to change back to forest.

The fur trade changed all this, but not in clear or simple ways. Even after the beaver vanished, their ponds persisted. Succession in these areas was rarely straightforward: instead of moving in an orderly fashion from pond to marsh to meadow to forest, there were complex jumps and pauses. Some marshes, bogs, and forested wetlands remained in a surprisingly stable condition for a century; others quickly reverted to forest. Beaver ponds in various stages of creation and decay formed a shifting mosaic of diverse patterns across the landscape. By buffering the effects of floods, drought, and fire, and by providing a source of nitrogen in a nitrogen-limited forest, beavers may have allowed many forests to persist in an otherwise dry landscape.

Missionaries

When the fur trader Nathaniel Wyeth ventured into the Blues in 1834—in yet another vain attempt to establish an American fur empire that would rival the Hudson's Bay Company—a missionary named Reverend Jason Lee joined the party. Lee brought with him two things that drastically altered the local landscape: missionary zeal and cows. Together, these transformed the inland West more thoroughly than had the British fur desert.

Protestant missionaries were dedicated to redeeming savage souls, but felt that they must first convert those souls to a more American relationship with the land. This meant farming. As Henry Spalding, a missionary from the American Board of Missions who worked with the Nez Percé, said, "While we point them with one hand to the Lamb of God which taketh away the sins of the world, we believe it to be equally our duty to point with the other to the hoe."[39] Missionaries, Spalding wrote, should be both "teachers & preachers, to call in as it were, the people from their wandering mode of living & settle them upon their lands." As he put it more succinctly: "Nobody yet has been saved on the wing."[40] The Protestant missionaries, as well as the settlers who came in their wake, felt that the only proper relationship to land was one of labor. Farming was the way you earned a right to a place. Since Indians hunted, gathered plants, and fished—activities most whites considered play, not serious work—the tribes had little claim to the land.

On the grasslands at the northern edge of the Blue Mountains, Protestant missionaries and Indians met in mutual bewilderment and then anger. In 1836, Marcus and Narcissa Whitman opened a Protestant mission among the Cayuse at Waiilatpu (near present-day Walla Walla), and Henry and Eliza Spalding established a school and farm among the Nez Percé at Lapwai (near present-day Lewiston).[41] The tragedy that resulted was in large part a clash between two very different philosophies about the proper human relationship to a particular place. Both Americans and Indians learned to see these lands as home. Both invested their hearts in one spot of land, but there was clearly something different about the ways Americans and Indians approached a given plot of land, and that difference is critical to what happened in the Blues. It is too facile to say that Americans wanted to control the land, simplify it, and treat it as a commodity—an object that could be robbed of its sacred character and thus sold and plowed and clear-cut and sliced into bits. But there are elements of truth to this. Americans loved the places they settled, and often they even loved the forests they cut. Yet in large part, the American relationship with the land developed from "working" the land, which meant changing it to fit a changing ideal.

One way of looking at the tensions between Americans and Indians is to contrast patterns of land use. In the most general terms, whites settled and Indians wandered. Not all whites fit this pattern: miners and industrial loggers and sheepherders were anything but settled, and the settled farmers in the Blues usually lost their farms as soon as hard times struck. But transforming a place by putting up a house and a fence and a garden was an American ideal, even when it rarely worked well in the dry grasslands or forests of the Blues.

Henry Spalding argued that nomadic tribes lived a pitiful life on the edge of starvation, and survival lay in changing to American ways and settling. But his judgment of what was a decent situation was obviously colored by his own ideals. He wrote: "On arriving in this country we found this people in a most pitiable situation as it respects the means of subsistence, depending entirely on roots fish & game. To obtain these precarious sources, requires . . . an intensity of labor which but few white people could endure."[42] This statement reveals two crucial misperceptions about both the land and the Nez Percé's relation to the land. First, Spalding assumed that the Nez Percé's diet must have been poor since it was not an American diet. What the Indians perceived as abundant, Spalding saw as inherently inadequate because it was wild and not cultivated. Second, Spalding at first assumed that in an arid and marginal land, agriculture would be easier than a migratory hunting and gathering system.

Ironically, reliance on imported agriculture made the Indians much more susceptible to drought than they had been before, because the exotic crops could not survive without intensive irrigation. Migrations and the use of a wide variety of resources had helped reduce vulnerability to drought. Without irrigation, crops failed; with the limited technology the Protestants brought with them, irrigation was extremely difficult. The Cayuse and Nez Percé appeared to have thought the whole process silly after a while. They soon refused to work on the mission farms, and the missionaries beat them for their "childishness" at refusing to work. At that point most of the Nez Percé and Cayuse lost interest in the whole enterprise and went back to their migrations.[43]

Although the missionaries at first assured the Indians that they had not come to challenge their right to the land, the missionaries eventually felt that whites had more of an inherent right to that land. What gave whites that perceived right was their labor—the act of transforming the land into an agrarian landscape, an act that was prerequisite to ownership. Marcus Whitman wrote in frustration, "For the Command is multiply & replenish the earth neither of which the Indians obey. . . . How then can they stand in the way of others who will do both."[44] If the Indians refused to settle and farm, then they lost their God-given right to live on that land. Whitman soon began to argue for settlers to come and form an American agrarian society.

The Protestant missionaries tended to see wild nature—land that had not yet been farmed or made familiar—as a barren and potentially evil region separating humanity from God. Not all whites felt this way; many had read the Transcendentalists and saw wilderness as a source of spiritual sustenance. Phoebe Judson, a settler who crossed the Blue Mountains in the 1840s, quoted Emerson in her diaries, writing that nature brings "one close to the divine." She felt that when she walked out alone in the wilderness, she was closer to God, even if distant from organized religion: "in this secluded, romantic spot we were free to worship our Maker according to the dictates of our conscience." Judson wrote that when she had set off across the plains, she had possessed a deep sense of evil fostered by her religion, but soon her experience in the open western landscapes had changed that, lessening her sense of inherent evil in both humans and nature.[45]

The missionaries' experience of the western landscapes was strikingly different. Their journey away from eastern civilization did little to alter their sense of the evil inherent in humanity, and even less to make them feel that the natural world was a place with spiritual value. Narcissa Whitman, when she crossed the plains, felt extremely exposed in the open space. She felt unable to worship out in the wilderness, longing for a private tent, a place where she could enclose herself and pray. She could not stand the sense of being watched, either out on the plains or once she reached Waiilatpu, where she felt that the eyes of the Native Americans were always upon her.[46] This absorption in their inner struggle closed the missionaries off from the outside landscape. Asa Smith's diaries of his overland journey are filled with extensive meditations on his own sense of sin, while all he wrote about his surroundings was: "Traveled over hills and mountains as usual."[47]

According to the teachings of the American Board of Missions, both nature and the human heart needed to be changed; to know the land and to know the heart meant knowing that both were in a state of sin. This view of land and self appeared to have been utterly foreign to the tribes. Narcissa Whitman wrote about the chief Umtippe, "His heart is still the same; full of all manner of hypocrisy deceit and guile. . . . They know [no] knowledge of the heart."[48] To Narcissa "knowledge of the heart" meant a sense of one's own evil. Asa Smith said of the Nez Percé: "The more I see of these people, the more I see of their wickedness their deep rooted selfishness & their hatred to the gospel."[49] If both nature and the heart were evil, both needed to be reformed—the land through farming, the heart through conversion.

The Protestant missionaries were the first white men and women who came intending to make this dry inland region their home, and that may have been at the heart of their desire to convert the strange landscape to a more homelike, Christian-seeming place. Most missionaries loved the forests of the Blues, but when they reached the grasslands at the north end of the forests, they found the landscape alien, exposed, and frightening. There were no trees; nothing seemed welcoming and familiar. And so they planted familiar trees and brought in familiar animals, and tried to carve out of the grasslands a small, manageable view. One way to make the land seem more familiar was to introduce exotic species, both of plants and animals. Their cows assumed an emotional role far beyond what one might expect, with feuds breaking out between the Spaldings and the Smiths over cow ownership. Planting trees from home was another way of lessening the sense of strangeness. Narcissa Whitman wrote in a letter to her family soon after they arrived in Oregon, "Husband has sent for the seeds of the large Locust, Chestnut & Walnut trees. . . . When Brother Weld comes please remember to fill his pockets with peaches, plums & pear seeds."[50]

The Protestants' attempts to convert the Nez Percé and Cayuse to agricultural Christianity were disastrous, and ended in tragedy for nearly all concerned. As the tribes refused to settle and become Americans, and as the Protestants grew increasingly bitter over rejection of their culture and religion, tensions mounted and eventually led to war against the Cayuse. The missionaries saw their role as teaching the Indians "such arts of civilization as shall enable them to improve their condition," as one missionary wrote.[51] The irony was that horse grazing, which was at the center of the northern tribes' way of life, can be more productive and less destructive than trying to convert the land to small farms. The Jeffersonian agrarian ideal, that the good and moral life in a democracy was lived by a family on a small farm, might have worked in the humid East, but without irrigation it was ineffective in the West. After frustrating years watching crops fail, Henry Spalding finally realized that he needed to learn new tricks for a new land—a new vision of the ideal relationship between humans and land, one less bound by ideals based on eastern landscapes. He now argued that grazing, a system the Nez Percé had been using for long before he arrived, might indeed be the best use of the land.[52]

Emigrants and the American Landscape

Even though the Protestant missionaries converted few Indians, they made it possible for other American settlers to envision the inland West as a place suitable for Christian homes. Following the paths first broken by Indians and then widened by trappers and missionaries, about 300,000 people traveled west on the overland trails between 1840 and 1860. Of these, 53,000 ended up in Oregon. The Oregon Trail took these emigrants through the gentlest part of the Blues. Travelers were cutting a thin line across a complex landscape, and they believed that what they saw was true of the entire region. Much of the Blues looked familiar and welcoming to whites. The forests seemed a reassuring sign of fertility, and settlers assumed that they could use this land as they had the humid forests of eastern America and Europe.

Most American settlers were not seeking to make a brand new society in the West, but to create a better version of their familiar world. They did not want to overturn a system in which some were rich, some poor; some landowners, some landless laborers. They wanted to be the ones who were landed and rich.[53] Most settlers were farmers, and they came wanting to make perfect farms. They brought with them familiar plants and animals, as well as farming practices—such as draining wetlands and plowing the soil—derived from humid lands. In the process, they catalyzed ecological changes they rarely understood or expected.

There had been numerous accounts of whites in the Blues, but most were heroic stories about the terrors and rigors of the mountains. Explorers and trappers had not minimized the danger—adventure was what sold books, after all. Irving, in particular, had brought the area to the world's attention, but hardly in a manner calculated to soothe the fears of emigrants, who wanted not stirring adventures at cliff edges but reassurance that paradise was waiting for them at the end of the journey. Reports of the Blues had portrayed the mountains as sublime but threatening, a place where no one could imagine themselves living on a small farm. John C. Frémont, an explorer and scientist with the U.S. Army Corps of Topographical Engineers, changed all that with his wildly popular reports on the Oregon Trail route.

Frémont's work made the Blues imaginable. He portrayed himself as a scientist and explorer conducting a careful survey of the West, but above all he was an expansionist tirelessly promoting both himself and the West.[54] To this end, Frémont was intent on naming, quantifying, and categorizing what he saw; he also was careful to make notes for a profitable guidebook for future settlers. As he went along, he conducted soil analyses, with the hopes of putting farming and settlement on a rational basis. His report offered a way to categorize the western landscapes: barren wasteland versus fertile farmland and useful timberland. The book also told settlers where to go to fulfill their agrarian dreams, and how to get there in one piece.[55]

Frémont did his best to think rationally about a land that was different from what he had been trained to judge. For example, when he described the soil along the Snake River just east of the Blues, he wrote, "The soil among the hills is altogether different from that of the river plain, being in many places black, in others sandy and gravelly, but of a firm and good character, appearing to result from the decomposition of the granite rocks, which is proceeding rapidly." In one passage, he also tried to steer easterners away from the mistaken notion that tree cover meant fertility, and the absence of trees meant sterility. When he moved from the sagebrush hills along the Snake into the higher grasslands of the Blue Mountains, he noted that although the sagebrush looked discouraging, in Mexico sagebrush-covered land had proved fertile enough to grow wheat. He recognized too that some things in the Blues were the reverse of what he had been taught back East: "On this western slope of our continent, the usual order of distribution of good and bad soil is often reversed; the river and creek bottoms being often sterile and darkened with the gloomy and barren artemisia; while the mountain is often fertile, and covered with rich grass, pleasant to the eye, and good for flocks and herds."[56]

Frémont's first description of the Blue Mountains also recognized their difference from what was familiar. He described a land "embracing many varieties of trees peculiar to the country, and on which the timber exhibits a luxuriance of growth unknown to the eastern part of the continent and to the Europe." There were different tree species, different patterns of growth, a new kind of forest here. When he reached the Grande Ronde, it seemed immediately to be a fine place for American settlement: "A beautiful level basin. . . . It is a place—one of the few we have seen in our journey so far—where a farmer would delight to establish himself, if he were content to live in the seclusion which it imposes." Even while recognizing the differences, Frémont responded with relief to what seemed most familiar about the mountains.[57]

Unlike Irving's exaggerated language of sublime wild nature, Frémont's was plain; his images were focused on utility. Much of his journal for the Blue Mountains consisted of a careful record of the forests: the density of stands, the heights of trees. He was overwhelmed at how huge the trees were, and by how "delightful and full of enjoyment" his journey through the pine forests was. Wild nature was not something distant, viewed from high peaks across lofty chasms. Nature was right beneath his feet; it was the soil crumbled into a cup to test for alkalinity, the sagebrush sniffed between his fingers, the needles of the trees pulled off so he could identify the species. In a way, this detailed approach to nature was a prelude to treating the land as a commodity—something to be divided and possessed. But it was also a process of forming an intimate connection with the land, of removing nature from the scenic vistas and bringing it underfoot.[58]

By the mid-1840s, the first emigrants drawn by Frémont's guidebook had found their way across the Blues, and almost without fail they expressed in their diaries pleasure at reaching the timbered mountains. Their pleasure had several sources: a sense of finally reaching Oregon and its promises of paradise, a relief at finding some shade in the forests, and an enormous joy at finding a place that looked like home. The emigrants had just crossed the Snake

River plain in the brutal heat of late summer, and most of them had hated every moment of it. Once they got up out of the sagebrush into the southern Blue Mountains near Powder River, they were happier, since the grasses looked more useful than sagebrush. But it was not until they saw the pine forests near the Grande Ronde Valley that they felt truly at home. The Grande Ronde was, in the guide James Clyman's words, "a Beautifull green spot in this region of interminable rocks dust and wild sage."[59]

In the first days after they reached the Snake River at Farewell Bend and crossed into the promised land of Oregon, the settlers were dismayed by what they saw. Expecting a fertile paradise for small farmers, they found instead sagebrush and scablands: a barren place, dry and forbidding and bleak and empty of trees and full of confusing canyons that led into blank walls of stone. Their intense desire to find something worthwhile in Oregon made them happier when they reached the open pine forests of the Grande Ronde Valley. If the Grande Ronde was this fine, surely the Willamette Valley would be even better. As John Kerns wrote, "this is the best and most beautiful place we have seen on the whole road, or, in fact, in our lives, and is said to be a fair specimen of western Oregon. If so, our expectations will be more than filled."[60]

The Grande Ronde Valley met the settlers' criteria for beauty: it was scenic, safe, and useful. The surrounding mountains made for a sublime view at a safe distance, and the valley had resources that seemed familiar. Sarah Sutton's diary made this clear: "the mountains are covered with tall pine trees down to the foot of them, and very rich perraries [prairies] joining and it begins to look a good deal more like getting to some place, than we have seen all the way. . . . It resembles our large prairies in Illinois."[61] The Grande Ronde was the first place that made sense to them; it was a real place, a solid place, in a way that the strange and confusing landscapes of the arid canyons were not.

Settlers were not looking for grazing lands for cattle; they were looking for places suitable for small farms. What made a place ideal was the presence of trees, but not too many trees. They liked the Grande Ronde Valley because the pine forests were not thick and choking but interspersed with prairies and parklike areas that seemed to promise that farming would be possible without undergoing the painful efforts of clearing farmland. What was so nice about the Grande Ronde was its closeness not to wild nature, but to something very different: it looked like an eastern, managed landscape. Space for farms was already cleared, and a pleasing, picturesque variety of streams, meadows, and trees made the place look homelike, not wild. The garden had already been designed; wild nature had already been tamed.

Trees assumed an almost mystical quality for some of the emigrants, for they made a place feel like home. These open forests stirred intense feeling of homesickness in many of the emigrants—a homesickness especially evident in the women's records. When she first saw the forests near the Grande Ronde, Rebecca Ketcham wrote, "We have seen so many hills and mountains without a tree or shrub, that seeing these really gives me a sort of home feeling. . . . They look like some of the spots on the hills about Ithaca."[62] Men also were pleased with what reminded them of home. James Nesmith wrote about the Grande Ronde Valley: "Had a beautiful prospect of the Grande Ronde from the top of the mountains. Found the mountains covered with evergreen trees which remind me of the scenes of my childhood."[63]

Trees helped settlers regain a sense of distance and perspective they had lost in the open plains. Cecelia Adams and Parthenia Blank wrote in their joint diary, "Blue Mountains beautiful in the distance covered with Pine looks as if we were coming somewhere."[64] Rebecca Ketcham wrote about the hills just north of the Grande Ronde: "Our road has been nearly the whole day through the woods, that is, if beautiful groves of pine trees can be called woods. . . . I can almost say I never saw anything more beautiful, the river winding about through the ravines, the forests so different from anything I have seen before. The country all through is burnt over, so often there is not the least underbrush, but the grass grows thick and beautiful. It is now ripe and yellow and in the spaces between the groves (which are large and many) looks like fields of grain ripened, ready for the harvest."[65] The trees were different from what they knew, but not too different: the strangeness was mild enough to be a curiosity rather than a terror. Much of what seemed so familiar and homelike about the forests came from their openness, which in turn came from their history of burning. Whites wanted to find a land that looked like home, only better.

After passing through the Grande Ronde Valley and climbing above the open ponderosa forests, they found themselves in forests that were far less likable. The higher grand fir and subalpine fir communities were hard on the emigrants, both emotionally and physically. Until several years of emigrants had pounded down a clear path, most whites promptly got lost in the high forests. W. T. Newby wrote, "The timber is so thick in meney places that you coldant see a man 10 steps."[66] They stumbled in the smoke from forest fires, wandered around in confusion on the crisscrossing networks of Indians trails, found their path barred by acres of dead and down timber that had to be hacked up and dragged out of the way, and eventually they looked at the forest with frustration. "We have been making our way over the Blue Mts through thick pine steep hills bad roads poor grass, Panthers wolves & grisley bears," wrote John Glenn in 1852, with obvious irritation.[67]

What impressed the emigrants most was the size of the trees. These were usually the first unlogged forests that settlers had ever seen, and most of them had never imagined trees could get so big. Numerous journals listed heights, diameters, and densities of the trees along the route. Emigrants valued a beautiful landscape, but only when it did not interfere with the real business at hand. As Harriet Loughary wrote about the area near the Grande Ronde Valley: "As we approach it we view a complete panorama of the beauty and grandeur of natures handiwork. . . . But beautiful as it seems, we hasten through it for no grass grows in these mountains, and grass is the chief commodity in demand every day."[68] In a statement that foreshadowed the Forest Service's attitudes toward the Blues forests, Armeda Jane Parker "regarded the trees as stately, but grumbled about the thousands of cords of wood that were going to waste."[69]

Miners and Settlers

In October 1861 a man named Henry Griffin found gold near Baker City, and eastern Oregon became a destination, not a way station. The mining boom in the Blues was brief, but nevertheless it was an ecological disaster. Miners burned swathes of timber off high elevation slopes to expose mineral outcrops, and when the spring rains came, the soils on these denuded slopes slumped, causing great landslides. Capital-intensive technologies—hydraulic pipe, reservoirs, long canals, and then steam dredges—soon replaced the placer miners with their simple pans, and the new technologies could sluice off entire hillsides. Watercourses silted in, destroying salmon habitat.[70] When miners started using steam dredges, they did not just alter riparian zones—they completely removed them. The massive dredges trundled down the streams, sucking up the streambed and spitting out the remains. The first large herds of cattle were brought into the Blues to feed the miners, and the first timber logged in any quantity was cut for mining timbers.[71]

A few people got rich off the minerals, but little of that money stayed in the region. Mining meant cutting open the land—often in the harshest ways—and then pulling pieces out to feed the demands of distant financiers. The effects could be as brutal on local communities as they were on local ecologies. Dredged streams were bitter with arsenic and mercury; ghost towns throughout the mining areas speak to how brief and unprofitable were the hopes of many.

Few of the whites who rushed into the mountains realized their dreams of striking it rich, but many of them took a look around them at the luxuriant grasslands and fertile prairies, and decided this would be a fine place to live. As the Willamette Valley began to fill up with settlers and the Indian wars died down, a migratory backwash began. Settlers who had crossed the Blues on their way to the Willamette Valley turned around and came back to the Blues. A year after the discovery of gold in 1861, a woman named Nancy C. Glenn staked a claim in the valley and wrote to her family: "This is one of the most beautiful valleys in the world. . . . Nearly all the emigration that has went down into Oregon this year intend coming back as soon as they can get back in the spring and I expect the land will then all be claimed up."[72] Five years later, General Rusling described a transformed landscape in the Grande Ronde Valley: "The whole as rich and fertile as a garden, already sprinkled well with ranches, while horses, cattle, and sheep by the thousand were grazing off in the bottoms. . . . The wheat crop of the valley

that year alone was computed at half a million of bushels."[73] Grazing and wheat displaced the native bunchgrasses, while the draining of wetlands for crops transformed the valleys.

Settlers came hoping for an ideal home. But having experienced
one dislocation, they tended to keep moving—from the eastern
seaboard to the Midwest, then to western Oregon, and finally to
eastern Oregon. The problem was not with the land but with their
expectations about the land. Even though they envisioned themselves as creators of the ideal landscape, they found it difficult to
form a permanent relationship with any single place. They came
West on what one emigrant, Phoebe Judson, called "a pioneer's
search for an ideal home," but once out West they found themselves restless.[74] A strange land ethic developed: since land was limitless, and the perfect home was just over the next mountain range,
you could always move on. One example of the carelessness this
philosophy encouraged was the settlers' attitudes toward fires.
Even though they criticized the Indians for setting them, they set
far more themselves—just for fun, or for reasons that seemed frivi-
lous even to the settlers.[75] Visions of quick riches conflicted with
visions of a perfect little farm in the distance, but neither view
of life fostered an ethic of taking care of one's immediate surroundings.

For all the settlers' high hopes, their attempts at farming in the
Blues usually ended in disaster. Where there was water, it was too
cold; the snow lingered into June, a fact that was not apparent
when the settlers passed through in late summer. Where it was
warmer there was not enough water, and irrigating by hand was
backbreaking and often heartbreaking labor. Still, settlers kept trying, well into the twentieth century. Few homesteaders ever proved
their claims; misery and poverty rather than profit usually marked
the end to their endeavors. Settlers struggled and starved and
froze—and in doing so, they spread myths of open land and the
good life in God's country.

Grazing and Grasslands

The presence of forests had reassured Americans who crossed the
Blues on their way to western Oregon, and the lure of quick profits

through a sudden gold strike had enticed many to come back and try their luck there. But what kept them was not gold or trees, but bunchgrass so thick and tall that many said it was the best range they'd ever seen, the best in the West. Grass was so thick that cattle could survive the winter without being fed hay. People could make a living just by reaching out their hands for it. The names chosen for ranching settlements in the bunchgrass lands reflected this sense of optimism. As the 1907 Chesnimnus report noted: "West of this line is surveyed country . . . the Lovely, the Paradise, the Promised Land and Garden of Eden country."[76] As one cattle owner reminisced fifty years later, during the droughts of the 1930s, when it looked liked easy times would never come again: "When the first settlers came to the county there was an abundance of fine grass. The valleys were covered with tall meadow grass that was cut and stored for winter feed. The open hillsides all had a heavy stand of bunchgrass and scarcely any sagebrush."[77] But now, he went on to say, it was all cheatgrass and scablands: paradise had been lost.

Ten years after whites first drove their cattle into valleys such as the Grande Ronde, the native bunchgrasses were already feeling the pressures of overgrazing. Stock soon needed hay to survive the winters, and whites began looking for better and bigger pastures— higher in the summer meadows and lower in the winter canyons. Competition for dwindling resources was soon intense, and tensions were strongest between three groups: the small local cattle ranchers, the itinerant and usually immigrant sheepherders running large bands of sheep owned by out-of-state corporations, and the large out-of-state cattle corporations beginning to bring their cattle to the Blues. The critical resource was the summer mountain range—fragile high meadows in the subalpine fir zone and above timberline. Because the lower elevation bunchgrass prairies could not support many cattle during the summer drought, herders turned to the much moister alpine meadows, which were even less resistant to grazing pressure than the bunchgrasses. Since the range was totally unregulated, control of the high meadows went to those who got there first each spring. Each year there were races to reach the meadows before snowmelt, to be the first to claim a section of range. Grasses were trampled and eaten before they had a chance to put on new growth, much less set seed. The result was a rapid die-off of perennial grasses in the high meadows. Since occupation meant possession, herders were unwilling to move their stock once the grasses started showing overuse, and 4,000 sheep would spend a month at a time in one small meadow until nothing was left but dust and rock.

When the transcontinental railroads opened up access to eastern beef markets in the 1880s, pressure on the range became insupportable. The Blue Mountains became the favored route for large herds of cattle moving from the Pacific Northwest, first to Wyoming and then to stock the Great Plains after the demise of the buffalo and eviction of the Indians. Spanish longhorn cattle from Texas could not survive the winters of the northern Great Plains, and the hardier stock from Oregon was soon in great demand. Stock trails meant much more than just a lot of cattle moving through the mountains on their way someplace else. As Jon Skovlin, a former Forest Service range scientist, wrote: "The Blue Mountains were a formidable crossing for cattle raised in the lowlands, and cowboys were sorely tried in trailing cattle through heavy timber. The main herds were often held on the Starkey Prairie while drovers went back for strays in the timber. . . . 25,000 head of cattle [were] bottlenecked between Pilot Rock and Starkey waiting for snows to melt."[78]

The cattle may have been in transit, but it was no simple matter to drive 25,000 cattle at a time through rough mountains, rimrocks, and canyonlands. Cattle eat. They trample grass. They wander off in the wrong direction and need to be found and brought back, while the rest of the cattle stand around and eat some more. And where do they stand? In the rich damp basins and in the riparian zones. Cattle like water. Unlike sheep, they need constant sources of water, and their favorite grazing is in the creeks and the wet meadows. This meant intensely concentrated use, with long-term impacts in localized places that were also prime spawning grounds for anadromous fish.

Still things seemed manageable—some people were making their fortunes on the bunchgrass, and ranching communities were thriving—at least for ten years or so, until the mid-1880s. Then the bubble broke. What had seemed abundant suddenly vanished without anyone really noticing. There just was not enough grass to go around, and small cattle ranchers were going under. The loss was immediately blamed on sheep, but they were by no means the only culprits. Concentrated bands of 2,000 sheep did damage the high meadows, but the loss of small cattle ranchers' range was not the fault of sheepherders. A more important factor was the out-of-state cattle operations that controlled summer range by filing claims on the few sections of public land containing springs and waterholes.

In the 1870s sheep had been a rare sight in the Blues. But by the mid-1880s they appeared to be everywhere; at least that was what cattlemen thought. These sheep herds were run by "tramp sheepmen"—foreigners most often, men who knew little English and were hired for slight wages by out-of-state corporations. Sheepherders were easy targets for local ranchers' frustrations over a dwindling resource. An illiterate herder who could barely speak English and had no local ties of property or family was easier to blame than friends, neighbors, or other cattle ranchers. The sheep herds wintered in southeastern Oregon or Nevada and were driven into the Blues for summer range. Local cattlemen saw this as an affront to their own rights, since the sheep used the lower elevation areas that local ranchers had been reserving for winter cattle range. Cattle could not use these areas in the summer because they lacked perennial water sources, but sheep could manage.

In the summer of 1882, the cattle rancher J. G. McCoy complained to the *East Oregonian* that within a ten-mile radius of his place there were 50,000 sheep. And that same year, John Starkey stated that the south-slope bunchgrass—normally winter range—was gone by mid-October.[79] As homesteaders complained to reserve inspectors: "Migratory bands of sheep, on their drive east from Wasco, Crook, Gilliam and Umatilla Counties to Idaho and Wyoming, ate the grass to the very doors of homesteaders; and tramp sheepmen [those with no home range] encroached on the range of resident stockmen."[80] Excessive as these sheep numbers were, they were not the cause of range destruction. They were the result. Cattlemen claimed that sheep poisoned an area, fouling the grass so that cattle would not use it.[81] Yet cattle had already overgrazed the range to the extent that sheep could do far better than cattle on what was left. As James Iler, the Malheur National Forest Supervisor, wrote in 1940, overgrazing by cattle created the conditions that led to their own demise: "Herds of cattle gave way to bands of sheep. History states this was due to the change in the condition of the ranges. Evidently at this early date the ranges began to show the effects of overgrazing."[82]

Sheep did better on poorer range because they required less water and they had a better chance of surviving harsh winters with little forage. In short, they were better competitors for scarce forage and overgrazed lands. Unlike cattle, sheep needed the close attentions of a herder. But with a herder, sheep could survive conditions that would kill a cow. Sheep raising also did well for reasons of economy and scale. Sheep were run in huge bands—usually 2,000 adult sheep in a band, plus their offspring. They roamed from one public range to another, and the men who roamed with them were placeless too, foreigners who had little status and made few demands on their employers. Sheep were owned not by locals, but by large corporations that had to invest almost nothing in land, taxes, equipment, or horses; just in the stock themselves. In contrast, small local cattlemen needed to overwinter their cattle with hay on their own lands, putting them in a tight financial situation.

Small cattlemen were in trouble not just because of sheep damage to the grasses. Laws and custom specified that the range was supposed to be open to all, and not the exclusive property of the wealthy. Grass in the mountains was free and belonged to those who got there first: the Enclosures Act of 1873 stated that no one could legally fence public domain. Larger corporations, however, found ways to control large sections of public domain and thereby exclude small local owners. By 1880 the larger and wealthier stockmen, most of whom came from California and had great amounts of capital to finance them, consolidated control of their grazing areas. Settlement of the small valleys would be a disaster for the large stockmen, because their cattle could find water only in those valleys. Whoever controlled that water controlled the range. The large cattle operations illegally paid cowboys to file homestead claims on the few sections that had water. One government inspector, H. D. Langille, wrote in 1906 that the Pacific Livestock Company "had taken up forty sections controlling springs and waterholes, directing their cowboys to locate homesteads on these tracts, and then paying them fifty dollars for their title and ranch. By ownership of these few sections they had control of thousands of acres of the range."[83] After this move, feuds broke out between large stockmen and small settlers and ranchers, resulting in hundreds of lawsuits and some killings in the south end of the Blues, in Harney County.[84] Trends in the cattle industry were increasingly favoring large ranches under individual owners or partnerships, and this left the small homesteaders with little control of either water or grass.

Land swindles were common, as cattle-owning corporations tried to get control of public ranch and timber land. Railroad and military road grants were also magnets for corruption. The largest ownership in Grant County—the Eastern Oregon Land Company—was formed by what most people agreed was a clever swindle. In 1867, Congress enacted a law that created a land grant for The Dalles Military Road. Along a strip three miles wide, the federal government agreed to give the cattle company every other section of land. In return, the company would build a road from The Dalles to Fort Boise, and this road would open the region to development, allow for the export of resources out of the region and money into the region, and generally lead to a brighter future for Oregon and Idaho both. The government's idea was that the company would sell the land piece by piece to investors, raising money to finance road construction. The only problem was that although the company sold the land and kept the money, it never finished the road. The case eventually went to the U.S. Supreme Court, which affirmed the original title, even in the absence of the road.[85]

By the mid-1890s, the situation was ready to explode. Large corporations were running cattle on public land, excluding the small ranchers from water sources. Itinerant sheepmen were trailing vast bands of sheep through the mountains, and herds of cattle were also crossing the mountains. There was an unregulated race for the summer range, and consequently the forage was nearly gone. As one rancher stated twenty years later: "The first man to an area generally topped it and later on other outfits used the same range with a damaging result, the results of which are still to be seen."[86] Not only that, but there was an agricultural depression under way. In 1940, James Iler, the Malheur National Forest Supervisor, wrote that in Grant Country between 1893 and 1897, "grain crops were below average; prices were low; wool sold for less than ten cents per pound; the price of wheat fell to 26 cents per bushel; and this general depression extended to the stock industry."[87]

Tensions finally spilled over into cattle and sheep wars throughout eastern Oregon. In Union County, cattle owners formed a group called the Sheep Shooters Association. They ran advertisements in the La Grande *Gazette* identifying certain cattle ranges where sheepherders were advised not to cross recognizable boundaries or "deadlines." They also announced that they would be placing lethal saltpeter mixed with stock salt in certain hotly contested range areas. Jon Skovlin wrote that "Andy Sullivan, who ran horses on the flats below the Campbell brothers' homesteads . . . burned out several night corrals built by itinerant sheep owners along what is now called Burnt Corral Creek. It is very likely that Sullivan also burned the accompanying tented camps of the herders. Blood was shed near the Starkey Range on upper Camas Creek when herder Lew McCarty was shot by unknown assailants."[88] Thousands of sheep were also killed in Grant County, where feelings were strongest because summer range was in shortest supply. The wars were not just between sheepmen and cattlemen; homesteaders and the large cattle operations also came to the point of violence. In the late 1890s, small homesteaders made a determined effort to break up the large blocks of land controlled by the Californian-owned corporations. Homesteaders settled on open meadows and, in defiance of the law, fenced the creek bottoms to cut off the water supply from the large stockmen. Bitter feuds resulted, and while many of the small settlers were driven out, enough survived to break down most of the large ownerships in Grant County.[89]

Outside eastern Oregon, however, the public was largely un-concerned. As the range historian William Rowley argued, many Americans saw this violence as the natural outcome of competi-tion—a competition that would inevitably lead to advancement and progress rather than chaos and resource depletion.[90] Urban res-idents paid little attention until they realized that overgrazing might be threatening their own financial interests. Irrigation com-panies were among the first to respond, since overgrazing promised to destroy the watersheds that protected their investments in water developments. For example, the Lewis-Clarkston Irrigation Com-pany petitioned for a forest reserve near Asotin, to preserve the headwaters upon which their investments depended.[91] Early forest researchers also identified serious overgrazing in the higher eleva-tions of the Blue and Wallowa mountains. In 1903 a flash flood "devastated the little city of Heppner nestling between the treeless hills," as the reserve inspector H. D. Langille wrote, and Langille easily persuaded Heppner residents that destruction of plant cover in the watershed by sheep grazing had contributed to the disaster.[92]

By the time federal inspectors came out West, everyone in-volved seemed to recognize that unregulated grazing was devasta-ting the landscape. Ranchers were ready for an end to the disputes, and increasingly welcomed government intervention. On the whole, local sheepmen as well as cattlemen were ready for regula-tion, even though they feared the government would rule in favor of cattle over sheep. Herders were sick of the bloodshed and tired of the struggles to grab the last bits of grass. Rampant competition had led to chaos, a situation that left no one happy.

Changes in Terrestrial Game Populations

Unrestricted use not only replaced lush bunchgrasses with rock and dirt, but it also devastated wildlife populations in the Blues. With booms in mining and railroad developments, markets for meat opened up, and commercial hunters were quick to exploit wildlife to fill the demand. Ranchers saw wild animals as competi-tors for increasingly scarce forage, and overgrazing by domestic livestock added to the pressures on wildlife populations. Although animal numbers had always fluctuated in the Blues independent of human agency, severe population crashes followed commercial hunting and livestock grazing.

Hunting pressures, ecological changes in plant communities, disease epidemics, as well as severe winters and droughts had tangled effects on game populations. According to Nez Percé traditions recounted by Gerald Tucker, a local historian and Forest Service employee, even before whites arrived, elk and deer populations had declined several times after severe winters.[93] During the Lewis and Clark expedition in 1805, game was at a low ebb just north of the Blues. Wilson Hunt and Robert Stuart, for example, both mentioned how few deer and elk were present in the 1810s. But soon afterward, game populations appeared to have increased rapidly, and by the 1830s whites began to comment on deer abundance. Surprisingly perhaps, wildlife increases may have been an indirect effect of European activity in the new world. Disease epidemics resulting from European contact had caused sharp declines in Indian populations during the early 1800s; malaria, for example, killed as many as 80 to 90 percent of the population of some villages along the Columbia River. When human populations crashed, hunting pressures undoubtably dropped as well, allowing deer and elk to increase.[94]

By the 1860s and 1870s, just as the population of whites began growing in the Blues, game was abundant. One resident of the Wallowa Valley wrote that when whites first arrived in the valley, "large herds of deer and elk were frequently seen crossing the valley, while bear were so numerous as to be a decided menace to the stock industry. Prairie chicken, grouse, pheasants, ducks and geese were also much in evidence. . . . The streams also abounded with trout, salmon, and red fish."[95] Abundance, however, was short-lived. Over the next thirty years, as white populations grew sharply, wildlife populations crashed. By 1905, when the Forest Service arrived in the Blues, what they saw was a land that seemed perfect for both deer and elk, but both were almost entirely absent.

A few people blamed wildlife collapses on an excess of predators. The part of wild nature that whites disliked was seen as responsible for destroying the part they preferred. As one Forest Service employee wrote in 1970: "Game animals, both elk and deer, were no more plentiful in 1906 than today. Coyotes, cats, cougars, and bear were plentiful, which undoubtedly kept other animals killed off."[96] For most whites, Indians were also part of the undesirable element of wild nature, so they were convenient targets for much of the blame. In 1903 H. D. Langille stated in his report on the proposed Heppner Reserve that game was not at all abundant, "probably due to the annual hunt of the Warm Springs and Umatilla Indians."[97] In 1907, Overton Price, the Associate Forester of District 6 (Oregon and Washington), wrote to Supervisor O'Brien: "I am very glad to note that you have been able to afford protection to the game on your reserves and I am highly pleased to hear of Ranger McClain's exploits in keeping the Indians out."[98]

Commercial market hunting, however, rather than predators, weather, or Indians, probably led to most of the declines in game numbers at the turn of the century. These market hunts could be extraordinarily intense. Howard Fisk, a resident of the Blues, reported that bands of commercial hunters shot herds of deer during the winters of 1903 to 1911 and shipped the meat back East, and "after that deer were so scarce that [Fisk's] father, who drove the stage between Wallowa and Elgin, would stop when he saw a track, it was so rare to see one." Rolland Huff, a rancher who spent his life in the Blues, recounted his father's work with these market hunters: "Many hunters who shot out the plains buffalo later moved westward to hunt deer for their hides. . . . In the summer of 1877 [my] father joined up with another hunter . . . [and] on July 4th they started out of Sumpter on an expedition, taking hides and leaving the carcass. The partners ended the season in September near Prairie City with 354 hides." It was 1910 before Rolland Huff saw a deer track, and 1915 before he got his first taste of venison. The abundance that had seemed so promising to whites vanished almost as soon as they arrived.[99]

Early Logging in the Blues

During the last years of the nineteenth century, the Blues were up for grabs, or so it seemed to government critics. People were starting to sense that there was an end in sight to the limitless abundance of western resources, and the mood was one of frenzy, as people tried to get control of the last few pieces before they vanished. While the rush for summer range was tearing up the high meadows, loggers were stripping the biggest ponderosas from the lower watersheds as fast as they could cut them.

The heaviest logging took place along railways built by David Eccles, who began logging in Utah in the 1870s and then in 1889 came to Baker to found the Oregon Lumber Company—just four years after the transcontinental railroad reached that small town, connecting the Blues resources to the rest of the nation's markets. Eccles soon realized that he needed his own railroad to funnel logs to his mills, so he financed construction of the Sumpter Valley Railway, which reached from Baker to Sumpter in 1897. In 1901 the railroad was extended to Whitney on the North Fork of the Burnt River. By 1909, the line reached Prairie City, and this single railroad carried out nearly all the ponderosa that was cut in the southern Blues. At first, locals were delighted to have the railroad, believing it would offer a cheap and easy way to ship their cattle, logs, and minerals to the rest of the country. But they found that the railway was not as helpful as they had hoped. H. D. Foster—the forester who had been so concerned about the Wenaha fires—wrote in 1908 that the Baker City Lumber Company (which was affiliated with Sumpter Valley Railway Company) owned "practically all the timberland tributary to the right of way, and even, it is claimed, the ranches in the Whitney Valley. . . . Since this company control most of the timberlands of this region outside of the National Forest boundaries, and own the railway, they are in a position to charge excessive freight rates on lumber, an opportunity which they do not neglect."[100] Eccles had a monopoly with his new railway, and his company seemed to mushroom: first it owned one timber company, then another, then it owned the railway, and then it gained control of the largest ranch operations too. Locals had thought that the railways would open up the future for them, but instead they seemed to be getting left in the dust.

Logging was particularly intense in the ponderosa forests within the upper watershed of the Grande Ronde River. In 1890, the

Smith-Stanley Lumber Company built a mill at Stumptown, later Perry, and installed the first bandsaw in northeastern Oregon. The mill was later sold to the Grande Ronde Lumber Company, a large concern funded by midwestern capital. In 1893, ten local ranchers built another mill in the upper Grande Ronde watershed, this one at the mouth of Spring Creek. Three times they depleted the pon-derosa pine in a local area and then moved the mill, rather than try to transport logs farther along the small creeks. A year later a man from Pendleton came in and set up a mill on his homestead along Meadow Creek, also on the Upper Grande Ronde. By 1895 there were two hundred loggers at work on the Upper Grande Ronde, harvesting between 15 and 20 million board feet each year from the watershed. A century later, many people were arguing that early logging was insignificant, and problems came from too little logging, not too much. But these figures are not insignificant; logging was almost as heavy one hundred years ago as it was in the late 1980s.[101]

Along the Grande Ronde River, loggers floated timber to the mills through a system of splash dams that blocked the small streams during high water. When enough water had accumulated, loggers dynamited the dams, forcing the logs far downstream in the explosion of high water. Splash dams were clever ways of trans-porting logs down streams that normally did not have water levels high enough to float logs. But as one can well imagine, they de-stroyed the structure of the stream bank, tearing away willows, alders, and cottonwoods—not to mention any fish that might be lurking in the pools.

At the beginning of the new century, only the most accessible lands had been cut, but this was soon to change. Starting in 1902, just before the Bureau of Forestry began inspecting for potential reserve withdrawals, heavy cutting in the large pine stands began. By 1906, even the least accessible pine forests had been scouted by locators. As one forest report stated in 1906, the Wallowa Valley had "passed into the hands of the mill men . . . [and] timber land is becoming hard to get."[102] M. L. Erickson, a government forester, argued that "this [open yellow pine] type is very characteristic of a large portion of the reserve, and is the kind of timber much sought after by the vigilant timber locators, who have been operating along the boundaries of the reserve for the past three or four years."[103] Farther north, in what became the Wenaha reserve and later the Umatilla National Forest, the foothills had once been unbroken conifer tracts. By 1904, W. H. B. Kent reported that these foothills were entirely cut, burned, and denuded by sheep grazing. At higher elevations, stands of pine and fir were still unlogged, but the lower elevation ponderosa stands were cut.[104]

Logging in the Blues, as in much of the West, operated right at the borders of legality just before the Forest Service arrived, often slipping over the edge into fraud. Most lumbermen wanted not title to the land, but just what was called "stumpage": ownership of the standing trees. But federal law had no provision for this. Timber speculators in the Blues got around this problem by advertising for men willing to file a homestead claim on forest land. The timber companies would pay the men $2.50 an acre for their claims, and then strip the land of timber. In five years, when it was time to prove the claim, the land defaulted back to the government.

The new federal foresters wanted timber companies to adopt the principles of scientific, conservative logging. In short, this meant logging in such a way that there would be trees left to log again in the future—growing trees as a crop, as Gifford Pinchot, the first head of the Forest Service, liked to repeat. But growing trees as a crop required three things: protection from fire so that there would be a crop left to log, tax laws that would make it possible to carry timber on land without being forced to harvest it, and land laws allowing owners to obtain pieces of land large enough to let some trees grow instead of being immediately harvested. American land policies of the late nineteenth century did not meet any of these requirements; they were based on agrarian assumptions and designed to meet agrarian needs, rather than the needs of timber or ranching industries. Even though much of the arid West was worthless for farming without irrigation, the laws affecting forest land reflected the general agrarian belief that the best thing one could do with a forested tract was to clear it and farm it.[105] Timber operators could buy land in the West, but it was rarely cheap, and until lumber prices rose, it made more sense for lumbermen to invest in manufacturing facilities or railways than in land.

Private forestry practices in the Blues at the beginning of the century were notoriously brutal. The timber industry was still mostly migratory, and thus had little commitment to the future welfare of the deforested area. To make a profit off railroad logging, cutting had to be extremely intense to pay for the rails alone. According to federal inspectors, all the Eccles timber companies—not just the Oregon operations—used very destructive methods. The head government forest inspector, H. D. Langille, complained bitterly that along the entire length of the Sumpter Valley Railway "the destruction of the timber is almost complete. Only the best portion of the trees is used, leaving a dense heavy litter on the logged off areas. The hillsides have been wiped clean of everything large enough for saw timber of any kind. In many places fire has followed the cutting and the destruction is complete."[106] After clearcutting the site, loggers left brush and debris "scattered in the utmost confusion."[107] Sparks from logging railways often ignited the logging debris, and catastrophic fires destroyed the upper soil layers, killed whatever young growth had not been destroyed by the skidders, and left the land in a condition from which recovery seemed unlikely. As Langille claimed, "a very few years of such work as is being done by this Company would denude the entire watershed of this stream [the upper Grande Ronde River]."

People had expected that after land was logged, it would be able to support the agrarian ideal: small farmers living the good life. It had seemed only logical that if a piece of land could support tall trees, it must be fertile enough for intensive farming. But this hope proved illusory: attempts to farm cutover lands usually ended in misery. The public looked at those barren lands and thought they would never grow anything again. The loss seemed irrevocable.[108]

Settlement in the Blues, as in the West at large, had been driven by a vision of limitless abundance. The forests seemed endless; the land in need of improvement; the world available for the taking. But as the timber industry reached the Pacific, people began to fear that there might be an end in sight. Many worried that if the nation continued to deplete its forests without thought of the future,

it might one day find itself without the timber upon which civilization depended. Federal scientists in particular were certain that,
because of wasteful industrial logging practices, a timber famine
was about to devastate America. By the first decade of the twentieth century, the Blues seemed to be in serious trouble. The bunchgrass was largely gone, depleted by intense grazing. Wars between
small cattle ranchers, itinerant sheepherders, and large cattle operations from California had left thousands of sheep and several
sheepherders dead. Timber locators and speculators were taking up
the best timber land; small mills and miners were illegally cutting
throughout the watersheds; irrigators feared that their investments
in water projects would be lost. It was in this context that federal
foresters came west—to save the Blues from unrestricted abuse fostered by the desire for short-term profits.

The Feds in the Forests

The Forest Service came to the Blues in the first decade of the twentieth century with the best of intentions: to save the forest from the scourges of industrial logging, fire, and decay. When they looked at the Blues, they saw two things: a "human" landscape in need of being saved because it had been ravaged by companies and the profit motive, and a "natural" landscape that also needed saving because it was decadent, wasteful, and inefficient. Not only were federal foresters going to rescue the grand old western forests from the timber barons, they were going to make them better. Using the best possible science, they would make the best possible forests for the best of all possible societies: America in the brand new twentieth century. But instead of an orderly and efficient forest, what resulted was forest chaos.

For all their mistakes, the federal foresters were doing something revolutionary: they were trying to come up with a different vision of the human role in natural history. Nearly all the whites who had preceded foresters to the Blues felt that they had stepped into a pristine wilderness—an unchanging place empty of all meaningful human influence. If the forest was a collection of separate parts, then people could either admire these parts or remove them. But they did not have to imagine themselves as participants in a history of relationships and interconnected effects. The foresters changed this by trying to see the forest as a complex web of indirect effects—with human actions as part of that web.

In 1900, federal forest inspectors came to the Blues to determine whether the forests were valuable enough to be withdrawn from the public domain and placed in the new forest reserve system. Rumors immediately spread of a railroad that would open up access to stands of ponderosa pine. Within a week, speculators came into the region by the hundreds from Wisconsin, Iowa, and Minnesota. A race between the government inspectors and the speculators began, with the inspectors' work driven by a conviction that land thieves were scouting the Blues for the best government forest land, which they would claim and strip of timber. But at the same time, the *Oregonian* accused the government inspectors of working in league with the speculators. It was a frenzied, chaotic time, as speculators tried to claim land before the government withdrew it, and everyone suspected everyone else of being a spy for the other side.[1]

The government's attempt to establish forest reserves in the Blues sparked an immediate and intense controversy over land fraud. The Forest Lieu Land Clause, an element of the Organic Act of 1897, allowed homesteaders to select lands from the public domain in lieu of any lands they had within the reserve boundaries before the reserve was declared. Although the purpose of this clause was to protect citizens against unfair seizure of private property, the result in the Blues was a series of scandals that made many Oregonians intensely hostile to the forest reserve system.

When the forests of the Blues were first being inspected for potential withdrawal as forest reserves in 1900, administrators in the Land Office leaked information on a proposed forest withdrawal outside of Baker City—the Blue Mountain Forest Reserve. Lieu land speculators paid their employees to file homestead claims on the land two days before the reserve inspectors arrived, and then the speculators forged a petition calling for a reserve on the land they had just claimed. Most of the signers were supposedly local citizens, but turned out to be, as one official put it, "barflies and roustabouts." Once the reserve lands were withdrawn, the speculators were able to choose land they liked outside the reserves, in good agricultural territory that was worth more than the land they had just claimed, but had already been closed to ordinary homestead entries.

Several types of speculation were common. Legally, a homesteader could buy land at the market price (if any was available) or could file a 160-acre claim on public land and then either "improve" that land for five years and own it outright or buy it for $1.25 an acre after six months. The latter was a popular option with bona fide settlers, because once they owned the land, they could mortgage it and raise money for improvements. In order to get the money for initial purchase, settlers could sign the title over to land agents, who advanced them the money at 40 percent interest. This system satisfied both parties: the land agents made a tidy profit, and the settlers ended up paying about $2.00 an acre for land worth much more on the market. Timber speculators also paid people to file claims on public lands, which the speculators could then strip of timber—not a legal operation, but one that was often impossible to control. After five years, the lands were defaulted upon, when the supposed settlers turned out not to have made the required improvements.[2] Finally, the lieu land speculators paid their employees less than $1.25 an acre to file claims on forest lands, and then the speculators acquired title to agricultural lands worth many times more than the forest lands, which they then resold. Thus homesteaders could file claims to land without paying a thing, but with the Lieu Land Clause they had a certain legal claim to the title, even though they had not yet proven their claim.

When the *Oregonian* broke the lieu land fraud story in 1903, the entire Oregon congressional delegation, save one person, was named in the fraud.[3] In addition, the *Oregonian* accused the Bureau of Forestry of colluding, by leaking information to timber operators about withdrawals. Surveyors for the reserves in the Blue Mountains, particularly H. D. Langille—the man responsible for promoting and surveying most of the Blue Mountains withdrawals—were said to be in the pay of the speculators.

Inspectors tried to get ahead of timber speculators by making large temporary withdrawals of both forested and unforested land—land that was potentially suitable for farms as well as forest reserves. These temporary withdrawals were vast: 668,160 acres for the Wallowa Reserve; 322,560 acres for the Joseph Reserve; 391,680 acres for the La Grande Reserve; and 3,133,680 acres for the Blue Mountain Reserve. The purpose of these temporary withdrawals was to legally protect as much land as possible before speculators could lay claim to it. After the situation had calmed down, inspectors planned to survey the forested lands and return the other lands to the public domain.

This logic did not impress the locals, who figured it was one more scam by corrupt officials out to steal good farmland.[4] The temporary withdrawals left much of the land in the Blues in a state of limbo. By 1903, nearly 5 million acres of land in the Blues went into legal uncertainty while the lieu land scandals were being investigated. During the tense three years between the breaking of the scandals and the repeal of the Lieu Land Clause in 1905, the Bureau of Forestry tried to clear its name by sending out scientists to do careful inventories of the withdrawals. These inventories are gems: they offer an excellent idea of what the land was like and what the federal scientists wanted from the land.

H. D. Langille, an inspector first for the Geological Survey and then for the Bureau of Forestry, wrote most of the Blues reserve inspection reports between 1902 and 1905. His "Report on the proposed Blue Mountain Reserve" (1906) is the best example of what the surveys were attempting to accomplish. Since Langille had been accused of corruption by the *Oregonian* and his name had not yet been cleared (as it would be a year later), he felt that everything was at stake: his good name, the land, the grass, the trees, the wealth of the region. Langille spent much of those limbo years traveling endlessly over the region, getting to know the land so he could speak with authority. In part he was trying to save the land from what he saw as the grip of vicious speculators. In part he was trying to clear his name of the accusations of carelessness and arrogance and ineptitude. In part he was trying to shift local opinion, trying to win locals over to his side. And in large part, he was trying to learn something about the strange, unfamiliar place in which he found himself.

Langille was a government bureaucrat, thus by definition an outsider. He had a hard time on his inspection trips. They always seemed to take place in midwinter, and the snows were deep, his horses recalcitrant, the locals suspicious. He wanted to persuade the residents that this reserve would be a good thing, not a private reserve for the wealthy, but he found the task a difficult one. His inspection reports are political documents—justifications for withdrawing the land before the eastern timber operators could grab it. But they are also emotional documents written by a man trying to understand the land, trying to name it and encircle it with words. The reports at first read like bare descriptions, dry facts. But beneath the rough surface, one can trace the memory of Langille's fingers on the cold reins, the moment when he leaned forward in his saddle at his first sight of the knife-edge ridges of the Imnaha. Words are like footprints, like stumps in the forest. They can reveal not just the facts—the number of pines in a watershed in 1906—but what motivated those men who recorded them.

After Langille had ridden five nights alone on a tired horse in an unsurveyed forest, he was regarded with suspicion by those who saw him. His head ached and he was cold inside his heavy, wet leather coat, and his horse stumbled and the water dripped off his hat in cold rivulets down his neck, and the forest seemed dark and alien around him. Every few hours, he wrote his notes, crouched over the saddle horn, his fingers cramped with the cold. To keep his spirits up, he reminded himself that this was an almost sacred mission. He was on a quest to save the heart of the country: to preserve the life-giving springs from those who would destroy their protective forests.

Langille was trying to judge the Blues as a region worthy or unworthy of government protection. To do this, he had to make some sense of it. Plenty of other whites had come to the Blues before Langille. They had come to mine, to trap, to cross the mountains in search of a complicated and unyielding agrarian dream. But these men and women had not felt the need, as Langille did, to name this area as a single place defined by its forests. The Blue Mountains were in large part defined as a region by the reserve men—outsiders. And their definition depended not on the mountains, because there are several mountain ranges in the area, but on the forests. What made the loose collection of places a whole was a shared economic resource, not any inherent cohesiveness. Langille's task was to define this area as a place no longer wild but securely set within federal boundaries.

Some of the railroad promoters and tourist agents and eastern travel writers had already come through, describing the area as a scenic and resource wonder. And then during the Nez Percé wars, white settlers had started talking about themselves as Americans, as a group with a claim to a place. But the government scientists looked at land in a different way: as a region that could become a particular government possession. Langille's classifications were driven as much by desire as by science. His reports are a sometimes sober, often exuberant record of desires and speculations, wild science, wild logic, all put forth under the pressure of time.

To begin his report on the Blue Mountain Forest Reserve, Langille located the region not within ecological categories but in the midst of an American political map. He wrote, "the proposed Blue Mountain Forest Reserve is situate in the Eastern part of the state of Oregon in Umatilla, Union, Baker, Grant, Malheur, Harney, Wheeler, and Crook Counties." With this dry sentence, he located the forest in relation to a set of known American political entities. He did this to lay claim to it as a known place: to draw the mountains out of the realm of confusion, into the linear frame of bureaucracy.

The push for forest reserves in the Blues arose in large part from the desire of western irrigation interests to protect their water supplies. Irrigators feared that lumbering, overgrazing, and fires were decimating the high elevation forests at the head of watersheds, the forests that regulated the flow of water into the valleys. Heavy spring floods and summer droughts would follow, destroying the hopes of farmers and irrigators. With the mountains' value for watershed protection as the basis for his claims, Langille tried to place the Blues at the heart of the Northwest. The mountains were at the center, he wrote, and from them streams "radiate in all direction from the summits and distribute their life-giving glow to nearly all parts of Northeast Oregon." Because of the importance of water to agricultural development, the mountains might be geographically isolated, but they were not therefore unimportant. Langille went on to write: "The water shed is of incalculable economic value to all parts of Eastern Oregon. . . . The geographic location of these

mountains, occupying, as they do, a peculiar isolated position . . .
[nevertheless] bears an important relation to the economic resources of the territory [of Oregon at large]."

When Langille listed the important biological resources of the
proposed reserve, he continued his emphasis on watersheds. Trees
were valuable not just for their timber, but even more for their
indirect effects on water, and this meant that Langille valued not
just a few timber species, but all plants that might slow the flow of
water over soils. For example, he wrote that mountain mahogany
"affords excellent fuel and is invaluable as a conserver of moisture
upon the timberless areas it occupies." Throughout all the early
inspection reports for the various Blues reserves, the major concern
was watershed protection. Inspectors listed every plant species they
could identify. In contrast, by the late 1910s when the timber sale
business had drastically increased in the Blues, the silvics reports
mentioned only trees valuable for timber.

Langille created a tale complete with suspense and heroes, writing that he came "just in time to prevent wholesale location upon
these tracts by parties under the guidance of professional locators
who had been at work for weeks and had formulated plans to secure every section of timber in that region." He worked in a "mad
rush" to save the watersheds from the dirty grip of timber speculators who would lay waste the forests and destroy their potential.
Timber companies were decimating the hills in their haste to cut
ponderosa pine, and "millions of feet have been logged and
shipped out of state by the Grande Ronde Lumber Company and
the Oregon Lumber Company." Much of this cutting was illegal,
and all of it was irresponsible. Simple greed, according to Langille,
drove the loggers, and only the government could protect the
locals from their depredations.

Langille portrayed himself as a friend of the working man and
a foe of eastern capital and the robber baron loggers. As he bitterly
wrote about the Grande Ronde Lumber Company, a Wisconsin
firm with close ties to the massive Booth-Kelly Lumber Company,
"the fact that the Grande Ronde Lumber Company desires these
lands not included in the reserve is to me sufficient reason to justify their inclusion within the boundaries." The Grande Ronde

Lumber Company, according to Langille, had illegally acquired lands which they stripped of timber and then used as lieu base. "All sections contiguous to the Grande Ronde River have been logged over by them and left in a hopelessly denuded condition. It is only natural that they should desire to continue their operation and cover all of the desirable timber bodies in that region."[5] What is most striking in Langille's reports is a rhetoric that portrayed the companies as inherently bad. The historian Samuel P. Hays has argued that the protection of federal forests was not motivated by a desire to protect the land from greedy lumbermen; but at least in the Blues, this anti-industry tone pervaded every government report for the first decade of Forest Service operations in the region.[6] It was not until the Forest Service began pushing heavy sales of ponderosa pine that the anti-industry orientation radically changed.

When Langille turns to grazing matters, his report reads like a dirge, a sad song of accelerating loss: "A few years ago Eastern Oregon was one of the best range sections of the West. The rich bunch grass waved knee deep on hill and plain in such close growth that it was mowed with machines for hay. . . . At all seasons of the year there was an abundance of feed on the open range. Now this is all changed." As further evidence of the past riches, he recounted what a sheepherder had told him: fifteen years before, in 1890, any herder could have bedded his band of two thousand sheep forty days in one place. Not only was this evidence of what had once been there, it was also evidence of why it was no longer there: the impact of two thousand sheep eating in the same place for forty days would have been devastating.

Langille's recommendations about grazing policy were carefully hedged. He urged that grazing should be allowed for two reasons: it was the economic basis for most local communities, and grazing in the forest could be done without destroying forest cover— an assertion he made without evidence. Langille retreated into vagueness at this point, unlike in earlier sections where he counted out the plants and gave precise estimates about timber yields and castigated the timber cutters for careless practices. Why was he so careful here to temper his rhetoric? Unlike the timber operators, the cattlemen and a few of the sheepmen were local and could not be antagonized if the reserve were to win local support.

In his consideration of mining, Langille again focused on the reserve's benefits to small local operators. Miners were among the reserve's most vocal opponents, and Langille tried to win them over by stressing three points: First, miners would still be allowed to mine and cut timber for mining within the boundaries of the reserve. Second, a reserve would offer local miners protection from out-of-state miners. Third, mining depended on a high elevation supply of timber, which was rapidly being depleted. For the future prosperity of mining, a reserve was necessary.

Langille's overriding argument was that reserves would not remove land from production, but rather conserve it for sustained production. Only with conservation could development prosper. In this sense, Hays's arguments are correct for the Blues: the issue was not one of setting the forests aside, but of protecting forests so that they would ensure economic prosperity. Conservation was not opposed to a vision of economic growth and progress; quite the contrary. Without conservation, economic development would falter. Inspection reports written during these years all stressed that because outsiders had plundered the land, only the reserves would offer prosperity for locals.

Protection of small local concerns was a theme Langille stressed over and again. Using this theme, he could portray any opposition to the reserves as motivated by greedy out-of-state capitalists. He was careful to portray the miners as essentially sympathetic to his cause, once they understand what it really meant; in one passage he reported that "many of the small miners are prepared to welcome the reserve as a means of protection to themselves from the large operators." Rather than accuse large companies of exploiting small miners, Langille was able to find miners who would do that for him: "Several of the prospectors offer the statement that the small miner or prospector who is developing his claim is, at the present time, at the mercy of the large operators who have large capital and paying properties." Langille always linked this theme of large against small, locals against outsiders, with his crucial theme of depletion. Greedy eastern capitalists—not the locals struggling to make a living off the resources—were the true source of depletion. Locals had more right to the resources: their place gave them some claim to what was there.

Langille and the other government inspectors did their best to create forest reserves, but the actual administration of those reserves turned out to be extremely troubled. Public forestry, for all its high ideals, got off to a rocky start in the Blue Mountains, as in the West at large. Westerners raised an immediate protest over the 1891 reserves, arguing that the government was seizing land that was rightfully theirs and impeding the development and full use of these lands. Between 1891, when Congress created the forest reserves under the authority of the Department of Interior's General Land Office, and 1905, when the Department of Agriculture finally got control of the Forest Service, the reserve system seemed doomed to chaos and inefficiency. By 1893, there were sixteen western reserves with more than 17 million acres. However, the 1891 legislation enabling the establishment of reserves had provided no means for administering or managing those areas, nor did the law state what kind of use could take place inside the reserves. It was increasingly unclear whether the reserves were intended for use—which most people interpreted as grazing and logging—or protection.

In response to protests, when Congress passed the Organic Act of 1897, it was careful to state the purposes of the reserves: to protect water flow and to ensure a continuous supply of timber.[7] The Organic Act gave the government the authority to use the forests and made it clearer that the forests were not preserves. But the administration of the reserves was still marked by corruption and confusion. A strange situation arose: the Department of the Interior, through the General Land Office, was in charge of the forests but had no foresters; whereas the Bureau of Forestry in the Department of Agriculture had foresters, but no forests to work on.[8] While the two departments struggled over control of the public lands, the forests got further abused—now by their supposed protectors as well as their traditional exploiters.

According to the memoirs of Smith Ripley, a forester who started working with the Bureau of Forestry in 1899, the reserve

system failed utterly. The high ideals of the professional foresters
had little basis in reality, and there was an enormous gap between
eastern ideals and the situation out west. Ripley was only seven-
teen when he heard about the new science of forestry. Fired with
enthusiasm, he talked his way into the Bureau, and with a team of
other young eastern foresters straight out of school, he headed west
a year later to inspect the new reserves. Here were twenty-year-old
boys with high ideals and little practical experience setting out to
tell loggers how to cut trees, and supervisors how to run reserves.
What resulted dismayed everyone involved. Reserve administration was corrupt and fraud was rampant, largely because of the
spoils system of the early reserves: supervisors and administrators
were political appointees, not scientists or foresters. Political influences won supervisors their jobs, and they often repaid the favors
with special breaks on timber contracts. Rangers took whatever
paybacks they could from timber sales. Few in the department's
administration knew anything about trees and even fewer cared;
outsiders tended to assume that the department was made up of a
bunch of criminals.[9]

The job of the reserve supervisors was to change wasteful logging practices and institute simple regulations for good forestry:
utilize logs fully to avoid waste; pile slash for controlled burning to avoid catastrophic fires in cutover stands; and, most important, leave a reserve stand to ensure that future generations would
have timber to harvest. But instead, under the reserves, nothing
changed. Traditional cut-and-get-out practices were still in effect,
but now with the connivance of the federal administrators who
were meant to transform forestry. Ripley wrote that the trees to be
cut in a sale were not marked by foresters, "but by men looking
primarily to what could be marketed. . . . It is needless to say that
the cutting area . . . was in wretched shape; in fact, it appeared as
though someone had gone to work to violate the very principles
of forestry." In the Black Hills Reserve, local Land Office officials as
well as the private contractors were extremely hostile when Ripley
tried to implement what he saw as good forest practices: "The contractors stood ready to trip the men should they make a false
step. . . . Then the local Land officials resented those men's intru-

sion . . . [because] the men were outsiders. . . . An entire disregard
of the simplest stipulations of the contracts was apparent everywhere." Regulations that were supposed to ensure scientific forestry existed, but the reserve supervisors had no interest in enforce-
ment. Nor were the companies going to change on their own,
because, as Ripley argued, they wanted "to make money and had
no intention of departing from their old methods any farther
than forced."[10]

One thing was clear to Ripley by 1905, when Gifford Pinchot
managed to win control of the federal forests and create the Forest
Service. No matter what, forestry had to pay, and "many matters
of theoretical forestry were possible . . . that the market conditions
did not justify."[11] The industry would consider scientific forestry
only as long as it made a profit. This lesson made a deep impression
not just on Smith Ripley, but on the young Forest Service as a
whole. The frustrations of management under the reserve system
made Pinchot—and his corps of young foresters—determined not
to repeat the reserves' mistakes by letting science get under the
control of politicians. In effect, the bad experiences under the General Land Office ensured that the young Forest Service would put
its faith in the clean, incorruptible light of science. This, however,
got them into severe trouble later, because the foresters were accountable neither to the locals nor to the land.

Old Growth and the Young Forest Service

For all the troubles with the reserve system, Gifford Pinchot's
young foresters were extraordinarily optimistic. They shared with
Pinchot a firm faith that science would allow them to understand
everything worth knowing about the world. Redesigning wild nature as an orderly, efficient machine was at the heart of their efforts. As one government scientist wrote: "The course of nature has
come to be investigated in order that it may be redirected along
lines contributing to human welfare."[12] Science, conscious purpose, and human reason would engineer a new world out of the
chaos of laissez-faire economics and short-term selfish interest. The
conservationists felt theirs was an almost sacred mission: to perfect

nature and civilization both. The goal was not just a better forest, but a better world. They assumed that human ingenuity could perfect nature without losing anything in the process. As scientists who had the interests of America and American forests at heart, they felt they were beyond criticism. Their very enthusiasm and faith—qualities that made them extremely effective—fostered an arrogance that often blinded them to the consequences of their actions.

In the early years of the twentieth century, America was in a furor over land management. Disposal of the vast tracts of western land was an enormously corrupt process, and to many Americans the federal government seemed to be more corrupt than anybody else when it came to managing land. The new forest scientists stepped in and said: science will show us a way out of this chaos of political corruption, if you just leave it to us. By turning to the clear, calm, seemingly universal rules of science, foresters tried to avoid the mess of contentious politics and the contingencies of history. They felt they could introduce science into the chaos of land management, making a better society as well as a better nature. They alone could serve the public good, they felt, because efficiency rather than short-term profit was their goal.

In the eyes of the early conservationists, western old-growth forests and the loggers who denuded these forests shared a basic flaw: both were wasteful. As the historian Samuel T. Hays argued, the point of American conservation was to reduce waste and increase efficiency. A Umatilla National Forest press release dated September 12, 1906, put it well: the intent of conservation was to "hunt down waste in all its varied forms" in waters, forests, lands, and minerals. Waste existed not when people overused resources, but when they failed to use them fully enough. Any water that wasn't used for irrigation was lost forever; any grass that wasn't eaten by a cow went to waste—or so the press release insisted. If people did not put everything to full use, it was a moral failure, not just an economic loss.[13]

Early government foresters had several strong articles of faith: First, the point of forestry was to reduce waste and make forests more efficient; this meant making them produce more timber, more quickly. Second, America needed wood, and demands would continue to increase as quickly as they had increased after the Civil War. Third, if harvesting continued as usual, the country would run out of timber in twenty-five to thirty years. Fourth, forests ought to be used, but scientifically, to ensure a perpetual supply of timber for a growing nation. Finally, scientists were best at solving land management problems, and so scientists, rather than politicians, ought to control the Forest Service.[14] Trained scientists— professional foresters—would redesign the old-growth forests, to improve them and ensure the perpetual supply of timber.

The basic premise of the new Forest Service was simple: if the United States was running out of timber, the best way to meet future demands was to grow more timber. More than 70 percent of the western forests were old-growth stands—what early foresters called "decadent and overmature," which meant forests that were losing as much wood to death and decay as they were gaining from growth. In order to prevent a famine, foresters believed that old-growth forests needed to be cut down so that regulated, sustained-yield forests could be grown instead. Regulated forests would protect the water supply just as well as old-growth forests, and furthermore would produce more timber. The best way to free up the land for timber production was to cut the old timber as soon as possible, which meant pushing sales. This logic shaped a Forest Service that, in order to protect the forest, believed it necessary to first remove it.

Americans have a long history of splitting the world into two parts: civilization versus wild nature. Forestry at the turn of the century was a brave attempt to find a way out of this dichotomy. The attempt failed, not because it was a bad idea, but because foresters soon developed an overreliance on universal scientific theories that made it increasingly difficult for them to value complexity, inefficiency, uncertainty, and redundancy—all the hallmarks of old growth.

Attitudes toward old-growth forests have changed dramatically over the last century, and these attitudes have played a critical role in how people shaped the western landscapes. The ways people envision the ideal forest and the "virgin" forest—and the relationship between the two—reflect underlying assumptions about the relationship between nature and culture. Ideas matter because they are shaped by what happens in the political and scientific world, and because they themselves shape what happens within the forest. Influences go both ways: from action to ideas, but also from ideas to actions. It is not quite accurate to argue that the early Forest Service subjugated aesthetic and spiritual values to utilitarian ones, and so approached the forest purely as a place of usefulness.[15] Something more complicated was going on. Ideas of value have always been intertwined with both material usefulness and spiritual or ethical standing. The utilitarian choices that the early Forest Service and Pinchot made were, in effect, a set of judgments about ethical and spiritual values.

Centuries before whites ever showed up in the Blues and before anyone conceived of a Forest Service, the Puritans encountered the American forest. Indians had done a great deal to alter the New England forests, so those landscapes were anything but untouched. Yet for the Puritans, Indians as well as forests were part of the "hideous wilderness." The forest was a "dismal thicket" separate from God, where Christians might lose their way both literally and spiritually, falling back into pagan heresies. Wild nature was evil, threatening, and scary, but most of all in need of being tamed. A place of terror, it was also a place of possibility—its wildness offering the opportunity to create the City of God on earth. Nothing would be lost in the transformation: the change from the wilderness of an uncut forest to the culture of an orderly town, farm, and woodlot was wholly positive.[16]

By the early nineteenth century, wild nature had lost much of its association with evil and ungodliness. American transcendentalists and romantics, particularly Emerson and Thoreau, argued that nature was sacred in its wild state. Forests could offer wearied Americans spiritual sustenance. Nature gained its spiritual authority from its pristine separateness, its independence from the messy contingencies of civilization. Nature stood outside history, bearing spiritual witness to the follies of culture. Nature, for all its virtues, was thoroughly at odds with culture, an attitude about the relationship between the two which was not so very different from the

Puritans' views. Proponents of wild nature portrayed the forest as a place valuable for moral reinvigoration but not crucial to society. Many preservationists worked in large part out of this tradition, trying to preserve parcels of the forest for holidays from the real business of life. Wild nature was a collection of scenic views— positive, certainly, but unconnected to civilization.[17]

The scientific reformers of the late nineteenth century came in large part out of this intellectual tradition, but they transformed it with a scientific bent. Nature was still a source of goodness and virtue, but culture was no longer opposed to nature. American civilization needed nature not just for its spiritual survival but for its material survival—for the timber and water that cities needed to prosper. In particular, America depended on forests for a host of indirect, difficult to measure, interconnected ecological functions. If people too rapidly degraded nature, then civilization would fall. Even in their unregulated state, forests had a strong moral virtue for the scientific reformers. But to serve humanity, forests needed to change.

George Perkins Marsh was one of the first scientific reformers to write about the complicated dependencies between culture and nature, focusing on the indirect effects of forest destruction. Marsh had been the fishery commissioner in Vermont, charged with restoring declining fish populations. After his fieldwork, he attributed the fish decline to water pollution from development, forest clearing that led to stream flow fluctuations, water temperature changes, and insect population declines that were side effects of deforestation. In 1864, Marsh published *Man and Nature,* a work which sparked concern over the fate of the forest and the approaching threat of a timber famine. In a passage concerning the indirect effects of deforestation on civilization, Marsh wrote: "When the forest is gone, the great reservoir of moisture stored up in its vegetable mould is evaporated, and returns only in deluges of rain to wash away the parched dust into which that mould has been converted. The well-wooded and humid hills are turned to ridges of dry rock, which encumbers the low grounds and chokes the watercourses with its debris."[18] The effects of deforestation, he argued, are far-reaching, but often invisible and unexpected. Part of Marsh's concern was to make people pay attention to indirect ecological effects: he was trying to point out that human beings are dependent on the land for things beyond simple commodities.

Marsh's emphasis on indirect effects marked a very different attitude toward the relationship between nature and history. When he argued that interconnected, indirect effects were important, what he meant was that when something happened in one place, other things happened elsewhere in response. If living things were bound together in a community, nature was no longer outside history, for changes were now an integral part of natural communities. At its heart, this meant a new way of thinking about the relationship between human culture and nature. Human actions were not only the cause of many indirect effects, they were also subject to these effects. People were part of an interconnected community of living things; what they did to the land was no longer somehow external or unimportant.

Marsh argued that to prevent timber famine and preserve civilization, science must be introduced into the forests. He was the first to reason that the only way to save the forests was to transform them to regulated forests. In a critical passage, Marsh insisted: "The sooner a natural wood is brought into the state of an artificially regulated one, the better it is for all the multiple interests which depend on the wise administration of this branch of public economy."[19] Civilize the forest or perish, was Marsh's challenge. His own immediate concern was an overlogged eastern forest, and he assumed that intense logging would continue, since civilization would not decrease its demands for wood. The choice was not between protecting forests or logging; the choice was between cutting trees carefully or cutting them without concern for other values. Marsh was writing in protest to an ethic of extraction, one of profit and shortsighted greed. Yet the irony is that, with his emphasis on forest regulation, he prefigured much of what went wrong in forest management in the Blues.

Understanding the importance of Marsh's reasoning requires us to step back and consider what regulation meant for a forest. Scientists of Marsh's time defined old-growth forests—what they called decadent or overmature forests—as those forests in which annual growth did not exceed annual decay. Within an old-growth forest, some trees were young and some old, and the forest as a whole was in equilibrium, with growth about equal to death. Regulated forests, in contrast, were those that were young enough and growing quickly enough so that they added more volume in a year than they lost to death and decay. Not only were they growing, they were growing in an orderly fashion: each year exactly the same number of trees became available for harvest. As the standard forestry textbook definition from 1966 stated: "A regulated forest has age and size classes that are in such proportion and growing at such rates that an approximately equal annual or periodic yield is continuously available for harvesting."[20] To envision a regulated forest, consider an 80,000 acre Douglas-fir forest with trees that would reach their maximum growth rates at 80 years. A forest managed on an 80-year rotation, if intended to be cut annually, would contain 1,000 acres of one-year-old trees, 1,000 acres of two-year-old trees, and so on to 1,000 acres of 80-year-old trees. Each year, a thousand acres of 80-year-old trees could be cut and replanted with saplings. In theory this process could go on forever.

Scientific forestry, later known as sustained-yield forestry, required regulated forests, so that the annual net growth could be harvested each year. The reasoning went that in a regulated forest, loggers could harvest the net annual growth forever without depleting the growing stock. The economic analogy is obvious: the harvest was equal to the interest; the growing stock was equal to capital; and no sensible businessman and no sensible forester would want his investment in a bank that paid no interest, or in an old-growth forest that produced no net growth. Old-growth forests were in equilibrium, so foresters felt that scientific forestry was impossible until the old growth had been cut and replaced with a regulated forest.

Marsh was a scientist trying to bring the light of reason to land use. His willingness to regulate and control nature for human use came from the best of intentions—to save both civilization and the forest. He exemplified a particularly American desire to have the world both ways: wild and tame. A regulated forest was one way of reconciling the opposition between nature and culture, and having both the wildlands and civilization.

Bernard Fernow and Economic Forestry

As foresters gained scientific respectability in America, their attitudes toward old growth shifted. Bernard Fernow, born and educated in Germany, was one of the first scientific foresters active in the United States. He moved to America in a conscious rejection of traditional European ways: he had married an American woman, which infuriated his German family and made it necessary for him to live elsewhere. Yet Fernow brought with him the attitudes and expectations of German silviculture and tried to apply them to American conditions. Like Marsh, he saw the old-growth forests as morally virtuous even in their natural state, but as economically inefficient. The ideas of efficiency and waste had assumed increased importance in the decades since Marsh first called for forest conservation, and Fernow mirrored this in his emphasis on the need to transform forests for efficient human use.

To understand the attitudes expressed by American scientific forestry toward old-growth forests, it is important to understand the profession's ties to European forestry. American foresters turned to European silviculture for their models of a regulated forest, but at the same time they reacted against those traditions. Most European foresters laughed at the idea of scientific forestry ever succeeding in America. Too much old growth, they said, far too many old trees. Germans in particular said that American forests were ill-suited to scientific forestry because they were too big, too wild, and too decadent. This in turn made many American foresters determined to prove that forestry was indeed possible in America. But their way to do this was not by transforming the ideals of European silviculture to fit American forests, but by transforming American forests to fit European ideals. This, in effect, meant cutting old growth, because old growth was what made American forests different. Americans perceived their grand old forests to be something special, but they were nevertheless uneasy about that difference.

From Fernow on, government foresters and teachers in forestry school expected to apply European principles of regulated forest management to American forests. When the new Forest Service completed their first rough estimates of the national forests, they were dismayed to learn that 73 percent of the western forests were in old growth and not in a growing condition. Yet they remained confident that these forests could soon be regulated. Henry Graves, the second head of the Forest Service, predicted that "in the long run, the application of forestry in this country will resemble very closely that in Europe, with such modifications as are required by the peculiar characteristics of our species and climate."[21]

Fernow came squarely out of the German regulated forest tradition, and in his writings, such as "What Is Forestry?" (1891), he hardly seemed to recognize the differences between the American and German situations.[22] Germans originated the ideal of intensive forestry, which, in addition to regulation, required the elimination of waste from the forest. When it was discovered, around 1810, that pure spruce outyielded a mixed forest, the Germans converted the forests of their entire nation to spruce by clearcutting and planting. As the wildlife biologist Aldo Leopold later argued when he visited German forests, this "wood factory economics" simplified the system and took too much out without giving anything back. By the second rotation of pure spruce plantations, timber yields declined sharply in Germany. For some poorly understood reason, spruce litter was not decaying, and the deep litter smothered the undergrowth. Roots failed to penetrate the soils, and as a result windfalls increased. Insect epidemics spread rapidly through the monocultures of spruces, particularly in places where the spruce was out of its historic range. Excessive acidity of the topsoil, or podzolization, became a problem. Since all the hardwoods had been removed, nothing was left to pump up bases from the subsoil. German silviculturists recognized that the spruce monocultures were not producing as intended, so in 1914, a century after their mass attempts at intensive silviculture, they turned to *Dauerwald*, or "permanent woods"—mixed forests that would ideally take care of themselves. *Dauerwald* did not solve all the problems, because the foresters were still keeping forests far too neat and tidy, but the concept was at least an attempt to reverse the effects of a failed experiment in intensive silviculture. Americans, however, were less influenced by *Dauerwald* than by the ideals of intensive silviculture that preceded it.[23]

As head of the Division of Forestry, Bernard Fernow had no power of administration over the forests, yet he had an enormous influence on American forestry ideals, largely through the publication of hundreds of bulletins aimed at private landowners.[24] His 1891 bulletin "What Is Forestry?" illustrates the fundamentals of his silviculture. This bulletin addressed three major questions: what is old growth, what is the natural forest, and what are the roles of people and scientists in reshaping this forest? The bulletin was suffused with the economic rhetoric of competition: forestry was a moral struggle for competitive superiority; only through struggle would the best trees emerge. Yet there was not the hysteria about the moral turpitude of old-growth forests that one finds in later Forest Service documents. Fernow wrote about old growth as a valuable resource, full of economic and moral virtue: "The 'forest primeval' is our most valuable inheritance. It is the ready cash of nature's bountiful provision for our future. . . . The accumulations of centuries are stored in the tree growth of the virgin forest and in the forest floor of decayed foliage." The perspective here was economic; the forest was both an "inheritance" and "ready cash." The point was to make a forest useful for civilization by converting it to something that was more productive economically. Forestry above all was the process of reducing waste and "applying economy in the use of natural resources" by treating the forest as a crop and "attempting to create values from the soil" (p. 11).

When Fernow viewed the forest from the perspective of human economy, it fell short—not because it was decadent or evil, but merely because it was profligate. He described the old-growth forest as a place where "Nature has taken no account of time or space, both of which were lavishly at her command; nor did she care whether the forest was composed of the timbers most useful to man; tree growth, whatever the kind, satisfied her laws of development." Yet he tempered his respect for the primeval forest with an emphasis on usefulness. No matter how lovely the wild forest might be, the needs of human economy had to come first, for "when a growing nation has need of the soil for agricultural use and for timber . . . it becomes necessary in time to introduce economy into the use of our inheritance, . . . to make the soil do full duty in producing only that which is useful to man" (p. 7). Fernow implied that people needed more from the forest than it ordinarily gave, but that did not mean the forest was immoral or wasteful, only uneconomic. The human role was to reduce this waste by reshaping the forest.

Lumber, Fernow insisted as Marsh had before him, was not the only value of a forest. What he called the "hidden indirect phases of utility" were even more important. Protecting soils from erosion and protecting watersheds from floods were things that only forests could do. This emphasis on indirect forest influences was at the heart of an ecological perspective in forestry, and likewise at the heart of an attempt to value what was difficult to measure in human economic terms. As Fernow put it, "another incalculable benefit of the forest cover has impressed itself upon the minds of the observing and thinking portion of mankind only comparatively recently, namely, *the part which the forest plays in the great economy of nature*, the recognition of which led the most eminent naturalist and philosopher, A. von Humboldt, to exclaim: 'How foolish do men appear, destroying the forest cover without regard to consequences, for thereby they rob themselves of wood and water'" (p. 9; emphasis added). Fernow, like Marsh, was arguing that since nature's parts are interconnected, any action done to one seemingly valueless part of the forest might have cascading effects throughout the landscape. In a limited sense, this was an attempt at a shift in values: from seeing the forest as simply a storehouse of extractable commodities whose value lay only in what it directly offered to human economy, to seeing the forest as a source of value through its indirect effects and ecological interconnections. Fernow still defined nature's value in relation to human economy, but his perspective had shifted slightly. He saw the forest as a complex whole whose functions people could only dimly understand and

which could be disturbed by shortsighted attempts to extract commodities.

As Fernow saw it, the central principle structuring nature's
economy was competition. He argued that "in the vegetable world,
as in the animal world, there is a constant struggle for supremacy
going on. . . . The methods used in this warfare are various, and
both offensive and defensive." The forester's role was not to over-
throw nature and substitute a human order but "to interfere in this
warfare in favor of the species which he desires to propagate . . . by
reducing the chances of reproduction and supremacy of the undesirable species" (p. 19). For all his economic terminology and
emphasis on struggle, Fernow's version of forestry was one that
interfered as little as possible with the forest's own processes. For
example, he advised the forester to avoid clearcutting, never convert mixed-species forests to monocultures, and always attempt to
use natural seeding rather than artificial planting. The best foresters would "study the natural forest" and mimic its processes, using
the ax to "assist with the struggle" by hastening natural thinning
processes. Fernow's forestry was content to let the forest take care
of itself. With thinning, he hoped to increase tree growth rates by
a factor of three, but he was not talking about razing the trees to
the ground and replanting with faster growing spruces. This kind
of mild forestry would work only in a regulated forest, and although Fernow assumed that regulated forests were best, he had
little to say about how to transform American old growth into the
ideal forest.

The Young Forest Service

Efficiency became increasingly important for the young Forest Service, and its foresters' attitudes toward old growth reflected this.
The wild forest was not evil as it was for the Puritans, but it was
something that was starting to impede progress. Yet in the writings
and reports of early Forest Service foresters, the men who were out
in the woods trying to decide what to do with all those trees, there
was a curious mixture of attitudes toward old growth. At first foresters expressed a degree of respect and awe often missing from

later writings. Above all, the young foresters in the field discovered that they needed to address the complexity and difficulty of old-growth forests. Mixed with their optimism, enthusiasm, and desire to put the forest to good use was a recurrent undertone of confusion, as if they were just starting to realize that the forest was indeed complex.

American forestry's hostility toward old growth came not so much from German silviculture as from an American anxiety about how different American forests were from the ideal European forests. Even while American foresters bragged about the grand, huge American trees that surpassed anything European forests could offer, they did their best to eliminate those trees and make their forests more European.

Foresters in America needed to prove the utility of their young discipline and justify forestry to the logging industry, and that meant regulating the forests as quickly as possible. American forestry, from Gifford Pinchot on, showed a curious mixture of indebtedness and defensiveness with regard to German silviculture. Pinchot—usually considered the father of the Forest Service and the father of American forestry—expressed this hostility throughout his autobiography, *Breaking New Ground.* He graduated from Yale in 1889 and went to Europe to learn scientific forestry, since there was nowhere in America to study the subject, and indeed no profession of forestry at all in the United States. In Europe he learned a system of forestry based on the regulated forest, and he returned to America with a great deal of enthusiasm for applying these principles to American forests.[25] Yet his enthusiasm was tempered with hostility, in part because he felt that Europeans, particularly Germans, were inclined to dismiss American forests. Pinchot declared in his autobiography: "we distrusted them and their German lack of faith in American forestry." When, in 1900, he persuaded his family to establish the Yale University forestry school so he would have professionals to run his new forests, the school's purpose was avowedly American: "What we wanted was American foresters trained by Americans in American ways for the work ahead in American forests."[26]

Pinchot and his young foresters were increasingly impatient—

and then hostile—toward decadent old growth, as the emphasis on eliminating inefficiency and waste increased. The best way to free up the land to grow better forests was to sell off the old-growth timber as soon as possible, which meant pushing sales, even in a slow market. On their first day in forestry school, foresters learned how to think about old growth. In 1911, C. S. Judd, the assistant forester for the Northwest region, gave the following warning to the incoming class of forestry students at the University of Washington. First, a timber famine was on its way unless the Forest Service did something quickly, for only "about 2,826 billion feet BM [board feet] of standing timber" was left in the entire nation. But since the annual consumption of timber was 50 billion feet; "at this rate the timber now standing, without allowance for growth or decay, would last only about 55 years. The present annual growth is estimated to be about one third of the present annual cut."[27]

Since the forest was running out of trees, the way to fix the problem was to get National Forest land to grow trees faster. As Judd put it, "the good of the forest . . . demands that the ripe timber on the National Forests and above all, the dead, defective, and diseased timber, be removed." The way to accomplish this was to "enter more actively into the timber sale business" and heavily promote sales. This would get rid of the old growth, freeing up land to "start new crops of timber for a future supply." Foresters saw old growth not as a great resource but as a parasite, taking up land that should be growing trees. Realistically, however, this grand dream of recreating the forest would take time, Judd warned the students. There were just not enough foresters and too much land. As he put it, "it will be many years before our Forests are managed in the same intensive manner that most European forests are managed at the present time."

The attitude of the young Forest Service toward its task of creating an American forestry for the American situation was well expressed in a talk given by District Forester Frederick Ames at the 1910 joint supervisors' meeting for the Northwest region (Oregon and Washington). In this early meeting, the regional forest supervisors were still trying to clarify the basic elements of their policies.

But there was excitement and a sense of challenge to their task: they had 63 million acres of land available to show what the new profession of forestry could do. More important, the foresters were given the responsibility of averting a crisis to American civilization itself: they must prevent a timber famine.

Ames opened with a reference to the threat of this timber famine: "Soon the timber resources of the eastern forests in the District will be tapped," he said, referring to the ponderosa pines of the Blue Mountains.[28] Because of the famine, the thing to do was to cut old growth as heavily as possible. Ames recognized that "the popular idea and probably the one most likely to occur to the casual thinker is that the best way the National Forests can meet the approaching timber shortage is to cut as lightly as possible and save this supply until then." The foresters needed to teach the public otherwise, for "this idea is probably erroneous. Though we must await the results of the reconnaissance studies to be sure, the data now on hand indicates that there is a large proportion of National Forest lands covered with timber which is past its maximum growth." Because the trees had slowed their growth, much of the timber was "decreasing in value, through deterioration, faster than it is increasing through volume increment and rise in stumpage value." Ames admitted that the Forest Service really did not know what it was doing, but one thing was certain: old growth had to go. "From no point of view can we make any mistake in cutting timber of this class," Ames insisted. "The more sales we make the better."

The foresters intended to devise sales that would improve the forest. But they were acting in the dark, and they knew it. By 1910, just five years after the government established the National Forests, they were already feeling the pressure of inadequate knowledge. Ames said: "We must try to put our timber sale policy on a scientific basis. . . . We do not know how much timber we have, how much our forests are producing annually, or how much they could be made to produce." Ames's words express a definite uneasiness that things might quickly go wrong. So far, he said, "we could not make any serious mistakes because we have had very few large sales. There has been no possibility of overcutting. *Within a very few years, however, we shall be called on to do an immense business, and we have got to know how to do it"* (emphasis added). Underneath the optimism and bravado of Ames's calls to transform the forests, there was anxiety in his recognition that they did not know what was out there, nor did they know what to expect from their efforts to eliminate old growth.

Pushing sales of old growth was not just a way for the Forest Service to increase sales receipts. As Ames acknowledged, the Forest Service would actually lose money by selling old growth: "No doubt a greater financial return might be obtained if some of this timber, which is not deteriorating too rapidly, should be held for a rise in stumpage values, but this consideration has little weight." Losing money was the necessary cost of improving the forest. Ames added: "It is more important that we should bring the Forests into a condition of maximum production than that the timber now on them should be managed to bring the greatest financial return." The overall goal, Ames stressed, must always be kept in mind: to make the forests efficient by cutting old growth, even though "it may not be the timber which purchasers want most."

In 1911, Gifford Pinchot was ousted from the Forest Service after a struggle with Secretary of the Interior Richard Ballinger over Alaskan public lands. Henry Graves, the second Chief of the Forest Service, continued Pinchot's emphasis on removing old growth to reduce waste and inefficiency. In his 1912 annual Report of the Forester, Graves wrote that the national forests contained nearly 600 billion board feet of merchantable timber, and nearly 60 percent of that was "ripe for the ax and deteriorating in value." The timber needed to be cut immediately, because "standing timber, unlike coal deposits, can not be held in storage indefinitely. To the extent to which the overripe timber on the national forests can not be cut and used while merchantable, public property is wasted."[29] For Graves, forests were just storehouses for public commodities; they had ceased to exist as entities with their own complex, indirect influences. Throughout all the years Graves wrote his annual reports, he ignored indirect forest influences—the original emphasis of the early forest reformers. As Graves added in the next year's report: "virgin forests are merely reservoirs of wood." If the forest was just a storehouse, then production was the main thing forest-ers needed to consider. And, as Graves added, "production can be secured only by converting them [old-growth forests] into thrifty, growing stands through cutting." The Forest Service's sale policy was clear: "the timber sale policy aims, therefore, as the first re-quirement of good management, to work over the old stands on the National Forests, utilizing mature timber . . . and putting the ground in such condition that forest production will be renewed at a much faster rate."[30]

The unregulated forest was something to be altered as quickly as possible for moral reasons, to alleviate what one forester, Thornton Munger, termed "the idleness of the great areas of stagnant virgin forest that are getting no selective cutting treatment whatsoever.[31] As one Blues forester, H. D. Foster, wrote in a silvics report on the Wenaha Reserve: "There is much yellow pine on the edges of the reserve which is beginning to deteriorate through decay and dying at the top. This material should be disposed of as rapidly as pos-sible."[32] The problem was not just old growth or dying timber; the problem was a forest that did not produce precisely what people wanted; a recalcitrant, complex nature marked by disorder. As George Bright, a Wenaha Forest silviculturist, complained in 1913, in a lovely turn of phrase: "In the general riot of the natural forest, many thousands of acres are required" to grow the trees that, under management, could be grown on far less land.[33]

Making Sense
of Strangeness: Silvics
in the Blues

The government had its forests, but what was it going to do with them? The foresters were faced with an extraordinary problem: how do you make sense of six million acres of land with few trails, no roads, no maps, and no history that you can understand—land that seems to you to be wilderness? Where do you begin? The foresters came laden with directives from the head office that often conflicted with each other as well as with the foresters' silvicultural ideals. They had orders to try to sell so much timber, protect certain watersheds, make the constituents happy, and support local enterprise—all while transforming chaotic, decadent old growth into a forest of young, vigorous, competitively superior trees growing as fast as they possibly could.

The Forest Service in the Blues began by trying to classify the forest, which meant first getting funds from Congress to survey and then categorize forest communities, so that managers could draw up working circle plans and sales plans. Very early the Forest Service recognized that it needed new tricks for a new land. Managers did realize that there was something new, something different, something unusual and special about this place. They knew they could not simply apply their German forestry training to the western forests. They needed some way of seeing what was out there, of naming and organizing what was different about the land. But ideals about science and the control of nature often seemed to blind them to what was present on the ground, so that they saw the forest first and foremost as a place to be changed. When they actually went out in the woods, they were confronted with an obdurate nature that resisted conforming to their ideals. For all their problems, the Forest Service in the Blues did make a real effort to pay attention to the land. The silvics reports were a way of naming complexity, not just a way of reducing complexity to fit simple theories.

From the first, forestry was the province of professionals in the Forest Service. But out West, the lines blurred. On paper, the Forest Service consisted of a cadre of professionals out to prove their new specialty. But in the Blues during the first decade, almost everyone—temporary forest assistants as well as professional foresters—wrote silvics reports; and those reports were exercises in seeing what was out there, and trying to understand it as well. Science was not just something reserved for elites with fancy degrees; it was the province of anyone who was interested in trees. There was an exuberant faith and optimism in the early Blues silvics reports that is extremely moving. We have got to manage all these trees, and we do not have a clue what to do, said the young foresters. But rather than retreat into specialization, into manuals and obfuscation, the Forest Service responded by saying: everyone can gather information, everyone can do science, everyone can understand this.

Each forest assistant in the Blues was required to make up an annual silvical report, which encompassed "general information concerning the silvical characteristics of the trees of that region, of the types, and of the general forest conditions and problems."[1] Each new forest got its silvical report, usually called simply "The Forest: Silvics," which described each forest, judged its value, and listed its potential problems. What is striking about the reports is how strongly these men felt that close, intimate attention to the life of the forest was part of their mission. In 1909, acting district forester George H. Cecil wrote to Gifford Pinchot describing the ideal forest assistant's silvical report as "a scientific monograph, a complete discussion of some single problem of live interest, . . . [based on] *intimate knowledge of local conditions*" (emphasis added). This problem should lie "close to the heart of the forest assistant." Throughout the year, the assistant would keep "constantly in mind the subject which is assigned to him" and take "every opportunity to make observations on the subject."[2]

As George Cecil admitted, some foresters saw these required reports as so much drudgery, but many of them were gems, marked by enthusiasm and close attention to the forest. Five men in particular—H. D. Foster, R. M. Evans, M. L. Erickson, George Bright, and W. H. B. Kent—wrote an excellent series of reports. These men were based at the District Office in Portland, in the new Section of Silvics headed by Thorton Munger, a recent Yale University graduate in forestry. Fred Ames, the District Forester, was their boss; later he became Chief of Silviculture for the entire nation. According to the historian Lawrence Rakestraw, Ames was a "quiet, competent man with a deep-rooted New England sense of honor," and he "quickly gained the respect of the lumbermen" as well as his fellow foresters.[3] Although the foresters were willing to work with industrial loggers, they were fierce in their condemnation of the ways those loggers had treated the land. Foresters were men with a mission; they felt that right was on their side. Most of them were young and well educated; some were recent graduates of Yale Forestry School, which Pinchot had helped found with the intention of shaping a generation of American foresters. Pinchot's foresters all seemed to have implicit faith in their chief, and Pinchot returned that faith. Even when money was tightest, he always made certain that silvics research got funded.

Foster, Erickson, Evans, Bright, and Kent did not spend their careers on a single forest in the Blues. Yet, even though they moved from place to place each year, their reports show that they had an ideal of their relation with the forest—a relationship not just of control, but of attention and curiosity. Although silvics had at its core an ideal of transforming the forest, it also offered a way of learning about the forest and making a connection between the individual and the wild nature out there. These two ideals were often in tension, and it is important to recognize this ambivalence.

Complexity and Classification

What the foresters wanted was knowledge, an end to all their uncertainties. But what they had to face instead was confusion, for the Blue Mountains seemed a very strange place. Part of the problem was a lack of information: this was still unsurveyed territory. As M. L. Erickson put it in his report on a proposed sale in the

Wallowa Forest Reserve in 1906: "the maps are very poor, the region is largely unknown; it has not yet been surveyed."[4] But the lack of maps and inventories was not the only problem. If that were all, it would be just a matter of time and effort, a matter of patiently applying current techniques to a set of tasks that were finite. Sometimes the Forest Service managers seemed to imply that this was all that was needed; at other times a hint of fear crept into their reports. They could label individual grasses and trees and bushes and animals with their proper scientific names, so in a superficial way these things appeared familiar, but the pieces fit together in very odd ways. The plant communities were unlike any that foresters recognized, particularly in the matter of burning frequencies. This was a different kind of landscape, and foresters were uncertain how to proceed. As Erickson said when he opened his 1907 report on the Chesnimnus reserve: "the area is rough and wild and unlike anything." In 1904, W. H. B. Kent wrote that the Wenaha Reserve (now the Umatilla) still had 695,200 acres unsurveyed and essentially unknown by science or by whites. It was, as Kent described, a "strange and poor land: hard to classify," but classify it they must. "This region is a succession of high, narrow divides and deep gorges, with precipitous rocky slopes, usually without so-called bottom land," Kent wrote. "The soil is generally shallow and loose and the native rock everywhere in evidence." Even the water was unusual. Erickson reported: "A peculiar condition in respect to the Chesnimnus country is that the main heads of the important streams do not rise in the timber but have their origin from springs in the bare hills beyond the timber belt."[5]

In his 1906 report, H. D. Foster called the Wenaha country a strange country, with the streams running in precipitous canyons 2,000 feet deep. Between the canyons were broad plateaus, and on these "flats" grew the best timber. At the end of the report, Foster appended a careful species list of trees and plants, not just the money makers, but also all the forage and flowers and undergrowth. These lists were aimed toward figuring out what might be valuable, but they also showed an openness to the possibility of value in things that were not yet commodities. The real meat of Foster's report was a set of extensive tree descriptions: histories of what each individual species did in the forest in conjunction with the other trees. Foster's descriptions came from close attention to the forest, an attention blended with curiosity. He saw strange things, for example, when he went out to look at the firs and spruce growing at the upper limit of the forest edge. This was a place of no economic value, but one where he still paid attention: "The lower branches, which extend to the ground, are closely appressed to the soil and extend for a distance of several feet from the center of the ring. The result is a cone-shaped mass of dense foliage, often as regular as if pruned and trained by art."[6]

What was unusual could also be awesome: the foresters felt at times that they were on the verge of a grand discovery, that they had stumbled into a land that was not only strange but magnificent. A hint of excitement crept into Erickson's description of the ponderosa pine stands in the Blue Mountains Forest West, on the Strawberry Mountain range: "[The] forest in this region covers approximately an area of one half million acres, and the portion south of the Strawberry range that bears excellent yellow pine and tamarack covers approximately 800,000 acres. . . . The yellow pine is more abundant and is found in more suitable situations on this reverse than I have seen its occurrence in any other part of Oregon. It grows tall and straight. . . . Trees thirty to fifty inches in diameter, with height of 150 feet, furnishing four to six logs, are not uncommon. . . . [Tamarack] reaches immense size, I think its best development is found in the Blue Mountains west."[7] There was no disrespect or impatience with the unregulated forest in this passage; what the forest had to offer was more than enough.

Stories about History

The first task of the new foresters was to catalogue the forests, and these catalogues could begin to seem like little more than numbing details. Erickson, for example, wrote that on the Blue Mountains West Reserve (now the Malheur National Forest), the soil was very rocky and thin on the south side of the divide, so there was less yellow pine than was normal for south slopes. On the north slopes there was mostly larch and lodgepole, while on the south and east slopes there was lodgepole alone, not the more usual Douglas-fir and yellow pine. But these descriptions were more than simple lists; they were attempts to make sense of the land by piecing together its communities: which tree was found with which others and why. Erickson observed that ponderosa pine was "usually mixed with red fir [Douglas-fir], but [was] often in pure stands." Douglas-fir, however, was in a "mixture with tamarack, white fir and yellow pine, and lodgepole pine." High up, tamarack was mixed with lodgepole; lower down it was mixed with Douglas-fir and ponderosa pine. A history of the land emerged from Erickson's lists: "Spruce also was noticed to follow the course of the creeks, where it was in mixture with both firs and lodgepole pine. Juniper occurs on the high, dry, exposed ridges or mesas. It seems to grow on the lava and rocky points on the watersheds of the Crooked River." What was notable here was the generosity of Erickson's attention, his willingness to be open to stories about the land. Spruce liked water, so it followed the creeks; juniper liked sun, so it followed the ridges. Plants were not just set at random upon a blank canvas; they fell into patterns, and those patterns told tales that people could interpret if they learned the forest's language.[8]

Science offered foresters a way of telling stories about history: about how the world had become the way it was. For example, someone unburdened by an interest in natural history might go out in the woods and look at trees. There is a green tree here, another big green tree there, one more tree over there. Big deal, he thinks. Maybe he notices that some trees look different from other trees. End of story, end of thought for that person: the forest is just a bunch of trees. But when H. D. Foster, Forest Assistant of the Wenaha Reserve, went out into the forest armed with his natural history and his rules about competition and succession, he started noticing certain repeatable patterns. Spruce seemed to grow mainly in wet places, at the heads of draws and along the streams. Yellow pine seemed always to be near one particular grass and on the south sides of slopes. On the north slopes, there was still yellow pine, but less of it, and it was always with Douglas-fir. When Foster walked high enough, another kind of spruce took over. Maybe this sounded like just a list of details, but it was not. It was a set of stories with plots and motives and questions. Foster started asking: Why is yellow pine always in hot places? Why is spruce always in damp places? Why do we see lots of old tamarack in a stand, but underneath the tamarack all the young trees are firs? He came to the forest with a set of general rules borrowed from ideas about competition for light and water, and the rules let him make sense of those patterns. More important, they enabled him to *see* the patterns in the first place. The rules were simplifications, but they gave him a way of seeing, so he could notice something more than just a lot of trees.

Some philosophers of science have argued that schemes of classifications determine what you notice, and blind you to what does not fit.[9] But the alternative would be even more blinding. If you do not go out with a set of rules and questions, you do not see anything at all: the differences are lost to you. Your eyes are closed to the fact that spruce never grows out in the open, that tamarack stands change to fir stands after a time, that lodgepole changes to spruce, that yellow pine changes to fir. You see a static mass of green, not a history of change, not a forest in motion.

Numbers and lists could offer a way of paying attention to the natural world, but they could also do the opposite. Systems of classification—lists and tables and careful columns of numbers precise far beyond the limits of the tools available to the foresters—could sometimes seem like strategies for simplifying the complexity of the world and thereby limiting its fearfulness. Submerged under the optimism of the Blues silvics reports, one detects a barely repressed panic. The foresters walked on the edge of confusion: all was new and frightening; nothing was quite understandable. All of Foster's reports reveal a sense of human limits, the need for caution in the face of complexity. He opened his 1908 report on the Blue Mountains East National Forest with a warning: "This report will of necessity deal simply with those parts of the National Forest with which I am personally familiar, which is of rather limited area. . . . Of the northern part of the forest I know nothing, nor of the high mountains in the former Baker City Forest Reserve, except what can be seen from a distance." And then he added that his notes "have been meagre" and so "my report must be based on memory." One could only know what one could touch and see, Foster implied, but that was little of what needed to be known. Foster noted that "to give an estimate of the standing timber on the public land of the National Forest of any one, or all species, is exceedingly difficult, even after careful valuation surveys. . . . [There is] confusion of records and surveys . . . which further complicate matters."[10] Foresters turned up in a place that was completely new and bewildering, and their first response was fear: not so much that something might leap out of the woods and eat them (although at times that had been a reasonable fear), but that nothing might ever make sense again. The forest was a frightening, disturbing place; forestry was a way of managing this fear. If the men could name everything in the forest and then clean it up, reduce what George Bright called the "general riot of the natural forest" to a managed stand, they could keep the confusion of natural history from overtaking their efforts.

Foster's reports bore a surprising resemblance to the comparably detailed—but no less ambiguous—records which one of the first European explorers had made in the Northwest. In 1792, when George Vancouver was sailing around Puget Sound looking for the Northwest Passage, he kept a meticulous journal of his wanderings.[11] Vancouver opened each entry with a rash of numbers— sextant readings, depth readings, compass readings, temperature readings—a reassuring list of precise numbers in neat columns. But these numbers were in a sense meaningless, because Vancouver had no maps of the place where he actually was. He was carefully orienting himself, but in relation to an unknown world. All his expensive and accurate equipment told him that he was 1822.321 miles from some data point, and he carefully wrote that number down, but what did it mean? Very little. What is so moving about Vancouver's entries is how careful he was to persuade himself and his benefactors that he really did know where he was and what he was doing there, when obviously he didn't have a clue. Vancouver created a fragile shell of certainty with his impressive quantification, and what this shell covered was all the newness of the New World, the disturbing unknowable savage Others who might kill you if you turned your back (as indeed the native Hawaiians had killed his friend Captain Cook, with whom Vancouver had made his first voyage to the New World). Vancouver's numbers were real and they came from expensive equipment, but what they described was imaginary, at least on one level. Vancouver's entries, as well as the Blue Mountains silvics reports, are records made by people trying hard not to be overcome by doubt. Everything was new, and nothing made sense. So they tried to describe everything; whenever they saw something half familiar, their relief was palpable. Obsessive quantification was one way to contain their unease that familiar rules might not work in a new world.

Foresters crammed their silvics reports with lists of numbers: tree species, rough estimates of timber yields, precipitation, soil types, elevation, longitude, latitude, and anything else they could think of that could be quantified, whether or not it had much to do with trees. In part, they were attempting to mention everything that might someday matter, but they were also attempting to locate themselves in geographical space as well as in conceptual space. They were trying to figure out where they were, what these forests were about, how they were different from the rest of the world that they already knew. They were explorers in unfamiliar territory, and they were desperate to get their bearings.

Explaining Forest Changes: Succession and Competition

Blue Mountain foresters in the 1990s often claim that what went wrong with the forests was simple: early foresters did not realize that succession would be a problem, or that their actions might cause unwanted changes in the forests. Current managers tend to portray the problems as caused by simple ignorance or ecological innocence. Just a bunch of guys out there cutting trees, not intending any harm, is the way one forester described the early Forest Service managers to me.[12] Yet silvics reports as well as working circle plans show that early foresters in the Blues were immediately concerned about forest change, and indeed obsessed with ecological theory.

When foresters arrived in the Blues, they looked upon millions of acres filled with millions of trees, and every tree was different and every acre of land was different too. Nobody had any real idea what was going on. Obviously, things were changing; where there used to be trees, now there were none. Where the old stand was yellow pine, now the young trees were firs. Where timber cutters came in with a railroad and logged, there were no more trees but a lot of brush. The foresters saw these changes and, as their silvics reports show, they worried about the changes they themselves might be causing. How could they ever control these changes? Science, foresters hoped, would offer them a way to predict the future and avoid the problems that had overtaken past efforts at working the forest. Foresters seized on simple ecological theories—in particular, succession and competition theory—as a way of reducing the mass of potential information to something they could hope to manage. Every species might be different, foresters reasoned, but with any luck they all followed the same simple rules.

Competition and succession seemed to offer foresters a way out of chaos. But by focusing on competition and succession, foresters discounted other ecological theories: disturbance, unpredictable change, and particularly a recognition of the intricate, indirect effects that tied communities together. The irony was that foresters had begun their work in the forests because of an initial concern about indirect ecological processes within the forest—the complex network of cause and effect that connected humans and nature through water. But in their attempts to create an ideal forest through competition, managers increasingly ignored these interconnected ecological processes.

To understand how the Forest Service managed the inland forests, we need to look more closely at the two ecological theories foresters relied on the most: competition and succession. According to the succession theory foresters knew, changes in the forest should follow orderly laws, and competition for space, light, and water would determine the patterns of those changes. After fire or logging destroyed the forest, succession theory predicted that grasses would first invade the site, followed by shrubs which would crowd out the grasses. Soon certain tree species would displace the shrubs, and under the shade of the first trees, other species would come in and eventually eliminate the original species.

Competition—for light, for water, for space—would determine the patterns of forest changes. Foresters did not conceive of the forest as a static entity, but rather as something marked by constant flux. Even though succession and competition theories led foresters into trouble—for these theories minimized the importance of disturbances such as fire—seeing the forest as a changing landscape was still a major, and potentially revolutionary, development.

Before the federal foresters arrived, most whites in the Blues asked few questions about why one tree was here, another there. Trees were there because that was where God, or nature, put them; not because of biological relationships—not because one plant altered its habitat, making it possible for another plant to survive. Most people thought of nature as unchanging, at least on any time scale that might matter to humans. Nature would not always remain unchanged, of course; it was their role, whites felt, to alter the land for productive use. While their conception of the world did not preclude change, in a sense it did preclude natural history—a history of a forest in motion, a biotic history made up of changing interrelationships. Seeing the land as a static entity, rather than a place whose history was shaped by complex biological relationships, allowed people to pull out certain pieces—beaver, for example—without worrying much about the indirect effects on the rest of the community. God made one forest, now man was going to make another, or at least man was going to cut it down and put up something different.

When Forest Service scientists came to the Blues, they brought with them a new curiosity about the history of the forests. In trying to make sense of the patterns they saw, they at first focused on what are now called abiotic factors: nonliving aspects of the landscape that would not change very quickly, such as rocks, climate, elevation, aspect, and soil (which they thought was abiotic, although it is biologically active). Temperature, water, and sun seemed to determine which trees ended up where: the higher you went, the colder it got, and the fewer ponderosas you saw. Each tree had a reason for being where it was, and the development of a forest followed a few orderly rules. For example, R. M. Evans's goal in his 1912 silvical report on the Wallowa and Minam Forests was to explain the forests by giving a geological history of the region, starting with the lava flows that covered much of eastern Washington, Oregon, and Idaho. The patterns of rock and ash explained forest diversity, Evans went on to argue. Basaltic soils supported denser growth because the soil was well decomposed and retained moisture. Granitic soils were much worse, even at the same elevations, and supported a different forest. Forests, Evans asserted, were the way they were for orderly, sensible reasons: they had a predictable and knowable history that was determined by geology first, and moisture and sunlight second. These ideas made some sense in relation to humid forests, where stable states could appear to exist for centuries. But these ideas about orderly change made it very hard for foresters to imagine that disturbance—particularly fire—had played critical roles in shaping the dry inland forests.[13]

Throughout the nineteenth century, most plant biologists had focused on individual species rather than plant communities and the complex interrelationships between plants and animals. In part, this reflected lay people's attitudes toward nature as a collection of separate parts. But even though forests did consist of individual trees, thinking about trees as isolated individuals was certainly not the only way to think about a forest. As the nineteenth century drew to a close, plant ecologists began to develop a radically different way of seeing the forest: they focused on interconnections between plants, not the plants in isolation. Biologists began to note which plants tended to grow near which others, and then they thought about how one plant might affect the presence or absence or growth of another plant. In other words, biologists thought about the ways plants fit into communities. The foresters who came to the Blues were part of this new tradition, so they saw the forest not just as a collection of individual trees, but as changing patterns of trees in groups. This was a critical difference. Once people started thinking about plant associations, they soon realized that they needed to consider the ways these associations formed: the history of communities as they grouped and regrouped. Thus when people moved from seeing the forest as a collection of separate objects to seeing a complex community, they were much more likely to imagine roles for change and history, as well as interconnections and indirect ecological effects.

Although most Blues foresters might not have recognized the names of two critical American plant ecologists—Henry Cowles and Frederic Clements—foresters' ideas about the inland forests developed in the context of the research of those ecologists. Henry Cowles, working on the sand dunes of Lake Michigan, had formalized the idea of dynamic vegetational succession—an orderly sequence of changes in plant communities. After a major disturbance, such as a fire that burned down all the trees on a site, the first species to colonize were those that could best exploit the conditions of the disturbed site—lots of sun but little water or nutrients. Soon, however, those colonists would change the environment in ways that made their own survival difficult; they would create so much shade that their seedlings could not survive. Yet those changes favored the invasion of the community by other species: they cooled the soil surface, contributed organic matter to the soil, and increased soil moisture, all of which the more shade tolerant species needed for their survival.

The idea of plant succession was not new. Thoreau had written about it in his "Natural History of Massachusetts" and "Succession of Forest Trees," where he argued that shade tolerance was critical in determining successional changes. Oaks succeeded pines because young oaks could grow in the shade of pines, whereas pines could not grow in the understory unless the forest was thinned by burning or logging.[14] With the development of succession theory, foresters gradually came to believe that what existed in a particular place was not only a matter of predetermined, abiotic factors, but also a product of biological history. A given plant existed in a particular place because of the other plants that had once been there.

But would succession continue forever, or was there some end to all that change? Frederic Clements, one of the most influential ecologists of the twentieth century, proposed in 1916 that succession led to a stable climax—a community in which the vegetation was in equilibrium with the climate. When new species no longer changed the patterns of light intensity and soil moisture, then succession stopped. Plants in the climax community could grow as well under their own parents' shade as those parents had grown under the species they replaced. Eventually all forests would arrive at the end point of their strivings: the climax forest, a place with the potential to remain essentially unchanged forever. Different plant communities might begin with different species, but in a given climatic region they would all end at the same climax: climate and not biotic interactions determined the final forest.[15] The individual habits of the species on the site, the local environment, the soil, interconnections between plants and animals, disturbances such as fire and grazing, the plant and animal species available to colonize an area after disturbance, and finally chance—all these mattered little compared to climate. As Clements argued, the chance accidents of history mattered for only a short time, until finally the end point of succession was reached.

Most important for the Blues foresters, in Clements's theoretical framework, disturbance was a rare, external event, not an intrinsic property of the community. Succession, Clements insisted, was an orderly process. If foresters could not predict the exact forest that would come in after disturbance, they just did not know enough yet about the situation. Clements's ecological framework suggested an inevitability about the development of a forest. It became an often rigid orthodoxy that treated disturbances such as wind, fire, insects, and diseases as external problems that foresters could, and should, eliminate.[16]

Blues foresters who needed a conceptual framework for managing plant communities eagerly seized on succession theory. The alternative—that natural history might not follow orderly laws, and that nature might be so complex that people could never precisely predict the result of any action—was not something foresters wanted to contemplate. Moreover, they interpreted succession theory in a particularly narrow way. Succession, they argued, was driven almost entirely by competition for light, sun, and moisture. George Bright, for example, wrote in his 1911 report on the silvics of the Umatilla Forest that "all species of trees prefer full light with an abundance of moisture, but it is the lowest degree of moisture and light on which each of the various species can survive which determines the species of tree for each locality." In a struggle that approached warfare, each tree species tried to control limited commodities. Bright noted that lodgepole was the only tree that could "invade the territory of the typical Yellow Pine," because it was a prolific seed producer, so it could "rush in after a burn or cutting and usurp the territory."[17]

Competition was an inevitable part of nature, in the foresters' eyes, but the outcome of competition was something foresters could, and should, manipulate. Managers wanted to create their own changes: to alter the processes of succession so they could extract the best from the forest. If forest changes followed simple laws of competition, foresters could manipulate those competitive struggles, speeding up succession to quickly arrive at the most desirable plant communities. Forestry, as Bernard Fernow had said, was simply a matter of manipulating nature's own competitive struggles, so as to tilt the balance toward economically useful species.[18] Foresters could play favorites, sending their own troops onto plants' natural battlefields, speeding up or slowing down succession, depending on the desired final forest. The Forest Service was confident that it could simply step in and play, if not God, then Competition.

"What kind of a forest will result from different kinds of management?" W. H. B. Kent asked in the Chesnimnus report of 1907. "This is the Forest Service's major concern." Changes after logging became a major issue very early, in part because the Forest Service was reacting against a perceived devastation of forest resources by timber speculators. An early emphasis on forest influences had meant that the Forest Service recognized that actions could have unintended, unpredicted, far-reaching effects. But although the foresters worried that logging could have unpredictable consequences, they soon tried to appear confident that with succession and competition theory, they could control those effects. Yet just beneath the confident tone of the reports runs a current of anxiety.

Like most foresters, Foster worried about the competitive balance between ponderosa pine and true firs in a mixed-conifer stand. The problem, as he wrote in the 1906 Wenaha report, was that "yellow pine is intolerant of shade throughout life. . . . When shaded by dominant trees the suppressed tree dies. It does not seem to be able to continue to live under shade, and when the dominant tree is removed by wind, fire, or logging, it is not often that the suppressed tree regains its vigor." Douglas-fir and grand fir "cast a dense shade," and usually "get the better of yellow pine when there is competition for growing space." Kent elaborated this argument in his report on the proposed Wenaha Reserve in 1904: "The natural tendency in this bull pine [yellow pine] and white fir belt is toward an extension of the white fir at the expense of the pine." Even though white fir grew more slowly than ponderosa pine, it was nevertheless competitively superior because it was "far more [shade] tolerant than bull pine" and so fir, under "*normal conditions* would naturally supplant the pine in time" (emphasis added). Fir was the last thing foresters wanted to encourage. Since fir liked shade and pine liked sun, the best way to halt succession in its tracks was to ensure that pine had plenty of sun. The general agreement was that pine regeneration was best assured by cutting heavily, which would allow the young pine trees unlimited light.

This was exactly how the industrial loggers who preceded the Forest Service in the Blues had cut mixed-conifer forests. But what came up afterward was fir—not the expected pine. Foster observed that on parts of the Wenaha Forest, "black pine [lodgepole] and tamarack are the principal commercial species, largely, however, because these species have supplanted the yellow pine after logging."[19] Evans, in his 1912 report, argued similarly that on certain sites within the yellow pine zone, mixed-conifer stands were present, and that "the proportion of this type in the yellow pine zone is undoubtedly increasing" after logging. Why were pine trees diminishing on the sites that industrial loggers had clearcut—sites that had unlimited sun? One obvious explanation was that when loggers high-graded—taking the good pines but leaving behind the firs—all that was left for the next forest was fir. The natural increase of fir in mixed-conifer stands, Kent wrote in 1904, "has been greatly aggravated in the portions that have been lumbered by cutting the pine and leaving the white fir. The fir, often already on the ground under the pine, springs up, and pine reproduction is thus impossible. This is unfortunate since bull pine is by far the more valuable species." In other words, industrial logging had accelerated natural processes of succession—even though foresters had thought it ought to reverse those processes.

Manipulating Succession in the Forest

The early silvical reports sometimes revealed a quickly repressed fear that human-induced changes might have begun to swing out of control. As Foster wrote about the Wenaha, in his 1906 report, "old cuttings have modified the forest." These modifications were not only undesirable but often difficult to understand; for example, Foster noted that "on burned areas the new growth is apt to be either white fir or lodgepole pine" instead of the ponderosa predicted by succession theory. Changes multiplied at such a rate that soon everything appeared to be in a state of constant and confusing flux. Foster wrote in bewilderment that "the yellow pine type may change after logging to the mixed conifer type, the mixed conifer type after burning may change to the lodgepole type, while after clear-cutting the lodgepole type is prone to deteriorate to the white fir type." At times, some tree species began to seem like chimera. Larch, in particular, which Foster wanted to favor in the north-slope communities, resisted all his attempts at control. He complained that larch "is not common, and appears to be transitory, being easily modified by art or nature into one of the types enumerated above, as for instance into the lodgepole type."

As Foster argued in a 1907 report on the Blue Mountains East National Forest, it was not just the industry that could create havoc. Even the Forest Service, for all its good intentions, might inadvertently create the same problems caused by former industrial logging. He warned that "in all sales on this Forest, care should be exercised in marking the timber not to leave the cutting area in such condition that a valuable stand be supplanted by inferior species. . . . Unless care is taken this species [white fir] is prone to supplant such species as yellow pine and tamarack since it is much more tolerant of shade in early life."[20] Yet soon this note of caution disappeared, as foresters become more convinced of their ability to reshape the forest, and less able to notice their own effects on the land.

Early foresters in the Blues realized that their science was not exact: one silviculturist would see the same set of circumstances as another, but the two might then come up with entirely different recommendations. Throughout the first ten or so years of the Forest Service, foresters groped for the best ways to manage forests. Each forester was briefly convinced of the merits of his own ideas, but what was striking was how readily researchers admitted their own confusion and the limits of their data.

For example, how best to manage larch? The problem, as Erickson noted in his 1906 silvics report on the Blue Mountains National Forest, was that lodgepole was "seemingly encroaching upon areas formerly occupied by tamarack, where fires have occurred," even though the fires rarely killed the mature larch but did kill mature lodgepole. Why would fire favor the species it killed, while the species that survived ultimately lost out? Erickson reasoned that although "the large tamarack, because of its thick bark, is seldom killed by the fire leaving the mother trees standing," fire appeared to dry the soil, which was "not favorable for tamarack seed," but furnished "the best seed bed for lodgepole." Underneath the mature larch trees were not young larch but "a dense reproduction of lodgepole pine with none or very little evidence of tamarack seedlings coming in." Yet the situation was even more complicated. Erickson noted that lodgepole might sneak in after fire, but eventually it might change the soil enough to allow another generation of larch to take back the site, though only if the tamarack was able "to hold its own until the lodgepole pine stand has nearly matured and *brought about better soil conditions*" (emphasis added). Keep fire out and the larch seedlings would "secure [the] opportunity to come up in the more open blanks, resulting from the falling of matured lodgepole pine, and only in this way can a more desirable species of tamarack be brought about to cover these areas again."[21]

If nothing was stable in the forest, how should a forester manipulate processes of change to favor desirable species? Erickson recommended that lodgepole should all be cut, tamarack left for seed trees, and the slash lopped and scattered—not burned, because a burnt soil seemed to favor lodgepole. Evans, in his report on the Wallowa and Minam Forests, came up with the exact opposite recommendation for the same problem. In 1912, he argued that the best management to favor larch over Douglas-fir in mixed-conifer sites was with scattered seed trees and broadcast burning. George Bright, working as a regional forester, came up with a third idea: clearcut to favor larch. In a study titled "The Relative Merits of Western Larch and Douglas Fir in the Blue Mountains, Oregon," he argued that larch was the ideal tree—almost better than ponderosa pine. Not only did it have valuable timber, it was "singularly fortunate in the means of protection against the natural enemies of forest trees which it possesses." The only problem was that it was shade intolerant. Therefore, he argued, one needed "clean cuts"—or clear cuts—to get larch reproduction.[22] The Blues foresters had a seemingly simple goal—to manipulate the forest by capitalizing on the abilities of different species to compete for sun and moisture—but this single goal could produce drastically different plans.

Fire and Succession

As Erickson's report on larch showed, early foresters had no trouble seeing that fire played a critical role in shaping the direction and speed of succession. All the foresters recognized as well that this was a landscape shaped by frequent fires, sometimes by catastrophic fires. Kent, in his inspection of the proposed Wenaha reserve, mentioned that "practically every portion of the reserve has suffered more or less from fire." Nor did foresters have any trouble taking the next step of arguing that they could use fire or suppress fire to manipulate the direction of forest changes. Nevertheless, they still thought of fire as an unnatural agent of destruction. Because Clements's monoclimax theory—their theoretical framework for thinking about the forest—assumed that disturbances were external irritants rather than intrinsic properties of the community, foresters felt it was their responsibility to exclude fire.

In part, this belief came about because foresters recognized that

Trees this big were once common in the Blue Mountains; now they are the exception. This tree was found along the Minam River trail high in the Wallowas, in a forest of larch mixed with Douglas-fir, grand fir, and some lodgepole and ponderosa pine. *USDA Forest Service photo, date unknown.*

Fighting a ground fire in ponderosa pine near Billy Meadows, about 1910. Old growth ponderosa pine forests containing large trees in an open, parklike setting were once common throughout the inland West. Light fires burnt about every decade, and kept the forests open.

Another kind of ponderosa forest grew on sites that were cooler and moister. These mixed-conifer forests were dominated by ponderosa pine, but a few Douglas-firs and grand firs could also survive. Light, frequent fires swept through these forests every 10 years or so. After the Forest Service suppressed fire, grand firs crowded out the pines. This photo was taken in the 1920s, in northern California on private lands owned by the Collins Lumber Company. *Photo courtesy of Trygve Steen.*

By 1964, when this photo was taken near Burns, Oregon, firs were beginning to dominate the understory of the mixed-conifer forests. Some ponderosa remains, but the largest pines are long gone to the mills. The suppression of light fires has allowed grand fir to fill the understory, and as firs have increased, so too have the insects that feed on firs. The grand fir trees in the background show topkilling caused by Douglas-fir tussock moth larvae. *Photo By W. C. Guy; USDA Forest Service photo, PNW Research Station, Forestry and Range Sciences Laboratory, La Grande, Oregon, #PS-3147.*

Not all forests in the inland West were big open ponderosa forests. What early foresters called the *north-slope type* were also common. Grand fir and Douglas-fir crowd together, competing for the little light that makes it through the canopy. Defoliating insects have attacked the Douglas-firs in this photo, taken near Meadowbrook Creek, Dale, Oregon, 1946. *USDA Forest Service photo, PNW Research Station, Forestry and Range Sciences Laboratory, La Grande, Oregon, #PS-724.*

When light fires were keep out, conifers grew too closely together, and "self-suppressed." The growth of all the trees slowed since there was not enough space to grow or water to thrive, and the stand became stagnated and vulnerable to insect attacks. This 1964 photo shows a stagnated ponderosa pine stand on the Yakima Reservation in Washington, with Forest Service entomologist K. Wright in the foreground. *Photo by R. G. Mitchell; USDA Forest Service photo, PNW Research Station, Forestry and Range Sciences Laboratory, La Grande, Oregon, #PS-7990.*

A Ford tri-motor plane spraying in 1955, along the Powder River. In the 1950s, the Forest Service tried to control a spruce budworm outbreak in the Blues with aerial spraying of DDT. Insect attacks have always been a part of the forest, and are essential for the forest's long-term persistence, since they recycle nutrients and open up space for young trees to grow. But as firs have come to dominate forests where ponderosa once reigned, attacks of spruce budworm and Douglas-fir tussock moth have become increasingly devastating. *USDA Forest Service photo, PNW Research Station, Forestry and Range Sciences Laboratory, La Grande, Oregon, #PS-1430.*

Fire-fighting does an excellent job of delaying catastrophic fires, but people can never hope to remove all fires from the landscape. When light fires are suppressed, the forest becomes denser and fuels build up—so future fires are more intense and destructive. Yet even though catastrophic fires were once rare in the forests dominated by ponderosa pine, they were fairly common at higher elevations. This photo from about 1913 shows the effects of a stand-replacing fire in the high-elevation subalpine fir forests on the Umatilla National Forest, near Table Rock Mountain. *Photo probably by M. N. Unser, USDA Forest Service.*

Before the Forest Service came to the Blues, most logging was basically clear-cutting. The Forest Service insisted that loggers instead selectively cut, leaving a reserve stand to become the basis for the next generation. Loggers usually left about 15 percent of the volume. This 1919 photo shows a reserve stand in the Whitman National Forest five years after it was logged. *Photo by M. H. Weidman, 1919, USDA Forest Service.*

A logging steam train in 1908, north of Imbler, near La Grande. After horses dragged the logs out of the stand, steam trains carried them to the mills. As this photo shows, not all of the Blues were forested. *Photo by Joseph McKenney, Courtesy of Wallowa County Museum, Joseph, Oregon, gift of Dean Morrow, 1937.*

Grazing has changed the landscapes of the inland West as much as logging and fire suppression. In the early twentieth century, grazing pressures on the high elevation forests were intense, in part because sheep were herded in bands of two thousand. These sheep were bedded in a corral on the Wallowa National Forest in 1909, as part of research on protection from coyotes and wolves. *Photo probably by James T. Jardine, 1909, USDA Forest Service.*

Such huge bands of sheep damaged the meadows to the extent that only stones remained. This photo was taken *outside* a corral near the Clearwater Ranger Station, on the Wenaha (now the Umatilla National Forest), in the north end of the Blues. The forest in the background is a lodgepole stand. *Photo probably by M. N. Unser, 1913, USDA Forest Service.*

Small settlements in the Blues relied on resource-based industries—grazing and logging, and some agriculture. This is the ranch of John Kirk Hayes, outside of Joseph in the Wallowa Valley at the edge of the Wallowa Mountains. Dense fir forests grow on the north-facing slopes of the mountains. *Photo courtesy of Wallowa County Museum, Joseph, Oregon.*

The remote Wallowa Mountains are high, cold, and rugged. This pack string is making its way up the west fork of the Wallowa River in 1929, heading for the Lake Basin. The riparian vegetation is dense, and there is a good deal of dead and down wood in the water and on the forest floor. Such streams were once excellent fish habitat. *Photo by N. J. Billings, USDA Forest Service.*

Hunting and fishing parties often camped in the high country of the Wallowas, in the Lake Basin at Horseshoe Lake, about 9,000 feet high. *Photo by N. J. Billings, 1929, USDA Forest Service.*

Above the Lake Basin in the Wallowas, meadows and subalpine fir forests give way to granite peaks and snow. *Photo by N. J. Billings, 1929, USDA Forest Service.*

North of the Wallowas, instead of granite peaks there are rolling hills, steep canyons, and dense lodgepole forests. This was the Clearwater Ranger Station, set in a logged-over lodgepole forest in the Wenaha Forest, now the Umatilla National Forest. Before becoming a ranger station, this was a trapper's cabin, when fur-bearing mammals were still abundant. *Photo probably by M. N. Unser, 1913, USDA Forest Service.*

Not all of the Wenaha was lodgepole forest. Near the Tucannon Ranger Station, the south-facing slopes have open forests dominated by ponderosa pine, while the north-facing slopes have denser forests with more fir. This area was where H. D. Foster and George Bright did much of the silvics work that set the foundation for forestry in the Blues. *Photo probably by M. N. Unser, 1913, USDA Forest Service.*

The north-south contrast is even sharper where the forests edge into grasslands. Forests grow densely in the wetter, north-facing draws, but on the ridges and south slopes it is too hot and dry for most trees to survive. *Photo probably by M. N. Unser, 1913, USDA Forest Service.*

Shady, protected riparian zones are critical in a place as dry and extreme as the Blues: they cover only 4 percent of the area, but are home for 75 percent of the vertebrates. The white patch in the center is a plowed field where a family was homesteading; few of these families managed to make a living. The scattered timber growing on protected places on the canyon walls is mainly small Douglas-fir, while much denser vegetation grows along the streams. Near Tucannon Creek, on the Wenaha; *photo probably by M. N. Unser, 1913, USDA Forest Service.*

One of the extremely isolated homesteads on the Imnaha River in the late 1800s. Note the elk antlers, the six children, and the heavy wool clothing in a place where summer temperatures often exceeded 100 degrees. *Photo courtesy of Wallowa County Museum, Joseph, Oregon.*

Another shot of the Imnaha River canyon, showing the steep rimrock terrain across from Five Mile view point along the Grizzly Ridge Road. The canyonlands were steep and rugged, and on the south- or west-facing slopes few trees could survive. But bunchgrasses were once abundant in such canyons, until heavy grazing depleted them. *USDA Forest Service photo.*

Even in the extreme landscapes of Hells Canyon, huge trees managed to grow in protected draws. The grasslands at the right edge of the picture show the effects of heavy grazing. *USDA Forest Service photo.*

Some of the most spectacular and most vulnerable canyons in North America are found in the Blues. When this photo of the Imnaha River canyon was taken in 1941, riparian vegetation was still lush, and salmon were abundant. *USDA Forest Service photo.*

stand-replacing fires often resulted in lodgepole. Erickson argued that "the fact that extensive forest fires have denuded the slopes on the south side of the Wallowa Forest Reserve accounts largely for the large areas now covered with lodgepole pine timber."[23] But what foresters had more trouble recognizing was that not all fires led to the same results. Foster noticed in 1906 that "in mixt [sic] forest, fires tend to bring in lodgepole pine which tends to supplant the more valuable yellow pine, thus injuring the commercial value of the forest." He was right in noting that crown fires within a mixed-conifer stand could exclude ponderosa; what he did not see, however, was that fire exclusion would do the same thing.

After only a few years of fire exclusion, Evans noted in his 1912 report that a series of changes was accumulating—some desirable, from his perspective, others much less desirable. Sagebrush was taking over the grasslands—not good—but then, yellow pine was "slowly encroaching upon the sagebrush . . . provided fire is kept out," a very good thing. Evans reasoned that before the Forest Service began suppressing fires, whenever young pine "pushed out from under the protection of the parent trees, the periodical fires . . . killed it back, thus keeping the timber line practically stationary." But with fire suppression, "conditions have improved, and it is noticeable that the pine is reaching out." On the less desirable side, fire suppression meant that some pine forests were "being occupied by a thick stand of fir reproduction." Evans could not see fire as anything other than a problem, or the exclusion of fire as anything other than an improvement, even though he found the results less than desirable. Fire was an unnatural agency; by implication the Forest Service's role was to remove this unnatural force and allow the forest to return to its more natural, more productive existence.

Early foresters realized that there were different types of fires, and they also recognized that surface fires did not damage older ponderosas. Kent mentioned that only young trees died in most fires, while mature trees were not damaged unless covered with dry moss. Evans added that in mixed conifer stands within the Wallowa Forest, crown fires in old-growth stands were extremely rare. Foster even noted that white fir—a tree they wanted to eliminate—

was killed in mixed-conifer stands by light fires, while ponderosa remained unharmed. Nevertheless, these three men recommended the exclusion of all fires, because fires seemed to damage soil, lessen germination, and kill the seedlings. Foster argued that "the worst effects from fires upon slopes is the destruction or injury to the forest floor. The humus is burned off leaving a shallow soil unprotected from erosion. . . . The soil is left dry and is destroyed in patches furnishing but a poor seedbed for further restocking." [24] But these effects were rarely consequences of light fires. Part of the foresters' confusion arose because, although they knew there were differences between high intensity and light fires, they found it hard to move beyond simple associations. Some fires damaged trees, harmed soil, and killed seedlings, so all fires seemed bad.

Reproduction

Foresters came to the Blues with a heavy sense of responsibility that grew from their understanding that good land had already been destroyed and wild nature had already been lost. As Kent wrote in 1904 about the hills south of Walla Walla: "Originally this range of hills was practically surrounded at low altitude, by an excellent belt of timber which doubtless encroached more or less upon the neighboring plains." Much of this area was probably grasslands rather than forests when whites first arrived, but Kent assumed that if trees were absent, loggers were to blame. Government foresters firmly believed that industrial cutting practices produced sterile lands, and as Kent put it, "in these [logged] portions no forest can ever be expected again." The waste left on the ground invariably caught on fire, burned ferociously, sterilized the soil, and destroyed the young growth. Young trees were the future of the forest, and industry seemed to have sacrificed future forests for short-term profits. Because of this, Forest Service managers felt that their major responsibility was to reverse the devastation caused by industrial logging, and so ensure that there would be forests for the future. This meant encouraging reproduction—the best conditions for germination and seedling survival. Foresters did their job so well that thickets of overcrowded seedlings resulted, and the forests they were trying to save changed in ways they had never intended. In their haste to fix what was wrong with industrial logging, the foresters created other problems that proved much more difficult to mend.

Even if all the foresters agreed that their task was to ensure forests for the future, the next step was not clear. What exactly were the best conditions for regenerating pine trees? Since fir liked shade and pine liked sun, foresters agreed that pine regeneration was best guaranteed by clearcutting small sites. But then why were not pine trees taking over the sites that industrial loggers had clearcut—sites with unlimited sun? The foresters were observant enough to realize that theory and the forest did not mesh; moreover, they firmly believed that theory had to be tempered with on-the-ground studies. So in the summer of 1910, George Bright went out to the Whitman National Forest to find out exactly which local conditions favored pine regeneration.

The problem Bright faced was that, strangely enough, reproduction appeared to be good everywhere. Young yellow pine flourished "on all kinds of sites and on all kinds of seed beds, from nearly barren scab rock flats and on ridges, to the partial shade and thick pine grass found in mature Yellow Pine forests," he wrote in his 1911 "Umatilla Studies" report. This abundance made his task difficult: "Where reproduction is so universally good it is difficult to determine which conditions are the most suitable to Yellow Pine seedlings." What could be simply deduced if everything seemed to do well? Was germination higher on loose rocky bare soil or in shaded sites? Even though Bright was observant enough to recognize that a lack of variability made his task difficult, he was working within a framework that assumed if some reproduction was good, a lot of reproduction was better. He could not go one step further and imagine that if natural reproduction was so very abundant but pine still seemed to be decreasing, then the best way to ensure that pine remained dominant might not be to favor more young pine. Bright's task was to decide under what conditions young pine did best, and he missed the evidence in front of him that suggested this goal might be ultimately problematic.

Part of the difficulty of scientific forestry—of all land management—was that in the laboratory, theory might predict a simple cause-and-effect relationship. More sun, more pine regeneration. But out in the forest, numerous other factors come into play— confounding simple cause and effects. In the lab, for example, there was no question but that ceanothus shrubs competed for sun and water with pine; when ceanothus was present, pine got a smaller share of the water and sun that researchers made available. But in the field, although ceanothus might reduce some of the light pine needed to grow, it would also increase the amount of nitrogen that pine needed to grow—indirectly favoring pine. And shading out one pine tree might release more nutrients for other pine trees. These indirect effects stymied the foresters, because they complicated matters that had seemed to be simple. Was competition good or bad? Was sun good or bad? Was fire good or bad? Was reproduction good or bad? It all depended; but that was not an answer that helped foresters decide how to cut trees.

George Bright, like most of the early foresters, was observant enough to note that the forest was a complicated place, where simple scientific theories were not always as helpful as managers had hoped. This complexity was at the root of many of their problems. For example, Bright noted that climate variability made scientific conclusions extremely difficult: "This matter was further complicated by the fact that the most favorable localities in a wet year would very likely be the most unfavorable sites on a dry year." Bright set up sample plots and came up with a few contrasting observations. Open sites led to the best germination, but "the mortality of the seedlings during the first year was often 100% over considerable areas." On mature forests with competing vegetation, there were "seedlings which had finally succeeded in getting a foothold through the pine grass" but those few seedlings "revealed a much larger per cent of living over dead, than the less shaded and protected seedings." These were potentially revolutionary observations: what Bright was noticing was that simple associations of good and bad did not make much sense. He recommended that managers focus not just on germination, for "it is the living seedlings that are of importance."

If managers had followed Bright's recommendations, ponderosa pine might have had more of a chance in the Blues. His advice fell by the wayside, however, because the Forest Service was convinced that the more young pine they had, the more old pine would necessarily follow. Managers suppressed fire because they thought light fires would kill all the young trees. Competition, which dense stands of young trees fostered, would surely create vigorous, manly trees; without competition, weaklings would result—or so the foresters reasoned.[25] The opposite turned out to be true, unfortunately. Firs and pines failed to thin themselves, nor did they recover from suppression when they were artificially thinned after their first decade or so. Without fires to thin them, what resulted was not a few big trees, but a thicket of stagnated trees all the same age.

Monitoring Actions

In trying to manipulate the forests through management, the foresters recognized that for all their theories, they were acting in the dark. Given their limited knowledge, the Forest Service agreed that foresters should try to monitor the effects of their actions on the land. In 1907, forest officers in Washington and Oregon were asked to "make a particular effort to examine the cut-over areas on your Forest from time to time and to keep the records accurately and up to date." Why? As Frederick Ames, the Chief of Silviculture stressed, they needed to get away from theory derived from German forestry and try to see the forest clearly. Ames wrote: "The practice of forestry is still young in this district and we have much to learn regarding the practical management of forests. We do not yet know under just what conditions the best second growth of Douglas fir is secured, whether reproduction in the dry yellow pine region takes place best when the brush is burned or when it is scattered over the ground."[26] Because they knew so little, they needed to be alert to the possibilities that their attempts might go wrong.

Ames was describing a forestry that did not rest on hard certainties, but was a flexible process based on the recognition of human fallibility. He wrote: "The forest descriptions and record of cut-over areas should be so complete that, if twenty years after a couple of

timber sales were made, we find on one sale-area good reproduction and on the other little, we could turn to the records and find
out just what conditions were different on the two areas." Ames
called for close attention to both the forest and the effects of human actions on the forest. He detailed an extraordinarily ambitious
amount of monitoring: he wanted all supervisors in the Blues to
send a forest officer out every three or four years to examine the
cutover areas, write concise descriptions of the changed forest,
then clip these reports to the description of the original forest so
they would have a record of changes. As Ames urged, they needed
to learn to see all of sales as a vast experiment. In modern terms,
he was telling his foresters that they needed to practice "adaptive
management"—management that recognized that they could not
always predict the effects of their actions. Ideally, if someone such
as H. D. Foster reasoned that the best way to ensure pine regeneration was to clearcut, he would first try it on one area and follow
the progress of that site. If the clearcut did not produce pine, it
was Foster's responsibility to try something different. This kind of
responsiveness was much more easily advised than done: George
Bright had tried to do exactly that with his yellow pine study, but
his results had little effect on Forest Service logging practices.

The implication in Ames's report was that by 1907, only two
years after the Forest Service took over administration of the forest,
matters seemed to be getting out of control. Already, forest officers
were not keeping close enough track of their actions and were overwhelmed by attempts to keep records up to date. Monitoring
proved to be an impossible task. Even when conscientious assistants gathered all the data Ames called for, these reports accumulated dust, first on the top of the supervisor's desk, then in the
office's filing cabinets, then in cardboard boxes in the storage
attics. No one knew what to do with all this information, and it
continued to multiply exponentially while managers tried to figure
out a solution. This difficulty in comprehending complexity was
one of the core problems faced by the Forest Service—in the 1990s
as well as in the 1910s. Very early, managers recognized that sales
were massive experiments with unknown results. They had no pos-

sible hope of monitoring, or even thinking about, the data that they generated.

When foresters did try to monitor the effects of their logging practices, superiors in the regional offices usually shied away from making recommended changes. Caution seemed easier, given the uncertainties, than trying to revise theories. Logging in ponderosa pine stands provides yet another example of these difficulties. In 1915, foresters began to notice that the mature pine trees they were leaving behind for a reserve stand were knocked down by the wind five times more often than mature pines in unlogged forests. If all the reserve trees were going to fall down, there might be nothing left to cut in sixty years—a possibility that would overturn the foundation of scientific forestry. Kan Smith, a forest examiner studying windfall patterns in the Whitman Forest in 1915, recommended that the Forest Service forget the reserve system of cutting ponderosa and harvest all pines greater than 12 inches in diameter. Foresters had expected that when logging opened up a stand, the reserved trees would grow more quickly, given that they received more light. They would also extend their root systems, to take advantage of the extra space. After his field studies, Smith argued that "the theory sometimes advanced that old and mature trees . . . will upon exposure by selection cuttings develop root systems and strength to meet these new conditions, hardly seems reasonable." He observed that the part of the tree above ground did not respond to the new light and space with vigorous growth, and therefore, by extension, "it does not seem probable that such vigorous accelerated response will be found in the root systems."[27]

Smith's study was extremely detailed: he did a 100 percent cruise of 1,624 acres of the Eccles sale site, which had been subjected to the heaviest windfall. This 100 percent cruise meant that he mapped and measured every tree on 1,624 acres—a monumental task that led to an overwhelming quantity of data, much of it uninterpretable. For each tree that had fallen in the windstorms, Smith recorded its size, trunk, roots, crown, relation to neighbors, soil hold, and topography. He then compared these windfalls with data from windfalls on two other sites: the Baker sale cutover area, where losses were one-sixth as great, and an unlogged stand of old-growth pine, where losses were one-fifth as great. What he came up with was "an enormous mass of data," in his frustrated phrase, that allowed him to make several tentative conclusions. The size and shape of the tree most strongly affected the probability of windfall: wider, taller trees with denser crowns were more likely to fall than thinner, shorter, looser-crowned trees. Clumps of trees were more likely to fall than individual trees. This surprised Smith; he had expected that an unstable tree would gain protection from neighbors, but instead it seemed as if one unstable tree could pull stable trees over with it. Slope, aspect, topography, and soil depth had no apparent effect on windfall. Most surprising, the effects of cutting continued into the uncut forests: there was a significant edge effect no one had expected. Smith wrote, "The wind throw is very much greater on the edge to the windward, adjacent to cut-over lands, than in the interior.[28] On one 40 acre square cutover plot, 20 chains wide on each side (a chain measured 22 yards, and 40 acres is the current size now allowable for clearcuts), Smith reported that the windfall effect continued for 5 chains (110 yards) into the uncut forest, resulting in an affected area of 50 acres: an edge effect larger than the cutting area itself.

Fred Ames, the district forester who had recommended intense monitoring, wrote a response to Smith's studies, and this response reveals how difficult it was for early managers to make decisions in an unfamiliar world. Ames had begged all his foresters to do exactly what Kan Smith had done—to go out and measure the effects of their logging, and change anything that was not working. But after describing and interpreting Smith's results, Ames drew back from recommending any changes in cutting policy. He acknowledged that they had to do something, but they did not know what that something should be. The problem was that they did not understand what was special about the site, or even why the trees fell down. As Ames explained, "whether the Eccles area is topographically such that it is subject to very high winds or whether its timber is especially susceptible, we do not know. Neither do we know why the loss was four or five times greater on the Eccles Lumber Co. sale area than on the adjacent Baker White Pine Lumber Co. area."

He did recognize that something needed to change, and he admitted that "in localities like the Eccles area . . . we must adjust the method of marking so that this great loss will not be suffered." But even though Smith had strongly recommended that the Forest Service reevaluate its policies for all pine areas, Ames turned away from such drastic measures. He reached the slightly more comforting conclusion that only Smith's single site faced such odd difficulties: "The problem, however, seems to be local. . . . I do not propose to make any District-wide changes in our methods of marking. Nothing in this letter, therefore, authorizes you to make any changes in the method of handling yellow pine sales."[29]

Foresters simply did not know what was happening. They were swamped with information about the history of every tree on the cutting area, but they had little idea how to reduce this complexity into general observations and trends. They had no statistical techniques beyond comparing averages and percentages, so they did not know which differences were significant and which were random. Nor did they know how to extrapolate from one site to other sites. Ames was the man who wanted each cutting area to be closely monitored, but when he received the information from that monitoring, he realized that their troubles had only begun. Rather than change the techniques, he advised caution. But caution was not really an option. Refusing to change meant they were, by default, managing millions of acres of pine lands with logging techniques that were not producing the desired effects. Yet foresters were afraid that if they changed things now, those changes might produce worse effects.

Water

Ecology can sometimes seem like the science of grim warnings: everything has indirect effects and interconnected functions, so if you alter one process, you are bound to disturb a thousand other processes that you do not even know exist. Scientists such as George Perkins Marsh and Bernard Fernow had used this as their major argument for forest protection. Because there were always indirect effects of an activity, what one did to the forest's water-holding capacities in a single place would affect many other places in unexpected ways. Beginning with Marsh's writings, a concern about watershed effects was closely intertwined with an interest in ecology. For the first Blues foresters, the purpose of forests was not just to produce timber, but also to protect the surrounding lands by preserving the water supply. Their responsibility, they felt, was to keep a dry area from turning into a desert. Only vegetation cover could protect the water supply, they argued, but a regulated forest could do just as good a job protecting the water, while also producing timber.

Forest reserves in the Blues and across the West had gained much of their support from the desire of western irrigation interests to protect their water supplies.[30] Irrigators feared that lumbering, overgrazing, and fires would decimate the high elevation forests at the head of watersheds—the forests that regulated the flow of water. Heavy spring floods and summer droughts might follow, destroying the hopes of valley farmers.[31] Because the movement of water connected one patch of land to another, many of these indirect effects were mediated by water. Water was the critical and often limiting resource in a semiarid region such as the Blues. The health of riparian zones—the winding ribbons of forested land along streams and rivers—was particularly critical; they formed only 4 percent of the forest area, but supported 75 percent of the vertebrates.[32] Healthy riparian zones could act as filters, buffering the effects of one action on another place; likewise, unhealthy riparian areas would magnify the destructive effects of an ill-considered action on a distant place. Foster, for example, wrote in 1906 that irresponsible grazing and logging had already devastated the Wenaha Forest. These poor land-use practices had to stop, because "if it were not for the forest growth upon them, the soil would soon wash off, exposing the bare rock. This has happened where the bunch grass has been overgrazed by sheep, and there are no trees to hold the soil." As Kent put it in his inspection of the proposed Wenaha reserve, the forest was absolutely necessary to protect the streams and return them to their even flow, so irrigation would be safe and land values could be increased.

Forest Service scientists were initially adamant that forest cover played an essential role in protecting water. They based their arguments on a comparison of conditions in 1900, after thirty-five years of logging and grazing, with conditions in 1865, before white settlement began in earnest. Before industrial loggers had ransacked the forests, foresters claimed, the water ran all summer long; but after greed had denuded the hills of their cover, the streams turned to dust by July. For example, Kent wrote of the Wenaha in 1904: "There has been a decided change in the manner of [water] flow. . . . The tendency, according to the farmers and water power millmen, is toward heavy and annually increasing floods in the early spring, followed by long periods of low water. . . . The trouble is not in the rainfall but in the manner of delivering this rainfall to the streams." Why had the delivery of rainfall to streams changed? Kent argued that to find the answer, one needed to look not at the farms where people noticed the problems: "the trouble is to be sought in the hills among which these streams find their source." In just a few decades of logging and grazing, Kent wrote, "conditions have undergone decided changes. Thirty-five years ago the foothills presented a practically unbroken body of heavy coniferous forests." Not only had the forests fallen, but the high meadows, where the streams found their sources, had been ravaged by sheep: "Thirty-five years ago the summits and upper slopes of the high interior hills probably had but little more forest cover than at present, but these high hills were then covered with a profuse growth of bunch grass, weeds, and shrubs, which have since been destroyed by small fires and sheep grazing. This growth of weeds and shrubs has been replaced largely by hard, baked earth, and often by bare rock from which the scanty soil has been completely eroded." As a result of compaction and erosion, the soil could not hold water, and floods and drought had become common, because "in these hills a forest cover is a positive necessity for the regular flow of the streams." Human-induced changes were usually dangerous, Kent claimed, and loggers had harvested without knowing the indirect effects on water, on soil, on trees, much less on the future of the farming industry in distant places.

Nothing about water and forests was entirely clear, because people defined water in ways shaped by their own cultural perspectives of value. Did logging increase or decrease water supply? The answer depended on how people measured water, and how people measured water depended on what they valued about water. Many observers had noted that after intense tree harvests, spring floods seemed to increase whereas the summer dry-up came earlier. They argued from these observations that forest cover was necessary to maintain hydrologic continuity—to keep water levels more constant. Tree cover, they reasoned, would increase the total water present in the local environment and raise the water table by making snow stay longer in the spring and slowing its evaporation. But there was little experimental evidence to support this contention, and people could always find examples that supported the exact opposite arguments. For example, many loggers argued that cutting trees *increased* water, because more water ran off clearcut sites. Engineers argued that because trees consumed and transpired water, the net effect of tree cover was to decrease water levels in the area, not increase them.[33] But engineers and ecologists were measuring different things: there was no single essential property of water that people could measure and then determine if water increased or decreased.

When the Blues foresters had first argued that forests protected the water supply, some of them went one step further and suggested that forests also increased rainfall. This was a far more radical claim, and much more difficult to substantiate. Kent, in his 1904 report on the Wenaha forest, proposed that "it is very probable that the annual precipitation of 17.70 inches at Walla Walla . . . is due to this high, cool range of hills against which the rain laden clouds are forced by the prevailing winds from the southwest." Removing the forests would not just change the water flow, it might also *diminish* rainfall: "Once the vegetation is removed from these hills, turning them from cool, snow-holding slopes into bald ridges of bare rock, they will become in summer a region of intense heat and the rain clouds on contact with them will have their moisture holding capacity increased instead of lowered as at present. The result will be a decided diminution in the rainfall over the great grain belt west of these hills . . . [which] will seriously cripple its greatest industry." Kent realized that many people would laugh at his conclusions: how could trees possibly affect the rainfall? He defended himself gamely: "Nor is this conclusion at all far fetched. In case the present stripping of the higher foothills for timber and severe over-grazing and consequent erosion and total destruction of the vegetation of the moist ranges are continued . . . drought . . . is none the less certain."

The association of forests with water made intuitive sense. Because forests were wetter than the surrounding grasslands, it seemed reasonable that if people removed the forests, the land would dry up and the rains would stop. These were the ideas that drove the massive plantings of trees in the Great Plains: if trees affected the movement of rain after it had fallen, then trees might affect rainfall, by increasing transpiration—the moisture passed from plants to the air. Most people now dismiss the idea without serious consideration, as evidence of the quaintness of early scientists.[34] Yet this scorn partly grows out of our own current world view, one shaped by the competition theory.

Recent studies have suggested that, at least in some tropical rainforests, forests do alter precipitation, and moreover this effect is felt outside the individual stand: if one forest is logged, rainfall decreases in nonadjacent unlogged patches.[35] Even more interesting, botanists have known for many years that tap-rooted trees (and tap-rooted bushes such as sagebrush) draw water from the deeper layers of soil and then transpire it through their leaves. This fact was central to both sides of the debate about trees and water. The climate-change advocates argued that the water transpired by trees would condense and return locally as rainfall. The alternative view held that because trees draw water out of the soil and then lose it by transpiration, trees contribute to a net soil water deficit. For years, people argued that we should cut trees down to increase water levels, because trees were water hogs and kept water from more useful plants like wheat.[36]

Which side of the water debate was right? Did trees steal water from their neighbors or did they give water away? The correct answer depended on which effects people decided to measure. The foresters were partly right: trees often did show a net water loss. But the water they transpired was not water from the upper levels of the soil; trees prevented evaporation from the upper layers by shading the soil, and they also decreased runoff. So they were not stealing water from the levels of the soil where it was most useful to other plants. But more important, trees were not just drawing water from the deep soil and transpiring it to the air. At night they leaked this water out to the upper soil levels, in effect watering the plants around them in a process called hydraulic lift. Hydrologists suspected this for years, because trees did not transpire during the night. Since tree roots leaked water, it was difficult for hydrologists to imagine how trees could hold onto stored water at night. But until 1993, when the ecologist Todd Dawson showed that certain trees watered nearby plants during a drought, most ecologists refused to consider the possibility.[37] Why? In part, because the idea violated competition theory. Trees would not release water through their upper roots into the surrounding upper soil; it was simply unimaginable, even though hydrologists might say that root membranes leaked water. Why would it not be possible? Because that would be sharing: why would plants give up something valuable to other plants without being paid back in turn?

Much of ecology and most of forestry assume that resources such as energy, water, and food are limited commodities. There is only so much time in the world, so much energy, so much food. Tradeoffs are therefore incessant: any time or energy spent on one activity is time taken from another activity. Any water you give out to the soil or to other plants is less water for you. Any nutrients another plant takes mean less for you. Competition—between species, between individuals, between every single activity—structures the world, according to this framework.[38] It is difficult for us to imagine a world organized otherwise, a world where tradeoffs are not incessant. Yet there are two assumptions at the heart of competition theory: that resources are limited, and that using a resource lessens the available supply. Both assumptions envision the world as a collection of separate, exchangeable parts. There are, however, other ways of seeing nature.

The forest might be a place where resources are not always limited—where a plant or animal could give something away without using it up, where giving might increase abundance, not decrease it. Maybe this sounds farfetched, but it is how most people imagine emotional relationships. Expressing love or anger to someone does not mean you have less love or anger left over for yourself. We tend to see objects as essentially different from emotions, but they are not necessarily so. The whole point of ecology is that the natural world is not merely a collection of separate objects but a web of relationships—relationships we might as accurately call emotional relationships, instead of commodity relationships. If a ponderosa pine releases water to surrounding shrubs, that does not mean there is less water for the pine. Those shrubs might in turn increase the local population of mycorrhizae, some of which might join with the pine and make it better able to absorb the nutrients in the soil. Do the shrubs compete with the tree? That question assumes a simple relationship of gain and loss; it is a human framework for seeing the forest, rather than the way the forest really is. Nor is the forest really an interconnected web of relationships—both competition and interconnection are human metaphors which help people work with the forest.

The forest that people have seen has always reflected what they wanted from the forest; the same is true for water. At first, the Forest Service in the Blues argued that, for the sake of water, forest cover needed to be preserved at all costs. But once timber sales had become the top priority after World War I, the Forest Service reversed its position and declared that cutting trees was best for the water supply. How could anyone argue this? Foresters had decided that the important aspect of water was the "water yield"—the amount of water that ran off the forests into the streams. By that definition, water yield would be greatest off a paved parking lot. Since forested soils absorbed much more water than clearcut soils, the Forest Service could honestly argue that clearcuts were good for water.[39] Any moisture that soaked into the soil was wasted, lost forever to farmers and irrigators. Water was no longer the link between members of the community; it was an output, one out of many isolated resources that ought to be put to good use.

When the government wanted to exclude the timber industry from the Blues, foresters found evidence that cutting trees hurt the watershed. When the government wanted to justify clearcutting, they found evidence of exactly the opposite. Both times, nothing was wrong with the data. What changed was the way foresters framed the questions—and the way they saw the forests. Ideas about indirect effects and forest influences on water had found fertile ground in the young Forest Service. Soon, however, this perspective vanished, as foresters focused on manipulating competition and succession to produce more commodities. Throughout the history of forestry in the Blues, a lack of information did not determine the ways people altered the land. Bad science was never to blame. Instead, the ways different people envisioned the land— as well as the kinds of relationships they wanted with the land— shaped how they used the information available to them.

Redesigning the Forest: Eliminating Waste and Insects

Guided by competition and succession theories, foresters set out to redesign the forest. They wanted to clean up the forest—to make it as efficient and productive as possible. Decadent trees, inferior trees, diseased and snag-topped and defective trees were not going to be part of the future. The Malheur report for 1911 ordered foresters to "mark for cutting all diseased, butt-burned, spike-topped, and other defective trees."[40] A perfect forest would contain only the very best trees. Evans advised in his 1912 report that "yellow pine, alone, should be favored and an effort should be made to get rid of the Douglas fir, larch, grand fir, and lodgepole. . . . Pure even-aged stands of larch should be clear cut and planted. Mixed stands should be cut upon the selection system, favoring the larch and leaving sufficient seed trees to restock the area." Every early sales contract and management plan stipulated that contractors had to remove all snags, dead-wood, insect-damaged, and fungi-damaged trees from the cutting site. At first, contractors tried to ignore these requirements. But the Forest Service persevered, and eventually persuaded loggers to clean up the forest. Unfortunately, the eventual result was not an efficient forest, but a forest so overrun with insect epidemics that it horrified the foresters.

Why did eliminating waste create havoc? What was wrong with the attempt to make the forest efficient? To understand this, we need to know the assumptions behind the desire to clean up the forest. Foresters believed that disease, dead wood, old growth, and fire all detracted from efficient timber production. In other words, they were assuming that the role of the forest was to grow trees as fast as it could, and any element that was not directly contributing to that goal was bad. What was the matter with a stand of old growth that was not growing quickly? Why were a few fir trees a problem? Why did insect activity take away from forest efficiency? Whatever was not producing timber competed with trees that could be producing timber, foresters believed. Any space that a dead tree took up, any light that a fir tree used, any nutrients that an insect chewed up—those were stolen from productive trees. At the heart of this were the assumptions of competition theory: that the forest was a collection of resources, and that those resources were limited. If timber trees did not use all the available water, that water was wasted. If young, vigorous pine did not get all the sun, that sun was lost forever. Clearly, foresters' faith in competition theory was inextricably linked to their fear of waste and their desire for efficiency. These assumptions made it difficult for foresters to imagine that insects, waste, disease, and decay might be essential for forest communities; indeed, that the productive part of the forest might *depend* on the unproductive part of the forest.

Some early foresters recognized that insects, fires, and fungus diseases had interconnected effects on other parts of the forest. George Bright, for example, noted in his 1911 report on the Umatilla that "especially thick clumps of reproduction are almost invariably found coming up beneath bug killed timber." Why would insect damage favor the next generation of trees? Bright suggested three possible factors: "It seems that the cause of this is the partial protection from the sun which the dead trees form. The shade of living trees is too heavy, but the light shade which the dead trees cast is especially favorable to seedling growth in a dry climate. Also the decaying roots provide a certain amount of fertilizer and moisture which the seedlings use." What appeared damaging to most foresters could have benefits, Bright recognized. But for most foresters, insects, as well as fires and disease, were external disturbances, not part of the essential nature of the forest, and therefore something that science should eliminate. As Evans wrote: "of the *external* influences . . . [on the forest], fire, insects, lightening, grazing and fungous diseases are the most important. It is difficult to determine which is the more destructive, fire or insects, for the relation that exists between them is very close" (emphasis added).[41]

To gauge the health of the forest, people tended to focus on the health of trees. If they saw something killing a tree, that must be bad, even if they knew a few dead trees were not necessarily a major problem. A focus on insects as agents of waste—killers of individual trees—made it difficult for foresters to recognize alternative evidence in front of them. For example, lodgepole was usually seen as a pest, because it took over after a fire and forced larch out. The foresters devised complicated policies for trying to eliminate lodgepole from burnt areas. Yet when they saw lodgepole dying from insect attacks, their first impulse was to control the beetle and borer epidemics, to rescue the lodgepole they did not want in the first place. As Erickson wrote in 1906, 35 percent of all lodgepole on the north side of Wallowa was infested or killed by mountain pine beetle. He worried that the "immense damage will result in a complete annihilation of lodgepole," so he called for help from the Bureau of Entomology to stop the epidemic.[42]

Not all foresters immediately assumed insect damage was bad. Evans suggested that they ought to let the beetles control the lodgepole. If foresters kept out fire and let the insects kill the lodgepole, he argued, what would come up in the bug-killed stands was larch, a valuable tree. Another strategy that Foster proposed in 1906 was to encourage mixed stands and uneven-aged stands to control the spread of insects and disease. Because large stands of ponderosa pine were subject to bark-borer attacks, Foster reasoned that a "mixture with other species might tend to check their ravages if the insects became numerous." Even foresters who recognized pest benefits, however, held contradictory beliefs. George Bright had noticed that squirrel caches produced the best ponderosa saplings, and that the overwinter mortality of saplings planted in caches by squirrels was much less than from wind-scattered seeds. He recommended eradicating squirrels nevertheless, because they ate some seeds. On one page of his report a forester might outline the positive effects of pests and the impossibility of eliminating them, but then three or four pages later recommend policies that would attempt to remove insects and disease entirely.

Foresters in the Blues thought their mission was to clean up the forest, and insects, disease, waste, and old growth were not part of their plan for a redesigned forest. But it was dangerous to simplify the system by eliminating elements that seemed irrelevant or wasteful; only after foresters got rid of them did they learn what critical function those elements had performed. What seemed unequivocally bad—such as defoliation or dead trees—turned out to be something quite different in the long run; human conceptions of good and bad meant little in the forests' terms.

What were foresters missing when they tried to make an efficient forest? H. D. Foster was an observant man, but he still assumed that if a bug killed a tree, foresters needed to get rid of first the bug and then the dead tree. If a dead tree was taking up space that a live tree could use, someone needed to cut down that dead tree and plant a young one in its place. Dead wood on the ground raised the danger of fire and put timber resources at risk. What was Foster missing when he kicked aside a log and told his assistant to come in and clean the dead trees off the forest floor? The dead tree had provided habitat for insects—which Foster certainly noticed; that was probably part of why he wanted his assistant to get rid of it. The insects living in that dead tree, however, were probably not defoliators; they were most likely the *predators* of the insects that harmed trees. Or the relationship might be more indirect. Carpenter ants, a major predator of defoliator larvae, depended on dead wood for both forage and nest sites. At the same time, because carpenter ants carried wood-decomposing pathogens into logs, they helped degrade dead wood and return it to the soil. Carpenter ants were also part of at least one complex regulatory cycle. They provided 98 percent of the diet of pileated woodpeckers.[43] Pileated woodpeckers did not eat spruce budworm or tussock moths, so no one thought they were important in regulating pest populations. But pileated woodpeckers did excavate cavities in dead trees, and those cavities provided the nest and roost sites for the birds that did eat spruce budworm and Douglas-fir tussock moth. By eliminating dead wood from the ground, the Forest Service set into motion a chain of events: they decreased the carpenter ants, thus decreasing the pileated woodpecker populations, which decreased populations of the secondary cavity nesters that had been eating the insect pests.

The insects and disease that Foster and his colleagues noted were certainly killing trees, a situation the men assumed was bad for the forest. But there were other ways of viewing insect damage. Insect epidemics happened in part because of nutrient stress; resistance to insects was largely a matter of toxin production, and stagnated trees with low growth rates rarely produced much in the way of defensive toxins.[44] The outbreaks themselves corrected that nutrient imbalance. On dry, south-facing sites, when trees crowded together too closely, growth rates slowed and trees began to die from water stress. In Foster's time, those dead trees would have provided excellent fuel for fires, and those fires would have thinned the stands, allowing surviving trees to grow faster. If Foster had managed to keep fire out of the crowded stands, insects would probably have attacked the stressed trees. Either way, the result would have been a thinned stand. On a landscape level, insect damage opened up the patches in the forest, allowing trees access to the space, light, and nutrients they needed for growth. Trees damaged by insects could provide habitat and food for predators, helping to control insect outbreaks. Bark beetles provided bird food, and woodpeckers used decayed sites for nest excavations. In other words, negative feedback mechanisms tended to regulate insect populations: overcrowded stands produced conditions that favored either fire or insects, which in turn would correct the overcrowding. Insect attacks in a forest would produce conditions that favored the predators that would regulate the insects.

These regulatory mechanisms did not lead to stability, but they did create an intricate network of relationships within the forests. For example, monocultures of single species provided excellent habitat for insect epidemics. Once a population of spruce budworm established itself in a large expanse of fir trees, those budworms found themselves in bug heaven. Wherever they turned, there was a host tree. But while monocultures favored insect epidemics, those epidemics in turn favored forest diversity, by creating mosaics of different-aged stands within the forest. Low levels of insect infestation could increase the health of neighboring trees by increasing light levels, changing plant structure, increasing photosynthetic efficiency, and triggering changes in plant chemistry that decreased herbivore efficiency.[45] More surprising, insect attacks could sometimes benefit the damaged tree. When spruce budworms and tussock moths defoliated conifers, they ate needles, which reduced needle area and therefore reduced carbohydrate synthesis. But after the outbreak, trees that insects had partly defoliated could grow faster than trees that had not been attacked by insects—perhaps because of increased nutrient cycling from insect droppings and litter fall.[46] Likewise, Douglas-fir trees partly defoliated by spruce budworm survived droughts better than undefoliated trees, perhaps because of reduced photosynthetic rates.[47] Back in 1911, George Bright had a hint that these complicated webs might be important, when he speculated that insect attacks might fertilize the soil for the next generation of trees. But even though foresters could imagine that insect damage might have benefits, they found it difficult to act on this knowledge.

Part of the difficulty foresters faced was their definition of a vigorous, healthy forest. A healthy forest was one where trees were not dying; where growth was greater than mortality.[48] By that definition, old-growth forests were in terrible shape. Because foresters measured health by measuring outputs, everything else in the forest gradually faded in importance. For example, foresters tended to think that soil was little more than the stuff that held up trees. They knew that organic matter was critical; remember how disturbed Foster was when he saw fires burning up the Wenaha's forest floor. But foresters had no idea that the soil was full of living creatures, much less that those creatures were what enabled trees to grow. Although the forests in the Blues might have survived the loss of all their trees, those forests could not have survived without their soil invertebrates. Arthropods—insects and their allies—acted as system catalysts; without them, the soils could not have supported trees. Soils might have been loaded with nitrogen, potassium, and phosphorus, but those nutrients were usually bound up in a form that roots could not use. When invertebrates defecated, for a few seconds there were soluble nutrients available to plant roots, and if they were released close enough to the roots, the roots could take them in. Soil invertebrates crushed up nutrients, mixed organic and inorganic soil components, and drove the complex processes of microbial succession. Not dirt, but the bodies, skeletons, and droppings of invertebrates, fungi, and bacteria made up the forest floor.[49]

Soil arthropods were much more abundant in old-growth forests than in young forests, so those old-growth forests may have provided nutrient sources for young, rapidly growing forests. The very first stages of forest succession—clearcuts—had the lowest levels of soil arthropods; yet the plants that were trying to get established there had the greatest need of what those invertebrates provided. When Foster was working on the Wenaha, natural events such as windstorms and fires were the major disturbances. Disturbed patches were usually fairly small, and there were many refuges available for soil insects to wait out the disturbances. Because most soil arthropods lacked wings, they could not disperse very far; so as foresters cut down the old growth and removed dead wood from the forest floor, insects found it more and more difficult to recolonize forests after fires or logging.[50] Dry sites such as those in the Blues on south-facing slopes could lose their ability to support forests when the soil was damaged past certain thresholds— when dead wood was lost and insects abandoned the forests.

H. D. Foster and George Bright, along with their fellow foresters, had no way of predicting the consequences of their efforts to clean up the forest. What they saw was dead trees. How could they imagine those dead trees might be important; how could they think that death was not always a loss? A tree that died in the forest and rotted on the ground was a tree stolen from the mills. A tree that grew slowly usurped the space that rightfully belonged to a vigorous tree that could earn its keep in the efficient, businesslike forest that the Forest Service desired. Yet the Blues forests were anything but efficient; their very inefficiency—their redundancy, their seemingly irrational complexity—may have been what allowed these forests to persist on dry, marginal sites. When Foster walked the forests, he noted that spruce budworm and Douglas-fir tussock moths were feeding on the needles of firs. But what he could not see was that at least 120 different parasitic wasp and fly species, 150 spiders, and 32 birds were in turn feeding on the spruce budworm and Douglas-fir tussock moths.[51] In trying to eliminate forest enemies, Foster and his fellow workers destroyed the habitat for the enemies' predators, making future outbreaks ever worse. Redundancy allowed the forest to buffer disturbances; complexity allowed the forest to ride the waves of fires and epidemics and droughts.

What foresters saw when they looked at old growth was not diverse habitat for predators and prey, but a chaotic mess. At times, foresters' impatience with what George Bright called "the general riot of the natural forest" became so great that they longed for the day when they finally had the money and the clout to raze the hills and plant exactly what they liked. As Bright wrote in 1913, on north slopes, white and grand firs predominated over larch and Douglas-fir because of their greater shade tolerance. But "as no big use has been found [for the firs] . . . a method of management should in future be used which will prevent their appearance in succeeding north slope stands. This can only be accomplished by clear cutting all species and leaving only seed trees of Douglas fir and larch.[52] Unfortunately, these north-slope types were "so decadent that it will probably be many years before there will be any inducement to log them." In the natural forest, there was "not more than a fifth or tenth of the possible stand. The average stand of timber in the north slope type on the Umatilla National Forest is below 5,000 [board] feet. Under management these same trees would easily be expected to produce 50,000 feet in a rotation of 180 years." This was just a dream: under the intensive management in place 80 years after George Bright wrote, most areas of the Umatilla produced only about 5,000 board feet an acre, if even that—one-tenth of what Bright predicted.

Intensive management often decreased timber production instead of increasing it, but this was difficult for early foresters to imagine. The natural forests were obviously imperfect and wasteful; how could people do any worse? As Bright complained, "the North slopes are at present understocked and nearly hopeless from a logging point of view but could be made to grow, under management, an amount of timber greater than the south slopes and typical yellow pine types." Bright envisioned a day when the Forest Service could operate its own mills, and therefore set its own timber policy, for "these slopes might then be logged off and be prepared for raising crops of timber of good quality and volume." Foresters tried to create a different forest, a better forest. Their efforts were severely constrained by the tools they had, by the markets they lacked, by the railroads they wanted. But all the same, they still managed to set in motion a chain of events that quickly accelerated out of control. As Kan Smith's windfall studies indicated, before they knew it, they had instituted radical changes in the forests, and the tools they had available for comprehending those changes were not adequate. Even when they recognized that unexpected things were happening, they had no idea how to approach the baffling world of indirect effects. Their first—and understandable—response to the complexity of the forest was to transform it into something simple, regulated, and manageable.

What emerges from the silvics reports is a sense of urgency and optimism combined. The foresters were trying to work in a complex and unfamiliar world, hoping to make it more efficient and productive. Even though they knew they had insufficient information, they were part of an agency with a mission, and they felt compelled to produce results. They were the heroes in an almost epic struggle against big business, outsiders, insects, disease— against the forest itself. Foresters had begun their work in the forests because of a national concern about the intricate indirect ecological effects of logging on water—the complex webs of cause and effect that connected man and nature. But in their attempts to create an ideal forest, managers increasingly ignored those indirect ecological processes. Much of what went wrong in the Blue Mountain forests, and in land management across the nation, came from the problems of trying to simplify and control the bewildering complexity of the natural world.

Liquidating the Pines

While the young Forest Service was trying to introduce scientific forestry and transform riotous old growth into a regulated crop, the timber industry was going through its own turmoil. Ultimately, the dreams of the Forest Service depended on markets for timber; they could hardly liquidate old growth if nobody wanted to buy it. Before we can understand the logging that went on in the Blues under the new Forest Service, we need to consider the position of the timber industry. During the years that the government was trying to gain control of the forests, federal inspectors such as H. D. Langille had accused the timber industry of savaging the western forests in its greed for ever-larger profits. But from the perspective of lumber companies, they were barely breaking even. Between 1890 and 1910, the industry had loaded itself with a fifty-year supply of raw material, much of it on borrowed money. Weyerhaeuser's purchases of timberlands from the Northern Pacific Railroad increased the prices lumbermen had to pay for both land and standing timber, but overproduction drove down the price of manufactured lumber. The industry could not afford to harvest and sell the timber because of low sales receipts; nor could they afford to hold onto the uncut trees since they had to pay taxes and interest on their investments. In 1906 timber taxes rose, largely because northwesterners were angry about the perceived profits of timber speculators. Many people wanted to force immediate harvests rather than institute scientific forestry, because they felt that by holding onto growing trees instead of cutting them, timber speculators were forcing up prices. As taxes on standing timber increased, the industry was forced to cut more heavily to make the same profits, which in turn drove lumber prices even lower.[1]

At this point, government foresters—eastern elites trained in eastern forestry schools—told lumbermen that they ought to institute scientific forestry and forgo some of their short-term profits for the good of the nation. Lumbermen thought this was absurd. An industry spokesman said in 1905 that "forestry advocates were of two classes, either sentimenalists or technicists; the latter being trained in the forest methods of the old European countries where conditions were entirely different from those that obtained in the United States. [They] proposed the impossible."[2] Gifford Pinchot was impatient with this characterization, and he set out to prove to the industry that good forestry could make a profit. Pinchot's three principles of forestry were clearly economic rather than ecological: "First. The forest is treated as a working capital whose purpose is to produce successive crops. Second. With that purpose in view, a working plan is prepared and followed in harvesting the forest crops. Third. The work in the woods is carried on in such a way as to leave the standing trees and the young growth as nearly unharmed by the lumbering as possible."[3] When the Forest Service gained control over the reserves in 1905, it was in an odd position. Pinchot and fellow forest conservationists had based their calls for reserves on the threat of imminent depletion by the industry. But now that the Forest Service had control of the reserves, it wanted to show that scientific forestry was profitable. That meant increasing sales to the big out-of-state lumber companies they had demonized several years earlier.

The lumber companies, however, refused to cooperate, at least until the First World War. From 1905 to 1916, the Forest Service's emphasis on redesigning the forest had little effect on timber sales. As Henry Graves, second Chief of the Forest Service, noted in his annual reports, sales were slow for two reasons: the inaccessibility of National Forest timber, and the fact that timber from private holdings had glutted the market.[4] Graves neglected to mention a third problem, one he might have been able to alleviate if he had not been so stubborn: the Forest Service valued its timber too highly, setting stumpage prices so high that few lumber companies were willing to invest in the timber.[5] Nobody wanted government timber, and even if someone had, it was too inaccessible to reach cheaply. As R. M. Evans glumly noted in 1912, "Owing to the inaccessibility of the Government timber and to the large amount of privately owned timber surrounding it, there is no immediate prospect of a large sale."[6] And on the Wenaha Reserve, H. D. Foster admitted that the forest was filled with less desirable timber, "which should be cut," but he could see "no hope for its early exploitation" because of the cost of transport out of the "inaccessible interior."[7]

After the war, the situation changed. The war converted the industry from what the historian David Clary termed a "migratory consumer of virgin forests" to a "network of stable regional enterprises engaged in long-term production."[8] The war also lessened tensions between the industry and government foresters. Demands for national forest timber did not increase much during the war, but demands for private timber did. Thus when the war ended, industry was more willing to consider investing in national forest contracts.

With the opening of markets for national forest timber, the Forest Service began to push sales of ponderosa pine in the Blues. This provided the momentum needed for a serious campaign to regulate the forests. The resultant emphasis on liquidating old-growth ponderosa motivated timber policies that established conditions leading to the problems being experienced today. Throughout the heavy cutting years of the 1920s, foresters dismissed their own calculations showing that a second cut would be much reduced, given current logging rates. By the late 1920s, as the industry went through a major slump and the Forest Service was under pressure to decrease production, sales planners and managers in the Blues began to realize that they were in trouble—economically and silviculturally. The heavy sales of the 1920s, and the resultant problems in the 1930s, foreshadowed the situation currently faced in the Blues. These problems developed as much from silvicultural decisions to push heavy cuts in the 1920s as they did from decisions to suppress fires.

Overcutting in Enterprise: A Case Study

The town of Enterprise was high in the Wallowa Valley, an extraordinarily beautiful place that was the home of Chief Joseph's nontreaty band of the Nez Percé. Whites came to the valley in the 1870s, after they had begun to exhaust the best grass in the Grande Ronde Valley. The area was high and cold, set in the heart of the Wallowa Mountains, a place so lovely that most people who came wanted to stay. After increasing tensions between settlers and Indians led the U.S. government to renege on an agreement that had given the Nez Percé title to the valley, federal troops and militia drove out the Nez Percé in 1877. Whites then settled rapidly, concentrating on livestock grazing and some minor farming. But for all the place's lavish beauty, it was never easy to make a living; frosts could destroy crops all summer long.

Enterprise lay at the north edge of the Wallowa forests, and on three sides it was surrounded by high rolling bunchgrass hills. To the south, however, rose the steep wall of the mountains, thick with lush fir-larch forests. These were not commercial timberlands during the glory years of ponderosa pine. But ten miles or so to the north of Enterprise were the Chesnimnus plateaus that in 1900 were covered with open stands of fine ponderosa. And these forests soon caught the attention of lumbermen and the Forest Service both.

Just after the turn of the century, a Kansas City corporation called the East Oregon Lumber Company (named to sound local, like other companies operating in the Blues, even though midwestern money financed them all) started buying land north of Enterprise. By 1914 they had accumulated about 42,000 acres in the headwaters of Trout Creek, Swamp Creek, and Courtney Creek. In the fall of 1914 they started laying railroad track from Enterprise north to their holdings, and by April 1915 they had completed a small mill at the edge of the holdings. At this mill, they sawed out timbers for a huge mill at Enterprise that had an annual capacity of 35 million board feet. In view of the small size of their private holdings, this mill was astonishingly large.

On November 15, 1915, the first trainload of logs showed up at the Enterprise mill. Over the next twelve years, the town boomed as the mill prospered. The Forest Service pushed sales to them heavily. Over twelve years, the East Oregon Lumber Company bought 131.5 million board feet of public timber, all near Sled

Springs at the edge of their private holdings. This was the largest Forest Service sale on the Wallowa forests—the first large sale in the Blues. A new regional policy stipulated that the district foresters' office in Portland would administer the sale, rather than the local district ranger—the man who knew the area best. The idea was to centralize the administration of large sales, making the sales more efficient and also preventing any possibility of collusion on bids. But this meant that the local men in the Forest Service had less say than they might have liked over the depletion of their timber. Any forester who submitted a working circle plan that called for sales lower than the district forester expected had to revise his plan, or offer some very good reasons why he could not support the sales the regional office wanted.

By 1925, the East Oregon Lumber Company had cut the best timber off its own lands, leaving no reserve stand of ponderosa. Financial troubles started up that year. The company was hoping to meet all its future timber needs from Forest Service sales, but there were no accessible stands left. The best ponderosa was gone much more quickly than anyone expected. By 1928 the company was forced into receivership, and soon the business failed and the mill closed. Gerald Tucker, a local Forest Service employee, wrote that "the results were tragic for the town and some people expressed the thought that the town would have been better if the mill had never located in Enterprise."[9]

What is so depressing is that there was nothing at all unusual about this story. A small town pinned its hopes on a single natural resource, and soon that resource was exhausted. The capital for development came from somewhere else, and that company pulled out after the lumber was cut and the investments met. The locals were left holding an empty bag. This was the story of the West over and over again: residents eagerly gave up control over the rate of resource depletion, and were soon left with very little. Money and trees both followed the railroads out of the region.

The irony was that although proponents for the federal reserve system had argued that the Forest Service would protect locals against large out-of-state corporations, the opposite usually happened. As Langille had written in his 1906 plea for forest protection in the Blues, a reserve would be "invaluable not only to the industrial interests of the immediate, contiguous sections but to the entire surrounding country."[10] Langille had stressed that "under the usual [pre-Forest Service] methods of cutting this timber supply will not long continue, but under proper restrictions and protection from fire I believe the supply can be made permanent." Protection of local concerns—in timber, grazing, and mining—was one of Langille's central concerns. In one inspection report, he wrote that miners would welcome the reserve once they understood that a reserve would be "a means of protection to themselves from the large operators and saw mill companies which would secure the best of the timber and ship it out of the state." Locals, he went on, were "at the mercy of the large operators who have large capital and paying properties." All the inspection reports played upon the same refrain: outsiders had plundered the land, and only the Forest Service could protect local industry from the depredations of out-of-state capital.

The reality of trying to manage public lands, however, meant that the Forest Service was soon doing its best to form coalitions with the large corporations they had earlier charged with untrammeled greed. The emerging federal bureaucracies, particularly foresters and grazing managers, found it far easier to work with large corporations than with smaller operators. The larger lumber concerns owned substantial private lands and were better able to institute what the government called "scientific forestry" practices. Likewise, larger cattle ranchers could afford grazing improvements better than smaller ranchers. Small mills, small logging operations, small farms, small ranchers, were less efficient, and efficiency was something the new Forest Service was unwilling to give up.

Throughout the Blues the Forest Service pushed huge sales and often stunning rates of railway cutting in the late teens and early 1920s. By the twenties they discouraged small local mills and did their best to draw in big capital from out of state. The Forest Service mission was to regulate the forests, and big companies could do this better than small companies. They could log faster and could afford to log more carefully, leaving a decent reserve. As the Malheur River Working Circle plan stated in the late 1920s, the intent was to "vigorously discourage sales to small operators." Their "inability or unwillingness to adhere to contract stipulations," coupled with their financial instability, made the Forest Service reluctant to work with them. Most important, the Umatilla Hilgard Project Report (1926) stated, small sales interfered "with efficient logging by the larger and more important operators."[11]

The Forest Service soon held to a perverse-sounding formula: we must cut the forests in order to save them. The faster we cut the forests, the faster they will become regulated, and only then will we have a continuous crop of timber that can support local businesses forever. But this formula never worked. Mills closed, towns collapsed. In the 1930s the Forest Service blamed such failures on the Depression—which was certainly in part responsible. In the 1990s environmentalists have been getting the blame. But then, as now, the data did not support the story. In their haste during the 1920s to regulate the Blues forests, planners authorized extremely rapid harvests, well knowing that those harvests would ensure the collapse of the local timber industry by the 1990s.

Deciding on the Cut

Before the young Forest Service could regulate the forests, it needed plans, and to make plans that had some basis in reality, it needed far more information than it had. As Fred Ames told his fellow foresters at a supervisors' meeting in 1910, "just as fast as sufficient information is collected, we shall put our Forests under working plans and our cutting in order."[12] Sales were always part of an overall plan to rework the forest. Instead of just going in and cutting trees, the Forest Service tried to organize each sale so that it fit within a complicated ideal. Each tree cut in a particular place was supposed to play its part in recreating the new forest; each sale would bring the Forest Service one step closer to its dream of regulating nature. But how to translate these ideals into logs? To make sure that every sale fit into the grand plan for the landscape, the Forest Service broke each forest into several units called *working circles*, which were areas of land whose boundaries were defined by markets for the timber. A working circle usually included all the timber that would feed into a single large mill. Working circle boundaries most often coincided with major watersheds, because the easiest access to the timber for rail lines was along the creeks; few timber rail lines crossed over ridges into neighboring watersheds. Each working circle had a management plan that outlined the orderly harvest of the timber within that circle, and these working circle plans were combined for each forest to produce a forest plan. The silvics goals behind the plans were simple and clear: to grow sawtimber, to harvest mature and overmature timber, and "to insure regeneration and bring the forest into maximum production," according to one early working circle plan for the Middle Fork of the John Day.[13] Production of a crop was the emphasis here; concern about the watersheds—and any other aspect of the forest—vanished when the Forest Service set out to calculate annual cuts. When foresters tried to plan for the landscape as a whole, they focused on one small fraction: the timber outputs.

Rotations and Cutting Cycles

Before the Forest Service could determine how much to harvest and how fast to harvest it, planners needed to decide how long they should allow the trees to grow. Would it be best to cut trees only when they were ready to die—say, at 300 or 400 years for a ponderosa pine? Or would it be better to cut trees when they were still growing at their maximum rates—when they were only 40 or 50 years old? Whatever a forester decided, tradeoffs were involved. The longer he let a tree grow, the bigger it got and the more money that tree would fetch. But trees did not grow at the same speeds all their lives. A young tree started out slowly in its infancy, then sped up in its youth, then eventually slowed in its maturity. If a forester let all the trees remain after their growth rates had slowed, the trees would continue to put on volume—but not as much volume per acre as young trees. As trees matured and their growth rates slowed, however, their wood grain became denser, fetching higher prices on some markets. For maximum profits, foresters calculated that they should harvest trees as soon as their growth rates slowed. This decision, of course, assumed that the only value of a forest was in its ability to produce financial profit.

In the early decades of the Forest Service, mills in the Blues preferred to work with trees 19 inches in diameter. Because ponderosa took on average 180 years to reach 19 inches in diameter, the Forest Service managed it on 180-year rotations, even though the land would not be producing the maximum timber volume per acre. Rotations of 180 years meant that each tree would grow for 180 years before being cut, but it did not mean that the entire stand would grow for 180 years. A single 180-year rotation included three cutting cycles 60 years long; during each cutting cycle, loggers cut up to 80 or 90 percent of the stand. Thus during one rotation, loggers would have harvested 80 percent of the forest three times (Figure 1). Each time, they would leave about 20 percent of the mature trees over 12 inches in diameter for a reserve stand, and all of the reproduction (the youngest trees). Reserve trees were "thrifty trees"—pines between 12 and 19 inches in diameter. The hope was that removing neighboring trees would release the reserve trees from suppression—slow growth caused by competition for light and water. When released, reserve trees would grow rapidly and form the basis of the next two cutting cycles, while the reproduction would be cut once it reached 180 years of age. After three cycles, the result would be a regulated stand of trees—an equal fraction of trees in each age class, all growing as fast as they could. Then, for the rest of time, the Forest Service would have an unvarying percentage of 180-year-old trees ready to harvest. This, of course, was the ideal, not the reality. No one had ever tried to regulate an American old-growth forest before, so no one knew if it would work. But that did not make the Forest Service hesitate long before making plans that ensured that millions of acres of old growth would rapidly fall to the ax (and eventually the chain saw).

Cruises and Estimates of Volume

Before foresters could make plans to liquidate old growth, they needed to know how much merchantable timber was present. Estimates of timber volumes were not value-free numbers; they con-

Cycle 1

*Cut 80 percent of mature stand
Leave 20 percent for reserve*

*At the end of 60 years, this reserve stand
will double in volume*

*Let reproduction grow each year;
do not cut it until end of 180-year rotation*

Cycle 2

*Cut only 80 percent of the
reserve left from Cycle 1*

*Leave 20 percent of this as the
reserve for the next cutting cycle;
this reserve will double in volume*

Allow all reproduction to keep growing

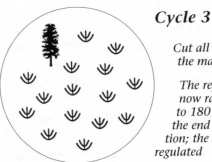

Mature trees
for harvest

Mature trees left
for reserve stand

Reproduction left
until end of 180-
year rotation

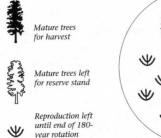

Cycle 3

*Cut all the rest of
the mature stand*

*The reproduction
now ranges from 1
to 180 years old by
the end of the rota-
tion; the stand is
regulated*

Figure 1. Diagram of three idealized 60-year cutting cycles in ponderosa pine. Each tree represents 10 million board feet of timber. Note that the harvests in the second cutting cycle are less than half the harvests in the first cycle. This diagram assumes—as the early foresters assumed—that the volume of the reserve stand will double in 60 years, which requires an annual growth of about 1.5 percent. Few of the reserve trees grew at this rate, however.

tained a host of implicit assumptions about nature that affected how the Forest Service treated the forest. For example, the Burns Working Circle Plan from 1923 stated that the 600,000 acres of commercial forest on the circle contained 6,696,000,000 board feet of merchantable timber. When a forester such as M. L. Erickson wrote down such a number, people tended to assume it was a precise and accurate representation of the forest. But timber stand estimates were just that—estimates. Erickson certainly did not go out into the woods and measure the volume of every single tree; that would have taken a lifetime. Instead, he based his estimate on what foresters called a *cruise*. Different people did different kinds of cruises, but all were samples of a small fraction of the forest, which foresters then extrapolated to the entire forest. For example, when Erickson cruised a stand of timber, he walked a thin line across the forest, counting some small percentage of trees—say, every twentieth tree. For each tree that he sampled, he recorded its species, then he peered into the canopy and estimated the tree's height, and finally he took out a pair of calipers and measured the tree's width four feet above the ground—its diameter at breast height, or dbh. Once he had the diameter and height, Erickson could flip through a set of tables organized by species to get an estimate of the volume of wood that a mill could profitably cut from that tree. When he was done with the cruise, he had estimates of timber volume for 5 percent of the forest, and he multiplied that by 20 to come up with an estimate for the entire forest.

On paper, the estimates might sound accurate enough, but on the ground they led to problems. A small fraction of the forest could accurately represent the entire forest only if the forest was uniform, or if Erickson was extremely careful to sample equally in each different forest patch. Cruises worked best on single-species forests; in the Blues, however, where the forests varied from acre to acre, cruises could only be guesses.[14] Being human, Erickson probably spent more time on easier terrain, where the trees were bigger and more regular. If so, he overestimated the proportion of high volume forests and underestimated the proportion of sparser forests. Thus his total estimate was probably too high. When a planner wrote down a number like 6,696,000,000 board feet of pine, a lot of variability and doubt lay hidden in those digits.

There was nothing unusual or nefarious about the Forest Service's survey techniques; everyone who has ever worked with natural resources has had to use partial samples to estimate the whole. Nevertheless, the uncertainty in timber cruises affected what people did to the forest. If a planner calculated harvest levels based on an inflated cruise, he started a cycle of depletion that outsped the rate at which a forest could recoup its losses. For example, when a planner decided to cut 1 percent of the estimated volume each year, he was assuming that after 100 years, when all the mature timber was cut, the reproduction would be ready to harvest. But if the cruiser had mistakenly doubled the volume, after only 50 years all the mature timber would be gone but the young trees would be nowhere near big enough for the mills. At first, the Forest Service tried to correct for this potential problem by sending different people out on each cruise to check each other's estimates. Different estimates could vary by 100 percent; this was not a precise or objective business. If someone wanted to sell lots of timber, it was in his interest to overestimate the amount of timber available; likewise, if someone wanted to slow sales, he might tend to underestimate the amount of timber left on the ground. Just because numbers looked precise, they did not necessarily reflect what was out in the woods.

Calculating the Allowable Cut

Only after planners had estimates of the timber volume on the forest could they calculate the allowable cut—the amount of timber that the Forest Service could put up for harvest each year. According to theory derived from European models, allowable cuts would eventually be the same as the *sustained-yield output*—the net annual growth of the forest, or the interest, so to speak, which could be removed in perpetuity without affecting the capital of the forest. But this assumed a regulated forest, one that was still young enough to add more volume in a year than it lost to death and decay. Because western forests mostly consisted of old growth, their net annual growth was basically zero. By European standards, there would be nothing to harvest, nothing to sell. How then could the Forest Service get the forests regulated? Most foresters agreed that that old growth needed to go, but how fast should it go? How could foresters remove it rapidly and still be sure there would be something left to cut after the first cutting cycle, before the forests were perfectly regulated? To address these problems, planners had to distinguish between two different kinds of allowable cuts. The first was the theoretical sustained-yield output of the forest—what the regulated forest could produce forever. But then planners also had to calculate the annual harvests during the liquidation phase, a matter that proved far more troubling.

At first the Forest Service confused the two kinds of allowable cuts. Harvest levels should be equal to the annual growth, *The Use Book* of 1907 proclaimed.[15] But what was the annual growth? Most foresters knew it was close to zero, so instead they decided to set harvest levels on *potential* annual growth—basically the sustained-yield outputs of the ideal future forest. But of course planners had no idea what this might be: there were no regulated western forests to measure. To estimate potential annual growth, managers needed to know the total volume of timber in the forest, the age at which different species reached their maximum growth, and the typical rate at which seedlings replaced mature trees. They knew none of this. They did not even have maps, yet they had to somehow figure out how much timber might grow on millions of acres of national forest land, much of it unsurveyed. As George Bright wrote in disgust when he set out to quantify the timber available on the Wenaha, "the Atlas Folio sheets . . . were found to be very inaccurate and out of date, and it was accordingly deemed best to draw an entirely new map. . . . Roughly, a third of the Forest has never been surveyed by the Land Office, and the data on topography and stream flow was here apt to be particularly unreliable and meager."[16] Tables of predicted yields derived from European forests or from tree farms gave vastly different estimates of how fast foresters could expect young trees to grow. Nobody knew what the productive capacity of the forests might be, even assuming European standards of a regulated forest; nevertheless, managers were determined to come up with site classifications and then shape the forest to meet their goals.

Edward J. Hanzlik, a Forest Service biologist who worked for years in the Blues, reasoned that for each site, one could figure out exactly how much "biological potential" it had: exactly what the growth and yield of its forest would be.[17] Using the site classification, a forester generalized across all that varied from place to place and came up with a predictive estimate of timber yield. Soil, slope, aspect, and moisture were collapsed into one measure of place— the site's potential for growing a timber crop. Everything that made a specific place unique was by necessity ignored. At first foresters scoffed. How could someone say what an acre of land could produce if they had never walked between those trees and wrapped their arms around the bark to measure a tree's width? Foresters found it difficult to believe that they could forgo detailed cruises and instead rely on an estimate based on generalized ideals rather than on experience of the specific place. But in 1912, Hanzlik tested his theory on Douglas-fir in western Washington and Oregon, and showed that his site classifications gave estimates of timber per acre nearly as good as the estimates experienced timber cruisers came up with after exhaustive—and expensive—surveys on the ground. Even though Hanzlik's classifications were less accurate on the drier forests east of the Cascades, foresters used them for decades to derive extremely simple measures of the sustained-yield cut.[18] In the Blues pine forests, for example, foresters assumed that each regulated acre should produce a net annual growth of 100 board feet. To get the sustained-yield harvest, they simply multiplied the growth rate by the total number of acres on the forest. For a working circle with a million acres, each acre would produce 100 board feet a year for harvest, so the total sustained-yield harvest would be 100 million board feet per year.

Even though the old-growth forests were obviously not growing at 100 board feet per acre each year, the Forest Service decided to harvest that amount. But there was an essential confusion, for the distinction between ideal and actual growth rates got lost in the planning process. First, managers guessed what the idealized growth of a regulated forest should be, and then they planned their cuts, assuming that the forest would grow at their ideal rate after loggers had finished cutting. In 1907, for example, California foresters estimated that the total stand on 450,000 acres of one national forest was 8 billion board feet of timber, mostly ponderosa pine. They had offered for harvest 40 million board feet that year; to calculate their future allowable cuts, they merely projected that harvest into the future. With a 200-year rotation, if they cut 0.5 percent of the stand each year, it would take them 200 years to cut all the trees. Foresters then estimated that the reserved trees would increase their growth rates after their neighbors had been harvested, so that the amount of timber grown each year would exactly equal the amount of wood cut. This assumed an annual growth rate of 0.5 percent (meaning that the total volume of all the wood on the forest would increase by 0.5 percent each year), allowing annual harvests of 40 million board feet forever.[19] But all this was based on a guess. Foresters really had no idea how fast trees would grow after a partial harvest; they did not even know how fast trees grew *before* a harvest.

The Regional Office looked at the California figures and decided that the allowable cut was not nearly as large as they wanted it to be. The easiest way to justify a larger harvest was to state that the annual net growth on each acre was really *four* times the rate the California office had come up with. This then allowed an annual allowable cut of 135 million board feet. Since the growth rate was only an estimate—well, then, the Regional Office would come up with its own estimate. The local supervisors protested the Regional Forester's change, so they called on the Washington office to mediate. The Washington office set the allowable cut at 80 million board feet, but it based this more on a desire to compromise than on any data that suggested pines could grow at 1 percent a year after harvest. Since most foresters in the West favored an immediate heavy cut to put the stands into maximum production, allowable cuts were set quite high, at 1 percent of estimated live timber every year—the figure the Washington office had suggested. This high figure may have been offered as a compromise, but it assumed that the actual net growth on the forests was high and steady, even though most foresters knew that this was only the *potential* growth.

Planners were confused: they felt they needed to cut old growth quickly, but they also needed to leave enough timber growing to justify another cut in 60 years. They could not harvest *all* the old trees at once, because there would be nothing left to cut while everyone was waiting around for the forest to become regulated. At first foresters recommended leaving about 30 to 40 percent of the timber then salable. How much would then be left for the next cutting cycle? For a working circle with, say, 100 million board feet, if the planners cut 60 percent in the first 60-year cutting cycle and left 40 percent to double in volume, that would mean 80 million board feet would be present at the beginning of the second cutting cycle—enough to justify another harvest, although a slightly smaller one. Foresters breathed a little more easily when they saw these numbers. It looked as if they could regulate old growth quickly—cutting 60 percent of it in the first 60 years—and still have almost as much timber for the mills at the end of that first cycle. But a few foresters decided to test the key assumption here: would the cutover forest really double its volume after 60 years?

Foresters had obtained this estimate from the site potential calculations, in what was basically a process of circular reasoning. Because, ideally, a regulated forest could grow at 100 board feet per acre per year, planners assumed—or just hoped—that cutover timber would grow at the same rate. The number may have looked reasonable, but it contained several critical assumptions. On one level it simply reflected the fact that young trees grow faster than old trees. But it also implied that after cutting, the reserved trees in cutover stands would suddenly increase their growth. Old-growth ponderosa in the Blues had taken, on average, 180 years to reach a 19 inch diameter, but maybe the yellow pine would reach 19″ dbh faster "after a selection cutting due to stimulated growth," the Burns Working Circle Plan suggested hopefully.[20] An interesting assumption, but unfortunately when tested, it often did not hold. By 1915, field studies in the Blues were already showing that pines did not recover from suppression after other trees in the stand were cut. Hanzlik did a series of growth and yield studies which suggested that trees in thinned or cutover stands often did not increase in growth.[21] Kan Smith's study of windfall in cutover lands showed that young trees under 12 inches in diameter sometimes increased their growth after the stand was thinned, but other trees did not.[22] Other planners in the 1920s stated the problem succinctly: allowable cuts were basically unfounded guesses. As one unnamed Malheur National Forest planner admitted, "they were based on very meager information on growth of Yellow Pine. Nothing is known about the growth of inferior species either in virgin forests or on cutover land."[23] But all this uncertainty got buried within a single hopeful number that could justify planners' heavy cuts.

Even though by 1915 foresters had begun to realize that the reserve stand might not double its volume after 60 years, when the Forest Service revised its policy of selective cutting on pine stands in 1916 it assumed that cutover stands would grow much faster than 100 board feet per acre per year. The Forest Service quietly changed to heavy selective cutting—largely to make the sales contracts more attractive to buyers—and contracts allowed for the harvest of 80 to 90 percent of the pine in a given working circle, instead of the former 60 percent. The "Timber Sale Policy of the Forest Service" (1920) stated: "It will be necessary in some instances to cut more than the annual growth for a time because of the presence of large quantities of over-mature stumpage which is in danger of deterioration and retards the production of which the land is capable."[24] In 1922, Hanzlik argued that before the forest was regulated, the annual cut should, in addition to the sustained-yield output, also include enough old growth that by the end of the rotation all the old growth would be cut. Hanzlik offered a formula for calculating the first cutting cycle's annual harvests: the Forest Service should sell an amount of timber equal to the projected growth of young trees (the sustained-yield harvest), *plus* all the mature timber divided by the number of years in the rotation.[25] After the first rotation, when all the old growth and mature timber was gone, the Forest Service could return to selling an amount equal to the annual growth.

On the Blues, however, most planners decided to liquidate all the old growth and mature timber during the first 60-year cutting cycle, rather than allowing it to sit around for 180 years. The Hanzlik formula might not have been so disastrous if Blues planners had allowed the old growth to be removed in 180 years rather than 60 years. Ignoring for a moment the biological implications of removing all old growth, there were severe economic implications as well that planners failed to acknowledge. According to the Hanzlik formula, if one took 180 years to remove all old growth, then when it was all gone, at least the new forest would be regulated and ready to cut. Instead, Blues planners calculated harvests that would remove all the mature timber in 60 years, but at that point, their new forest was nowhere near rotation age: it was only 60 years old, not 180. Planners hoped that the reserve stand—the 10 to 20 percent of trees they left uncut—would form the basis of the next two cutting cycles, but this proved an illusion. What would a 90 percent harvest leave for the second cutting cycle—the cutting cycle that would have started in the 1980s? Using the 100 million board feet forest from the earlier example, a 90 percent timber removal would leave only 10 million board feet for a reserve stand. Even if this doubled in volume after 60 years (which planners knew was unlikely), only 20 million board feet would be left for the next cutting cycle. During the second cutting cycle, therefore, mills would have only *one-fifth* the timber they had come to rely on— not a recipe for community stability.

Patterns of Cutting: Clearcuts or Selection Cuts?

After foresters decided how much pine should be harvested, they drew up a plan that translated that ideal harvest into specifics. Should foresters remove the trees all at once in huge blocks, and then go in and plant their favorite trees? Or should they cut just a few at a time? Since ponderosa was shade tolerant in the first year and intolerant after, and since it generally grew in uneven-aged stands, most silviculturists recommended what they called "light selection cutting" rather than clearcutting. Actual patterns of cutting, however, varied in the Blues.

At first, the reserve stand was supposed to be evenly spaced out over the entire cutting area, but by 1913 the policy changed to group systems of cutting: reserve trees were left in large, nearly intact groups, with clearcutting of mature timber between them. Clearcutting at that point meant not cutting every living tree down, but harvesting all the sawtimber over a minimum diameter (usually 12 to 19 inches) and leaving everything smaller. The point was to release young trees from suppression by older trees, and to disturb regeneration as little as possible. In 1918, policy in the Blues changed back to an evenly spaced distribution of reserved trees, leaving 15 to 25 percent of the stand over 12 inches in diameter. On the ground, however, these policy changes meant little. Because of the widely varying density and condition of old-growth stands, loggers used a great variety of cutting patterns in the Blues during the late 1910s and early 1920s. On cutover areas, site examiners found all gradations—from clearcuts, to harvests that left scattered seed trees, to group selection cuts, to evenly distributed reserve stands.[26] Unfortunately, few foresters found the time to compare how different harvest patterns affected the subsequent growth of pine. This variability, however, means that it is now impossible to blame current problems on historic light harvests, as many people in the Blues have recently done.

Sales before the First World War

For all these optimistic calculations of allowable cuts, sales of Forest Service timber in the Blues were quite small. The *Annual Reports* show that only one-tenth to one-sixth of the allowable cuts were sold and harvested during the first decade of sales, before 1916.[27] In 1906, for example, M. L. Erickson—the Forest Assistant who wrote many of the Blues silvics reports—set up the first timber sale on the Wallowa Reserve, offering 80 acres of timber with 12,000 board feet of white fir and 15,000 board feet of Douglas-fir. What was striking about this sale was that these were not the big yellow pines. As the sales plan stated, the Forest Service was trying to force cutting of less desirable species so that better trees would have more room to reproduce.[28] Yet, as Erickson noted, forcing the harvest of undesirables was not going to work very well if nobody wanted to buy those trees. Private buildings outside the reserve were supplying the demand of the local settlers, and there was no way to get this timber outside of the local area. Transport costs were far too high, for there were no accessible railroads.

Most other sales on Blues forests were equally small until just before World War I. The first large Forest Service sale in the Blue Mountains came, surprisingly, in the midst of a major market slump in 1916. On 14,600 acres along the lower Middle Fork of the John Day River, the Whitman National Forest offered buyers 124 million board feet of timber—a huge amount for the time. Of this sale volume, 92 percent was ponderosa, and the government required the buyer to cut 8 percent of the so-called inferior species: mainly Douglas-fir and lodgepole. Stumpage prices were very high: $2.70 per thousand board feet for ponderosa and $0.50 for the rest. Planners derived the stumpage prices not from the market value of the lumber, but from a formula based on estimates of a "fair" profit, which meant the local company's standard margin of profit on private lands.[29]

The site was 60 miles southwest of Baker and 5 miles west of Austin, where the Sumpter Valley Railway already extended. Since only 5 miles of rail would need to be laid to the area, costs would be relatively low. The contractor would build a small mill on the site, and then ship the rough lumber to Baker for finishing. Investments in railroads and a new mill would necessarily be substantial: $170,000, plus the cost of the timber, for a total of at least half a million. The Forest Service aimed the sale at a large corporation, hoping to bring into the remote region capital that would catalyze development. This would then enable other sales of mature ponderosa timber, opening eastern Oregon timber to national markets. The prospectus urged buyers to recognize that consumption of good yellow pine was increasing in the northeastern United States. Freight rates were still relatively cheap from Baker to Boston and New York, the prospectus reported, clearly hoping to entice eastern lumber companies. Even the lower grades, promised the Forest Service, could profitably be sold in Utah, Colorado, and Idaho.

The contract for this initial large sale was restrictive enough that nobody seemed to expect loggers to follow it exactly. Yet, compared to the Forest Service's original intentions of good forestry, it was a mild contract. For example, instead of leaving 30 to 40 percent of the mature stand, the contractor would need to leave only 20 percent of the ponderosa and lodgepole greater than 12 inches in diameter. Although private companies did the logging, government foresters went in first and marked the trees for harvest. If loggers cut or injured unmarked trees, the contract stipulated that they would have to pay double the price, a penalty that the Forest Service hoped would help loggers refrain from making profitable mistakes. Any marked trees that loggers missed would still have to be paid for—again, at double the rate. This severe financial penalty would, the government hoped, ensure that contractors refrained from *high-grading*—the common practice of removing only perfect ponderosa pine, which meant that less desirable species would form the next stand. Although the contract did require the harvest of inferior species, loggers could cut 92 percent ponderosa—a higher proportion of ponderosa than was present in the forest. Even if the loggers followed the contract perfectly, they still would have high-graded off the best ponderosa pines. For all these concessions, however, the contract held to the ideals of using logging as a way of cleaning up the forest. Loggers would need to remove all the dead-and-down ponderosa that was still merchantable. Moreover, they also had to take out all snags, and diseased or defective trees.

The Oregon Lumber Company purchased the timber, and then they did exactly what the Forest Service had hoped: they began buying more and more timber across the Blues. From the first sale, they cut 20 million board feet a year, and by 1928 they had stripped 380 million board feet of yellow pine from that single watershed—three times the original contract.[30] When the Oregon Lumber Company signed two additional large contracts—one in the Prairie Working Circle near the Sumpter Valley Railway line, and another in the Baker Working Circle near Whitney—the Forest Service began to believe that regulating the forests would be possible. By 1930, the company's annual harvest exceeded 45 million board feet a year. These were tremendous harvests: the timber sold in 1993 on the entire Wallowa Whitman National Forest was less than 40 million board feet.[31] Even though the Forest Service sales program started out conservatively, it quickly gained a momentum that seemed to overwhelm the good sense of foresters.

The Bear Valley Timber Sale

Within six years of that first large sale in 1916, the Forest Service was making extensive concessions in the hope of attracting business. In 1922, nearly one billion board feet of government timber was offered in a single sale, south of the Strawberry Mountains in the Bear Valley of the Malheur National Forest. Local residents, rather than foresters, had demanded this sale, petitioning the Forest Service to put the timber on the market. Locals did not want to buy the timber themselves; they wanted to attract eastern capital and spur industrial development in the area. This sale is critical, not just because it illustrates the push to sell timber, but because it reveals how quickly silvicultural principles changed to meet political demands. The Forest Service's goal was to sell timber, and everything else had to bow to that desire.

The government angled for a single buyer powerful enough to finance an intimidating quantity of railroad: thirty miles of railroad extension from the mill site at Burns to Crane (where a railway branch already extended off the Union Pacific); another fifty miles of tap line from Burns to the cutting areas near Seneca, twenty-three miles south of John Day; and numerous five- to ten-mile branch lines leading to the timber up in the Bear Valley. The company would get to remove the branch lines after harvest and use them elsewhere, but the main lines had to remain in place. Local residents wanted the sale for two reasons: the mill would offer jobs, and the railroad would ship their livestock to eastern markets. Railroad development had stopped short of the Blues, and while rumors were constantly circulating about plans to build a line down the Snake, nothing had materialized. So, from the locals' perspective, anything that would end their isolation from national markets was desirable.

The Forest Service prospectus was so enthusiastic, it almost sounded as if they were trying to sell patent medicine, not government timber. "The time is ripe," it declared, "to bring about this development and to begin the use of the timber. Seldom, if ever again, will such a business opportunity in National Forest virgin pine timber be offered."[32] The Chief of the Forest Service himself signed the prospectus, indicating that it was not just a local or Portland office initiative. This sale would be a chance for the Blues to pull their weight for the Forest Service as a whole, while at the same time opening a remote region for development—making it less of a wilderness and more a part of industrial America. As the prospectus stated, the sale had a fourfold purpose: to open up the area to modern development, to catalyze railroad development and agriculture, to start a permanent timber industry, and to meet the demand created by exhaustion of pine timber resources in the Lake States and the South:

It is the policy of the Forest Service to make the timber resources of the National Forests available for use and to have the sale of the timber aid in the development of the neighboring agricultural territory. In accordance with these policies the Service is now offering the opportunity to open up one of the finest large compact bodies of yellow-pine timber in the West. . . . The pine timber on the south side of the Blue Mountain region, in east-central Oregon, has never been operated except in insignificant amounts for local use. Railroad development has stopped just short of the point where it would tap the timber and just short of opening up fertile irrigable valleys. . . . The establishment of this lumber manufacturing business, based on the contract now offered, will bring much-needed railroad transportation into a region of large possibilities for agricultural development.

The prospectus stated, surprisingly, that although the initial outlay for the Bear Valley timber would be large, the government would assume most of the economic risk, while assuring a supply of timber well past the end of the contract. The Forest Service was willing to pay heavily, for this was a sale it envisioned in grand terms, as "an unusual opportunity for establishing a new permanent unit of pine lumber production, to meet the demand caused by the rapid exhaustion of the pine timber in the Lake States and the South." The company, however, would need to come up with an initial outlay of more than $2 million ($1.5 million for the rail-

road, and half a million for the mill). Only extremely intense—
and rapid—logging could pay these costs. The Forest Service promised a continuous yield of 68 million board feet annually. Furthermore, an additional 210 million board feet of private pine was
within or adjacent to the proposed sale area, and could be bought
at a reasonable price.[33]

Three things about the sale are particularly striking, and all are
related to the Forest Service's emphasis on drawing capital into the
region and making the financial outlay worthwhile. First, the allowable cut was heavier than normal: 85 percent rather than the
standard 60 to 80 percent. Second, loggers would be allowed to
skid out the timber with Caterpillar tractors, even though in previous sales the Forest Service had discouraged tractor skidding because it damaged young growth. Third, and most important, the
contractors would not be required to cut "inferiors." They could
cut only ponderosa if cutting other species was not financially
profitable. In other words, they could high-grade all they liked.

Considering what later happened with firs in the Blues ponderosa forests, allowing high-grading was a critical concession on
the part of the Forest Service. The planning report for the Bear Valley sale noted that the "big problem is to prevent the spread of
inferior species as white fir and lodgepole pine which are invading
the pine stands where the type merges from [south] slope to north
slope."[34] But then the sales report ignored this caution, and merely
assured potential buyers—who were, after all, supposed to be buying enough ponderosa pine to run their mills for centuries—that
there was sufficient reproduction across the area. The report did
not mention, however, that it would be fir and not pine reproducing, and therefore providing the future harvests that the Forest Service had so generously promised.

When the Forest Service offered this sale in 1922, it had just
changed the official policy on high-grading. Loggers had been refusing to cut inferiors, preferring to violate their contracts rather
than cut timber they viewed as worthless. Instead of forcing them
to meet their contracts and run the risk of losing sales, the Forest
Service quietly looked the other way. But soon contractors began
demanding a reduction in stumpage prices, claiming that they

should be given a discount on ponderosa if they had to cut any other species at all. Not only did they refuse to pay for the firs, they wanted to be *paid* to cut them. When the loggers made this demand in 1922, the Forest Service decided that if it kept insisting that contractors cut firs, no one would buy the ponderosa—and nothing at all would get cut. So, rather than run the risk that their ponderosa sales might slow, the Forest Service decided that cutting inferiors would be optional.[35] E. A. Sherman, the acting District Forester, commented in frustration that "there is no intention on the part of the Foresters' office to go to extremes in urging the cutting of inferior species at a loss and consequently at the expense of yellow pine stumpage."[36] Trapped by their conviction that old-growth ponderosa had to be regulated as quickly as possible, foresters made a decision which accelerated the loss of their favored pine forests.

In spite of all the efforts to make the Bear Valley sale attractive to buyers, the Forest Service received not a single bid for the timber, in part because minimum stumpage prices were unrealistically high: $2.75 per thousand board feet for ponderosa. The Forest Service sent telegrams and letters to several midwestern lumber companies, asking them what changes would make them willing to bid on the contract. The Edward Hines Lumber Company said they were not interested, and the Shevlin-Hixon Lumber Company said no price would be low enough to make the investments in railway lines feasible. The Forest Service reduced the minimum price to $2.00 and finally received two bids. The Herrick Lumber Company began work on the railroad—not, of course, with their own money, but with money raised by selling options on the timber. After spending a great deal of other people's money, the company finally built 30 miles of the railroad before defaulting on the contract. Local residents were furious, and blamed the Forest Service.

After the company defaulted, the *Blue Mountain Eagle* charged Forest Service employees with colluding in fraud by offering the company low prices on a contract it never intended to meet. Forest Service Chief Greeley asked the U.S. Senate to investigate the charges. The Senate exonerated all Forest Service employees and, in 1927, terminated Herrick's contract. At that point, the Forest

Service contacted the Hines Lumber Company in Chicago again, and Hines submitted a bid which the Forest Service accepted. A contract was signed in 1928, and in January 1930 the Hines mill went into operation, eight years after the sale was first offered. But Hines soon made local residents no happier than had the Herrick Lumber Company. Railroads were expensive, and the money to finance them was never easily come by. Huge fortunes could be made in railroad speculation, but huge fortunes could just as well be lost.

Hines had invested $7 million in building the railroad and mill, but $4 million of that came from the sale and distribution of a bond issue—basically junk bonds issued on the expected future worth of the company. In 1932, Hines defaulted on the bonds, and for a while it looked as if the timber was no closer to getting cut. But then a committee of infuriated bondholders took over the company's affairs and finished the mill and railroad. The committee managed to sell enough pine to make a profit, and by 1941 they had bought an additional 405 million board feet of government timber in nearby watersheds. But instead of the usual twenty-year contract, they persuaded the Forest Service to allow them to cut all that pine in six years—so they could meet their railroad debts. Then with the money they gained from liquidating nearly 1.3 billion board feet of ponderosa in less than a decade, they bought out the Oregon Lumber Company's holdings within the Malheur National Forest—another 137 million board feet of ponderosa.[37] The Forest Service thought it could sell pine to finance local development, but had not realized how tangled the webs of financial obligation could become. At each step of the contract disputes, the Forest Service ended up selling timber much more quickly than it had ever intended—just to keep the companies from defaulting.

The Bear Valley sale was ultimately successful in meeting the Forest Service's aims. The southern Blues got its railroad connection to the rest of the world; Burns got its mill; and the pinelands got their first taste of regulation. These initial sales catalyzed the rapid harvest of nearly two billion board feet of ponderosa pine off three southern watersheds: the Silvies River, the Middle Fork of the

John Day, and the Malheur River. But the heavy investments were anything but stable. Companies regularly defaulted on their contracts, because they had financed construction by selling high interest bonds that attracted eastern capital but inflated the real value of the railroads. The result was that a few men made huge profits out of failed timber and railway companies, and timber got cut at rates that far exceeded sustainability. Local residents did attract the development they had sought, but at a price they had never expected. The pine that was going to bring them centuries of stability and prosperity was gone in less than a decade.

Plans in the 1920s

By the 1920s, Forest Service planners knew they were authorizing logging that would ensure that harvest levels would collapse by the 1990s. Figure 2 shows the rapid increase in logging during this decade. An examination of one plan, the Burns Working Circle Plan of 1923, shows how foresters calculated harvest levels that would inevitably lead to mill closures in the late 1980s. First, the Burns Working Circle planner calculated what the annual sustained-yield harvest would be after the forest was regulated. In 1923, the working circle contained about 600,000 acres of forest and 50,000 acres of unforested land. The planner started by assuming that the 50,000 acres barren of timber in 1923 would, through the efforts of foresters, soon be growing commercial timber. This meant that he could estimate growth on 650,000 acres. With net growth rates of 100 board feet per acre per year, on 650,000 acres, the maximum sustained-yield production would be 65 million board feet a year. This calculation made several important assumptions: (1) that all species of trees would grow at equal rates and produce timber that was equally usable; (2) that all stands on the 650,000 acres of forest were equally dense and productive; and (3) that at the end of 60 years, the Forest Service would have figured out how to change 50,000 barren acres into commercial forest at maximum production. And finally, it was assumed that disease and insects and fires could be excluded from the forest, and that growth could be maintained without them.

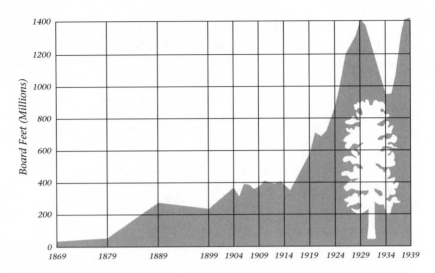

Figure 2. Trends in ponderosa pine production in eastern Washington and Oregon, 1869–1939. From R. W. Cowlin, P. A. Briegleb, and F. L. Moravets, "Forest Resources of the Ponderosa Pine Region" (USDA Miscellaneous Publication 490, Washington, D.C., 1942), 32.

Even given all these assumptions, the maximum harvest rate, under the most impossibly ideal conditions, would be 65 million board feet a year. Was that then the amount loggers should harvest? Not at all. For the first cutting cycle on the Burns Working Circle, the planner recommended that instead of cutting at the rate the forest could theoretically produce, harvests should be *increased* 50 percent: from 65 million board feet to 95 million board feet per year. A series of calculations attempted to provide scientific justification for this increase over the sustained-yield capacity. The actual volume of timber in the forest was 6.7 billion board feet, in an open, uncrowded stand of big trees (average 32 inch dbh) with an associated high volume of timber. But in an ideal forest, the planner argued, the trees would be smaller, so they would have a smaller volume, and the "normal" growing stock as calculated by the Munger formula would be only about 3 billion board feet. Since the actual growing stock on these 600,000 acres was 6.7 billion board feet, there was then a "theoretical surplus" approaching 4 billion board feet. According to the planner, good silviculture demanded that this theoretical surplus be cut as soon as possible. The forest was doing too well for its own good. Theoretically, forests could not support so many large trees, so the extra volume should be rapidly removed. The best forest was not what existed, but a forest that met a scientific ideal. But the real reason for the increased harvests was that, as the planner wrote, "this virgin yellow pine timber is in notoriously bad condition from a silvicultural point of view. There is an over-supply of decadent timber and an under-supply of thrifty middle-aged timber. . . . To put the forest in good condition for growth a heavy cutting is necessary in the next few decades."[38]

The planner argued that during the first 60-year cycle the Forest Service should sell 85 percent of the trees over 12 inch dbh, leaving only 15 percent of the trees as the basis of the next stand. Given that the circle contained an estimated 6.7 billion board feet of timber, an 85 percent harvest would meaning cutting 5.7 billion board feet in 60 years—or 95 million board feet a year. What would then form the harvests for the next cutting cycle, if only 15 percent of the trees were left? The planner admitted that the harvests would indeed drop: "Good silviculture dictates a heavy cutting in the present cutting cycle, i.e., heavier than the sustained production and this may result in a lesser cut the next cutting cycle. But it is not considered bad management if, in the interests of good silviculture, the cut during the next decade is somewhat in excess of the potential sustained production, which must be the limit of the sustained cut in later cutting cycles." Nowhere, however, did the planner consider exactly how much harvests would decline. Even assuming maximum growth rates in the reserved stand and maximum release from suppression, harvest levels would still drop 50 percent by 1983; but the planner did not bother to make this calculation.

As the 1920s drew to a close, fear rippled through the local communities, first in Enterprise when the East Oregon Lumber Company closed its mill, and then throughout the southern Blues when

Herrick defaulted on its loans and the Hines Lumber Company almost closed the mill in Burns. Concern about the effects of intense harvests on local communities began to emerge in working circle plans, even though foresters did not allow this concern to decrease their recommended harvests. In the Malheur River Working Circle Plan from about 1927, the planner did attempt to calculate the annual yield of the second cutting cycle. He realized, with dismay, that it would be at least 40 percent less than in the first 60-year cycle—a drop from 38 million board feet a year to between 21 and 24 million board feet a year. Fire protection would not help make up the difference, the planner added, "if there is any adherence to the 180 year rotation"—because the extra trees saved from fire would ideally be allowed to go through the full three cutting cycles. But his tone leads one to suspect that he did not place much faith in the ability of future Forest Service officers to hold onto reserve stands. The Malheur River planner acknowledged, as the Burns planner had not, that projected net yields of 100 board feet per acre per year were little more than guesses, because they were "based on very meager information on growth of Yellow Pine."[39] But then he consoled himself with the thought that because these figures were just rough estimates, perhaps they would turn out to be underestimates, and then there would be more timber than anyone expected. Of course, they could just as likely turn out to be overestimates, and the situation in 60 years would be even worse, but he neglected to mention that depressing possibility. He also hoped that "utilization efficiency will have greatly increased"—so less waste would mean more wood for the mills.

What is interesting here are the hints that things might go very wrong, as indeed they did. In 1927 planners were predicting that by 1987, at the end of 60 years, their heavy cuts would lead to drastic reductions in wood available for harvests—which was exactly what happened. Firs did not make up the difference; they only magnified the effects.[40] Why did the planners not recommend lower cuts when they realized what the effects would be on future harvests? Because they felt obliged to get the forest growing. For the same reason, they let operators skip cutting inferiors when it might lower stumpage prices of pine and result in fewer ponderosas being cut. "There is no data to show that the silvic benefits derived from requiring the inferiors to be cut would offset the monetary loss involved," stated one working circle plan.[41] Economics now took first place, because the Forest Service in the Blues more than anything else wanted the pine cut.

Management in a Climate of Selling Pine

Management of the stands shifted as the sales policy changed to favor rapid liquidation of pine. For example, in the 1920s the Forest Service stopped leaving seed trees for ponderosa pine. Sales plans stipulated that all big tress were now to be cut, and the only trees left to make up the reserve stand would be "bull pines" (ponderosa under 15 inches in diameter that were not producing seed). Markers were specifically told to leave seed trees only where no other reserves were present.[42] This change in policy helps explain why mixed-conifer stands changed to stands dominated by firs: foresters were no longer leaving anything that would have seeded ponderosas, which in their eyes represented prime timber. Why not? First, contractors wanted the big seed trees. Additionally, silvics taught the foresters that the big pines were not putting on enough volume to make them worthwhile. Finally, foresters had lost their faith that the forest could reproduce itself successfully. They decided that because of arid conditions, there was no point in leaving seed trees because seeds dried out instead of germinating. It was better to favor conditions that promoted the survival of the young saplings left behind after logging. The best way to ensure future stands, the author of the Malheur Working Circle policy statement argued, was not through seed trees but through fire protection. Fire, the report argued, was the enemy of future ponderosa stands, because fire killed the reproduction and left the stands thinly stocked. With fire protection, they could produce twice the timber off these forests, by doubling the stocking levels, the report continued. One forester had just concluded that the ponderosa lands were overstocked, because they had more big trees than a theoretical stand. Now another forester had concluded just the opposite: the stands were understocked, because the trees did not grow as close together as trees in an ideal stand ought to grow.

Both foresters had trouble seeing or valuing the actual forest because their vision of an ideal forest got in the way: all they could see was the forest's distance from their ideal. The author of the Malheur policy statement reasoned that if fires continued, the youngest trees would all die, soon only decadent stands would remain, and eventually ponderosa would disappear. But if ponderosa pine really needed foresters for its own survival, how could the forests that loggers were cutting have appeared in the first place? Forest Service planners were in a strange position. They had come so far from earlier foresters' respect for old growth that at this point they could not even imagine how a forest could survive without the Forest Service around to protect it. They wanted to favor pine, but their efforts to create ideal pine stands resulted in overstocked stands from which pine was soon excluded.

In the first silvics report, foresters had perceived the open stands as a good thing. But by 1927 on the La Grande Working Circle plan, this openness seemed problematic, and the irregularity and mosaic quality of the forest also worried them. Hanzlik—the forester who developed site classifications and much of the policy for ponderosa pine—was working on the Umatilla National Forest in 1927. In a memorandum concerning the La Grande Working Circle Plan, he wrote that the ponderosa stands were "more or less broken up by openings or blocks of lodgepole and larch, making a rather irregular and spotted stocking of yellow pine.... Satisfactorily stocked advance growth covers about 60 to 70 percent of the yellow pine type; the remainder is open or sparsely stocked, which will be very difficult to stock up to a satisfactory stand of young growth."[43] Foresters' emphasis on getting the forest regulated made them favor crowded stands over open stands, and thereby contributed to the emerging problems. Overstocking and stand conversion happened because foresters were trying to regulate the forest—not just because of fire suppression or natural succession.

The Forest Service's push for sales led to a striking shift in the ways foresters valued what they saw in the forest. In the early silvics reports, foresters had only praise for the huge larches. But by

1927, planners wrote of the massive trees with scorn. A report on the Hilgard Project from the Umatilla National Forest implied that smaller trees were better because the lumbermen preferred them: "Douglas fir and white fir trees do not here attain the real large diameter sizes as found commonly in the Blue Mountain region, and, therefore, are looked upon with more favor by the lumbermen. This is also true in the case of the western larch, where the lack of *large worthless* trees of this species is readily noticeable."[44]

The Hilgard report added that the lodgepole pine type "now has its chief value for watershed protection," a statement that at first glance sounds much like statements made two decades before, when watersheds were the highest priority. But as the report pointed out, lodgepole "exploitation for lumber purposes is not expected" for several decades, so watershed protection mattered only because the logs were not yet large enough for the Forest Service to sell profitably. Foresters' perceptions of forest values had changed dramatically since the time, just two decades earlier, when watershed protection had priority over timber sales.

Forest Service managers were not greedy or deluded; but they found it increasingly difficult to pay attention to the forest itself as they focused on a single output: harvests. In their hurry to clear the forest of decadent old growth, they became blinded to abundant signs that things were going wrong. By and large, they were intelligent men dedicated to a vision, and it was this vision that failed them. As foresters lost respect for the forest that existed outside their office windows, they closed themselves off from the information given to them by the forest and worked in a self-referential world of ideal stocking levels and theoretical surpluses.

The 1930s: Markets and Timber Sales

By the 1920s, lumber overproduction forced prices down, making pine a much less valuable resource. Lumber was not the only industry in trouble. Across the West, during a long economic slide that preceded the Great Depression, resource industries faced a glut in markets and decline in prices. When prices began falling, farmers and loggers produced more to try to keep their profits intact—

creating a spiral of declining prices and mushrooming surpluses. As the economic vise tightened, Forest Service planners began to look more closely at the economic effects of inflated pine harvests, and they winced when they saw what their predecessors had wrought. With its generous sales contracts, the Forest Service had encouraged the construction of several huge mills, which had annual milling capacities far above what the Forest Service could supply if logging was to be on a sustained-yield basis. On the Malheur Forest alone, for example, two large sales had totaled 2 billion board feet of pine, out of only 7 billion on the entire forest. Two mills followed—one capable of processing 60 million board feet a year, and another that could process 70 to 75 million board feet each year.[45] With mill capacities exceeding 135 million board feet a year, it would take only 15 years—not the 60 years of the cutting cycle—to process the 2 billion board feet in these sales, and only 52 years to process all the ponderosa on the entire forest. The mill capacities were far too large for the timber on the forest, but once mills were in place, the Forest Service was caught in a tangle of demands, and it could never easily resist the pressures to keep the mills running. And so, even though planners knew they were harvesting pine at far more than sustainable rates, they felt they could not stop without further devastating local communities.

In the Malheur River Working Circle Plan from about 1927, some concern over large sales emerged. The planner wished to hold onto timber in the upper watershed so there would be some pine left to cut in the future, but he acknowledged that it would be impossible once private landholders began cutting on their blocks within the forest. A checkerboard pattern of private and public land made the Forest Service vulnerable to pressures from private holders. As a memo between this planner and the Forest Supervisor acknowledged, in the east block there was one-half billion board feet of private timber lying in alternate blocks. If this was sold, the government timber would also be forced to sale.[46] Once a company laid rails in a watershed, any timber that was not immediately cut would not be cut at all, because the company removed the tracks after harvest. If private landholders demanded that the Forest Service make its checkerboard lands available for harvest, the Forest

Service usually agreed. They were reluctant to forgo the opportunity to access the timber while the rails were in place. High-grading was also a renewed concern. Inferior species made up a third of the volume in at least two blocks on the working circle—a substantial increase in the six years since sales policies had allowed contractors to leave all the fir. As the planner pointed out, no more pine at all would remain for the next cutting cycle, so harvests were going to depend on the inferior spaces. Yet there were still no hints that any of the companies would ever agree to cut the inferiors.

On the Whitman Forest, letters between sales planners, the Forest Supervisor, and the Regional District Forester show that by 1927 the Forest Service was beginning to feel trapped by the mill capacities it had encouraged. E. A. Sherman, the Acting Forester in Portland, criticized a draft of the management plan for the Baker Working Circle, complaining that the mill at Baker was too large and was using up too much wood, in excess of annual allowable cuts. He wrote: "the present milling capacity at Baker of between 40,000,000 and 50,000,000 feet annually . . . greatly exceeds the possible sustained yield from the Government lands in this working circle, and . . . is probably greatly in excess of the yield in the second or third cutting cycles . . . It does not look as if a reduction in the milling capacity at Baker, sooner or later, could be avoided."[47] The sales planner agreed that harvest reductions would certainly come by the second cutting cycle (which would begin in the 1980s). But then he pointed out that these reductions were not the Forest Service's concern: "The Service has never assumed any obligation of keeping these mills going to capacity. A reduction in milling capacity as the private holdings become depleted is a foregone conclusion." The planner persuaded the Supervisor that because they could not prevent the second-cutting cycle declines, they might as well do their best to meet the mills' demands for timber, and avert mill closures in the present. As private holdings were depleted, the Forest Service increasingly felt obliged to increase harvests on public lands to avert mill failure. Because the mills were dependent on Forest Service timber, Forest Service planners had to close their eyes to overcutting.

The Great Depression hit the West hard in 1930, and an already depressed lumber market crashed. In Washington, the largest producer of timber in the nation, the harvest in 1929 was more than 7 billion board feet, and by 1932 it had plummeted to 2 billion.[48] Many mills increased production to make up for losses, but this offered only a temporary respite. Mill closures devastated towns in the Blues. To add to the hard times, many companies became delinquent in paying taxes on their cutover lands—overturning the foundation of the local government's tax base.

Complaints arose from the Oregon Legislature that federal timber sales in Oregon had crippled the timber market. The Forest Service, accused the legislators, had set artificially low stumpage prices to push heavy sales, and liquidation of old growth had glutted the market.[49] Under pressure, the Forest Service decreased sales, and as sales dwindled it changed its definitions of sustained yield and allowable cuts. An economist named David Mason, who had worked for the Forest Service and then left to start his own consulting firm, crusaded for a new concept of sustained yield. Mason's version of sustained yield sowed extensive controversy, for its goal was not to regulate the forest but to ensure continuous industry production. As Mason stated, "sustained-yield forest management consists for a given forest in limiting the average annual cut to the continuous production capacity."[50] This was a compromise between the European concept that the annual harvest should be no more than the annual growth, and the Forest Service's practice of rapid liquidation. Mason's concern was industry stability—not a more perfect forest. And by 1927, the Forest Service was becoming more concerned about community stability. The chief, Robert Stuart, in his *Annual Report of the Forester,* stated that the Forest Service had once wanted to cut the old growth as fast as possible to get new growing stands, but now it preferred a slow cutting of old growth, to ensure steady harvests in the future.[51]

Working circle plans from the Blues reflected these policy changes. By 1930, the goal was no longer to liquidate mature timber as fast as possible, but to cut at a rate that would produce a second cut as large as the first one. As the 1930 Middle Fork John Day working circle plan put it, the new management goals were "to provide a continuous yield of sawtimber," while also maintaining "permanent industry" and "steady employment," encouraging private timber lands to be left in good condition, and discouraging "increased milling capacity in the region."[52]

The Middle Fork of the John Day—where the Forest Service had sold 124 million board feet of timber in 1916—was, in the planners's words, "the scene of the earliest and most continuous cutting of National Forest stumpage." Although the planner admitted to a "widespread impression of disastrous overcutting," he argued that the cutting had not been so very intense. Although the average annual harvest for the preceding 19 years (1910–1928) was 20 million feet board feet, the planner calculated, "sustained cutting for the remaining 41 years (1929–1969) can be maintained at the average annual rate of 15 million [board feet], with a estimated second cycle cut of 16 million yearly." In other words, average harvests were only a little more than what seemed sustainable. But his estimate was unfair, because cutting did not start until 1916, so the actual average for 1916–1928 was nearly 30 million board feet annually—far in excess of what was sustainable, even under ideal conditions. As the plan reported, by 1930 most "over-mature [yellow pine] areas have been cut-over" in far fewer than the 60 years originally planned.

This planner argued that the Forest Service should immediately reduce the annual cut to 15 million board feet, but he admitted that there was no way to enforce this. The Oregon Lumber Company mill had an annual milling capacity of 30 million board feet, which they planned to double, working on a two-shift basis to recover their initial investments. The company was supposed to cut half its harvest from Forest Service land and half from its private lands, but the District Forester stated that he feared the company would insist on cutting the Forest Service land first, in only 25 years and with no guarantees for the rest of the cutting cycle. Additionally, another company on the working circle operated a mill with an annual capacity of 45 million board feet, and to meet *their* investments they demanded an increase to 60 million board feet. All together, the mills in the working circle needed 120 million board feet of timber a year to run at full capacity; this was in a circle that was planning on a sustained-yield harvest of only 16 million board feet a year. Something was very wrong here, as the Forest Supervisor, the working circle planner, and the Regional Forester in Portland all agreed. Private land could not make up the difference of 104 million board feet a year, even for a short time; but the Forest Service lands could not meet the difference either.

These planners were admitting to a nearly tenfold discrepancy between the mill capacities and the sustained-yield harvests (which were themselves based on overestimates of growth). In other words, the local community depended for its long-term stability on a supply of trees which, between the Forest Service and the mills, were vanishing ten to twenty times faster than they could regrow. Something was wrong, and this was not an isolated case. A policy statement from 1938 detailed an even more extreme situation on the La Grande Working Circle. Within 11 years, two sales policy documents appeared for this working circle, one in 1927 and one in 1938. In that short span of time, it seemed the world had changed. All the cheery confidence expressed in the first report vanished in a fog of grim despondency.

E. J. Hanzlik, one of the Forest Service's leading researchers, wrote the first sales policy in 1927. His statement was filled with grand dreams: to cut and cut and get the land in shape. Hanzlik's enthusiasm led him to some astonishing figures. He planned to cut over the entire stand of 1 billion board feet of ponderosa in 30 to 40 years (rather than the usual 60 years), harvesting 25 million feet a year and leaving a sparse 10 percent reserve stand (rather than the usual 20 percent). What would happen at the end of 30 years, when all the ponderosa was cut, and the reproduction was only 1 to 30 years old? What would the mills use for lumber? The vague expectation was that larch and Douglas-fir left for a reserve stand would make up the difference. Hanzlik assured his readers that "an annual output of 25 million feet a year and a 10–20% reserve would cut this stand of yellow pine in about 30 or 40 years, at which time no doubt the other species, principally larch and Douglas fir, would be in greater demand and would give an extension of the cut for another 20 or 25-year period."[53] And after that period? Something else would come in to make up the difference. Perhaps the mills would retool and be able to use the 50-year-old ponderosas that had grown since the first cut, he suggested rather blithely. Or perhaps someone would think of a use for fir. Hanzlik shrugged at extreme high-grading; in fact, he encouraged it because firs had higher initial growth rates, so they would grow faster and make up the difference in harvest levels faster. He worried little, if at all, about the future effects on local communities—much less on the forests.

In 1938, J. Kier, the Assistant Forest Supervisor for the Umatilla National Forest, wrote another report on the same working circle, and the differences between the two reports are striking. Kier's tone was one of loss and anger.[54] As he argued, the Forest Service's estimates of sustainable allowable cuts had already been reduced, from 25 million board feet in 1927 to 6.5 million in 1938. The milling capacity, however, had continued to increase, and had reached 108 million board feet—with an annual harvest of 57 million. This cut was nine times the sustained-yield capacity, while the sustained-yield capacity was less than one-sixteenth of mill capacity. Companies were liquidating their private stock as fast as possible and when they finished, they planned either to pull out or to demand that the Forest Service meet their mill capacities.

The situation on the La Grande working circle was particularly difficult, since much of it was broken into little chunks of private land controlled by several individual companies. The total area on the circle was slightly more than 1 million acres, and 50 percent of this was private land. By 1938, only a third of the remaining forest was ponderosa pine, partly because some blocks in the circle were too high and damp for anything but fir forests, and partly because fire exclusion had changed the composition of the forest. But much of the change was simply the result of liquidating ponderosa. Kier wrote that at one time the circle had contained "a wonderful stand of ponderosa pine," mostly in private ownerships. Yet now the pine was almost gone: "Continued liquidation of private holdings, with no thought of a second cut, over a period of about 40 years, has depleted the standing pine forests until there is only about one half billion feet of accessible pine left, half of which is in private ownership. The allowable annual cut under sustained yield management on the remaining timber would be near 6.5 million feet, if private and public holdings could be managed now as a unit." But since companies were liquidating their private holdings even faster than their government holdings, there would be nothing left to fill the gap. The Forest Service could not hold back its timber, because it would be little more than a drop in the sea. All it could do was encourage better private practices and try to get cutover lands on exchanges of timber.

Kier argued that the timber companies were abandoning the practices of good forestry and reverting to their old cut-and-get-out policies. One by one, he listed the companies' abandonment of scientific forestry: "Bowman Hix [i.e., Hicks] Company are liquidating their private holdings rapidly and are then going out of the picture, about 8 years hence. Mt. Emily Lumber Company are buying all available private holdings, within economic reach, and are negotiating with the Forest Service for all its available timber. H. F. Reed Lumber Co. has asked for government timber on different occasions as his private holdings are about exhausted. The Oregon Trail Lumber Company at Union, with an installed capacity of 10 million feet, is destined to go out of the scene within the next five years." The solution that the mills proposed was simply to increase the working circle size, which would magically appear to increase the available cut. But this, Kier argued, could not work, because surrounding blocks were also depleted.

Part of the Forest Service's frustration came from trying to manage fragmented land, because so much of the circle was owned privately by out-of-state corporations. For example, Bowman Hicks planned not to let their cutover lands reforest. They intended to burn them heavily to increase the grazing rentals they received, then in eight years they would pull out of the region entirely. The Forest Service had little power to enforce particular cutting practices on private holdings. What leverage it had came from land exchanges. Rather than charge companies for the timber on Forest Service lands, the Forest Service would let them cut it for free, in exchange for title to the private holdings the companies had already cut over. This way, the Forest Service had some say over private cutting practices, because it could refuse to exchange timber for private land that companies had cut carelessly.

The Forest Service hoped to obtain title to private lands that lay within the boundaries of the National Forests (and also land that lay outside Forest Service boundaries but still within the watersheds that contained Forest Service timber). Eventually, the Forest Service wanted to put this private land into public, regulated timber production, to help maintain stability for dependent towns. As Kier stated, "since sustained yield cannot be attained in this circle, to keep La Grande and other dependent communities at their present prosperity as long as possible and to obtain good forestry practice on remaining private holdings, timber will be sold to established operators only, in exchange for cut-over lands in good growing condition within the circle, provided acceptable offers have been received and also provided that the operator practices good forestry on private lands cut over by his operations." But this kind of manipulation was less effective when timber prices were depressed. It was completely ineffective with companies such as Bowman Hicks that planned to cut quickly and move on.

Kier's 1938 plan expressed the first concern for labor evident in the Blues Forest Service reports. The labor situation in La Grande was, he wrote, "acute." Two large mills had been operating "spasmodically," and employment was unstable. When timber prices were high, things were fine. But at other times, large numbers of workers were thrown out of work, a situation that did not change for decades. Kier's proposed solutions to the timber and labor problems mirrored proposals current in the 1990s; mills should diversify and reduce their dependence on old-growth ponderosa. They should turn to specialty products and attempt "closer utilization" of wood, which meant wasting less at the harvest site and the mill. Kier promoted the Ponderosa Pine Lumber Company in Elgin, which made small wooden specialty products such as bread boxes and venetian blinds out of lodgepole and fir, as a model of a local firm that provided steady employment.

Increased forest production through harvests of old growth was still Kier's primary silvicultural objective, but the ways loggers

should accomplish that task had dramatically changed. "Ponderosa pine . . . grows best under a light selection system of cutting," Kier wrote. Instead of cutting 80 to 90 percent of the trees
over 12 inches in diameter, loggers should cut only the "over-
mature and low-vigor mature trees . . . except where thinning is
required." Most surprisingly, Kier acknowledged that old growth
had a certain value for soil and seed trees: "Over-mature trees of
good vigor and mature trees of fair vigor will be retained if needed
to insure adequate regeneration or to preserve soil values." This
was something that no plan written during the 1920s had ever
suggested. Loggers should also protect the soil, Kier urged, by leaving slash untouched on scab areas to "retard erosion and provide
cover." Finally, Kier gave a nod to multiple-use values. Sales planners should preserve recreational values, and logging on watersheds "should be carried on in such manner as not to materially
accelerate erosion." Timber was still top priority, but by 1938 the
emphasis had clearly changed.

Even though the Depression ended the push for heavy sales,
foresters still had a vision: to regulate the forest as quickly as possible, given economic constraints. As markets for government timber dwindled, the Forest Service began to consider the value of
lighter cuts. Yet foresters gave more efficient liquidation of old
growth as their justification for these lighter cuts—showing that
the basic ideals had not fundamentally changed. In 1936, the Forest Service decided that instead of heavy cuts that left only 20 percent of the forest as a reserve stand, foresters would now plan more
frequent but lighter cuts, each of which left 60 percent of the volume. The total volume removed from a stand during a 180-year
rotation would not change, just the timing of removal. Thornton
Munger argued that Forest Service silvicultural goals "can be
achieved better by light and frequent selection cuttings than by
heavy and infrequent cuttings." Tractor and truck logging would
give them the flexibility to do lighter cuts. "This has been in the
minds of many foresters for some time," Munger wrote, "but the
exigencies of horse and railroad logging did not permit light cuttings. Now tractors and trucks give a flexibility to logging and
lower the fixed per acre costs to a degree that makes light cutting

not only possible but apparently more profitable."[55] Truck logging, because of the expense of building roads, soon led to constraints that helped force the Forest Service into heavy logging; but when it first became available, it seemed to offer more control over silviculture. Only with tractors did it seem that light logging might become financially feasible, because the cost of building railways into an area necessitated heavy logging.

The great virtue of light cutting for the regional forester was not that it was less likely to change the forest by disturbing the soil or altering the multi-aged character of the stand; rather, it offered *more* control over manipulating the forest. In Munger's words, "the gradual removal of the timber . . . permits corrections and modifications not possible under heavy cutting, and thus gives rather complete control over the composition and character of the forest." Thus one could convert the forest to something more productive: "The removal of the overmature element of the stand . . . converts the stationary forest to a growing forest. . . . It is sound policy for both a public and private forest owner to liquidate the low-earning trees and to reserve for volume and/or value increment the high-earning trees." With shorter cutting cycles, "the quicker will the whole working circle be put under control with roads," and the faster the better, since "it is more desirable to remove the most overripe half of the mature trees from the whole area in 30 years than to take twice that length of time to get over the whole area with a cutting that takes all the mature trees." Ironically, it was probably this decision—to make light but frequent harvests in ponderosa pine stands—that accelerated the conversion of pines to fir.

Sales policies in the Blues developed out of silvicultural concerns, but they were simultaneously shaped and undercut by markets and technology. After the First World War, the main goal of the Forest Service in the Blues was to cut ponderosa pine in order to get the forests regulated, and this focus led to decisions with unexpected effects. An emphasis on liquidating old growth was the basic motivation for foresters' decisions about high-grading, selection cutting, fire regulation, and sales—decisions that established conditions responsible for the problems now faced by forest managers in the Blues. By 1930, as the industry went through a major slump and the Forest Service was under heavy pressure to decrease production, sales planners and managers in the Blues began to recognize that the heavy cutting of the previous ten years had led them into trouble—economically and silviculturally. The heavy sales of the 1920s and the resulting problems in the 1930s make it clear that the situation the Forest Service would face in the 1990s was nothing new.

Animals: Domestic and Wild Nature

Trees were not the only things that grew in national forests, much as the Forest Service sometimes seemed obsessed with timber. Under the trees, and in the places where trees did not grow, were grasses and shrubs—and the herbivores, both wild and domestic, that liked to eat them. The Forest Service understood that forage plants as well as trees could become commodities. Managers needed to make sure, therefore, that people put those resources to full and productive use.

Timber, grazing, and wildlife policies developed within a similar economic framework that promoted full use of resources, but they veered in different directions during the upheavals of the Great Depression. Timber policy in the 1930s underwent a major shift in focus, as the Depression forced the Forest Service to slow its heavy sales programs. When markets for Forest Service timber vanished, foresters reconsidered their emphasis on heavy sales. Yet the critical assumption underlying heavy sales—that people should put the land to full use, making it as efficient and productive as possible—changed little. Foresters during the 1930s noticed that intensive sales policies had threatened a steady supply of pine for the future. But because they did not question the belief that silviculture could improve forests, they failed to see the ecological effects their policies were having on the forest. In contrast, the Depression forced grazing scientists to pay attention to the ecological havoc their policies had wrought, and range researchers—unlike silvics researchers—eventually came to question the virtues of full productivity.

Bunchgrass Ecology and Grazing Effects

Although Indians had grazed great herds of horses in the Blues and across the inland Northwest, two decades of cattle and sheep grazing overwhelmed the effects of 150 years of horse grazing. When Lewis and Clark came through the inland Northwest in 1805, they remarked both on the Indians' horse herds and on grasslands that were still luxuriant after three-quarters of a century of horse grazing.[1] Seventy years later, when whites first brought cattle and sheep into the region, the range was still among the best in the West. But after the grasslands experienced just a few decades of cattle and sheep grazing, they collapsed.

By the time the Forest Service began to regulate grazing in the Blues, immense tracts of native perennial bunchgrasses from British Columbia to Nevada were succumbing to the rampant weed cheatgrass (*Bromus tectorum*), an invader from Central Asia that made for maddeningly poor cattle forage. Why did the bunchgrasses collapse under cattle grazing, when they had resisted horse grazing for 150 years, and the pressures of native ungulates such as elk, deer, and antelope for millennia? And most puzzling to the whites who watched the changes: Why were the grasslands east of the Rockies in the Great Plains able to resist heavy grazing damage, while the grasslands west of the Rockies changed almost as soon as cattle reached them? Both places were dry; both places were covered mostly with perennial native grasses; both places looked pretty much the same. What in the world was so different?

The ecologist Richard Mack has argued that to make sense of these differences, we need to consider the evolutionary history of the two regions. The grasslands of the intermountain West had formed quite recently in evolutionary time—only six million years before, when the Cascades and Sierras rose and blocked the Pacific winds. What little rain reached the east side of the mountains fell mainly in the autumn and winter; summers were extremely dry. In contrast, grasslands in the Great Plains evolved millions of years earlier, when the emerging Rockies blocked moist winds from the western oceans, creating a much drier region on the leeward side of the new mountains. Yet even though the Great Plains were quite dry, rain fell throughout the spring and summer, during the growing season. Because of their summer rains, the Great Plains could support grasses that were rhizomatous—meaning that they formed a sod, a continuous mat of stems and roots. Sod-forming grasses needed rain during the spring and summer, so summer aridity excluded them from the intermountain West.[2]

Instead of sod-forming grasses, the intermountain grasslands were dominated by bunchgrasses—plants growing in tufts—with lichens and mosses covering the spaces between the tufts. The bunchgrasses dealt with the summer drought by going completely dormant, finishing growth and seed production by mid-July. No photosynthetically active grasses were present during the summer. Thus large native ruminants could not survive in any numbers on the grasslands, because they required green forage for several months after calving to support milk production. The sods of the Great Plains, however, were home to vast herds of bison because the grasses stayed green and nutritious throughout the summer. A few bison did roam through the intermountain West, but they seem to have kept to the river bottoms, where grasses had enough water to stay green. The Great Plains grasslands, therefore, co-evolved for millions of years under heavy grazing pressure, while the grasslands of the intermountain West evolved in the absence of intense grazing.

Millions of years of bison pressure on the Great Plains selected for rhizomatous sods that responded well to grazing. Large herbivores such as bison and cattle did not simply eat some grass; they trampled the rest of the grass, depositing great heaps of nitrogen-rich dung and kicking up chunks of soil. Why could the sods of the Great Plains survive these disturbances while the bunchgrasses could not? Rhizomatous grasses did not need to germinate from seeds; they could grow from roots or chunks of broken sod. When an animal dislodged a hunk of rhizomatous sod, new grass could propagate from roots at the hole, and the kicked-up pieces could often reroot. But bunchgrasses grow from seeds, not from root masses. If herbivores trampled bunchgrasses, the plants would often die, because the damaged stems could not set seed. Additionally, many of the western bunchgrasses could not replace much leaf area if grazed. The elk, antelope, and deer that did graze in the Blues had much smaller body sizes than bison, and their total numbers were restricted by the summer drought and the need to migrate to higher, wetter elevations during the summer. Their grazing, therefore, did not select for adaptations to continual disturbance.

Indian horse herds must have damaged the bunchgrasses to some extent, but since tribes migrated to the mountains for the salmon runs and the hunts, grasses had a chance to set seed without heavy grazing pressure. Lichen and moss communities between the bunchgrass tufts formed a crust which was extremely vulnerable to disturbance, and once a grazing horse's hoof broke through this crust, weeds had the perfect site for colonization. Before white settlers, native annuals would have invaded these disturbed sites, but these natives could not outcompete the bunchgrasses. In contrast, settlers brought cattle and sheep onto the range much earlier in the season, and did not take them off until the animals started losing weight, long after the bunchgrasses were permanently damaged. Seed production, therefore, plummeted, and the bunchgrasses began to lose ground to foreign colonizers. Chance events after settlers arrived guaranteed that a very different weed would come into play, one that was preadapted to displacing bunchgrasses and native annuals because it had evolved under millions of years of grazing pressure.

Plowing the bunchgrass prairies was a relatively easy task, since there was no sod to break. Soon farmers were planting millions of acres of winter wheat at the north end of the Blues, and an uninvited weed—cheatgrass—waited in the seed stocks. Cheatgrass had evolved on the steppes of Central Asia, a place with a dry climate and pattern of rainfall strikingly similar to the inland Northwest. The critical difference was that the Asian grasslands had evolved over at least 60 million years, and grazing pressure by horses and camels had been intense for much of that time. Cheatgrasses started their invasion slowly—a few unusual plants between the rows of wheat. They soon swept through the intermountain West, because they had one major trait that allowed them to outcompete the native grasses: their germination strategy.

Cheatgrass seeds could sprout in pulses over an eight month span, unlike bunchgrasses that all sprouted at once. Because cheatgrass seeds germinated only a few at a time, some would remain dormant in the soil for months. This made the species extremely resistant to drought; if one group of seedlings withered, more seeds were waiting in the soil for another chance. This trait also made the grass nearly impossible to eradicate. Mowing a field before seed production did no good, because undeveloped seeds were still waiting in the soil. Fire only helped the grass, because seed reserves in the soil survived fires, and nitrogen pulses after fire led to lush new growth. Grazing also favored the domination of cheatgrass over native grasses, because livestock and native ungulates hated cheatgrass and searched hard for what little bunchgrass they could find, killing it back and making the proportion of cheatgrass to bunchgrass greater each grazing season. As Aldo Leopold wrote in *Sand Country Almanac,* "one simply woke up one fine spring to find the range dominated by a new weed."[3] With striking speed, cheatgrass took over the inland grasslands, as the native bunchgrass communities collapsed under the impacts of grazing.

Forest Service Policies

The wretched condition of the range was largely responsible for the establishment of the forest reserves in 1897. But even though concern about overgrazing was widespread, stocking levels rapidly increased after the reserves were created (Table 1). Throughout the West, half again as many animals grazed the forest ranges a decade after the Forest Service got control of the forests.[4] Although the Forest Service came intending to save the grazing resources, they ended up making the situation worse.

Depending on the perspective of the viewer, high levels of grazing could mean either that the range was overstocked or that it was in such good condition that it was doing just fine. Alternately, reductions in grazing numbers under the Forest Service could mean either that the Forest service was correcting the situation or that it was doing such a poor job managing the resource that the range could support fewer and fewer animals. For example, in 1914, the

Table 1. Changes in livestock numbers on the
Malheur National Forest, 1906 to 1921

Year	Cattle and horses	Sheep	Total "cow equivalents" (5 sheep = 1 cow)
1906	17,584	154,980	48,580
1911	23,389	143,268	52,043
1916	30,514	150,029	60,520
1921	38,561	124,975	63,556

Source: Iler letter (1940)

Forest Service saw the increase in stocking numbers under its management as proof that carrying capacity was increasing, not as proof of overgrazing.[5] The data that many observers now interpret as evidence in support of the hypothesis that the range was getting worse were then often interpreted as evidence of the alternate hypothesis, that the range was improving. According to many contemporary observers both inside and outside the Forest Service, if cattle were not starving to death, the more cattle you put out there, the better the grass must be.

In 1909, the *Annual Report* stated that the six goals of national Forest Service grazing regulations were to prevent injury to stands of timber, protect watersheds, "accomplish a complete utilization of the forage crop," prevent range monopoly, avoid unfair competition in the use of the range, and "accomplish a more equitable distribution of grazing privileges."[6] Preventing or reversing overgrazing was notably absent in this list of goals. "Complete utilization" took its place, an emphasis that contributed to most of the overgrazing problems that soon developed.

Unregulated grazing before the Forest Service era had depleted the forage because no one person or family had control over the health of the resources that they used. Ranchers could not survive without recourse to the public range, since the land disposal sys-

tem guaranteed that no one could claim title to the acreage necessary for supporting a family. Yet ranchers were unable to conserve
forage on the public lands they used, because there was no way to
ensure future access to that forage; moreover, any grass a rancher
did not use would be used by someone else. In the Basque country
of Spain, where many of the herders originated, grazing coopera-
tives had moderated the intensity of livestock use. The only attempts at regulating grazing in the American West, however, were
violent and ineffective attacks on transient sheepherders. What
was needed was some way of making sure that the people who
used the resource would have a stake in its future health. John
Minto, a political opponent of John Muir's and a prominent
rancher who had strongly advocated grazing on public lands, argued for adopting the Australian leasing system. In Australia, the
government leased a given acreage to a family for at least twenty
years, and they—not the government—decided how many animals to run on the land. The American government was reluctant
to adopt this system, because ranchers had never shown that they
could regulate their own stocking numbers. Those who had a financial interest in stocking levels should not be the ones to regulate those levels, the government decided. Stocking decisions
should rest purely on ecological grounds, and Forest Service scientists felt that they were the ones best qualified to make impartial
judgments based solely on ecological health.[7]

At the heart of Forest Service grazing management was a permit
system which established a legal means by which the government—rather than the individuals using the land—would monitor
and regulate grazing pressures. To prevent injury while also ensuring full economic use, the Forest Service relied on the concept of
carrying capacity, which Forest Service scientists defined as the
largest number of animals that the range's grasses could support
and still grow back the next year. Once range scientists determined
carrying capacities, the Forest Service would distribute permits that
set a minimum and maximum limit on the number of head a permit holder could graze on the allotment. Yet even though the Forest Service decided stocking levels, long-term permits meant that
ranches could have faith that they would stay on the land. Ideally,

this would motivate ranchers to improve the condition of their allotment because they had a financial stake in its health: the better the land looked, the more animals the government would let them graze.[8]

Despite their apparent attractiveness, permits proved to have a surprising problem. While private ranchers may well have had financial pressures making it difficult to pay attention to the signs of overgrazing, Forest Service employees faced pressures nearly as strong. It was no easier for them to judge the health of the land, because the Forest Service defined ecological health within economic terms. As part of a growing bureaucracy, managers' ability to respond to the information they got from the land was very limited.

The first major decision the Forest Service faced was choosing who would get permits. There were at least three possible ways the Forest Service could have distributed permits: supervisors might have chosen permittees, the government might have sold permits to the highest bidder, or local stockmen's associations might have been given the power to decide. The Forest Service chose the third option, in hopes of appeasing local opinion and increasing stability. Committees of local stockmen worked out the distribution of the grazing privileges on a priority basis in their respective districts. Permits were granted first to those who owned land adjacent to the forest; next came those who owned land locally but not along the borders of the forest; and last were the out-of-state owners or transient herders. "Commensurate property ownership" was a condition for receiving grazing privileges—meaning that a permit holder had to own enough land to support stock during the winter, when forest lands were closed. Cattle had priority over sheep, local landowners over transients, and small operators over large operators.

Members of local stockmen's associations met among themselves and presented recommendations to the forest supervisor that outlined allotment boundaries and the ownership of grazing permits. Ranchers' primary loyalties were to their local livestock associations, not to national livestock associations; this relationship ensured a certain measure of loyalty to the Forest Service, but also meant that forest supervisors were under intense personal pressure to meet stockmen's desires. As one Forest Service grazing report stated, "disgruntled grazers at first appealed to their congressmen, to the disgust of the regional staff,"[9] but soon most disputes were resolved locally. But this did little for the health of the range. In theory, a forest supervisor could force reductions in stock numbers, but in practice that was difficult. As a district ranger wrote in his 1958 Malheur range management plan, "the industry is still very dependent on forest range for summer grazing use to round out their yearlong operation. Such reductions in grazing use as have been made over the years were, in most cases, vigorously protested. A grazing preference is a very real economic asset to the ranch owner and the value of that preference has, if anything, increased over the years."[10] Supervisors found it easier to make concessions that brought peace to the community, rather than cause hard feelings for the sake of a few forage plants.

The Forest Service's goal of breaking up large stock monopolies and bringing about a fairer distribution of grazing privileges struck many ranchers as verging on socialism, and led the Forest Service into a series of confusing and often contradictory policies. The Forest Service seemed to want to favor both large and small owners. Large owners were more efficient, had better breeding stock, and could afford fences, salting, and stock tanks, thus potentially reducing damage to the range. Small owners, however, were more in tune with the antimonopoly social policy that the Forest Service was trying to enforce. During some years, managers in the Blues tried to help small operators by redistributing grazing privileges. Simultaneously, however, managers were trying to bring about more economically efficient operations. This amounted to encouraging small operators to go out of business while also supposedly helping them.

The Forest Service's antimonopolistic intentions inadvertently laid the foundation for overgrazing. Efforts to encourage small operators made it nearly impossible for the Forest Service to reduce stock numbers, because whenever there was a reduction on a large owner's permit, those stock allowances were immediately transferred to small homesteaders. When the Forest Service distributed extra allotments to new local homesteaders, it was supposed to reduce the number of stock that large owners could graze. But large allotment holders usually kept their stock numbers, often by appealing to their senators in Washington, D.C., who then pressured the forest supervisor not to decrease stock numbers.

Political pressures not to decrease livestock numbers allowed on permits could become extremely intense, and each Forest Service official did his best to shift the responsibility for vexing ranchers to someone else. In 1906, Senator Henry Cabot Lodge wrote to the Secretary of the Interior to complain about proposed grazing reductions, and not surprisingly, the reductions did not go through as planned.[11] The controversy started when E. H. Libby, president of the Lewiston-Clarkston Irrigation Company, asked the Forest Service to remove sheep from the watershed to protect his irrigation investments. The Clarkston Chamber of Commerce got up a petition in favor of sheep removals. But then Senator Lodge wrote to his friend James Wilson, the Secretary of the Interior, protesting the planned sheep reductions. Unfortunately, Senator Lodge's letter is missing, so it is not clear whether he was protesting the exclusions of his own sheep or the sheep belonging to a constituent.

The Secretary of the Interior passed the matter to L. Hall, the acting head forester in the Washington D.C. office. Hall wrote the Forest Supervisor a letter that was a masterpiece of careful pressure. "Your attention is called . . . to the enclosed copy of my letter to Senator Lodge," he began. "Please look into the matter carefully and make such definite recommendations as may be warranted by all the facts in the case as you understand them, giving all interests fair consideration." The supervisor passed the matter to the lowest man on the totem pole, Ranger John M. Schmitz. Schmitz was exasperated by the controversy, and replied: "your petitioner, the Lewiston Clarkston Company, has handed me an application for grazing 140 head of cattle. . . . They seem to lose sight of the damage done by [their own] cattle while protesting against sheep grazing."[12] Schmitz was quite correct in noticing that self-interest, rather than concern for the health of the watershed, motivated each party. Likewise, each person could accuse the other group of causing ecological damage while ignoring their own role in the matter. Such accusations were tools people used to justify their own overgrazing damages. In the end, Schmitz bowed to the pressure placed on him and allowed Senator Lodge's favored sheep to remain.

The problem was not just that supervisors were under political pressure to keep stock numbers high. A deeper issue was that Forest Service officials had trouble recognizing the signs of overgrazing, and not solely because of a lack of information. During the years just before the Forest Service was established, numerous government scientists had criticized overgrazing in the Blues. But a decade later, government officials were claiming that things were just fine, that in fact the land could support twice the former numbers of stock. The grass had certainly not recovered in the interim; something else had changed instead.

Why could Forest Service officials not see the overgrazing that was so obvious to earlier and later researchers? There were three major reasons. First, rangers and supervisors were not trained to know the signs of plant succession or overgrazing, and often they thought if any grass was left at all, things were fine. They had no way to compare what was present to what a healthy range might look like. In 1907 and 1908, summers had been very wet in the region; thus the recommended carrying capacities were set at high levels. Some researchers did continue to say that grazing levels were too high, but they were ignored by their supervisors.[13] Forest supervisors learned to use science as a justification for delaying, rather than enforcing, reductions. The easiest way to avoid the political fallout of cutting a wealthy stockholder's allotment was simply to call for more research.

At the root of overgrazing, however, was the ideal of *full utilization,* an ideal that underlay the scientific concept of carrying capacity. Carrying capacity was the Forest Service's legal instrument for enforcing reductions, since the law stated that stocking levels could not exceed the carrying capacity of the forest. The Forest Service had once hoped that science would remove it from political pressures. But instead science turned out to be shaped—at least in part—by politics, and definitions of carrying capacity were biased toward the fullest possible use. As the 1958 Range Management Plan for the Long Creek Ranger District expressed it, scientists in

1934 performed a grazing reconnaissance—a study of the range's ecological health. "The resistance to reductions in stocking," the report explained, "is perhaps best evidenced by the fact that the range management plan which resulted from this survey used a forage acre requirement . . . derived by dividing the survey cow-months capacity by the preference obligations then current. Hence no reductions resulted as a consequence of the survey."[14] In other words, the Forest Service was supposed to use the survey data to calculate the carrying capacity, and then use the carrying capacity to support its stocking reductions. But how did it determine carrying capacity? By dividing the current number of cattle by the area: a method ensuring that the current state of affairs would continue, but now with "scientific justification."

One could argue that this was not science but carelessness. Yet the scientific concept of carrying capacity itself grew out of culturally shaped ideals of efficient and full use. Estimates of carrying capacities had begun in 1908, when the Forest Service researcher Alfred Potter wrote instructions to all range officers, detailing exactly how they ought to determine the number of animals an acre of land could support. Potter stressed that estimates must grow out of a close knowledge of local conditions, not out of idealized site potentials. To calculate carrying capacity for a specific place, a forester needed to know a daunting list of specifics: any water sources on the site that were accessible to animals, soil types and their susceptibilities to erosion, forage values of the plants, and local climate variations. Close attention to the land would, Potter hoped, prevent overuse. But he was naive in his faith that foresters would base their estimates of carrying capacities on what they found on the land. Trends in carrying capacity estimates closely followed changing economic pressures, rather than ecological changes. During World War I, when foresters were under pressure to increase livestock numbers for the war effort, carrying capacity estimates for both cattle and sheep swung sharply upward. In the late 1920s, when overproduction decreased markets available for livestock, carrying capacity estimates dropped as well. If livestock numbers alone had changed with market conditions, it would have been unsurprising. But when scientific calculations of the land's ability to support herbivores reflected market conditions as well, scientists' claims to impartiality were clearly unfounded.[15]

The intention of the grazing program was that researchers would continually monitor the effects of grazing on plant communities, and then use those data to adjust the numbers of animals grazing on the land. But how would researchers know the signs of overgrazing on a plant community? The new sciences of community ecology and succession theory seemed to offer the answer. Arthur Sampson, one of Frederic Clements's students, came to the Blues in 1908 to begin the first attempt in the West to apply climax and succession theories to range management. Since grazing was disturbance, and different levels of disturbance returned communities to different successional stages, managers hoped that they could use grazing as a tool to hasten or slow succession. Moderate overgrazing would theoretically force a plant community to revert to the early weed stage of succession, while the erosion that resulted from intense overgrazing might take the community back to the pioneer stage of establishment. On the other hand, an intermediate level of grazing might maintain the community not at climax but at a stable mid-seral stage. Without grazing, the grasslands would succeed to forest; with excessive grazing, plant communities would continually be reset at the first stages of succession and never have a chance to develop complexity.[16] Range ecologists could see a role for repeated disturbance in the evolution of complex plant communities, while foresters tended to think disturbance was always destructive.

Frederic Clements, who had developed the climax theory of succession, pioneered a method of studying plant associations that allowed range researchers to examine changes over time in one specific place—to study dynamic ecology, rather than static associations of plants. Instead of just looking at the land and classifying it as being in good or bad condition, they could use a snapshot in time to give them insight into both the history of change and the direction change was taking the community. A plot was fenced in to protect the grasses and shrubs from grazing, and then researchers could compare changes in plant communities between grazed and ungrazed plots. This technique allowed scientists to examine experimentally the effects disturbances had on the direction and pace of succession. Successional theory transformed range ecology, since it offered researchers a way of thinking about history.

Because grasses grew far more quickly than trees, both damage and recovery in a grassland community happened on time scales that range ecologists could monitor. Arthur Sampson could observe cycles of community breakdown and recovery that happened over a period of years, not centuries. Since foresters rarely lived long enough to watch changes in tree communities, it was hard for them to balance their theories about forest change with evidence of change. Likewise, it was hard for foresters to trace the indirect effects of their actions, because it could take decades for those effects to manifest themselves in visible or measurable ways. Each year, a few more young firs survived in the understories of mixed-conifer forests, but the changes happened so gradually that although some people noticed them, identifying the causes was far more difficult. Range scientists, on the other hand, were continually confronted with conditions that tested their theories. Graze too many sheep on a meadow one year, and next year certain grasses did not return. Graze far too many sheep on that meadow, and three days later all you had was mud. Some changes in grassland communities, of course, could be slow and subtle. But those communities changed on scales that most people could intuitively comprehend. Twenty successive foresters' careers would pass before a single generation of ponderosa pine started from seed, matured, and died—but a single range scientist could watch twenty generations of grasses develop. Not surprisingly, perhaps, forestry concerned itself with ideals and site potentials, while range ecology focused its attention on the ground.

In 1908, one of Sampson's colleagues in the Blues, Jim Jardine, began range reconnaissances, intending to develop a quick visual method for rating the successional stage of the range. These visual methods could be very simple: for example, in certain meadows above 6,000 feet in northeastern Washington, yellow flowers tended to bloom on early-seral plants that came in after excessive grazing. If a meadow was yellow in the spring, animal numbers needed to decrease. The virtue of such methods was that anyone could learn to monitor the range; a degree in botany was not a necessity. Other studies quickly got under way in the Blues, and within two years it was the site for the most intense range research in the West.[17] In 1907, a sheep range study started at Billy Meadows on the Wallowa National Forest. Experiments with artificial reseeding of overgrazed areas began on the Wallowa Whitman Forest in 1909. These attempts failed, and a year later, researchers were arguing that range reseeding was best done not by artificial seeding but by natural methods—grazing livestock in such a way that ensured plants would be able to set seed before a sheep or cow ate them back. In 1910, Sampson argued that three critical methods of stock handling—bedding out, deferred grazing, and rotation grazing—would reverse overgrazing damage, and do a far better job than people could ever do of encouraging perennial grasses.[18]

When a sheepherder practiced bedding out, instead of returning with his flock to the same camp each night, he and his sheep slept wherever they found themselves. This may have sounded trivial, but it kept sheep moving each day, thus reducing their pressure on any one place and giving grazed areas time to grow back. Returning to the same camps each night had proved disastrous, since that focused most feeding and erosion on one locality. In addition, predator damage was much greater when herders used a camp repeatedly, because coyotes and wolves both preferred to scout out a band of sheep for a night or two before attacking it.[19]

Deferred grazing delayed the entry of stock onto meadows until after the preferred grass species had matured and developed their seeds. If an animal ate back bunchgrasses early in the season, those grasses would never have a chance to set seed, and after just a few years of this, the adult plants would die without ever having reproduced themselves. But if livestock came onto a meadow after plants had set seed, ideally they would trample the seeds into the ground and fertilize them a bit—thereby increasing germination of next year's grasses while eating back this year's crop. Instead of killing desirable grasses, livestock disturbance would spread the seed and eliminate the need for artificial seeding. But while favoring germination of new plants, deferred grazing would not much help the parent plants.

Rotation grazing was Sampson's real brainchild, one that had a revolutionary potential for it challenged the ethic of full use. In rotation grazing, ranchers would divide the range into several equal sections, and each year allow one section to go entirely ungrazed. This would give mature bunchgrasses a chance to recover from disturbances affecting their root systems, so that they would return much more vigorously the following year. Since bunchgrasses were perennials, rotation grazing helped increase not only germination of new plants but also the longevity and vigor of adult plants.[20]

Waste and Full Utilization

Given the intensity of grasslands research in the Blues, why were stocking numbers doubling at the same time researchers were quantifying the effects of overgrazing? Part of the problem was the ideal of full utilization. Supervisors and ranchers, as well as many researchers, felt that all forage plants should receive full and equal use. Therefore, if some patches of forage remained at the end of a season, clearly not enough animals were using the plot. But animals preferred certain plants and would overgraze them before turning to less palatable plants, an observation that eluded managers for decades. As a range specialist on the Umatilla National Forest, John Clouston, argued in his memoirs, "not only this region but the whole Forest Service, was permeated with misconceptions of the degree of use under which forage plants could survive." In 1907 many thought that livestock could eat 100 percent of the above-ground vegetation without harming the plants, because the roots were left behind to provide the next year's crop. By 1931, researchers acknowledged that 100 percent use harmed watersheds and soil fertility, so they figured that livestock could safely eat 75 to 90 percent of the herbaceous vegetation each year. As Clouston wrote: "Witness a quotation from the National Forest Manual of 1931. . . . 'The maintenance of soil fertility and watershed protection are also important considerations. For this purpose . . . not less than from 10 to 25 percent of the herbaceous vegetation should be left on the ground at the close of each grazing season.'" By 1957, when Clouston was writing, people believed that only 50 to 60 percent of herbaceous perennials could safely be removed each year; by 1990, this figure had dropped again.[21]

In 1907, people thought that any herbaceous vegetation not eaten was wasted. As in forestry, there was no sense that waste might have indirect effects people did not know how to measure. "Is it any wonder that there was failure to recognize what was happening?" Clouston wrote. "Is it any wonder that needed reductions were not made? Could it be expected that untrained people would see that stocking was too heavy or would argue successfully against the pressure of permittees who were even more blind? A stock saying of the time was, 'The opens and flats are grazed pretty short but the stock haven't used the timber feed yet.'" John Clouston argued, quite charitably, that it was scientific ignorance and not political pressure or greed that led to overestimates of carrying capacity. But science and economics cannot so easily be separated, as Clouston himself acknowledged in his recollections. Every supervisor was under intense pressure to meet the output estimates, Clouston wrote: "Another factor working against good management was the annual authorization letter sent to each supervisor. This letter authorized the grazing of a definite number of cattle units and sheep units on each forest. . . . Most supervisors took this as a requirement that the full number be grazed and many livestock associations and individuals knowing about it insisted that the authorization be filled." Basically, people hated to see good grass go uneaten. Everything ought to be used or else it was lost forever, and this reasoning made it hard for rangers and supervisors to believe what their researchers told them, and it made it hard for researchers as well to see the evidence of overgrazing.

A look at several range reconnaissances reveals how ideals of use and waste affected management. Scientists, rather than rangers or supervisors, wrote the range reconnaissances. These were men whose careers centered on determining carrying capacities and preventing grazing damage—the men who would have been most attentive to signs of overgrazing. In 1917, researcher F. Horton wrote a reconnaissance for the Camas and Hideaway Cattle and Horse Ranges on the Umatilla National Forest. Horton noted that overgrazing had led to the replacement of native perennials by weeds. He wrote of one pinegrass forage type: "it is believed that this type once supported a fairly good stand of grasses but continued abuse before the creation of the National Forest has so disturbed the economic [ecological?] balance that at present it is difficult to determine whether these south slopes and open ridge tops should be classes [*sic*] as grass or weed areas."[22] But after ten pages devoted to a detailed description of overgrazing on the allotments, Horton concluded with a curious about-face, writing that "it is thought that in a few years it will certainly be possible to increase the number of stock now allowed. There is apparently no great amount of forage unused and no great area over used hence it is said that if the whole is equally utilized there need be no fear of over grazing." Even though he had just detailed extensive evidence of overgrazing damage, Horton reassured his supervisor that there was no need for stock reductions; on the contrary, stock numbers might even increase. This might sound very odd, but what lay at its heart was an assumption about use and waste. If managers could only get "the whole equally utilized," Horton argued, then both overgrazing and waste might vanish.

A year later, Horton wrote another report for this same range. By 1918, war fervor was at its height. Supervisors were under intense pressure to increase their livestock production, and researchers felt these pressures as well. Horton made his point even more clearly: waste was bad, full use was ideal. The loss he now worried about was not loss due to ecological damage, but loss due to less than 100 percent utilization of grasses. "Pine grass furnishes the main part of the forage from a quantitative standpoint," he wrote, "but as a rule this grass is partly lost to the stock as they will not eat it completely after the first few weeks in the spring, and during this time they prefer to feed on the open south slopes. It is considered that this grass can never be used to its fullest extent, i.e. at its economic maturity, so long as it is used in connection with open grassland type."[23] Horton went on to give more evidence of grazing damage, suggesting the standard remedies for overgrazing: shorten the grazing season and draw the cattle away from overused areas with salt and water troughs. But then he admitted that these reme-

dies—the same ones recommended by Sampson ten years earlier—
would be impossible to enforce. For example, the season for cattle
was May 1 to October 31. Horton stated that "if the primary forage
of the range is to be brought back" managers needed to shorten
this season and postpone letting cattle on the meadows until the
grasses had put on more new growth. But then he admitted that
economic pressures would make this unlikely. Cattlemen would
protest because they would have to pay for more hay. A shortened
season would also mean less than full utilization and would "result
in the loss of some of the pine grass range."

Horton, like other authors of range reconnaissances, hoped to
learn to identify the amount of disturbance that would produce a
plant community useful for society. In that sense, like all scientists,
he was motivated—however indirectly—by cultural ideals. The
government paid Horton and his colleagues to determine changes
in community structure, then recommend patterns of herbivore
use that would keep the plant communities within a given range
of ecological health. But because they believed full use was a necessity, it was difficult for range scientists to read ecological signs indicating that full use was causing deleterious changes in community
structure. This emerged as a genuine confusion in their reports.
The first ten pages of each report were filled with carefully detailed
evidence of overgrazing: columns of precise numbers showing advanced erosion, and statistics noting the replacement of desirable
perennials with cheatgrass and weeds. But then the reports retreated from the implications of their data, refusing to recommend
stocking reductions. Horton, for example, ended his 1918 report
by stating that "the range is carrying its full limit and only by the
most careful management can be expected to maintain even its
present stocking of forage plants." A note in the margin indicated
that the supervisor approved the reconnaissance and simultaneously increased stocking levels.

Even when researchers were articulate and forceful about damage to certain plants, supervisors often found economic reasons to
ignore scientists' recommendations. The researchers Jim Jardine
and Arthur Sampson had shown in 1910 that overgrazing was causing less valuable weed species to replace the perennial bunch-

grasses, and they argued forcefully that deferred and rotation grazing were necessary to prevent these successional changes. Supervisors, however, dragged their feet for decades on both changes, since deferred and rotation grazing meant reductions in use. As Mr. Aldous, a grazing examiner, stated in his 1915 report on grazing conditions in the Umatilla National Forest, grazing was killing off the best forage species and worse species were taking their place.[24] Deferred and rotation grazing would help, Aldous conceded. But managers were unlikely to institute any changes that would offend users. Will Barnes, the Acting Assistant Forester in Portland, responded to Aldous's recommendations, writing that "it may be not be possible to apply an intensive system of deferred or rotation grazing, but it is believed that certain portions of every allotment can be protected each year until after seed maturity without making any great changes in the present method of grazing the allotment, or *without affecting the present carrying capacity to any appreciable extent*" (emphasis added).[25] Note that Barnes had changed the definition of carrying capacity: it had formerly meant the number of animals that a plant community could support without damage; now it meant the number of animals the supervisor gave permits for that year.

Barnes made it clear why he could not apply deferred or rotation grazing, or reduce stock numbers: "It is evident that the demand for grazing privileges on the Umatilla is so great that every effort should be made to reduce this overgrazed condition without either reducing or excluding stock unless it finally appears to be the only possible means of bringing about a better condition on these overgrazed areas." Finally, it was easiest just to use science as an excuse to avoid offending the users. Aldous, the examiner, concluded by stating: "we need to experiment with deferred and rotation grazing and open herding." Everyone knew these measures would be effective, but they also knew that stockmen would protest, so it was simpler just to recommend more studies.

Effects and Place

One might conclude that the major influences on grazing decisions were local—as if individual supervisors were simply trying to help their friends and neighbors. But much more than this was going on. Influences contributing to overgrazing damage formed a complex, interconnected network: within the small area, within the Blue Mountains, within the Pacific Northwest Region of the Forest Service, within the Forest Service as a whole, and within national livestock associations and national markets. Cows and sheep first had very local effects—they ate a blade of grass, which altered the plant, which altered the community on that acre. But grazing effects also rippled across a watershed, and eventually across the region (Figure 3).

The most obvious external influence on grazing levels was the effect World War I had on grazing numbers. During the war, the Forest Service pressured supervisors to increase stocking levels for the war effort.[26] The historian William Rowley argued that the external war fever did not force the Forest Service into overgrazing, but the Forest Service interpreted wartime policies to justify an already existing belief that heavy grazing was good for the range. As Table 1 above shows, livestock numbers had begun to increase well before the war began. After the war, instead of reducing stocking levels to the already highly inflated prewar levels, the Forest Service opted for more research, allowing stocking levels to stay high in the meantime. Science became a supervisor's excuse for delaying reductions, not a means of enforcing reductions.[27] When supervisors did acknowledge overgrazing, they often expected scientific research to overcome problems that only reductions in stocking levels could solve.

Researchers, however, were beginning to be more vocal about overgrazing, and many users as well as researchers were noting that cattle and sheep coming off the forests were in poor condition. Stockmen had long used the state of their animals as an index of the range condition. This measure of range condition led to overuse, as cattle and sheep could still find nutrients and forage long after they had exhausted the ability of bunchgrass to recover from disturbance. The decline in sheep and cattle weights toward the end of the war meant that ranges were extremely stressed. Even when stockmen began complaining that their cattle gained little weight on government land, supervisors and regional foresters still did not insist on reductions.

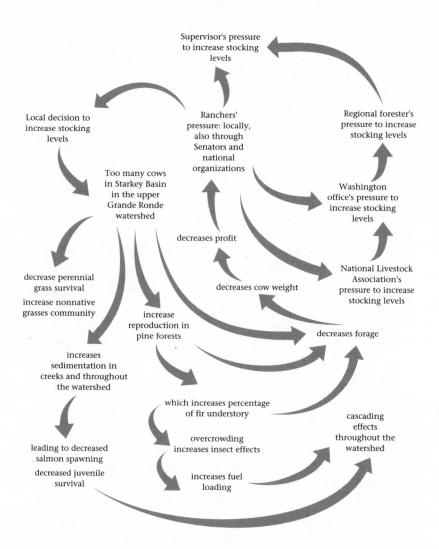

Figure 3. Grazing's web of interconnected effects, showing that grazing has both local and distant effects, and pressures to increase grazing come from local ranchers as well as national organizations. As the number of cows increases on an allotment, the forage declines and the animal weights decline, decreasing per-animal profits. To make the same profit, ranchers need to increase the stocking levels further, which decreases per-animal profit more, creating a cycle which can lead to rapid overstocking and rapid range deterioration.

An agricultural depression set in after the war, and national livestock associations demanded that the Forest Service ease the economic strain on stockmen. Stockmen's associations wanted two
major concessions from the Forest Service: fee decreases and, most
important, ten-year permits that guaranteed stocking levels would
stay constant. Forest Service employees resisted this, for inflexible
livestock allowances would remove the power of managers to use
carrying capacities as a tool for restoring the range.

The U.S. Supreme Court in 1911 had ruled that the Forest Service could charge fees to cover the administrative costs of permits
and also to regulate overgrazing. There was no clear legal context,
however, for setting fees at market value. And it was never clear
exactly how the Forest Service could use fees to regulate grazing
numbers. The Forest Service clearly hoped that by raising prices, it
could make overgrazing too costly, and thus avoid the controversy
of directly cutting stock or permit numbers. But disputes grew
around the legal status of permits. Did the numbers of stock allowed on a permit assume a legal obligation, for which the Forest
Service or ranger was accountable regardless of the land's condition? Did a permit assume financial value? The Forest Service was
reluctant to recognize the financial value of permits, because then
permit holders could claim permanent right over use of the range.
In effect, the Forest Service would be giving away public property.
But banks and courts did give financial value to permits: ranches
with Forest Service permits were judged to have up to three times
the value of comparable ranches without grazing permits.[28]

In 1916, the Forest Service unsuccessfully tried to raise fees to
market value. Three years later, Congress tried to push through a
300 percent fee increase, but by this time the Forest Service had
reversed its position on fee increases, in part because it did not
want to appear to be harming users in the glum postwar financial
climate. By the 1920s the Forest Service tried to revive fees based
on market value. This time, however, Congress objected. At least
Senator Robert Stanfield—a rancher from the Blue Mountains who
clearly had personal financial interests at stake—strenuously objected. Stanfield led a major challenge to the Forest Service authority, and eventually introduced bills that gave private property

rights to users of public ranges. To hold onto its rights to administer rangelands, the Forest Service made deep concessions in 1926. Ten-year permits became legal contracts that the Forest Service could revoke only in the case of permittee violations. Stock numbers on permits could not be reduced even with evidence of severe overgrazing. Further redistribution of grazing privileges ended, and local grazing boards gained an increased role in administration.[29] The effect was to make reductions far more difficult for the Forest Service to enforce, even though researchers were becoming increasingly vocal about continued overgrazing.

Cattle and sheep numbers were more than a local matter. The Forest Service in effect allowed damage to the range in order to keep its control over the range. Scientists saw evidence of overgrazing but were slow to translate this into clear calls for reductions, and supervisors were increasingly adept at using science as a way of delaying reductions.

The 1930s—Grazing Shifts Focus

Not until the Great Depression did livestock numbers substantially decline, and with the reductions came significant shifts in focus. Throughout the grazing reports, plans, letters, and reconnaissances, a new emphasis on ecology appeared. Even supervisors became attentive to signs of ecological damage, and increasingly began recognizing the history of overgrazing on their forests. Most important, by the late 1930s supervisors as well as scientists began to admit that full use was not possible or even desirable. What allowed the Forest Service to finally recognize the overgrazing and overharvesting that had been accumulating all along? The short answer, of course, is the Depression and the severe drought of the 1930s: nobody could close their eyes, not at least during the 1930s, to the evidence that diminishing resources had led to human catastrophe. But the long answer is more complex, since a serious depression and decline in markets after World War I had produced the opposite response.

Decades of intensifying stress from poor grazing, logging, and farming practices had made the dry western lands extremely vulnerable. When drought hit in the 1930s, the results were devastating. But in the Blues, drought was not the only culprit. Total annual precipitation during the 1930s remained close to the 80-year average (14.99 inches a year, versus the 80-year average of 15.2 inches). This was a sharp decline, however, from the previous decade; the years between 1911 and 1922 had been extraordinarily wet, with an average annual precipitation of 19.5 inches. Some of the managers' difficulties in recognizing overgrazing may have stemmed from the abundant rainfall of the 1920s, since annual grass growth appeared fairly luxuriant, and most supervisors knew little about long-term effects. Although annual precipitation in the Blues during the 1930s was not unusually low, the summers were extremely dry. July and August averaged only 0.16 and 0.25 inch of rainfall each month over the decade, compared to the 80-year average of 0.45 inch. This meant that during the 1930s, summers experienced less than a third of the normal rains.[30]

Ranchers claimed that the poor range condition was just a temporary effect of drought, and not the effect of overgrazing. This made the condition of the range an Act of God, not the ranchers' fault or responsibility.[31] But, as Malheur National Forest Supervisor James Iler responded in 1940, drought had not caused the range's poor condition. During the 1930s, although summer rains had practically vanished, the June rains were nearly twice the average: 2.75 inches rather than 1.5 inches. Since the June rains determined the annual forage crop, increased rainfall would not solve ranchers' problems, as the supervisor had pointed out to a rancher arguing against stock reductions. The Forest Service should increase stocking numbers, ranchers argued, because summer drought rather than overgrazing had caused declines in grasses. But the supervisor argued that overgrazing, not summer drought, was responsible for the poor forage. Because June rains determined forage abundance, and they had been double their normal levels, forage would only become more scarce when climate patterns return to normal. The ranchers were basically arguing that after the rains returned to normal, forage levels would recover. The supervisor was arguing the opposite: grasses would decline even further in the absence of stocking reductions.

Social Policy and Redistributions

Even though in the 1930s supervisors began to recognize overgrazing effects and the need for livestock reductions, those reductions were slow and limited because the Forest Service was also trying to protect local communities. Managers were in a tricky position, since they feared that sharp reductions would lead stockmen to abuse their allotments. As Carl Ewing, the Supervisor of the Umatilla National Forest, wrote in 1938, people who were not certain they would still be on the range in the future were unlikely to treat the land well. "One of our greatest difficulties in securing [permittees'] thoughtful interest . . . in better range management practices," Ewing wrote, "is the fear they have felt . . . that distribution reductions would be applied, and that their tenure of use would be short-lived." If the Forest Service did enforce reductions, powerful ranchers would object, Evans added: "It is true that we have very few permittees who would be affected in any event by such reductions, but it is equally true that the few we do have also happen, in most instances, to be leaders of thought in our communities." Therefore, reductions should not "be advocated any more than is absolutely necessary," and managers should enforce them "quietly and on an individual basis."[32]

The Forest Service felt it had to give the appearance of working to preserve local communities. But at the same time, it wanted more efficient operators who could afford to treat the range better. In effect, the Forest Service attempted to force small operators out of business while appearing to protect them. As Ewing stated, along the Grande Ronde River near Troy, people were poor and cattle ranching was their only livelihood. The Forest Service needed to be more relaxed about grazing limits; otherwise Troy's economy might fail. The supervisor intended, however, to eliminate small operations: "Ultimately ranch property and range will need to gravitate into the hands of fewer owners and permittees. . . . This will be done slowly and without announcement of our objective, but even so will be detected and no doubt resisted by the present permittees on the Asotin range."

Ewing intended to help the land by consolidating holdings in the hands of a few wealthy owners. Surviving ranchers, Ewing hoped, would become economically efficient, so they could afford improvements that would ease pressure on the range. But the Forest Service's goals of protecting communities and protecting resources were often in conflict. A series of letters written in 1940 made these tensions clear. R. E. Brooke, the Grant County Agriculture Agent, wrote to Malheur National Forest Supervisor James Iler in March 1940, complaining of three things: stock numbers were too low, the Forest Service was driving small operators out of business, and Forest Service policies had damaged the range by increasing tree reproduction, which crowded out grasses.[33]

Supervisor Iler responded that "range depletion through overstocking, overgrazing, premature use, improper management, and physical factors" made stock reductions necessary, for abuse had reduced "carrying capacity far below normal." Iler's justification for this statement revealed an ecological focus that would have been unimaginable coming from a supervisor during the previous decades. "In many places," Iler argued, poor grazing "resulted in a material recession of plant life, the more stable, highly productive and palatable species being replaced by less desirable ones. The breaking of the turf on mountain meadows caused erosion, lowered the water table which turned moist mountain meadows into dry flats. The destruction of beaver further aided in drying up many small meadows." Iler had not abandoned economics, however, when he turned to ecology. "Our forage is similar to any other asset," he argued. "By overstocking (with cattle or sheep) we are merely depleting the value of our capital stock (the forage). . . . When we graze our pasture beyond its average production, we are merely depleting our range, the same as we would deplete our cash savings by continuously drawing a little more than the average interest." In response to the accusation that the Forest Service forced small operators to fail, Iler blamed market forces. Stockmen who could survive the postwar crashes, Iler argued, were those with private forage—who happened to be the larger operators. The fault was not the Forest Service's. But, as Ewing's letter revealed, at least on the Umatilla National Forest, supervisors were in fact quietly plotting to eliminate small operators. Market forces alone were not to blame.

Use and Ecology

By the 1930s, supervisors could finally see ecological damage. The damage had been apparent for three decades; what changed was the supervisors' perspectives. As the faith of managers in full utilization declined, ecological signs that had been invisible became obvious. In 1938, Carl Ewing, the Umatilla National Forest Supervisor, complained that "the open ridge tops, particularly in the north unit, are so completely denuded of both forage and soil. . . . The steep slopes in the north unit are at best difficult to graze, and many of them are so thinly covered with light soil that it is believed impossible to graze them intensively without excessive damage."[34] Ewing still focused on intensive use, but he did recognize a history of damage.

These local changes reflected national changes in perspective. Soil damage in particular became a focus for national attention. After the drought conditions of the mid-1930s, public concern for dwindling forage resources on western lands motivated the Western Cooperative Range Survey, a joint state and federal effort to reverse range deterioration. A Senate document of 1936 on the state of the western range, nicknamed the Green Book, aroused concern throughout the nation.[35] The Green Book, which Forest Service researchers largely wrote, opened with the accusation: "there is perhaps no darker chapter nor greater tragedy in the history of land occupancy and use in the U.S. than the story of the western range." The report then claimed that the range was still overstocked by 43 percent. Many stockmen agreed, but others scorned its conclusions, charging that they were a Forest Service ploy to secure more control over the rangelands.

With the concern about overgrazing came a shift in the ideal of full utilization. Charles De Moisy, a range administrator in the Intermountain Region, was in 1926 among the first to argue that 10 to 25 percent of annual production of palatable perennial species should remain at the end of the season. Supervisor Ewing, in his 1938 report on the Umatilla National Forest, saw full utilization as a danger rather than a goal: "At least during drought years such as we have recently experienced, it should be recognized and admitted that many of our allotments are being utilized to a degree dangerously approaching complete utilization." In addition, managers finally realized that a simple reduction in cattle number would not fix the range. As Ewing stated, even though he had decreased one allotment from 2,500 cattle to 500, that allotment was still a mess, because the cattle continued to overuse the best areas near water while ignoring the rest.

As emphasis shifted in the 1930s, Forest Service employees could see value in what they had previously scorned. For instance, managers began to think beaver might be useful, in an enormous change from 1920s attitudes. In 1922, planners had blamed damaged riparian areas on beaver, rather than on logging or grazing. As a Malheur Timber Sales plan noted, "the area is heavily grazed, but no appreciable damage has occurred except along the stream bottoms where unfavorable soil conditions due to an excess of moisture, often caused by beaver dams, . . . has kept out reproduction."[36] The Forest Service, in effect, had blamed excessive moisture for what cattle did to creeks: If the riparian zones had not been wet, they would not have been damaged. Since beaver dams kept riparian areas wet, beaver were the source of riparian damage, not cattle. By 1938, however, the situation had changed enough so that range examiners wanted to reintroduce beaver. The Bear Valley grazing survey reported that "observations during the past summer showed that beaver have been responsible for building up bottom lands and meadows by checking the water and thus permitting sedimentary deposits. Meadows have been flooded and irrigated and the quantity of forage during the dry summer months was thus increased for both game and livestock."[37]

Grazing and Forest Reproduction

In the 1930s, foresters also reassessed the role of grazing in forest ecology. In 1906, reproduction had been the ideal: the more young pines, the better. Foresters thought sheep were bad because they browsed on young pines and decreased reproduction. As Chapman wrote about the Wallowa Reserve in 1906: "In the past, much country has been overgrazed by sheep, and reproduction retarded. As soon, however, as the number of sheep is reduced to the proper capacity of the range, grazing should not materially interfere."[38] By 1915, foresters had noticed that in areas of heavy grazing, reproduction actually increased, since the sheep killed back the grass that competed with young seedlings, and heavy grazing exposed mineral soil, which aided germination. Since the focus was still on increasing reproduction, F. Horton, the range examiner, saw this as a justification for increased grazing.[39] But by 1940, timber managers had developed a sense that thickets of reproduction might be an ecological problem and, furthermore, that heavy grazing might contribute to the problem. As a timber report from the Malheur stated, "overgrazing caused soil disturbance and no doubt the thickets of reproduction are a direct result of overgrazing and soil disturbance."[40]

Timber managers could see the ecological damage poor grazing practices created, while grazing managers could see damage resulting from timber programs. It was much harder for both groups to see the damage their own programs created. For example, range managers complained in a 1938 report that timber managers were allowing loggers to operate in the spring, when the ground was wet. As a result, logging reduced carrying capacity, destroyed meadow and hillside turf, and worst of all, led to sheet erosion, which exposed bunchgrass roots and washed away litter and topsoil. Finally, logging had led to "excessive reproduction of timbered types, especially in lodgepole and ponderosa pine types."[41] Range managers found it easy to see the problems caused by heavy logging, since their livelihoods were not dependent on keeping sales high. Likewise, timber managers were quick to note ecological damage caused by grazing—which range managers had trouble perceiving.

Throughout the late 1930s and early 1940s, range scientists developed a new awareness of erosion, soil damage, stream damage, and overgrazing effects on forest ecology. The Forest Service had a rare opportunity to institute radical changes in the way that the western range was managed. Scientists were arguing that a new kind of management was necessary, and many lay people agreed. The Dust Bowl and prolonged droughts during the Depression were enough of a shock that lay people recognized that overuse of natural resources affected their own lives. But little of this awareness translated into significant reforms. Even after Forest Service supervisors began to recognize damage in the 1930s, changes were few and grudging. Supervisors had lost much of their power to enforce grazing reductions a decade earlier, when the Forest Service gave up its legal authority to reduce stock numbers on the basis of ecological damage. As the historian William Rowley argued, the Forest Service may have missed its chance in the 1930s. Because Congress and the Interior Department challenged its administrative power over the range, the Forest Service became defensive and narrow-minded. In large part to hold onto its administrative powers, the Forest Service became quite conciliatory to interest groups and local stock associations. By the end of the Depression, many workers within the Forest Service felt betrayed, for the ranges were still badly overused.[42]

Restoring the Range

A lack of scientific information was never the problem in correcting range damage. For the last eight decades, researchers and grazing reports have recommended exactly the same remedies for overgrazing: reduce animal numbers; reduce the amount of time the animals spend on the allotment; use deferred and rotation grazing; and control animal movements through salting, water troughs, and drift fences. Since 1907, the Forest Service has known that fencing creeks to keep out cattle would lead to riparian zone recovery, and that deferred and rotation grazing would reverse or at least slow the replacement of native perennials with annual grasses. But Forest Service employees have found themselves unable to keep cattle out of creeks and out of the high meadows until the grasses set seed.

Arthur Sampson showed in 1907 that overgrazing in the Blue

Mountains was causing less valuable weed species to replace the perennial bunchgrasses, but that deferred grazing, rotation grazing, and bedding out could reverse these changes. A year later, in 1908, several reports and letters between supervisors and inspectors on the Malheur National Forest show that supervisors understood but were not following Sampson's recommendations. Range inspectors urged supervisors to gently "encourage"—not force—compliance. Regulations stated that all sheepherders must bed out their sheep. Instead, however, herders held to the old ways of trailing back to camp each evening. As a letter from the inspector stated, "You are requested to encourage the sheepmen to camp with their sheep wherever night overtakes them, as much as possible."[43] Salting too was required, but as the inspector noted, it was neglected. In 1918, F. Horton's reconnaissance reports listed the same problems and the same solutions, and then stated that the supervisors should try to enforce them if possible—indicating that the Forest Service was not yet following Sampson's recommendations.[44]

Supervisors dragged their feet for decades on both deferred and rotation grazing, since both techniques would mean reductions in use. A 1915 Umatilla National Forest report stated that grazing was killing off the best forage species and worse species were taking their place. Deferred and rotation grazing would help, the report conceded. But the supervisor was extremely reluctant to institute any changes that might offend users. "It may not be possible to apply an intensive system of deferred or rotation grazing," the report stated. But even so, managers should protect "certain portions of every allotment . . . until after seed maturity" if they could do so "without making any great changes in the present method of grazing the allotment, or without affecting the present carrying capacity to any appreciable extent."[45] In other words, managers could try to protect the land, but only if they could do so without threatening current levels of livestock grazing.

A 1938 list of problems on the Malheur National Forest shows how thoroughly range examiners recognized the causes of grazing damage. Overstocking, poor sheepherding, localized overgrazing, cattle concentrating along streams and small meadows, premature grazing, late grazing, and bad logging—all were devastating the grasslands.[46] Two years later, Supervisor Iler listed the exact same problems, adding soil deterioration, the lowering of the water table in mountain meadows, the invasion of grassland by sagebrush, and insect and rodent infestations to his list.[47] What was so depressing was that Iler's suggested remedies for the problems besetting his forest were, in 1940, exactly the same ones Arthur Sampson had recommended in 1908 and which nearly every report had repeated each decade since. In 1938 the regional supervisors agreed that it was finally time to decrease stock numbers, institute deferred and rotation grazing (but only "where possible"), and thin excessive tree reproduction in mixed conifer stands.[48] More than half a century later, the 1991 Malheur National Forest supervisor stated the same solutions to overgrazing problems.

Managers recognized the problems and knew the solutions, but they found it very hard to implement these changes. In the 1938 Bear Valley progress report, one reason was offered: "A majority of all the meadows examined on the cattle ranges showed over-use. It appears that this condition could be corrected by fencing and deferred grazing. However, there are only a few meadows . . . that are of sufficient size to justify the expenditure."[49] Remedies would be expensive, and the meadows were small enough that it was difficult to feed enough stock to cover the costs. Rather than exclude high-meadow grazing on the grounds that it was an uneconomical use of natural resources, managers rather hopelessly acknowledged that deterioration would continue. On the Umatilla National Forest, the supervisor Carl Ewing made the same confession: his grasslands had deteriorated beyond recognition, but "deferred and rotation grazing, while highly desirable, appears to be a long way in the future."[50] Twenty years later, in 1958, the district ranger's report admitted that "through a long period of overuse" meadows had been "reduced to gullied weed patches." The report suggested the same remedies for the same ranges, in the same resigned tone that implied nothing would actually change.[51]

The irony of overgrazing was that denuded grasslands could revegetate fairly quickly when protected from livestock. As Sampson's studies showed, high mountain meadows that looked as if they would never grow a blade of grass again were well on their way to recovery after just three years of livestock exclusion. Recovery, however, was rarely complete. Especially at high elevations, the new communities tended to lack a full range of native bunchgrasses. After ninety years of protection, perennial grasses were still rare in the meadows Sampson had studied, because grazing had been so intense that no native plants remained to reseed the protected areas. But because the life cycle of grasses was so much shorter than that of trees—on the order of months, rather than centuries—grasslands were in many ways more resilient than forests. Fence a creek, and in just a few years the willows would begin to recover, annual grasses would become thick, and intermittent streams would retain their water for longer each year. People knew what they needed to do to restore the grasslands, but implementing these changes was never easy.

The Forest Service's grazing program, like its timber program, originally aimed for full and efficient use of natural resources. The ecological devastation of the Great Depression forced grazing scientists to reevaluate the assumptions that underlay their program. But even when range scientists told managers that the health of the grasslands was at stake, forest supervisors often refused to revise economically based grazing policies. Although range scientists eventually rejected the ideal of full utilization, they were unable to displace a framework which saw the land as a collection of competing resources, whose disposal another collection of competing users would always quarrel over.

Wildlife

As range scientists wrestled with the problems of overgrazing during the 1930s, their attention turned to competitors for scarce forage: wildlife. Seeing the forests as a set of commodities had meant that managers discounted anything they could not transform into an economic benefit. If a wild animal ate the grass that a cow might have eaten, surely that grass was wasted. On the other hand, if the wild animal was one that people liked to hunt—and paid good money to hunt—perhaps the tradeoff was less clear. Game protection in America began, in large part, as a reaction against the commercialization of wildlife. Yet the irony was that game management also externalized wildlife as an economic resource which humans should harvest. The definition of wildlife included only those game animals that hunters liked for their sport; animals that threatened hunters' bags fell into the category of vermin. If animals neither threatened nor served people, they simply vanished from the concern of Forest Service managers. Yet profit was not the only lens through which whites viewed wildlife. As America became increasingly industrialized, whites mourned the loss of wildlife with the nostalgia and regret that accompanies a fall from grace. Americans made strenuous efforts to preserve wildlife, but the act of preservation destroyed the wildness that people had hoped to capture.

"Wild nature" was, for most whites who came through the Blues, whatever they did not yet control: the land, the flora, the fauna, and the Indians. But the very presence of whites led to the loss of wild nature. In 1925, more than a century after whites first arrived, one Forest Service game report mourned the loss of this wildness, noting that the blue grouse population had dwindled "due to close grazing, settlement and cultivation . . . also the building of roads and trails which has *an attendncy to inhabit the country and take away the wild nature* that this class of game birds require" (emphasis added).[52] Wild nature, in this passage, meant the world without evidence of whites. Wild nature was what disappeared when whites started to work the land. Some whites saw this loss as all to the good; some saw it as a pity; nearly all saw it as irrevocable and inevitable.

Not long ago, the Blues were a paradise, people now saw. Salmon thronged the creeks, deer and elk frolicked in the meadows, and great flocks of wildfowl darkened the skies. Now little is left; roads and houses litter the wild country. One hundred and fifty years ago, whites had the same complaint: paradise had been lost, just before their time. Each successive group of whites in the Blues has usually imagined that before they showed up, the Blues were an untouched, abundant wilderness. A settler named Daniel Williams, for example, described the Wallowa Valley as a kind of heaven when he arrived in 1880: "The valley was the hunters' paradise. There were deer, elk and mountain sheep; wild fowl by the thousands and a lake full of fish. There were berries and roots, everything the Indians desired, summer or winter."[53] Williams wrote this passage from the nostalgic distance of fifty years; when the settlers first arrived in the Blues, their journals expressed far less sense of wild nature. There was a certain irony in Williams's memories of the Indians in the Wallowa Valley, because he was the man who hauled supplies for General Howard when he drove the Nez Percé out of the valley that had "everything the Indians desired." Williams recognized that his own actions were partly responsible for the distance he found himself from paradise in 1930. Much of what motivated the nostalgia in this memoir, and in similar records, was a sense of having made choices separating oneself from an imagined innocent past, a time with no responsibilities and no work, a place where everything lay at hand for the taking.

Nostalgia for a lost wild nature came almost immediately on the heels of settlement. Loren Powers, son of one of the first white settlers in the Wallowa Valley, detailed what the place had been like when whites first arrived: "Large herds of deer and elk were frequently seen crossing the valley, while bear were so numerous as to be a decided menace to the stock industry. Prairie chicken, grouse, pheasants, ducks and geese were also much in evidence. Whooping or sand hill cranes also stopped in large numbers to feed. . . . The streams also abounded with trout, salmon, and red fish. . . . One could stand on a bridge and see that schools of these fish would darken the whole stream."[54] Whites saw what they had lost as a kind of Eden, a paradise to be mourned. But the sense of loss came almost immediately, even before they had a chance to deplete resources. It was not the actual grass and timber that people mourned; it was giving up the vision of perfection.

When people tell the story of wildlife in the Blues, they usually tell it as a history of loss. Yet clearly not all animal populations have declined: cattle, for instance, are far more common than they were in 1830, and elk and deer are probably more numerous than they were at any time since Lewis and Clark's explorations. What people are feeling is a loss of wild nature itself, not just a few animals. In 1925, the author of a Umatilla game report stated: "It is my opinion that stock grazing is the main or one of the main causes of this decreasing [of salmon populations], altho man is partly responsible as the more the forest are opened up, more people visit the back woods which has an attendncy to catch, kill and destroy the wild nature."[55] Even though populations of the principal game species—deer and elk—had begun to recover, people were still unsatisfied. Wildness did not return with the returning game populations, and it was the loss of wildness that many people mourned.

Elk Reintroductions

Elk disappeared so quickly in the Blues that many people now argue that elk are entirely nonnative to the Blues. But other people, still alive, remember their parents telling about seeing elk. Roland Huff, for example, recounted in an interview with Jerry Gildemeister that "around 1876 Joseph Huff was a hunter for a railroad crew somewhere around La Grande; he shot elk and other game to keep the crew in meats. . . . By 1892 elk and deer were nearly extinct in the Blue mountains between La Grande and Pendleton."[56] Another resident of the Blues, Ned Foye, remembered that one friend of his, T. Geer, saw twenty-five to thirty elk in the late 1800s. Another friend, Lee Thompson, told Ned Foye "about killing the last elk in Wallowa County in the early 1900s."[57] In 1912, only a few years after the elk population reached its lowest ebb, wildlife managers reintroduced Montana elk. The first introductions were slow and halting, but six decades later the woods were filled with elk and elk hunters.[58]

On the surface, elk reintroductions seem like a story of recovery: nature restored to its former bounty. But after even just a few minutes listening to these stories, it becomes clear that things are not that simple. In the 1990s, there are numerous elk in the Blues, but they are scrawny things that come down to the lowlands in the winter like cattle and ravage the ranches. As one game manager stated in 1992, the number of large bulls has declined, and "the habitat for both deer and elk is rapidly deteriorating due to present forest management practices of heavy roading and logging, plus widespread clearcutting and broadcast burning."[59] Forest management practices have forced deer and elk to lower elevations, where they compete with domestic livestock for forage, and even feed on haystacks and gardens like tame cows, not wild creatures. And the relationship between elk and people—between the hunter and the hunted—is also not what people had expected. Local residents complain that elk hunters from the cities swarm through the woods, shooting each other instead of elk and driving their four-wheelers everywhere, destroying the nature they are supposedly there to appreciate. "There is now a new breed of people who have no respect," locals complained in interviews with the Oregon Department of Fish and Wildlife. "Many people shoot at anything that moves and shoot animals only to leave them lay."[60] Game management has left people who live in the Blues disappointed, even though the elk have returned. Wild nature is no longer so wild, and the relationship between humans and wildlife troubles many people.

The history of elk reintroductions illustrates the ironic ways that attempts to save wild nature often led to the accelerated destruction of the wildness that people sought to preserve. In 1913, a year after the first elk reintroductions in Billy Meadows, Oregon, the Wenaha Game Protective Association formed, with members paying $10 each to restore elk to the Washington side of the Blues. They arranged with Yellowstone National Park to supply them with spare elk, and on February 3, 1913, the park shipped forty yearling and two-year-old elk from Gardiner, Montana. Along the way, there was a heavy storm, and the train was delayed twice. On February 10, it finally arrived in Pomeroy, Washington, and five of the elk lay dead in the car. The men had to feed the elk in stockyards for a month because of deep snow, and five more died and several calves were born prematurely and died. The members had originally agreed to haul the elk to the edge of the mountains and then release them into the wild. But it was muddy and no one "would be interested sufficiently to donate teams and wagons and their time." The Association had run out of money to buy hay, and the elk were in danger of simply starving in the stockyards. Some men decided to drive the elk out of the stockyards, but the elk refused to leave. Finally one afternoon they drove them up to Benjamin Gulch on the edge of town. By morning all the elk had returned to the stockyards to be fed. Finally, in March, they drove the twenty-nine survivors to the Tumalum Creek at the north end of the Blues and released them in the forest, and this time they were too far to find their way back to the hay.[61]

These are sad, confused stories of men who tried to manipulate wild things, which then refused to be wild, so people lost interest. Locals wanted elk back so they could hunt as their fathers had before them. More than just the elk, they wanted the return of wild nature. But reality intruded—mud and wet boots and hungry creatures—and people lost interest.

Reintroduction stories like the one recounted above are disturbing because people want wild nature to mean something. People who live in the Blues want to believe that elk really belong there. When I first tried unraveling the different stories people were telling me about whether elk were native to the Blues, I wanted to hear that there were some native elk roaming the hills when introduced elk showed up—old hands who could contribute their wilder genes to the creatures now filling the slopes and the grasslands. Elk mean something special to people in the Blues. When you walk the slippery cheatgrass-covered hills and see a band of elk on the other side of a steep draw, you feel like you have arrived in the heart of the land. It seems that the country is still alive, that it has not lost its wildness and become completely managed. Each time you see an elk, you feel that you have been given a gift, no matter how many times you have seen elk before. People hate the stories about starving elk coming down into the lowlands to eat grain each winter, because we want the elk to retain their wildness, their independence from our own machinations and management schemes. The people responsible for management are often among those most disturbed by it.

One of the curious things about the elk history is how muddled it is. People argue over whether elk ever existed in the Blues before the Forest Service introductions; and if they did, whether they had become completely extinct before the Forest Service reintroduced them. At their source, these debates are motivated by doubt

whether the elk really belong there—whether they are native, part
of wild nature. Yet what does it mean to be native? To have your
roots in a given place? Nothing is really "native." North American
elk are of old world origin, and they made their way down to Oregon during the Pleistocene, probably during the Sangamon inter-
glacial period between 120,000 and 70,000 B.P.[62] Yet if elk were present in the mountains before the Forest Service introduced Montana
elk, they seem somehow wilder to people than if they are just the
descendants of those pathetic creatures shivering in the Pomeroy
stockyards. Native does not necessarily mean to have been here
forever; it means to have been here independent of white men's
interventions.

When locals talk about elk in the Blues, they forget the details
of who brought elk where and when. Memories are inaccurate and
uncertain, and for a good reason: their uncertainty leaves possibilities open. We want native to mean something—to mean that the
animals are in their rightful place. Why? Because otherwise the
wild begins to seem as contrived as a zoo. Management can be
heartbreaking to people because it begins to create what seems like
an artificial nature, a tarted-up Hollywood version of the real thing,
just like conifer plantations seem to many like disturbing imita-
tions of real forests. But what is this real thing we miss? In part we
hate the evidence of human agency, of too much control. The forests are too simple, the trees are too straight, the rows are aligned,
the deer too tame: it is like Disneyland, not a real place, not a place
with its heart intact.

Management

Once the elk were back in place, the Forest Service had to decide
how they were to be managed. It was not entirely clear what managing wildlife meant; nor was it clear how much wildlife could be
controlled and still be wild. Aldo Leopold, who created American
wildlife management when he was working for the Forest Service
in the 1920s, originally argued that hunting restrictions and refuges were devices for "dividing up dwindling treasures"—holding
onto the remnants of lost nature. But Leopold wanted something

different. Instead of just trying to preserve the last few broken pieces, he argued that wildlife managers should apply forestry's sustained-yield concepts to game. In a perfect parallel to the Forest Service's attempts to transform wild forests into regulated forests, Leopold persuaded the Forest Service that rather than cling to the remnants of wild nature, managers could reshape that nature into a productive and sustainable commodity. Foresters could manage not just trees, but also game as a harvestable resource.[63]

From the inception of the Forest Service, the game management division was part of the grazing division; managers viewed stock and game as competitors for similar resources. Like grazing and forestry, wildlife science was based on studies of the land's carrying capacity for producing sustained-yield harvests. As in grazing and timber management, ideals of waste, use, and efficiency formed the basis of wildlife science. Management was the "art of producing sustained yields of wild game" by controlling natural forces of competition. As the historian Susan Flader argued in *Thinking Like a Mountain,* "Leopold simply extended to wildlife, through the medium of rudimentary ecological science, a faith in the possibility of intelligent control that goes back at least to W G McGee, Gifford Pinchot, and the origins of the conservation movement in America." This was an economic biology that, in Flader's words, conceived of nature as a "system of competitions and sought to give a competitive advantage to those species deemed 'useful,' whether corn or pines or deer, as against those deemed harmful or expendable."[64]

Just as in timber and grazing management, the first task of the wildlife manager was to figure out the carrying capacity of a place, then calculate the excess numbers above the breeding stock that could be harvested as a useful commodity. In 1920, Leopold called this harvest the "kill factor": the optimum annual kill from an area that hunters could harvest without decreasing the breeding stock. As in grazing and timber management, a key idea was that of "normal stocking": the optimum number of animals that a given site could support, given its biological potential. In the 1920s, normal stocking was defined as the largest number of individuals a given range could carry; the stability of populations and of habitat was simply assumed to follow. The concept of normal stocking was as flawed as the concept of full utilization in grazing management, and for the same reasons: it meant allowing overutilization of the most palatable plants, in order to get high use of range as a whole.[65]

A central goal of wildlife and grazing management was the elimination of predators, because predators stole the excess harvest of game that otherwise people could use. Killing predators meant eliminating waste—a goal at the very heart of conservation. Not until the 1930s did Forest Service employees begin to question the virtue of eliminating predators. Even Aldo Leopold, for example, was fervent in his drive to protect game by hunting down the very last predator.

Over and again people blamed the loss of one creature on the predatory actions of another creature. This meant that they could fix the problem—the loss of nature—by killing the predator, which was easier than correcting habitat degradation. "Varmints," as Leopold and the Forest Service at first called predators, were the animals that competed with hunters for access to wildlife. By calling them varmints, managers excluded predators from the category of wildlife, and from the idealized nature of hunters and game chasing each other in the managed forest. Varmints had to go, the Forest Service and hunters associations agreed, so that hunters could encounter more game and people could be closer to wild nature. Ironically, the elimination of predators took managed populations of wildlife even further from wild nature.

In the Blues and throughout the West, Forest Service officers joined stockmen in the war on varmints. The Forest Service hired gunmen to do nothing but kill wolves and coyotes, and Forest Service employees were also expected to kill any predators they came across. People thought cougar and wolves posed the main danger to elk, whereas coyotes seemed like a threat to sheep, deer, and calves. In 1915, Congress appropriated funds for the U.S. Biological Survey to start an intensive campaign against predators—a campaign that Aldo Leopold and the new practitioners of wildlife management threw all their influence behind.[66]

By the 1930s, as severe overgrazing became apparent, concern about increasing elk and deer populations developed. Populations had exploded in the absence of hunting and predators. Elk especially were seen as contributing to intense competition for livestock forage, because elk and cattle overlap in the plants they use, although not entirely.[67] Only a few people, however, saw the elimination of predators as a contributing problem. Some local ranchers had long objected to coyote killing, because they felt that coyotes ate mostly field mice, which devoured plants that game and cattle relied upon. As Howard Fisk recounted, "my uncle raised cattle in the Chesnimnus country and didn't want any coyotes killed because they ate the field mice which ate the grass. He also didn't like poison and used hounds for control of any problem critters."[68] Fisk's uncle knew what he was talking about. By the 1930s, with the decline of coyotes, prairie dogs and rodent populations had exploded, and the Forest Service had to spread poison over its grasslands and cutover areas to keep rodents from destroying new growth.

While the Forest Service was trying to decrease game populations to make the stockmen happy, the state game departments were doing their best to please hunters by increasing game populations. Both groups were squabbling over which was the "highest use" of the resource. As Dana Berghuis, a Malheur National Forest grazing manager, argued in 1938, the Forest Service's greatest grazing problem was not too many cattle, but "the competition between game and livestock." Although Berghuis did recognize that cattle competed with game, he argued that "great damage has already been done . . . by deer overbrowsing. The present tendency of our deer range is toward depletion instead of improvement, and the [deer] overbrowsing of bitterbrush, mountain mahogany and juniper is a very serious problem on the area surveyed. This cannot be remedied until the deer population is reduced to the carrying capacity of its winter ranges."[69] The irony here is that Berghuis was actually quite sensitive ecologically. No grazing manager ten years earlier would have bothered to mention bitterbrush, mountain mahogany, or juniper, because those plants had little economic value either for cattle forage or timber. Deer would eat those plants, but they preferred other plants—ones that cattle also preferred. For Berghuis, if deer were killing back less favored plants, there were too many deer. Although Berghuis recognized that cattle and deer were competing for favored plants, thus driving deer to settle for less favored plants, he did not mention that the problem might be an overpopulation of cattle rather than deer.

Recognition of the impact of big game on range capacity gained general prominence in the late 1930s, after a severe winter caused massive winter die-offs of deer on the Malheur. In 1942 a Umatilla grazing manager noted that some of the problem with reduced winter forage seemed to come from high mouse populations. Mice had killed both bitterbrush and bunchgrass "over a large part of the winter range . . . and there appears little we can do to improve or increase the winter forage on those critical ranges. . . . It looks like a heavy winter loss is imminent."[70] But the suspicion that this might be due to reduction of coyotes was slow to come.

Although most managers had focused on winter damage, when game animals starved to death if their populations were too high, Leopold argued that managers could use summer browsing to tell whether there were too many animals around to survive a winter. The virtue of this system was that managers could then set autumn bag limits high enough to trim game populations before they starved in the winter. Leopold was the first to argue that wildlife overgrazing might alter species composition of plant communities, by killing off the most palatable plants and allowing weed species to take over. If there were too many elk, they would eat off the most palatable species first, even though the unpalatable species were still untouched. In other words, clear signs existed of overgrazing before all the plants vanished and the animals starved.[71]

The ecological effects of increasing wildlife populations were far more complicated than expected. The combination of cattle grazing, deer and elk browsing, timber harvest, and fire exclusion led to a complex set of interrelated effects in the Blues. Deer and elk populations increased because of the cover offered by heavy pine reproduction, which had increased because cattle overgrazing had led to increased seed germination. This reproduction survived in thickets because of fire control and provided ideal cover, which increased juvenile survival of game, but did not provide forage. Fire exclusion drastically decreased forage, for two major reasons:

it allowed brush and pine reproduction to encroach on grasslands, and forage plants decreased under mixed-conifer stands as the canopy cover increased. As a result, cattle were forced into competition with deer and elk for palatable browse, and the combined pressure depleted palatable species and favored the less palatable species. As communities changed, people became increasingly dismayed. A wild and bountiful nature seemed to be degrading to a managed landscape that showed the clumsy hand of management all too clearly.

Even as wildlife managers became successful at increasing game populations, people's sense of loss only grew stronger. In 1992, Jerry Gildemeister, of the Oregon Department of Fish and Wildlife, talked with a number of lifelong residents of the Blues about their perceptions of wildlife. In these men's and women's voices, there was a recurrent tone of bitterness and sadness. What comes through their words is a sense that they did their best to manage the land well, but what resulted was a sterile, dying nature. The people speaking had spent their lives working on these lands; they were responsible for many of the changes they mourned. Although irrigated farming brought a certain level of prosperity to the Blues, many locals mourned the effects: "Wetlands have been drained, tree and brush cover removed from the streams and sloughs, miles of Catherine Creek meadows have been eliminated by the Government Ditch, and the plant cover along fencerows has gone along with the pheasant and otter,"[72] said Gildemeister. Several people agreed that greed for profit was at fault, for "many modern farmers want to cultivate every inch of ground and not allow any wildlife on their land."[73] Irrigation brought a great deal of money to the region, but also a deeper sense of poverty. What was once abundant came to seem barren and lifeless. For example, Harry Huffman's father "recalled great numbers of pronghorn antelope grazing lush bunchgrass. . . . The area, remembered for its abundant water, has since dried up and the bunchgrass covered slopes have turned to sagebrush and cheatgrass."[74]

Again and again, when people talk about wildlife, they give a list of what was once present, and then they tell a tale of bewildering loss. There is never any resolution to these stories, never any explanation for the loss of nature—just greed, idiocy, progress, our distance from childhood, our distance from Eden and from wild nature. What these stories recount is a longing for a lost paradise, a kind of childhood innocence. But paradise was never wild nature; it was a garden where the beasts lay down together and where death was unknown. Dreams of paradise made it difficult for people to interpret insects and disease and other animals that did not fit into the picture, and they made it difficult for people to imagine a place for themselves in nature. We feel exiled from the lost paradise, but we see this as an inevitable part of progress. It is this inevitability, this particular story of exile, that needs to be changed. At its heart is a story which says that humans and nature are inevitably separate and inevitably opposed; therefore the losses, while regrettable, could not have been prevented and are no one's responsibility.

Fire

The most widely told story about what went wrong with the Blue Mountains goes something like this: a century of fire suppression led to the replacement of open, parklike ponderosa pine stands with thickets of firs that have proven susceptible to insects and disease. Foresters fought those fires because no one in the Forest Service considered the long-term effects of fire suppression; fires killed trees and that seemed unequivocally bad.

There are elements of truth in this version of history, but foresters fought fires for reasons much more complicated than this suggests. Blaming what went wrong on simple ignorance implies an equally simple solution: now that we know more about the role fire plays in forest ecology, we can change our fire policy and fix the problem. If ignorance was the cause, knowledge will be the cure.

But, unfortunately, ignorance was not the cause. The image of early foresters as nice guys out in the woods with their Smokey the Bear caps and heavy tools, unhampered by research, needs some revision. Fire has always been a hotly contested issue in the Blues and in the Forest Service as a whole. The Forest Service, and specifically foresters working in the Blues, used elaborate scientific arguments to support their position on fire suppression. In addition, they backed up these arguments with research. When measured by certain local, internal criteria, most of their arguments were perfectly valid. The pro-fire contingent also used a set of scientific arguments that were equally valid. Which scientific "truths" a given side believed depended on their cultural and economic perspective: namely, what they wanted to extract from the forest. As the historian Stephen Pyne argued in *Fire in America,* fire is a cultural as well as an ecological issue.[1] There is no one right scientific position with regard to fire, and no one scientific cure that will correct our errors. All the problems the Forest Service saw with fire in the 1920s are still valid, and ignoring them will not make them go away.

Today, in the 1990s, most environmentalists see fire as natural and therefore good, but fire is neither good nor bad. Natural fire regimes cannot be created simply by withdrawing fire suppression. There is no natural state to which we can return, because thousands of years of human actions have thoroughly modified the Blue Mountains. I am not going to argue that we should therefore suppress all fires; I will argue, however, that there is no position in the fire debate that can claim the authority of being natural. The idea of returning to what is natural has influenced Blues fire debates since the turn of the century. By showing how both sides manipulated ideas about nature and science, I hope to throw some light on current fire issues.

Forest Service Fire Debates

After the Forest Service came to the Blues, fire policy took some time to consolidate and clarify. The first *Use Book* concerned itself mainly with small fires, advising officers to carry an ax or a shovel and to tell campers to put out their campfires. The book also advised that slash fires must be well controlled. Fires were unnatural events set mainly by careless logging, the *Use Book* implied. Now that the Forest Service was in control, fires would surely stop.[2]

In 1910, a summer of disastrous wildfires across the West shook the morale of the Forest Service. Many foresters were convinced that light burning (low intensity fires) was responsible, and this belief motivated the threefold strategy of fire control: prevent ignition, modify fire environments so that fires will burn with less intensity, and suppress fires while they are still small. In 1935, after a series of drought years and bad fires in the early 1930s (Matilija fire of 1932, Tillamook fire of 1933, Selway fires of 1934), the Forest Service adopted its "Out-by-10 A.M." policy.[3] To prevent catastrophic fires, all fires in all types of country had to be extinguished by

10 A.M. no matter how remote the area and how unsalable the timber.

But this policy of 100 percent suppression of wildfire was not a foregone conclusion. For decades, a controversy over light burning had flared. As forest reserves were established and given stiffer guidelines for fire protection, public protest became vocal. Numerous letters to the editor and editorials argued that fire protection allowed fuels to accumulate. Grazers had always liked light burning, because it increased the forage available for sheep. Settlers and timber owners also pushed for light burning beginning in the 1880s, reasoning that light surface fires would reduce fuels and lessen the chance of conflagrations. Others, such as the writer Joaquin Miller, said that light burning was good because it was a return to "natural" Indian ways. In 1889, John Wesley Powell joined his voice to those calling for light burning, alluding to the virtues of Paiute fire protection. Bernard Fernow, the head government forester, was sour about this, writing that "Major Powell launched into a long dissertation to show that the claim of the favorable influence of forest cover on water flow or climate was untenable, that the best thing to do for the Rocky Mountain forests was to burn them down."[4]

In light of public opinion that was often in favor of low intensity burning, why did the Forest Service eventually decide on 100 percent suppression? In arguing for fire suppression, the Forest Service was reacting against poor industrial logging practices that had resulted in conflagrations. The Forest Service saw burning as part of irresponsible laissez-faire logging practices—practices utterly opposed to scientific sustained-yield forestry. Migratory logging had resulted in disastrous fires, and tax policies encouraged this, because laws discouraged investments in cutover lands. Allowing cutover lands to burn, then moving logging efforts on to new lands, was cheaper for the industry than disposing of slash and encouraging regeneration. The spirit behind conservation at the turn of the century was antithetical to these laissez-faire practices. Scientific control and management, rather than policies that let forests take care of themselves, were the goals of government scientists. As Stephen Pyne wrote, "to suggest that fire could be controlled by more fire would be like the new Bureau of Reclamation suggesting that some periodic mild flooding was beneficial, or the reconstituted Biological Survey recommending an increase in coyote and wolf populations."[5]

The Forest Service agreed that light burning maintained open stands of mature ponderosa pine, but felt that this occurred at the expense of reproduction. Since future forests were the main consideration, anything that harmed reproduction was taboo. Forest Service scientists argued that light-burning advocates sought immediate rewards—the preservation of mature forests—at the expense of long-term forest values such as reproduction and soil protection. Stockmen, miners, railroaders, and loggers insisted they were only continuing Indian ways when they burned. When whites claimed that light burning was an Indian practice that maintained healthy open stands, the Forest Service met these appeals with cynicism, responding that westerners were only using Indian practices to justify their attempts to exploit public lands.[6]

Forest Service hostility against light burning was in large part cultural. If light burning was an Indian practice, then by definition it was superstition, not science. To an intellectual elite trained in Ivy League schools, Paiute forestry could hardly benefit industrial civilization. More important, perhaps, if light burning was accepted, that would threaten the Forest Service's very justification for managing the forests—a justification which came from its claims to technical and scientific expertise.

In 1910, extensive wildfires swept the western forests, burning more than five million acres. The Forest Service became convinced that light burning was responsible for these fires, and this made managers even less willing to consider the virtues of light fires.[7] Since under certain conditions that were impossible to predict, small fires became large fires, the Forest Service reasoned that there were no conditions under which small fires could safely be allowed. No one knew for sure what controlled the transition of a light fire to a conflagration.

The 1910 fires were a severe threat to the authority of the Forest Service. Government foresters had come to save the forests from greedy timber barons and instead the waste and destruction were worse than ever before. Richard Ballinger, the Secretary of the Interior, proclaimed that the Forest Service was at fault for the 1910 fires. Moreover, he added, the Forest Service was wrong about what had caused those fires: frequent burning was indeed necessary to reduce fuel loads and save the forests. Therefore, because the Forest Service had mismanaged its lands so badly in just five years, the forests should be transferred back to his department. The Forest Service was desperate to defend its own authority as manager of the federal forests, and fire suppression was one way to do that.[8]

The controversy evolved into a choice between two opposing philosophies of forest management. Laissez-faire industrial logging assumed that the only profitable forestry was one that simply cut all the old trees and moved to another stand when those trees were gone. Because regeneration and second growth were not part of laissez-faire forestry, and because most fires did little damage to mature trees, fire suppression was not worth the cost. The Forest Service accused laissez-faire loggers of having no concern for the future: they were engaged in nothing more than the prolonged theft of American resources. Light burning was a cynical sham promoted by companies that wanted to avoid responsibility for future forests. Sustained-yield forestry, the head of the Forest Service Gifford Pinchot argued, could eventually be both profitable and sustainable in America, but only if a strong Forest Service had the money it needed to protect young stands from fire damage.[9] The lines of debate hardened, and the Forest Service saw pro-fire arguments as slurs on its integrity and authority. As Bernard Fernow had stated when he was head of the Bureau of Forestry: "the whole fire question in the United States is one of bad habits and loose morals. There is no other reason or necessity for these frequent and recurring conflagrations."[10]

Fires and Natural Conditions

By and large, foresters saw fire in the Blues as unnatural, and they blamed fires on external disturbances: Indians and stockmen. For example, the forester R. M. Evans wrote in 1912: "In early times, the Forest was burned annually by the Indians: later, the stockman continued the same practice and it is only within the last few years that the fire situation has been brought under reasonable control."[11] According to the climax theory held by the Blues foresters, in the idealized natural forest, a mixed-conifer forest should give way to a stable climax forest of tamarack and grand fir. In his 1907 silvics report for the Chesnimnus Reserve, W. H. B. Kent noted that in the "usual forest" this stage had not been reached because of what he called "an unnatural agency of disturbance"—meaning fire. Kent added that *"natural conditions . . . rarely exist*. Fires have spread at some period over nearly the whole region and brought about an altogether different condition" (emphasis added).[12] What Kent and other foresters defined as "natural" was clearly a social construct, only tangentially connected to what actually existed on the ground. If fire was an unnatural, external agency of disturbance, that meant that in the natural world, so-called natural conditions did not exist—a muddled logic that helped the foresters little in their attempts to manage the Blues.

Even after 1935, when official policy was to suppress all fires— no matter how light or how remote—by 10 A.M., fire debates refused to fade away in the Blue Mountains. For example, the backs of forest tourist maps published in the early 1930s contained long sections on the fire debate, indicating that the Forest Service thought it was still a live issue for their public. On the maps, the foresters appealed to science, arguing that even though the damage done by light fires was not readily apparent, it was still significant. Light fires destroyed the humus, killed young growth, damaged mature timber, created an opportunity for disease and wind throw, led to western pine beetle attacks, and killed trees that protected forage. Next, foresters appealed to nature: fires might be natural, but natural was not necessarily good, because current undesirable barren areas were caused by fires. The Forest Service's goal, the map confidently assured the users, was to *improve* nature. Finally, they appealed to scientific authority: "The question of fire in the woods is a question to which many people, both in the Forest Service and out of it, have given much study and agree that there is no such thing as a fire in the woods that does no damage."[13] The tone here was one that became increasingly familiar in the Forest Service's statements to the public. We are the experts; let us decide; we know what is best.

Ideals of what was natural continued to play a central position in the debate, and either side could use the claim of "natural" to support its argument. Likewise, either side could make the claim that they alone were practicing "scientific" management, while the other side was merely trying to support its own selfish interests. A brief but intense local controversy in 1940 showed how vulnerable the Forest Service continued to be for its insistence on fire suppression. J. H. Allen, a county judge and stock rancher, wrote to his senator in 1940 complaining about fire policy on the Malheur. The senator sent the letter to the Acting Chief of the Forest Service, who sent it to the Regional Forester in Portland, who sent it to the Malheur National Forest supervisor. The issue eventually culminated in a congressional hearing on National Forest fire rules in the Blues, illustrating how vulnerable Forest Service personnel were to complaints by wealthy forest users.[14] Congress allowed the Forest Service to continue suppressing fires, but nevertheless foresters were well aware that many locals thought the fire policy was absurd.

Judge Allen was furious that he could not graze as many cattle as he once had, and to increase his permit allowance he had decided that the best strategy was to attack the Forest Service for mismanagement. He said to Congress: "Congressmen, I am now speaking for a large body of citizens who scarcely dare speak their voices regarding forest rulings, lest they be subject to losing their grazing permits."[15] Small operators were certainly vulnerable to changing policy, but Judge Allen surely was not. I can in fact find no record of anyone losing grazing permits for complaining about fire, or about anything else. Allen was hardly afraid that he would lose his permit; rather, he was voicing a strong anti-Forest Service sentiment. He appealed to the cause of the powerless little man who struggled against an impersonal bureaucracy, writing that "under forest service management, we have seen the timbered sections become jungles. We have had no voice in the matter whatsoever. Men behind mahogany desks dictate policies which the poor unfortunate stockman has to follow or leave the forest."

The political nature of Allen's complaint was evident, although concealed under layers of appeal to Nature and Patriotism. Allen was really protesting reductions to his grazing permit, which the Forest Service said were necessary because his cows had denuded the allotment. But instead of directly challenging his permit reductions, Allen decided it might be more effective to claim that Forest Service fire suppression, rather than his own cows, were to blame for the allotment's poor condition. But to argue that the Forest Service was at fault for destroying Paradise, he had to claim that grazing had not done any harm before the Forest Service arrived. Cattle, sheep, and horses were being "crowded from the summer grazing areas due to the accumulation of undergrowth and down timber in the Malheur forest since the forest reserve was created in 1906," not because of past overgrazing.

To support his claims, Allen turned to an appeal to nature. Fire exclusion was bad because it was unnatural, and with fire suppression the Forest Service had turned a paradise into a deathtrap: "Had forest service rulings added another 88,707 head of livestock to the summer grazing area; instead of decreasing that number; had the service not allowed the babbling mountain streams to dry up; had they not allowed the green mountain meadows to become waste lands; had the hills been kept free of down timber and the undergrowth, we'd have a different feeling in the matter. Had forest service regulations added more water to the streams, put more grass on the hills, kept the fire hazards below where they were when they took over the situation, we'd be happy to say with pride that forest management is perfect."

According to Allen, the problem with fire exclusion was that "nature has not been allowed to have its own way." Fire was natural, clean and pure. Without fire, this purity was fast vanishing: "Poisonous ticks . . . porcupines, insects, ants and other pests are all fast accumulating in our once pure green hills." Although light fires were natural and therefore good, catastrophic fires were unnatural, and entirely the fault of the Forest Service. As Allen put it, "man and man alone can be blamed when fires do come."

Now that the Indians had lost most of their political power in the Blues, it was safe to refer to them as idealized children of nature, symbols of natural virtue, freedom, and cleanliness. Allen wrote that "the American Indian roamed in the hills of the Blue Mountains thousands of years before White man was known in North or South America. The Indian hunted and he fished in our mountain by summer. He went to the hills when he pleased. He fired the woods when he pleased. He, together with Nature, lightning, kept a clean woods." What was being threatened by Forest Service policy? Not just Allen's grazing allotment, but women and children and finally nature itself. The woods had become deadly because of fuel accumulation, and if large fires burned "women and children would be the ones to suffer from our weaknesses."

Allen's objectives were clear: he wanted to get rid of grazing restrictions and run as many cattle as he liked wherever he wanted. To justify this, he turned to an idealized past, where Indians and white men roamed the hills in unregulated freedom, claiming that "when white man first came into this section, he took his sheep and cattle and grazed them on our higher mountain slopes. He camped where he pleased and he grazed and he salted his stock where he pleased, and when he handed the area over to the forest service, he gave them a paradise compared to what we now have." Allen was on some level right about his claims: fire exclusion did have some of the effects he claimed for it. But he was using these observations to argue his own agenda, which was one of unregulated use. His conclusion, that "Forest Service rulings, if continued, spell a destroyed forest so far as the Malheur is concerned," was a thinly veiled protest against any regulations. Although what Allen wanted was the freedom to abuse nature as thoroughly as he liked, he managed to justify this with a claim to natural virtue.

The forest supervisor and regional forester reacted to Allen— publicly at least—with a calm appeal to Science. Their tone had a certain edge of condescension; they were the experts patiently explaining to children that matters were very complicated. Lay people simply could not understand, so they should leave decisions to the scientists. Just as nature provided a way for ranchers to try to silence their opponents, foresters appealed to science to squelch debates and consolidate their own position in the face of threats to their qualifications as managers.

Lyle Watts, the Regional Forester, readily admitted that fire exclusion had increased pine reproduction, but he declared that grazing reductions were necessary because of past overgrazing and
drought, not because of increased tree reproduction. Furthermore,
Watts argued, although thickets of lodgepole reproduction did
eliminate grazing, "by far the greater part of the area now valueless
for grazing on account of reproduction . . . has become so as a result of forest fires that have occurred in spite of the protection
efforts of the Forest Service." Fires rather than fire suppression
created the thickets that destroyed grazing, Watts continued. After
a fire, what comes in are "large areas of lodgepole pine reproduction . . . as very dense growth." Ranchers, Watts said, "look upon
these areas as caused by protection of the forests from fire. In reality they are the result of fires."[16]

There were elements of truth to Watts's claim: lodgepole does
come in after certain fires, and no forage grows in the dense shade
under lodgepole stands. But Watts was confusing habitats and fire
types, and thereby muddling the issues. The fires the stockmen
wanted were low-intensity fires in mixed-conifer communities,
and the fires he was referring to were intense ones in much higher-
elevation grand fir and subalpine fir communities. He may have
been intentionally confusing the two fire types, because it is difficult to believe that the Regional Forester did not know the difference. By collapsing different forest types into one, Watts could
come up with seemingly neutral scientific evidence for his position
that fire is bad.

Watts then turned around and argued that, at any rate, increased reproduction was good, not bad, because it formed the basis of the future commercial stands. Therefore, if Forest Service fire
policy ever *did* increase the thickets of reproduction, this would be
was a good thing, because by definition, the more trees the better.
Another anti-fire Forest Service report went into more detail about
the benefits of dense thickets of young trees:

Anyone who knows anything about tree growth or plant growth and
who gives these "light-burning" arguments a moment's thought will,
of course, realize the utter foolishness of such an argument. Forest trees

start from seed, and grow very slowly during the first five to ten years. To our way of thinking, *Nature is notably wasteful,* under the right conditions, seeding up an acre with hundreds of thousands of tiny, young forest seedlings. Most of these will die eventually, but by the very fact of their growing so densely, we know that the ones which do survive will be hardier, taller, straighter and cleaner for having this heavy competition in their early lives. Dense young thickets of forest seedlings or saplings are what make our tall, straight, clean-limbed forest giants. Did anybody ever see a big, bushy-topped, limby tree that grew in the open, all by itself, that was worth a whoop as a sawlog? [Emphasis added][17]

The argument was that competition was a natural and virtuous process, which would ensure that only the best plants survived. Therefore overcrowded stands would be a good thing, because they would lead to vigorous, manly trees.

Either side of the fire debate, in other words, could use the arguments of natural virtue. Both sides could use Science to silence debate and an idealized Nature to further their own ends. Both sides were often right about the particular facts they cited in support of their claims. Yet the facts they chose were those that fit their prior viewpoint.

Restoring Fire to the Inland West

In the summer of 1994, as managers, ecologists, and the public struggled to define ecosystem management, fires began to burn across the inland West. Nearly 300,000 acres burned in Washington alone, and Idaho and Oregon suffered their worst fires in years. As the fires spread, pressures intensified for quick solutions to save the forests: salvage logging, commercial thinning, prescribed burning, ever more intensive management. People who had spent their careers calling for intensive management and fire control were suddenly calling for massive programs of prescribed fire to mimic nature. We need to burn 800,000 acres a year in the inland West alone, recommended James Agee, a fire ecologist at the University of Washington.[18]

Some environmentalists who had once argued that whatever was natural was good suddenly found themselves in the position of arguing that perhaps reintroducing fires was not such a good idea, because fire might harm old growth and wildlife. Other environmentalists took the opposite position, saying that if fires were natural, they needed to be restored.[19] But the kinds of fires that the Forest Service planned bore little resemblance to what most people imagined as natural. Lines of helicopters shooting fuel over the forests, barrels of chemicals spread beneath the trees—these hardly represented pristine nature.

Traditional managers, not to mention industrial foresters, were among the loudest voices calling for prescribed fire. Because of fire suppression, they argued, fuel buildup had led to fire temperatures much higher than natural. Intense fires had been rare in mixed-conifer forests, but by the 1990s they seemed increasingly common. Foresters thought they would be able to eliminate intense fires if they reduced fuel loads back to what was natural by cutting out all the firs, thinning the young pine, and logging heavily to open up the stands. But although managers might decrease the frequency of hot fires with prescribed burning, they would never end up with a precisely ordered system that guaranteed the absence of destructive fires. Fire would never become their docile servant.

When whites arrived in the Blues, there were probably three major fire regimes in the forests. Each regime consisted of two interconnected cycles: a pattern of light, frequent fires; and an overlying pattern of less frequent, stand-replacing fires. Pure ponderosa pine and mixed-conifer communities dominated by pine experienced light ground fires every 10 to 12 years, and stand-replacing fires at intervals of several hundred years. On the north-facing forests with lots of grand fir, low to medium intensity fires burned in patches every 40 to 80 years, while stand-replacement fires burned about every 150 to 250 years. At higher elevations, in subalpine fir communities, patchy light fires burned every 20 to 40 years, and intense fires every 80 to 200 years.[20] All these figures, however, are averages, and the averages hide a great deal of variability. In some mixed-conifer forests, fires might return at intervals of 5 years, then 3 years, then 23 years, but then 40 years might go by without a fire. There was no machinelike process ensuring that a fire would burn every 8 to 10 years. Because of this variability, no matter how much people might thin and salvage, no matter how much money they might spend on prescribed burns, fires will never be fully predictable. Management efforts might well make fires less predictable, because management introduces more and more disturbances—whose indirect effects are poorly understood.

Implicit in most arguments for prescribed fire is the belief that because frequent fires were natural, the forest will be better—healthier and more productive—if we restore natural processes. But how natural were frequent fires? And even if fires were natural, does that mean they are good for the forest, or good for what we want from the forest? What, indeed, does being good for the forest mean?

Fires were frequent when whites first arrived, but they were not necessarily natural. Lightning set some fires, while Indians set others—but there is no easy way to know how the balance fell. Explorers' accounts from the early nineteenth century give us clear evidence that fires were frequent when whites arrived, but they do not help us distinguish natural versus human-set fires. Yet if we assume that presettlement fire regimes were natural and therefore necessary, the logic falls apart if it turns out that those fires were of very recent origin, say only after the 1730s, when Indians acquired horses and wanted open forest stands to encourage forage for the horses and to make horseback hunting easier. If so, then frequent fires were an indirect product of European intervention in the New World, inherently no better or worse than the fire suppression that followed direct white intervention. Moreover, if the frequent fire regimes in ponderosa forests were of recent origin, there is every possibility that those fires may have been slowly depleting the soils of the nutrients necessary to sustain forests on those sites over the long term. The larger point here is that we cannot assume that just because something was happening before white people arrived, it was a good, natural, or sustainable thing.

One way to estimate the percentage of human-set fires would be to compare fire frequencies before and after the 1730s, when the Columbia Plateau tribes acquired horses. If Indians were the main source of fires in the ponderosa forests, the burning rates should have increased substantially after 1730, since the two major reasons Indians burned were to increase forage for their horses and to keep the forests open for easier horseback hunting. Another possibility is to compare burning rates before and after epidemics decimated the Columbia tribes, when there would have been far lower populations of Indians having an impact on the forests. If we find that fire frequencies increased sharply after 1730 and then decreased after Indian populations declined, it would suggest that frequent fires—and the resultant open stand structures of pine—lasted not much longer than fire suppression has lasted. That does not mean that fire suppression is a good or bad thing; it simply means that we cannot assume that ponderosa forests evolved in response to frequent fires and therefore the forests need fires to persist.

Restoring Forests and Fires: Returning to the Past

At the heart of the desire to save the forests with intensive fire management—thinning, logging, road building, prescribed burning—is a critical assumption that no one has yet tested. The hope is that by making the current forests look like they used to look, we will make fires behave like they used to behave. But the world has changed: simply rearranging the trees will not return a forest to its earlier condition. A hundred years ago, when intense fires were rare in some mixed-conifer forests, those forests were open, with minimal fuel loads, little organic matter on the ground, and few firs in the understory. But if we now go into the crowded forests and make them look like they once did, fire risk may not diminish. Intensive management—logging, thinning out the understory, and setting prescribed fires to reduce dead wood—may make tree patterns resemble earlier forests. But after all the management, fires may burn even hotter. Forests are more than just patterns of trees. Cutting down trees will not make forests function as they once did, nor will it make fires behave as they once behaved. After eighty years of fire suppression and intensive management, the forest is a very different place.

One of the great virtues of prescribed fire is the way it reduces fuel loads. Since so much fuel has accumulated that intense fires are more frequent than they were when whites arrived, reducing fuel loads seems like an obvious way to save the forests from intense fires. Another name for fuel loads, however, is dead and down wood: the material that forms such a critical component of the soil's organic matter and water-holding capacity. Burning certainly decomposes dead wood—while also removing organic material from the soil. Is this a good thing or a bad thing? It depends on your perspective. As the site gets drier, rotting wood becomes critical as a moisture source. First the wood has to begin to rot, and in dry sites this may take years. Fire can accelerate that process, but too much fire can eliminate dead wood entirely. Dead wood, of course, is neither good nor bad. Too little dead wood, and the soil would become impoverished. Too much dead wood, and fires would burn so intensely that there would be no soil left to become impoverished.

The structure of the forest floor has changed considerably with fire suppression. Forest floors are where most nutrients cycle, and soil fauna play vital roles in breaking down nutrients and releasing them to trees. As open pine forests have converted to dense mixed-conifer stands, the above-ground biomass has probably doubled, and thus the partitioning of biomass and nutrients has changed entirely. A Forest Service researcher, Arthur Tiedemann, has shown that in one ponderosa-dominated forest, about 17 percent of the total ecosystem nitrogen is now stored in the above-ground biomass—an amount probably much greater than would have been present ninety years earlier.[21] Nutrients such as nitrogen, phosphorus, and sulfur are now concentrated in foliage, small branches, and debris—where they are vulnerable to volatilization. Before fire suppression, plant biomass was concentrated in the large boles of trees, where fire could do little harm. With fire suppression, nutrient cycling in the forest has changed considerably, in ways that make the reintroduction of fire quite difficult. Even very light fires may now consume significant quantities of the forest floor. J. D. Landsburg showed that recent prescribed burns near Bend, Oregon, for example, consumed between 32 and 69 percent of the floor.[22] The effects on long-term productivity could be dramatic. After repeated light burns in ponderosa stands, growth slowed significantly. P. H. Cochran and W. E. Hopkins found that repeated moderate underburning led to a 4 percent reduction in site productivity.[23]

After nearly a century of fire suppression, the duff layer—the accumulation of undecomposed needles—has formed an insulating mat over the soil. Even very light fires may burrow beneath the duff blanket and smolder without dissipating heat into the air, thus prolonging the fire and concentrating heat into the soil. In the Southwest, prescribed burns ignited heavy layers of duff that formed an insulating ash cap, forcing heat into the soil, burning hot enough to kill small roots near the surface, and leading to the death of 40 percent of the stand after three years.[24] After decades without fire, increased litter cooled the microclimates near the forest floor and increased soil moisture, so root structures changed, with far more roots clustering close to the surface. In those conditions, even a very light fire could singe tree roots, destroying huge old ponderosa pines if the soil moisture was low.[25] If the purpose of reintroducing fire is to make ponderosa stands more productive, that goal might backfire. People need to think about what fire does in the forests we now have, not just what fire might have done in the forests we wish we still had.

Trying to recreate an ideal forest community from the past would be a hopeless task. After we interfere with a community, its history proceeds along paths quite different from those it would have taken without our interference. Each disturbance, whether human or natural, represents a branch in the path of forest history, and each action takes the forest in a slightly different direction. We cannot simply backtrack to a time predating some particular decision we now regret, because so many additional changes have radiated out from that original action. We cannot step back into history.

The point is not that we should not touch a thing because everything is interconnected and we will be pulling apart forest functions. Everything *is* interconnected, and pulling out certain components *will* change the forests, but doing nothing is no more reasonable than cutting down all the trees to "save" the forests. We have changed the forests so much that they are no more natural than what we would end up with if the proponents of intensive management got their way. If we want old growth, large verte-brates, and open pine forests, as well as logs for the mills, we need to try restoration rather than simply more intensive management or else preservation of the few remaining pieces.

Restoring the Inland West

J ust before World War II, the national forests had a total annual cut of about 1 billion board feet a year. During the war, harvests tripled, to 3 billion board feet a year. Like the livestock increases during World War I, these high harvest levels were intended to be a temporary adjustment to meet wartime demands, but they never declined. Instead, logging accelerated as road building and chain saws gave access to stands that had formerly seemed too expensive to cut, and as the postwar construction boom increased demand for timber. By 1965, the annual cut had soared tenfold, to 11 billion board feet. For the next quarter century, harvest levels just kept climbing. These heavy cuts were necessary, the Forest Service argued, for "evening out the timber supply of established industries and stabilizing communities as the private timber harvest declined."[1] In other words, since the industry was cutting its own lands heavily, the Forest Service felt it needed to fill the gap; otherwise total harvests would decline and communities might suffer. When the timber recession hit in the early 1980s, harvests finally dropped. But not for long. The Forest Service made a huge push to revive the faltering mill economy, and sales picked up again in the late 1980s.

As logging accelerated, managers became ever more enamored of intensive forestry. No one had yet proven any of the claims of intensive forestry; no one had managed to regulate a western old-growth forest. But the Forest Service was optimistic all the same. Surely, someday soon, with the help of loggers, silviculturists would be able to transform all the western forests into vigorous young stands growing at top speed. And when that day finally came, the Forest Service estimated that loggers could harvest

20 billion board feet a year forever. There hardly seemed to be an end in sight to what managers thought forests could eventually produce.[2]

The forest health crisis changed all this. In the late 1980s, after a decade of drought, a massive outbreak of spruce budworm began in the Blues, then a tussock moth infestation broke out, and on top of that came pine beetle infestations. By 1990, the Forest Service estimated that insect infestations had killed 50 percent of the Douglas-fir in some stands and damaged 63 percent of all trees throughout the region.[3] Everyone rushed to blame someone else for these sudden problems. Forest Service ecologists claimed that years of intensive management had weakened the forest and created conditions favoring an outbreak. Many Forest Service managers said just the opposite: the problem was too little management. And many local forest users were furious at the entire Forest Service. Trees were dying, and they wanted to know why the managers were not doing anything to stop it.

By 1993, lawsuits, injunctions, and the threat of further lawsuits almost halted harvests. Harvest levels on the three national forests—Wallowa Whitman, Malheur, and Umatilla—dropped from 706 million board feet a year in the late 1980s to less than 100 million in 1993. On the Umatilla, for example, the 1990 plan approved annual harvests of over 150 million board feet, but in 1993 less than 30 million board feet were actually cut, and most of this was salvage. Under pressure from environmentalists and its own research ecologists, the Forest Service began to reconsider what it had done with the 5 million acres in the Blues under its control. In 1991, the Forest Service published *The Blue Mountains Forest Health Report,* which stated, in an unusual admission of guilt and confusion, that the forest health crisis had been caused by its own history of forest management.

Intensive Management in the Blues

Fire suppression, overgrazing, and high-grading were not the ultimate causes of the changes in the Blues. These policies developed in large part because the central mission of the Forest Service was to make the forest more productive, eliminating waste by cutting old growth and simplifying forest structure. Early foresters, like many current foresters, had believed in the ideology of efficiency. Their goal was to transform decadent old growth into vigorous, efficient, regulated stands for sustained-yield production. Yet not until after World War I did they try to implement these ideals, largely because there were no markets for the trees. It was neither economically nor technologically feasible to cut the Blue Mountains forests heavily enough to bring about intensive sustained-yield forestry. After the First World War, the Forest Service's main goal in the Blues was to sell ponderosa pine in order to get the forests regulated. It was this focus, not a lack of knowledge about succession or fire, that led to decisions that produced unexpected and disastrous effects.

The initial push for forest conservation had come in large part from an emphasis on the indirect influences of forests on water. Foresters began by recognizing that ecological systems were complex and interconnected, so that things done to one element of the forest would have cascading effects elsewhere. Within the first ten years of federal forest management, however, the Forest Service dropped its emphasis on indirect effects and increasingly concentrated on commodity production. Forest management took as its mission the elimination of waste from the system. But what foresters defined as waste—dead and down wood, snags, insect and fungal damage, logs in the streams—were the components that kept a forest resilient and productive.[4] As managers tried to remove these elements from the Blues forests, they created a kind of Frankenstein monster: a brave new forest that would eventually run out of control.

Multiple-use planning, instituted in 1936 and then reaffirmed in 1976, did not displace intensive timber harvests; on the contrary, foresters used multiple use as an added justification for more logging. The historian David Clary has argued that all other uses were measured against timber; in fact, managers felt that intensive timber management (meaning clearcutting) was integral to every other use. As the Willamette National Forest plan in 1965 said: "Clearcuts break the monotony of the scene, and deciduous brush in these areas furnish fall color and spring flowers." Moreover, "the roads built in connection with timber harvesting furnish access for more people to enjoy the use of other resources." In an extraordinary twist of logic, the plan added that for soil quality, clearcuts were even better than old growth, because the harvest of old-growth timber "can reduce soil impacts from uproots."[5] To walk up to a clearcut—where bulldozers had gouged and scraped the soil, no trees remained standing, and massive smoking piles of slash and half-burned broken timber littered the torn ground—and to argue that clearcuts created better scenery, better recreation, and better soil took a certain effrontery.

Even ecologists such as Jack Ward Thomas and Fred Hall, two of the most respected and influential scientists ever to work in the Blues, had argued back in the late 1970s that "the silviculturist will be hard pressed to meet a goal of management for species richness using an exclusively uneven-aged timber management system." Even-aged management—which basically meant intensive management using clearcuts—was "a much better way to meet the goal of management for species richness because all successional stages are created. Early successional stages occur as a result of regeneration cuts [clearcuts] and the late mature and old-growth stages can be produced by commercial thinning and sanitation harvesting." Diversity, for the Forest Service, meant different successional stages, and therefore old-growth forests were deficient. "Under uneven-aged management early successional stages will exist only if stands are lost to natural factors such as wildfire or insect outbreaks, or if regeneration of stands is necessary," Hall and Thomas argued. "Such forests will lack the variety of distinct successional stages that insure diversity and a myriad of habitat niches."[6] Thomas and Hall were trying to convince traditional foresters that they needed to consider biological diversity when they planned timber sales. But the ecologists had persuaded themselves that the best way to get the greatest possible diversity was to substitute a simplified, managed forest for the old-growth forest. The problem with "the general riot of the natural forest" was no longer that it did not produce enough timber, but that it did not produce enough diversity.

The Forest Service recognized that its management was quickly depleting the big pines upon which the local mills relied, but managers convinced themselves that "untried opportunities for intensifying management" meant that after old-growth ponderosa was eliminated, scientists could produce something else to harvest.[7] Since grand fir grows faster than ponderosa, in the 1950s Blues managers decided that fir should be encouraged so that the mills would have something to cut after the 1980s. Ponderosa pines were underachievers compared with true firs, which grew faster and put on more volume at a young age. Once the foresters had site potentials listed in their handbooks, they felt honor bound to make the land produce at its full potential. By the time the Forest Service realized its mistake in the 1990s, it was too late. Firs grown on sites historically dominated by pine had already begun succumbing to insects and disease.

The point is not that true firs are bad trees. Precisely because they are short-lived and disease-prone, true firs add a great deal to old-growth forests. They decay quickly, providing habitat for numerous animals while the logs rot, and the dead wood gets returned to the system quickly. Firs were part of the Blues forests long before the Forest Service started fire suppression. Trying to eliminate firs because they get attacked by insects (as many people now suggest) would be as absurd as trying to convert the forest to firs because they grow quickly.

Intensive forestry never performed as well as everyone hoped, but that failed to lessen foresters' faith in it. In the 1990s, many planners within the Forest Service were still enamored with its ideals of maximum production. As the Umatilla Forest Service plan stated in 1990, its analysis "indicates that the Forest has an opportunity to increase its potential yields. Based on the use of intensive silvicultural practices and genetically improved stock . . . the long-term sustained yield level of the fully regulated forest is . . . approximately 309 mmbf [million board feet] a year. . . . A harvest rate *equal to the biological potential* would require 50 to 60 years to treat all the existing natural stands" (emphasis added).[8] In the late 1980s, during a period of extremely high timber harvests in the Blues, the harvests on the Umatilla were averaging 158 million board feet a year. By 1992 they had declined to about half that, and most ecologists—even those within the Forest Service—thought that harvests needed to decline still more to be ecologically sustainable. But in the 1990 Forest Plan, managers were talking about *doubling* the already inflated harvests of the late 1980s, an increase of five or six times over what most ecologists thought was feasible. The old dream of reshaping a forest to make it better and better had not disappeared.

Where was the Forest Service hoping to find these trees? The 1981 timber inventory (which was itself highly inflated), estimated that the Umatilla contained 11,772 million board feet of timber. Therefore, if loggers intended to cut all those trees at the rate of 309 million board feet a year, that would have meant only a 38-year rotation. Trees do not get very big in 38 years, even on tree farms, much less on the Umatilla. When foresters talked about a fully regulated forest, they meant a forest in which all the old growth was removed and replaced with young true firs growing as fast as they possibly could, producing the absolute maximum timber volume in the shortest possible time. No one really believes this any more. The last decade has persuaded most foresters who work in the Blues that true firs have an annoying tendency to get diseased and insect-ridden when they are grown in crowded stands on dry sites. But in the 1980s, the Forest Service was going by site potential, and site potentials were not always calculated by people who knew a piece of land by heart, who understood the constraints of a particular plot of land.

Ecosystem Management in the Inland West

In 1992, Dale Robertson, who was then Chief of the Forest Service, proclaimed that the era of traditional management had finally come to an end. Instead of maximizing timber outputs, the Forest Service would begin to practice something different: ecosystem management. This term, however, like biodiversity, was slippery enough to mean whatever people wanted it to mean. Many managers and industry representatives complacently assured the public that ecosystem management meant intensive management. Steve

Mealey, the head of the government team that was developing a new scientific framework for ecosystem management in the inland forests, voiced the feelings of many traditional foresters when he said: "In the inland west, ecosystem management may mean more management than before."[9] Representative Larry LaRocco, the Democrat from Idaho who was pushing hard in Congress for pre-scribed fire, thinning, and salvage to "save" the forests, agreed with Mealey, adding that "the scientific consensus is going to carry the day."[10] Fire and science, taken together, were suddenly providing managers the justification for something that looked very much like business as usual.

Most environmentalists, on the other hand, insisted that eco-system management meant not more management, but as little management as possible. The science of conservation biology, they claimed, made it clear that natural processes should be allowed to heal ravaged landscapes. For example, Dominic DellaSala, David Olson, and Saundra Crane, three scientists with the World Wildlife Fund, wrote that ecological processes necessary for maintaining the inland forests "cannot be effectively maintained or restored by intensively managing commercial forests to attain structural features resembling native forest systems." Only a "system of large reserves, corridors, buffer zones, and matrix areas" could save the forests.[11]

These two very different perspectives on the meaning of ecosys-tem management reflected the long American tradition of seeing nature and people as separate—a tradition that has led to two very different ways of managing land. Americans have either used land for maximum commodity extraction or have tried to preserve it in pristine wilderness areas, uncontaminated by human influence. Neither strategy has been terribly successful, especially in the in-land West. The increasing chaos of federal land management—fires, lawsuits, insect epidemics, and the collapse of faith in govern-ment policies—attests to that. But there are other ways of defining ecosystem management which may offer a way around the sterile opposition of humans and nature that has helped polarize envi-ronmental debates in the West.

Change and Ecosystems

As part of an attempt to resolve the conflicts developing over the best way to manage inland public lands, in July 1993 President Clinton directed the Forest Service "to develop a scientifically sound and ecosystem-based strategy for management of eastside forests." The next January, Jack Ward Thomas and Jim Baca, Director of the Bureau of Land Management, formed the Eastside Ecosystem Management Project, a joint effort chartered to develop an entirely different framework for managing public lands of the inland West.[12] Ecosystem management would rest on several critical principles, upon which the agencies hoped everyone could agree: Given that ecosystems are dynamic and often change in unpredictable ways, there is no natural balance to which managers can return ecosystems. Because humans have shaped the land for thousands of years, management must work within a human framework, not just a natural framework.[13]

Instead of resolving conflict, however, these principles only intensified it, as different groups interpreted them in radically different ways. Some argued that since people are part of nature, we can therefore do whatever we like to the land. Any changes we cause are not degradations, but merely new directions for the ecosystem.[14] In a furious response to such arguments, many environmentalists wanted to scrap the whole effort of management, and let natural processes run on their own.

Even though the conclusions traditional managers reached from the principles often seemed like thinly disguised justifications for their own agendas, the substance of the principles themselves— disturbance and change are a part of nature and so are people— can also be the basis for a very different ethic to guide working with the land. If we accept that people are connected to the land in intricate but poorly understood ways, there can be no stronger argument for living with ecological respect, as part of an interdependent community.[15]

At the heart of the controversy over ecosystem management is the old question: what is the proper place for human desires in nature? On what grounds can we balance one person's desire for a rapidly growing even-aged stand of trees with another person's desire for an old-growth forest? Traditional foresters have argued that because people are part of nature, ecosystem management is whatever gives people the commodities they want without damaging the ecosystem's ability to produce future commodities. If people decide they want tree plantations instead of old growth, that is fine; nothing is inherently better about natural forests, because no forests *are* natural. If some people want old-growth forests, they will have to prove either that the majority of people desire those forests or that some old growth must remain in order to sustain the industrial forests that are busy producing the timber people want. In a world where there are no more natural laws, the implication is that value lies only in what people desire.[16]

Ecosystem management, in this framework, is management that produces more of what people want, just so that the yields do not decline. The first draft of the Eastside Ecosystem Management Process scientific framework defined ecosystem management as "an adaptive management, learning, and planning process that attempts to ensure that people's activities and expectations are consistent with the limits and capacities of ecosystems." As James Agee and D. R. Johnson have argued, ecosystem management "involves regulating internal ecosystem structure and function, plus inputs and outputs, to achieve socially desirable conditions." The focus is on socially desirable, rather than ecologically desirable conditions, because what is natural "cannot be scientifically resolved."[17] Although this is certainly true, the problem with human-centered approaches to ecosystem management is that even when they acknowledge that there are limits to what people can remove from ecosystems, they still imply that the land is a collection of objects for human consumption.

Engineering and Control

Many of the Forest Service's attempts at defining ecosystem management show a stubborn faith in the engineer's paradigm of management: we can create any silvicultural system we desire, and

we can control the forest to make it do exactly what we want. As
the silviculturist Russell Graham wrote: "Silviculturists have the
knowledge and tools to complement, if not replace, many of the
processes associated with fire in many forest ecosystems. Silviculturists are just as capable of developing prescriptions to sustain a
wide variety of forests and forest amenities as they are of producing
forest crops. Nearly all of the effects a fire has on a forest can be
accomplished using traditional silvicultural treatments."[18] But this
reasoning assumes that the only important functions in a forest are
the ones we already know about. Graham adds, with a profound
optimism: "silviculture is the art and science of managing forests
to meet management objectives. If society desires forests to be
managed for sustainability and function, silvicultural prescriptions
can be developed to do so by using many of the tools that produce
timber crops." Tell us what you want and we can engineer it for
you; we can make the world look however you want it to look.
Graham is anything but a timber beast; on the contrary, he has
been instrumental in pushing ecological concerns to the forefront
of Forest Service management. One recent Forest Service report
that he co-authored, *An Ecological Basis for Ecosystem Management,*
is probably the best statement of conservation biology principles
in any government publication.[19] Yet although the Forest Service's
goal has changed—sustainable ecosystems rather than commodity
timber crops—the basic paradigm of control has not.

People will always manipulate ecosystems, and a goal of "sustainability and function" will probably cause less harm than a goal
of one billion board feet of prime timber harvested each year. Yet
manipulation does not mean control; when we manage ecosystems, all we are really doing is tinkering with processes we are just
beginning to understand. There is no doubt that we can push succession in different directions, but rarely are those directions the
ones we intended. In his affirmation of the powers of silviculture,
Graham quoted early Forest Service researchers who, in 1942,
called attention to ecological problems caused by overcutting.
"The picture that has been drawn thus far of the condition and
management of western forests can hardly be called satisfactory.
Overcutting of pines and undercutting of other species has been

widespread, causing an unbalanced drain upon the forests," wrote Forest Service researchers over half a century ago. After breaking the bad news, they assured readers that the Forest Service's new bag of silvicultural tricks would soon solve any problems. "There is no shortage of solutions," they promised. "The problem is to select the one which least disrupts the scheme of things." But in trying to disturb the political economy as little as possible, foresters ended up disrupting the biological economy far more. Fifty-two years later, the ecological situation in the West was far worse than it had been in 1942. For all the early silviculturalists' optimism, their solutions only worsened the problems, because their paradigm of management remained unchanged. Foresters assumed technology could fix the forests, but technology was causing the problems in the first place.

Attempts to engineer nature imply that the land is a predictable machine made up of disconnected parts. Any pieces we think are wasteful—insects, fires, vermin, dead wood, weed trees like alder— we just eliminate. A few years later, when the trees start dying, we wonder what went wrong. Only then do we notice that those wasteful parts had a critical function in the ecosystem, so we try to restore a few pieces, removing other weeds and vermin to make room for the ones we want to return. Managers call for more science, more experiments, more information about the functional roles those parts play. But more information will not save us from our errors, for we can never learn all there is to know. The world is far too complex. We need to change the way we think about the land, not just change the number of little parts we study, label, and preserve. Until we do that, current attempts at ecosystem management will have little more success than the 1942 Forest Service team had in its attempt to correct forest problems.

Balance and Disturbance

Much of the confusion and acrimony over the role of people in managing land arises from a basic philosophical difference. Left alone, is nature good or bad? Is nature self-regulating, or will it fall into chaos without human engineering to control it? Does nature need people to manage it? In other words, is nature inherently flawed and inadequate on its own, or is nature inherently self-stabilizing and complete without people?

Traditional management has, at its heart, assumed that the human relationship with land was "improvement"—to make nature more efficient and productive. Since Thoreau, environmentalists have largely rejected this, arguing that complex webs of interrelationships create a balanced system which self-regulates, preventing any major degradation. On the other hand, as Barry Commoner put it, "any major man-made change in a natural system is likely to be detrimental to that system." In the absence of human intervention, ecosystems would find their own natural balance, one that human intervention inevitably wrecks.[20]

Yet because natural systems are always changing and do not have an inherent balance or stability, disturbance processes often do not self-regulate. Even without human interference, forest ecosystems can change to the point where the land can no longer support similar forests. Although ecologists have been arguing this for decades, only recently did the ecologist Daniel Botkin make these arguments widely accessible in a book called *Discordant Harmonies*.[21] Traditional foresters have seized upon Botkin's arguments, seeing his work as justification for continued intensive management and extraction. If forests always change, then we do not need to worry about a web of interrelationships and interconnected effects. As Henry Alden, a forester for the Michigan-California Lumber Company, said in a speech, "The impact of the fire was more intense than any clearcut I have ever seen. . . . The Sierran forests are tough and resilient . . . If fire is a natural and essential part of the ecosystem we have been far too delicate in our attempts to simulate the natural cycles of the forest."[22] In other words, anything we do to forests cannot possibly be as rough as what they do to themselves.

All living creatures change the world; human changes are not necessarily worse than natural changes. But even when we recognize change, disturbance, and instability in ecosystems, we still need to make distinctions between types of change: all human changes are not equally acceptable if we want forests to survive our efforts.

Ecosystems may lack an inherent balance, but they do have different levels of resistance to disturbance—defined as the ability to undergo change and then return to a similar, but not exact, configuration.[23] Resistant forests may still experience catastrophic fires that reduce the forest to ash, but eventually trees return. On a site that has been degraded past its ability to resist disturbance, trees may not be able to recolonize the site. Resistance does not mean an absence of change; it refers to what happens after the change. Intricate biological relationships can contribute to resistance. For example, J. W. Byler and S. Zimmer-Grove use the term "biological balance" to describe the relation that develops between pathogens, hosts, and environments in complex ecosystems.[24] This relationship is dynamic rather than stable, fluctuating over time as climates and ecosystems change. Actions that upset those relationships, however, may bring about unpredictable, undesirable, and irreversible changes.

If people alter a system beyond a threshold of resistance, it may return to a new—and often much less desirable—community after a major disturbance. The same thing can happen in the absence of people, but that hardly justifies human-caused degradation. As the ecologist David Perry argued in 1988, certain levels of repeated human disturbance can push a forest over an ecological threshold so that it can no longer resist other disturbances.[25] For example, even when fires repeatedly volatilized nitrogen from the soil, the inland West still supported forests, perhaps because certain nitrogen-fixing plants such as alder and ceanothus came in after fires, restoring nitrogen in burnt-over sites. But when foresters excluded these uncommercial "weeds" from clearcut sites, they introduced a new, unstable disturbance that reduced the system's ability to resist other disturbances.

When we drop the notion of a fixed, unchanging balance of nature, we still need to recognize the importance of interconnected processes that allow forests to persist. Once again, focusing on single elements of the forest in restoration will not get us very far.

Ecosystems usually gain resistance to disturbance not because of the properties of individual organisms, but because of ecological interactions. Restoring ponderosa pine alone would not make a forest fire-resistant; it is the spacing of pine in relation to other trees in the forest (the landscape pattern), as well as the kinds of understory shrubs, the soil fauna, the mycorrhizae, and the water-holding abilities of the soil that allow certain forests dominated by pine to resist the effects of frequent light fires on soil nutrients. Resistance, in Perry's words, "emerges from a complex of factors, including interactions and landscape pattern." These interconnected relationships within a forest will change over time even in the absence of human disturbance, but human actions can nonetheless disrupt those relationships to the extent that forests will not persist.

The more managers alter a forest, the less they can predict the paths that succession will take. Each road we build, each stand we cut and replant with another species, each application of herbicide and pesticide adds another confounding layer of possibility. This is startling, since the changes managers have made to forests have all been done with the goal of making succession *more* predictable, not less—making more of what we want, and less of what we do not want. Managers have always insisted that they can engineer the forest to produce what people desire, but the forest is far too complex for this. No matter how many facts we accumulate and how many theories we test, we will never have the knowledge to manipulate natural systems without causing unanticipated changes.

Nature may not be stable, but that does not mean it is bad and therefore needs us to improve it: stability and virtue are not the same thing. Likewise, human effects on nature are not intrinsically good or bad. We need to learn how to make distinctions between which human effects are good and which are bad. This will be no simple matter, because definitions of good and bad depend on the context. From the forest's point of view, it is not a bad thing to burn up and be replaced by sagebrush. Brush replacing forest is undesirable only from a human point of view, and only if we happen to prefer trees. If we give up our simple associations—natural processes are inherently desirable, or else inherently bad—then we have no easy ways of making decisions about which goals to favor in ecosystem management.

Forest Health

One assumption at the heart of ecosystem management is that traditional management led to unhealthy forests. But what is forest health? Do dying trees mean an unhealthy forest? Definitions of forest health depend on what kind of forest people want, and the difference between their ideal forest and the actual messy plot of ground. Ideas of ecosystem health rest on our changing conceptions of the relationship between people and nature, because there is no essential ecological health or integrity independent of human perceptions. Some people see a healthy ecosystem as one which, by definition, is free of human contact. Others see a healthy ecosystem as just the opposite: a place that people have shaped to maximize short-term levels of commodity production.

Human desires will affect the way we define forest health, but our desires should not be at the center of the definition. In other words, a healthy forest is not one that gives us whatever commodities we want, whenever we want them. That is a storehouse, not a forest. One Forest Service report defined health in just this way: "A healthy forest is one that does not inhibit managers from achieving their objectives."[26] This kind of definition is what got us into trouble, for it assumes that any mortality interferes with human desires and therefore should be eliminated.

A recent report by the University of Idaho policy team illustrates some of the difficulties with a human-centered definition of health. "Concepts such as ecosystem integrity and balance are not measurable, and therefore not useful in judging forest health," the report argued.[27] Therefore, because people are part of ecosystems, definitions of forest health must be based on what people want. But human needs are no more objective, unchanging, or quantifiable than ecological integrity. Nevertheless, according to the Idaho group, "forest health is a condition of forest ecosystems that sustains their complexity while providing for human needs." This may sound as if the land has a place in the definition, but it is a very marginal place: human needs are squarely at the center. What kind of forest condition provides for human needs? According to the Idaho team, the best measure of forest health is when mortality is 18.3 percent of gross annual growth—the definition offered by the Society of American Foresters.[28] By this definition, intensively managed industrial forests in Idaho are in a much healthier condition than nonindustrial forests, and old-growth forests are in the worst condition of all, since mortality and growth are nearly equal there. The Idaho report thus triumphantly concludes that intensive, industrial management is what keeps forests healthy.

Early foresters justified liquidating old-growth pine forests for exactly that reason—so young, healthy, rapidly growing forests could take their place. This, of course, is what led us into our current troubles. When human desires for commodities become the definition of health, managers must eliminate anything that detracts from high annual growth rates: insects, disease, decaying trees, fire, anything that does not produce commodities. This definition of health is based on human conceptions of efficiency, not on an understanding of ecological processes of mortality and disturbance.

At the other end of the spectrum, some have argued that the only healthy ecosystem is one where human disturbance is minimized. As the *Blue Mountains Forest Health Report* put it, forest health is "the condition of the forest based on diversity of natural features of the landscape, distribution of plant communities exhibiting various stages of succession, and the degree to which naturally occurring fauna occupy habitats that are varied and equitably distributed across the landscape."[29] Ecosystem integrity, by the same logic, is an ecosystem without human disturbance.[30] But this too is problematic, once we recognize that there are no natural ecosystems in America, and that natural ecosystems are not inherently self-regulating. Both extremes of the definition, curiously enough, focus on people—their presence or absence—rather than on the ecological community. The point should not be the presence or absence of people; the point should be what is happening within the ecological communities in a particular place. Instead of defining health as either the minimization or maximization of human disturbance, it might be interesting to try to define health in ways that focus more on the specific places—a task that would mean giving up our absolute ideas, and allowing for variability and uncertainty.

Fragmentation and Restoration

At the root of our problems with managing land is fragmentation, both ecological and ethical. Our forests are fragmented, and so are we. We live like little islands, cut off from the places we inhabit. We have broken our forests into tiny stands of old growth lost in a sea of managed stands. We have cut ourselves off from place, from home; we have lost our knowledge of interconnections and dependencies. Fragmentation is a spiritual state, a moral state of disconnection, as well as a biological state. Removing this fragmentation between human and nature means moving away from seeing nature as something we can fragment into commodities and resources. As the philosopher M. Sagoff has argued, we have tended to see nature as a collection of resources put there for our use, and this has to change to seeing nature as habitat: the place where we live, a place to inhabit and become native, a place to sink our roots into.[31] Until we respect the land as a community, a complex and organic place with ethical value, we will not do much better.

Respecting the land does not mean leaving it alone; perhaps instead it means working with an ethic of attentive humility rather than an ethic of control. As the writer Michael Pollan wrote in reference to gardening, the lawn is a "totalitarian landscape" where nature has been "subdued, homogenized, dominated utterly"—a lawn is "nature under culture's boot."[32] Clearcuts are much the same thing; they represent our efforts to impose an impatient will upon the waiting land. There are alternatives, however; ways of working with the land that, as Alexander Pope advised in the eighteenth century, "Consult the Genius of the Place in all."[33] What Pope meant, I think, was an attentiveness to the local place—or as Michael Pollan put it, a "subtle process of give and take with the landscape" that roots itself in a respect for the particular plot of ground's ecological (and human) history.

Even though all lands have felt the impress of human activity, we still need wildlands—places where industrial effects remain at a minimum. Roadless areas matter for ethical as well as ecological reasons. Because everything we do has cascading effects we barely understand, we need to have some controls for our experiments in management—places where we do not extract commodities, places where we try to keep industrial disturbances minimized. People intended roads to be benign corridors for easing the flow of objects across the landscape, but instead they have fragmented the land into bits, allowing weeds, cowbirds, pests, and diseases access. Fragmentation is not inherently a bad thing, but in the last century the pace of fragmentation has accelerated to the point where the pieces overwhelm the whole.

Wildlands resist not just the land's fragmentation, but our own. They remind us of the limits to human knowledge and control, and while that can be unnerving, it can also be heartening. The spiritual solace of wild places is in the ways they seem whole unto themselves; they are places that let us know that the earth is not a collection of objects for our use. Wildlands do not need to exclude people; they can be places that remind us we are part of a community, not the engineer that created and shaped a machine.

Steve Fletcher, the forest health coordinator for the Wallowa Whitman National Forest, spent one hot summer day driving me around the back country, trying to persuade me of the virtues of intensive management. Each stand reaches its fastest growth and full potential only when humans are in there managing, he argued. Then he added: all forest problems ultimately come from a failure to manage enough. We drove up into the tangled subalpine fir thickets near the crest of the Elkhorn Mountains, and Steve shook his head. Trees were dying, falling over, their white stumps stuck into the sky. We should prevent this kind of waste, Steve said, by cutting down this messy forest and putting up a better one in its place. Then we drove on a little farther, and he stopped the truck and looked out. "This was wild country twenty years back," he finally said. "A wild country. Nobody knew what was back in here.

It was a place where men and animals ran loose." In his voice it was clear that he had a kind of grudging admiration for that kind of wildness, and he missed what was lost.

That night just before dark I went back alone and walked in a few miles to Black Lake. As night fell, something crashed through the dead trees behind the tent, and my dog lifted her head from her paws and whined softly. Bats flickered over the glassy lake and the mountains went scrubby and red against a darkening sky. An owl flew over my head, swooped down, and landed behind me silently. Then it flew low, over again, and a third time, in a calm arc around me and the dog, then across the marshy meadow. There was something wild, something out there, in the tangled and dead and decadent forest, with the bats and owls and pileated woodpeckers and salmon, the thronging spirit world and animate world. All this was missing in Steve Fletcher's view of the ideal forest, or at least in his words, and I wondered how these will ever mesh: desire for productivity with desire for all the rest, what is uncountable and silent and off in a thicket, some kind of tie to the damp meadows and the dirt.

As Gary Snyder and Edward Grumbine argued, ecosystem management must nurture both wildlands and the "wildness within human beings."[34] Just because we change the wild does not mean we are somehow outside it. The land is not, in Michael Pollan's words, a "neutral, fixed backdrop; it is in fact alive, changing all the time in response to innumerable contingencies," one of those being the presence of people. As wild places remind us, the land has its own will, its own genius; it is not a blank canvas upon which we write our desires for timber or scenery. Finding a place for human intervention in nature does not mean exiling wildness from the forest. It is when someone "respects and nurtures the wilderness of his soil and his plants" that the land flourishes the most. Wildness is out there, but also "right here: in his soil, in his plants, even in himself. Overcultivation tends to repress this quality, which experience tells him is necessary to health. . . . But wildness is more a quality than a place, and though humans can't manufacture it, they can nourish and husband it."[35]

Wildlands offer a refuge for wild things, but they also offer us a refuge too, a place and a way to remember what is wild inside us. What people have seen as an insult to man's industry and role on earth—decay and waste—is exactly that element of wildness, that quality wherein the forest's health and persistence lies. We need to learn to value it—the rot, the bugs, the fires, the fungi, the diseases, the dark, stinky, unnerving heart of the forest.

Extraction on Public Lands

Nourishing and valuing wildness does not mean we should necessarily exclude extractive uses from federal lands. Removing timber harvests and grazing from public lands would concentrate those activities someplace else, and no place is really someplace else; water ultimately connects all the separate fragments. Fully protected reserves that exclude timber and grazing will end up intensifying those uses elsewhere in ways that might be much worse than if they had been integrated. Conservation biology can help here, by giving us information comparing light cutting of mixed-conifer forests on midelevation south slopes with heavy cutting of low elevation forests and leaving the few high elevation forests alone.

We might eventually decide that for the goals of biodiversity, sustainable communities, timber extraction, and streams where salmon can spawn, it is more effective to concentrate extractive uses in a few valleys while leaving the rest in a more nonindustrial state. Then again, that might be worse for the watershed: it might be better to harvest selectively across half of the forest, rather than turning 20 percent of the forest into fertilized, herbicide-treated, even-aged monocultures and having 80 percent in nonindustrial uses. Pushing human uses out of the protected federal lands may be good, or it may be bad, for reaching our goals for a place. But before we know that, we need to define our goals, and that is a difficult task when we know so little about the effects of our actions.

Goals for restoration will reflect what people want from the land, but those goals need to be biologically centered and ecologically constrained. If they do not pay attention to the natural history of the place, they will be impossible goals. As Pollan wrote,

"How can we get what we want here while nature goes about getting what she wants?"[36] Figuring that out means paying attention
to the genius of a place—to the land, to its history, to its complexity, to the limits of what we know and can do. Respect for the
complexity and interconnections of ecosystems need not imply a
faith in balance or equilibrium. Such respect recognizes value not
just in what the land can give us but in a larger range of communities and processes that include us but are not controlled by us.

Efficiency and productivity have been very poor guides for management. This does not mean, however, that pristine nature or
unchanging natural laws would serve any better. As humans, we
inevitably have a voice in what the land becomes. We do have a
right to say that we do not want this kind of forest here, or this
kind of scrub there. But how can we define what we want and do
not want, if we cannot use natural laws or natural processes as
automatic guides to what is good?

Many conservation biologists argue that natural processes in
areas free of human disturbance offer an impartial, scientific basis
for making decisions about management goals. As a conservation
biologist, I have a certain amount of sympathy with this view, but
I still think it is wrong. Science is never impartial; conservation
biology cannot give us a set of laws to live by, much as we wish it
could. For example, DellaSala, Olson, and Crane argue that unless
managers follow a certain set of rules—set up reserves, corridors,
protect all old growth, and protect diversity at all levels—they will
inevitably run into error.[37] This may be right, but not necessarily
for the reasons the conservation biologists argue. Certain kinds of
forests may not continue without those reserves, and if people
want those kinds of forests, they will need those reserves. In other
words, human desires will not be met if we do not follow the rules.
But conservation biology does not give us a simple way of deciding what desires we should follow. Whatever we do, we are going
to favor one kind of forest or another, and the decision about
which forests are best is not a decision science can impartially
make for us.

This is why diversity was such a comforting concept to many.
The goal of preserving biodiversity seemed like a clear, scientific

goal upon which everyone could agree. But diversity, like health and sustainability, means different things to different people. Steve Fletcher, for example, had the biodiversity language down pat, but he was using it to justify clearcutting and even-aged management. Logging increased diversity by breaking up stands of single species, he argued, accurately enough. On a landscape level, the patchwork pattern left by heavy logging also meant diversity: a varied collection of even-aged stands scattered across the landscape. An ecologist might argue that instead of diversity across a landscape, we need within-stand diversity. But the replacement stands of true fir have more of this kind of diversity than did the presettlement communities of ponderosa pine. The new mixed-conifer forests have more age classes, a more complex shrub understory, and more organic matter in the soil; but does that mean we should convert all the remaining pine stands to fir, to increase within-stand diversity? Ten years ago, most foresters saw the creation of more forest edges as beneficial, since edges increased landscape-level diversity. Now edges are considered bad, since they reduce biodiversity elsewhere. When traditional foresters point out that the logging they have been doing makes the forest more diverse, ecologists tell them it is not the right kind of diversity. Foresters are understandably annoyed about this, and have begun to feel that biodiversity means whatever ecologists want it to mean.

The land has constraints, but because these constraints change as we change the land, we are never certain when we have overstepped a threshold. People want clear guidelines for management. We want someone to say: If you ever clearcut on ash soils, the sky will fall in. If you ever cut trees off a slope steeper than 45 percent, the world will come to an end. Absolute laws are something like living on top of a table, with the boundaries of allowable behavior exactly defined. We can run around all we like, with the comforting knowledge that if we get too close to the edge, a scientist will grab us and pull us back. Strict laws free us of responsibility.

But any single action will not destroy the forest; it will just change the land a little more, making it a little more impoverished, a little less resilient, or perhaps a little more diverse and a little more complex. But this is not to say that anything goes, just that we need to pay attention to the land. For there are no absolute constraints, only a changing continuum of possible degradation and possible alteration.

Foresters urge adaptive management, which at its best is a way of paying attention to what happens when we cut trees, burn forests, favor pine, or do anything else. As the first forest supervisors in the Blues recognized, everything managers do is an experiment. Experimentation means approaching the world with an open mind; scientists are supposed to treat their own ideas with humility, abandoning hypotheses if the results are not what they expected. This process is never completely open-minded; initial ideas about how the world ought to work shape what we see, what we think is worth noting down. But there is an important ideal here, of allowing the natural world to shape our ideas, and not just the other way around. There is a kind of give and take, a willingness to be surprised. The critical step for management, however, comes after the research: the hard part is using all that information to change how one works with the land. Monitoring does not necessarily mean big government programs; what it means above all is people on the ground being responsive to what the land is telling them, and being responsible for acting on that knowledge. It means a dialogue between people and land; it means people knowing the place they log, knowing the place they work.

Monitoring is never entirely objective, for it requires an implicit definition of what is healthy and what is not. Before people can decide if an action harms the land, they start out with an idea of what harm means. And that is where cultural conflicts are sharpest. People have always monitored, but we have changed our ideas of what are good and bad effects. Eighty years ago the sign of a healthy forage area was fat cows and fully eaten grasses—a perfectly reasonable way of monitoring the effects of grazing. But it focused on outputs—the cows—and neglected the information that ecologists were developing about the effects of disturbance on succession. When full use was the sign of health, monitoring meant checking to see that all plants were getting used. But now that we know that full use will lead to ecological outcomes we do not like—the replacement of native perennials with introduced annual grasses—we need to watch for different signs. Scientists can predict what kinds of outcomes different kinds of disturbance will have, and what early signs we can look for when monitoring to give us a better chance of reaching those goals. Science, however, cannot define the goals for us.

The Past as a Guide

The past can be our best guide in monitoring and restoration—a guide to how much recent activities have changed landscapes, and a guide to what once worked in a particular place. Many people think, however, that the goal of restoration is to make forests look like they used to look. As Eric Pryne wrote in the *Seattle Times*, "Careful logging and burning would help return the forests to their original condition, and reduce the scope of future wildfires." [38] Because presettlement mixed-conifer communities used to be open and parklike, managers argue that we should log out the dense understory of fir now present in these forests. As recent amendments to the 1990 forest plans make clear, the Forest Service is now legally mandated to manage the Blue Mountains so that forests return to their presettlement structure. No pine can be cut from watersheds where there is less pine than when whites arrived. No old trees can be cut from subbasins where there is less old growth than was there before white settlement. And by the same logic, if any subbasins have more old growth than used to be present, those old trees need to be cut. [39]

Descriptions of past forests can aid restoration, but they cannot tell us what is sustainable or desirable, nor will they tell us what we ought to do next. Emotionally appealing as open ponderosa forests might be, trying to change current forests back into historic forests will fail. The effort implies that what a forest looked like fifty or a hundred years ago is what it should always look like. But trying to replicate presettlement forest types on a subwatershed level means that we are in effect trying to fix patches of old forest on the landscape and keep them exactly where they used to be. This cannot work in inland forests, because disturbance processes kept old growth cycling through the landscape. [40]

The desire to return forests to their "natural" state grows out of a recognition that people have managed the forest to a point where it fails to produce what they want—pine for the mills. Nor do people emotionally like the current forests much, for they have become cluttered and insect-ridden. The overall fear, however, is that by creating an unnatural forest, people have degraded it to the point where it is no longer sustainable or self-healing, and its health will only deteriorate. As a panel of Forest Service scientists headed by David Caraher wrote, "When systems are 'pushed' outside the bounds of natural variability there is substantial risk that biological diversity and ecological function will not be maintained, and therefore, ecological systems will not be naturally sustained."[41] This may well be true; people have certainly degraded many lands in the past, to the point they could no longer support forests. But the presettlement forests were not pristine, and even if they had been, that would not necessarily make them sustainable. Many people assume that if repeated fires were burning every eight to ten years, the forest must have adapted to this, making sure that something was replacing the nitrogen that fires were volatilizing. Presettlement forests were not necessarily in any kind of long-term balance, however. They could have had so much of their shrub layer removed by Indian practices that repeated burning might have been pushing them toward a state where the soil would no longer have supported forests. Alternatively, presettlement forests might have been in a short-term equilibrium. But we have already added so many disturbances to the nonhuman disturbances that we cannot predict with any confidence what paths succession will follow once we try to change the forest back to what it used to look like. Structural similarities may not go very deep.

Knowing what forests used to look like will not give us any easy answers, but historical knowledge can be helpful in managing current forests. Although many elements of the forests constantly changed—such as the ratio of pine to other species—other elements remained fairly consistent across broad areas, at least during the hundred years for which we have records. These elements, rather than simply the ratio of pine to fir, may be what we want to restore. Across the Blues, historical surveys agree that 70 to 90 percent of the forests were mature or old. In other words, even though the actual makeup of the particular stand would change, and the ratio of pine to other trees would change, and the understory components would change, there always seemed to be a very high ratio of mature trees to immature trees, and a very high ratio of uneven-aged overstory to even-aged overstory. Diversity was another constant. Except for lodgepole pine forests, forests were patchy, with a variety of species in both the overstory and understory. All the forests were not, by any means, open pine stands; complexity was the rule, even in forests dominated by ponderosa. These are the elements that might have been important for allowing the forests to persist, and so these may be what we want to aim for—a high ratio of mature trees to young trees, predominately uneven-aged stands, and complex, patchy, diverse forests.[42]

Historical records also offer a baseline for monitoring the effects—both expected and unexpected—of management. In addition to the dramatic decline in large ponderosas and open stands, the clearest effects of Forest Service management seem to be a reduction in complexity, snags and deadwood, and mature and old trees of all species. Across the Blues, we have far less old growth, far fewer old trees, and far fewer stands with an uneven-aged overstory than used to be present. The average volumes of ponderosa pine, western larch, white fir, and Douglas-fir have all declined; we lack large trees of all major species, not just large pine. Very young forests were once small patches within a sea of mature forests; even-aged stands were once small patches within a sea of uneven-aged forests; monocultures were tiny patches within a sea of diverse forests. All these patterns have been reversed: now we have tiny uneven-aged patches of diverse old growth in a sea of young, even-aged forests. Even-aged management across large landscapes does not reflect anything we know about what the eastside forests looked like before the Forest Service started managing.

Records of historic forest conditions allow us to use the past as a way of monitoring the indirect effects of what we do to the land. We can look at past activities (say, group-selection logging of ponderosa on south-facing slopes), then use historical records to trace some of the ways the forest changed in response to those activities.

Historical records can also help unravel competing hypotheses about the effects of different activities on the land. For example, many managers hypothesize that forests changed the most during periods of lightest selective cutting, so heavy cutting is necessary to reverse changes. The history of management in the Blues shows, however, that light selective cutting was not the sole cause of current fir understories; high-grading and very intense logging of pine during the 1920s probably played more important roles. Therefore, heavy logging will not logically reverse the damage done by heavy logging in the first place.

Foresters have always based their decisions about cutting techniques on historical hypotheses, even though they have rarely stated these as hypotheses. Managers argued that pine grew up only in areas of substantial disturbance, so therefore clearcutting was necessary to regenerate pine. The historical record does not support this argument, because ponderosa did not often regenerate in areas of heavy logging disturbance. A new variant of the historical argument is that we should manage in ways that mimic natural disturbances. Because windstorms or fires naturally killed blocks of trees, foresters reason, clearcutting mimics natural processes. There are major flaws in that argument. First, clearcutting bears very little resemblance to fire or windstorms. Most inland western forests were uneven-aged: they did not grow up all at once after a major disturbance; young trees grew up in patches under small clumps of dead trees. In the inland forests, most disturbances were small and local. A tree fell, pulled down a few trees with it, and in the resultant patch of light, the young reproduction that was already biding its time there shot up, with the nutrients offered by the decaying tree contributing to rapid growth. Single-tree or group-selection harvests can better mimic this, but only when a chunk of the large dead wood is left on the site.

Natural and human disturbances may not be intrinsically different, yet recent industrial disturbances have surpassed in scale and intensity any preindustrial disturbances that forests managed to survive. Clearcuts now cover half the commercial forest area in some watersheds, and that level of fragmentation is probably nothing like what forests experienced in the past two thousand years.

Historically, disturbances were common, but disturbed patches were usually small. Burns, windstorms, and insect kills formed irregular patterns of disturbed and undisturbed forests, and the undisturbed patches offered refuges where organisms could recolonize after a disturbance. Nor do clearcuts mimic presettlement patterns of fiber removal. In most presettlement fires, small wood burned, but large-diameter wood—the dead standing trees and large logs—remained on the site. Timber harvests reverse the pattern. Clearcuts remove the big wood and leave behind the small bits, which increase fire danger but do not store water or contribute much organic matter to the soil.

There are larger theoretical problems, however, with the "even-aged management mimics natural disturbances" argument. Just because a disturbance is natural does not mean a forest will survive it. Even if clearcuts were exactly the same as natural disturbances, clearcuts would not *replace* natural disturbances; they would represent additional, cumulative impacts. If one level of disturbance was natural, doubling or tripling that level would not necessarily be natural. As disturbances accumulate, their effects can increase exponentially. Up to a certain level of pressure, a system may absorb the disturbance and keep functioning, but once a threshold is passed, the system may collapse. Much as we try, we cannot substitute our version of nature for the nature out there. We can only play around with it a bit, tugging on this process, pushing a little at that other process, adding our own agents of mortality—loggers—to the agents of mortality that are always going to be out there: decay, insects, fire, and wind.

Restoring Inefficiency: Death, Decay, and Waste

Restoring the inland western forests means not just focusing on ponderosa pine, but restoring the ecological processes that allowed forests to develop in a dry landscape. Death and decay are essential parts of these ecological processes; predators, insects, diseases, and fire are what enabled forests to persist. We have never been very comfortable with anything that reminds us of mortality, but the death of its parts is what allows a forest to live. Predators, for example, play critical but indirect and often subtle roles in shaping plant communities. Elk and deer drive forest succession by eating some plants but not others.[43] Mountain lions and coyotes in turn eat the deer and elk, thereby regulating the intensity of herbivory and indirectly affecting plant succession. Having a complex forest means restoring the habitat for predators, which tend to require space and structural diversity—forests with a large component of old trees and dead trees.

Traditional management aimed for full efficiency. And for trees this meant even-aged management, extracting as much timber as possible and minimizing the losses to mortality. Efficiency, however, is a lousy way to manage dry inland forests. Forests are not efficient. If they were, the first disturbance would have destroyed them. The monocultures that are planted after clearcuts may be economically more efficient, but as the history of the Blues illustrates, short-term economic efficiency tends to mean long-term ecological disaster. Preindustrial disturbances happened in a buffered, complex landscape, one that provided refuges for insects, soil fauna, and predators. Redundancy and duplication allow one part of the land to change for a while without killing off all the processes dependent on that part. When we make the land efficient, we eliminate that resiliency.[44]

We have no idea how much wood we can extract from the forest without harming ecological processes. Foresters traditionally believed that excess wood was available for harvest, and they tried to eliminate all waste so that trees would grow as fast as possible and mortality would be only a small fraction of growth. Many foresters still believe this, as the Idaho policy report makes clear. Trying to keep mortality so limited, however, seems like a recipe for ecological collapse, because dead wood is integral to many ecological processes. Environmentalists often imply that we cannot take anything out of the forest without causing it to lose its integrity as an ecosystem. If we remove trees, we will make the ecosystem unravel. The problem with this argument is that it assumes two things: first, that the forest is a closed system, and second, that the forest ecosystem is delicately balanced, and any external human pressures will cause that balance to collapse. But the forest is not a closed system; it constantly receives energy from the sun, and plants then convert this energy to carbon compounds. Presumably we can remove something, but not everything. The trick, of course, is deciding how much we can remove; and that decision needs to be attuned to the individual site.

Many people think of old growth or dead trees as something extra—either waste or else frosting on the cake ("amenities," in the language of the Forest Service's desired future conditions). Yet these elements may be what allows young forests to get their start. The initial stages of a forest, when trees are growing very rapidly, require more water, light, and nutrients than later stages. Young forests never occurred in very large patches in the inland West, suggesting that old forests—which create their own microclimates— might act as critical sources for the establishment of young stands. Since older forests are cooler and moister than surrounding areas, the young trees that can survive inside them may often not survive in the open. For the past centuries the inland climate has been warming, so many of the forests established initially when it was cooler and moister. Those forests can persist in the hotter, dryer conditions now present, because they have created local refuges for young trees—places where a patch of trees may fall over, opening up the canopy and letting in light, but where it is still cool, and slightly shaded. If we remove their overstories, however, forests might not be able to establish themselves again until the climate cools. People have assumed that if a forest is in a place, that place automatically supports trees: you can cut the forest down and grow another forest. But in dry, marginal places, the forest may be creating the moister conditions that allow it to persist. Cutting it down may mean no more forest for centuries.

Because of the aridity of the inland West, water is critical in restoration. Forests depend on the streams, creeks, seeps, and springs; but these in turn depend on the forests. If forests are poorly cut, streams can vanish, and then forests have a much harder time reestablishing. We cannot step back in time if we regret something we have done, because our actions change the relationships between elements of the ecosystem. Protecting water means in large part protecting the elusive, shifting margins between water and land. And that means encouraging vigorous populations of hardwoods along the borders. Riparian hardwoods are thirsty plants, and people have often cut them down for just that reason. They thought hardwoods were stealing water from livestock and more useful trees. But using water does not always mean reducing the supply for everything else, for riparian vegetation allows streams to continue flowing. Even while they steal water, those plants increase the available supply to other plants. Riparian plants make the boundaries between water and land more complex, slowing water flow, keeping dirt from flooding the streams and clogging the gills of fish. The leaves of these plants shade the streams, reducing water temperatures. Their branches and dead wood fall into the water, trapping debris, forming dams, and creating deep pools of scoured gravel where fish can spawn.

We tend to think that water and land are separate elements, but they interrelate in often surprising and ambiguous ways. Half the food that aquatic vertebrates eat comes not from the water but from the land. Where do fish get this terrestrial food, if they are staying in the water where they belong? The food falls from overhanging shrubs, and crawls along the dead and down wood that litters the creeks.[45] When foresters pulled the logs out of creeks, they thought they were cleaning up after themselves, leaving a good neat site. Trees obviously did not belong in the water; they belonged on the land or in a mill. Likewise, riparian plants blur the boundaries, slowing stream flow, keeping banks tangled, meandering, and uncertain. People used to think all this was bad. The purpose of a stream was to move water from point A to point B as efficiently as possible. But the more that people tried to simplify streams by channeling them and piping them and cleaning them up, the more the waters dwindled away.

If we cannot rely on presettlement forests for an indication of what is sustainable, what can we rely on? Relying on our own engineering to develop new forests is a terrifying thought, because our engineering seems only to lead us into ecological disasters. Every time in the past that we tried to manage for sustained yield and sustainability, we were actually pulling out elements of forests and soils that seemed superfluous, but were in fact critical. How then can we find a balance between our desires and the land's limits, in a world where we are no longer certain that we even believe in balance? When we set out to restore fire-resistant pine forests, we need to act with humility and circumspection. Everyone who has ever tried to fix the forests has ended up making them worse. Early foresters had good science, just as we do now, so science alone will not save us. Intensive management will not save the forests either. Further simplifying the forests is an absurd way to correct the problem of oversimplification. The kinds of goals we need to set are goals of living well within a community, of recognizing that we know so little that it behooves us to be humble, to pay attention to the effects of what we do.

Conclusion: Living with Complexity

Forest management led to a dizzying series of unexpected effects and unintended consequences. Every time a manager tried to fix one problem, the solution created a worse problem elsewhere. The best of intentions often brought about the worst of outcomes. As Stephen Pyne has argued in regard to fire, attempts to manage natural systems were often self-defeating: they introduced an element of instability into the systems they were supposed to be stabilizing. For example, fire protection and insect control involved efforts to control natural disasters by eliminating the unpleasantness and engineering it out of existence. Fire managers tried to prevent catastrophic fires by suppressing all small fires. Insect managers tried to control insect damage by killing all insects as soon as they appeared, or by simplifying individual stands so insects could not survive. In spite of these efforts, attempts at fire and insect control led only to worse devastation. Suppressing fires led to fuel accumulations, slowed the growth of many forests, and made future fires more intense. Changing old-growth stands to even-aged stands in order to control insects only eliminated insect predators, and contributed to the catastrophic insect damage now apparent in the Blues. A refusal to tolerate low intensity fires made moderate fires behave more erratically, just as a refusal to tolerate low intensity insect damage made future damage worse. Failures of fire and insect control generally led not to a reevaluation of the enterprise but to more engineering, more spraying, more fire fighters, more intensive management to fix the problems management created.

A kind of arrogance made it increasingly difficult for forest managers in the Blues, and throughout the Forest Service, to pay attention to signs that things were going wrong. Every time the Forest

Service's authority was challenged, its response was to consolidate its own power by appealing to its status as an organization of non-political, disinterested scientists with the best interests of the nation at heart. Increasingly, foresters refused to admit even to themselves that they might not know the best ways to manage forests.

Foresters have always found it difficult to imagine alternative consequences for their actions. They have also had a hard time recognizing that what they know about the forest is only a small part of the forest's story. This difficulty comes partly from the scientific optimism behind American forestry—the faith that whatever exists can be understood. Forestry has also run into problems with its urge to resolve nature's inefficiencies and make the world more productive. Yet it is unclear whether this kind of optimistic blindness, this urge to tell a simpler story about the land, is necessary to manage land. The line between trying to understand nature and trying to redesign it to fit certain narrow ideals is a thin one indeed.

Much of the difficulty in management lies in the complexity of the forest. As Jack Ward Thomas, the wildlife biologist who catalyzed much of the New Perspectives work in the Blues, and who is now the Chief of the Forest Service, once said: "The forest is an extremely complex place; in fact, it is too complex for us to ever hope to understand." Nevertheless, one still has to manage it; there is no neutral position possible, no way to say we are simply not going to manage land. All attempts to manage are attempts to tell a story about how the land ought to be, and by definition, all these stories are simpler than the world itself.

In many of the early silvics reports in the Blues, foresters would first admit that there were too many contradictory uncertainties to be sure of anything, and then two pages later they would reaffirm existing policy—thus suppressing doubts, uncertainties, and internal debates. The same thing is still happening. In *The Blue Mountains Forest Health Report,* for example, there is a recurrent confusion about the role of insects, disease, and fire; this stems from a larger unease about the role of waste and inefficiency in forests. Following New Perspectives guidelines, the report states that insects and disease are integral parts of any forest ecosystem. Yet in the individual chapters on insect management, the Forest Service's goal is still the eradication of individual insect pests—a goal that the report argues is best achieved through even-aged management of forest stands. In one chapter, foresters talk about how interconnected forests are and how necessary disease and fire are for forest health, and then a chapter later foresters recommend even-aged stands for maximum production. Foresters are still focused on individual forest stands, because it is extremely difficult to think about a forest without breaking it into pieces. To think about the whole you think about stands, and even when you acknowledge the interconnections between stands, it is difficult to know what to do with them. In the report, the authors retreated into old ways of thinking; perhaps because the alternative seemed to be paralysis. If everything is interconnected, anything we do will backfire, so maybe the easiest thing to do is business as usual—or else nothing at all.

Each time, when faced with complexity, foresters eventually denied it and retreated into their certainty. In their minds they partly acknowledged this complexity and partly denied it, just as the same forester could simultaneously have both a knowledge of ecology's interconnections and a faith in his own ability to redesign a more efficient forest. Foresters were not, as many environmentalists claim, greedy or stupid. Like everyone else, they needed to hold onto a story that made their lives make sense. Their work was based on the faith that they were making the forests better. If they let themselves see the evidence in front of them—that the forests were dying, not getting better—they would have to give up the vision that made sense of their lives. Instead, they blinded themselves to the consequences of their actions, ignored the doubts that crept in, and condescended to people who challenged their version of the forest.

Everyone does this, not just foresters. People are extremely skilled at believing any number of contradictory facts. If you believe in progress, if you have faith in the ideal of creating a good life in a good land, you rarely abandon that faith when facts suggest otherwise. You suppress or ignore the evidence. Each action makes sense in the light of what preceded it; in fact, each action seems like the only sensible, rational action to take at the time. Dim rumblings of trouble might come through, but you ignore them. You go back to shoring up the levees, fighting the brush fires, mending the ditches that irrigate your fields, spraying DDT on the insects that infest your trees. You cannot let yourself imagine that the forest might function better on its own terms, that things might be better off without all your efforts. And when the realization finally hits that you were wrong, you feel bitter and betrayed.

William Kittredge, a writer who grew up ranching on the high lands of eastern Oregon just south of the Blues, has expressed this sense of betrayal and confusion as well as anyone has:

> We summered our cattle on more than a million acres of Taylor Grazing Land across the high lava rock and sagebrush desert out east of the valley, miles of territory where we owned most of what water there was, and it was ours. We owned it all, or so we felt. . . . And then it all went dead, over years, but swiftly. You can imagine our surprise and despair, our sense of having been profoundly cheated. . . . We felt enormously betrayed. For so many years, through endless efforts, we had proceeded in good faith, and it turned out we had wrecked all we had not left untouched. The beloved migratory rafts of waterbirds, the green-headed mallards and the redheads and canvasbacks, the cinnamon teal and the great Canadian honkers, were mostly gone along with their swampland habitat. . . . We had reinvented our valley according to the most persuasive ideal given us by our culture, and we ended with a landscape organized like a machine for growing crops and fattening cattle, a machine that creaked a little louder each year, a dreamland gone wrong. . . . We thought we were living the right lives, creating a great precise perfection of fields, and we found the mythology had been telling us an enormous lie. The world had proven too complex, or the myth too simpleminded. And we were mortally angered.[1]

This sense of betrayal is echoed throughout the *Blue Mountains Forest Health Report*. As the report states, "past management practices such as fire exclusion and selective timber harvesting, though carried out with the best intentions and using the best information of the time, have led to potentially catastrophic [conditions]. . . . In offering this report, we realize that we may face the same situation as past managers who also used 'state-of-the-art' information. Their efforts contributed, to greater or lesser degrees, to the forest health problems we presently face; so we note that 'good faith' is simply not enough when it comes to managing entire ecosystems."[2] The authors seem to feel trapped by the confusion of their history: since they do not understand what went wrong before, anything they do now to correct problems may lead to worse results.

Everyone has a story they tell about their work, and about the way their work connects them to their place, their home. Environmentalists tell one set of stories, loggers tell a different set, managers tell yet another. The early Forest Service workers told a story that was full of promise and exuberance, and this story betrayed them. They saw their work as a heroic struggle; their efforts would make the land yield all its promised abundance; the world was open to them and they would make it better. It is a sad thing for foresters to give up that story and end up instead with pale green government offices and broken Xerox machines, endless meetings and petitions, and angry people grumbling at them all the time.

Histories of environmental change can begin to sound as if the moral is that there is no way people can work on the land without setting in motion its inevitable collapse. In these stories, people are inevitably separate from "wild nature," and their only relationship with that wildness is destructive. But there is no essential nature out there waiting to be saved. We tend to think nature is all the stuff out there—what surrounds us when we shut the door and step off the porch—but it is no more outside us than our breath or bones are outside us. The image of wild nature as a paradise uncontaminated by humans ultimately justifies the degradation of the relationship between people and land. We need another set of stories—a vision of wild nature that does not exclude people and cows and logs. We can never restore the Blues back to an idealized wild nature; trying to do so contributes little to the attempt to live in a place without destroying what one loves about that place.

Wildlife management, like logging and grazing, can be done very poorly. These activities generated a century of policy which led to depleted resources, silted streams, and seemingly endless difficulties. This does not mean such activities are bad in and of themselves. They can all seem to foster a lack of respect for the land, an arrogance about the ability of people to make things better. But the opposite can also be true: they can be ways of attending to the land's signs, reading stories in the land. Nor are they activities entirely without a spiritual or ethical dimension. It is too simple to contrast, for example, Native American hunters—whose hunting created a spiritual relationship with the prey—with white hunters who want to shoot something only for fun or food. An important part of Western tradition has been the belief that hunting can be a spiritual act. One of President Theodore Roosevelt's favorite books was *The Master of Game,* a medieval hunting manual written in 1407. In 1909, Roosevelt wrote an introduction for the book's London edition, and he undoubtedly shared his enthusiasm with his close friend and fellow hunter, Gifford Pinchot, who was then Chief of the Forest Service. *The Master of Game* justified hunting in a way that suggests why Roosevelt found the book so appealing:

There is no man's life that uses gentle game and sport less displeasurable unto God than is the life of a perfect and skillful hunter. Now shall I prove how hunters live in this world most joyfully of any other men. For when the hunter rises in the morning, he sees a sweet and fair morrow, and the weather clear and bright, and [he] hears the song of the small fowls, the which sing sweetly with great melody and full of love each in his language in the best way that he may. And when the Sun is arisen he shall see the fresh dew upon the small twigs and grass . . . and that is greatly liking and joy to the hunter's heart. He shall ride after them [his hounds] and he shall shout and blow as loud as he may with great joy and great liking and I assure you that he never thinks of no other sin nor no other evil.[3]

Hunting was a kind of prayer—a way of professing faith in creation not entirely unlike Native traditions. The hunter paid attention to the sunlight on the dew, the individual songs of individual birds, and by paying attention, he allowed himself to feel joy. By making connections to a particular place, one can see it as something valuable in and of itself, and not just something that produces useful commodities.

There is a certain paradox here, because the people in the Blues who caused the saddest changes were the settlers and foresters—those who were most connected to a place, those who tried hardest to make the land fit their dream. Migratory loggers and fur trappers took what they wanted and left, bringing about plenty of changes in the process. But for all their damage to beaver and pine, they never became entangled in the web of complications in which the Forest Service and settlers found themselves trapped.

Whites came to the Blues with preconceptions derived from experiences in frontiers that much more closely resembled Northern Europe, and this baggage caused many of the ecological and moral crises now facing us. Settlers wanted standard American dreams, "a new chance, a little gray home in the West, adventure, danger, bonanza, total freedom from constraint and law and obligation," in Wallace Stegner's words.[4] But these dreams, for the majority, just did not pay off. The act of work, the struggle with the land, can become a spiritual partnership. Yet there is a painful irony here, since the love of the land transforms that landscape. Stegner—one of the West's most perceptive writers, a teacher, novelist, and historian—argued that we need to let the western land shape us and stop trying to force the land to fit our ideals. We can work on the land, but only if we let the land itself draw the boundaries. When we try to play God, we create disasters like the Blues. Stegner quotes the writer Mary Austin, who wrote of the California Shoshones: "the manner of the country makes the usage of life there, and the land will not be lived in except in its own fashion. The Shoshones live like their trees, with great spaces between."[5]

It may well be that the system that works best on marginal, semi-arid land is one that mimics what worked before whites settled: namely, a wandering life. "Life on the wing," as the missionary Henry Spalding called the Nez Percé's way of life, is a lot less damaging than trying to settle and force the land to grow crops. Grazing is one kind of life on the wing that could work well in western lands, under certain conditions. Native ungulates trample and eat the vegetation in one localized place, deposit their bit of fertilizer and move on some place else. Movement is critical; and that is what cows are reluctant to do unless there is someone out there persuading them to do so.

Mobility is the usual way that animals and human cultures adapt to the constraints of limited water, but mobility is also at the root of our problems. As Stegner argued, the West "was largely a civilization in motion, driven by dreams"; being footloose "is associated in our minds with escape from history and oppression and law and irksome obligations, with absolute freedom, and the road has always led west."[6] This rootlessness can become a curse. Westerners have always been good at using up a bit of land and then going elsewhere. We have been reluctant to form close attachments with one place because there is always a better place over the next horizon.

So the answer perhaps is to figure out some way of working with dry lands and dry forests by forming close connections to a place but also being willing to adapt to the character of the place. A combination of mobility and connection: it may sound hard, but it's not impossible. That is what transhumance is—moving on fixed rounds, from the lower winter valleys to the high summer meadows. You take care of land, but you also move with it. You do not try to force an American version of irrigated, high production, high intensity efficiency on the land; you let the constraints of water and elevation and temperature shape your efforts.

Many environmentalists now call for a complete exclusion of livestock from the public lands; others call for exclusion from at least the wilderness and recreation areas. High meadows have made substantial recoveries since the 1930s, in large part because sheep are no longer common on the forest, due more to changes in markets than to ecological reasons. Cattle are still damaging riparian zones, however, as well as grassland communities. Yet even bunchgrass communities, which did not evolve under heavy grazing pressures, did evolve in disturbance regimes. Without some kind of disturbance such as fire or grazing, grasslands will succeed to something else. This is not necessarily a bad thing; but if one wants grasslands, one needs disturbances. Cattle are not inherently bad for bunchgrass lands; there are ways to have both cattle and native grass communities. Certainly, cattle favor riparian zones, but so do elk; a single cow does not do much more damage than a single elk to a stream bank. The 109,000 "animal units" (one cow and her calf) present on the Umatilla today, however, do far more damage than the 15,000 elk that are also present. Cattle and sheep have been badly mismanaged, and this had led to extensive ecological changes across the Blues—changes that are generally regarded as undesirable. Replacement of perennial bunchgrasses with non-native annuals such as cheatgrass, erosion in high mountain meadows, and damage to riparian zones are among the effects of Forest Service grazing management in the Blues. But it is the management that is at fault, not the animals. Livestock grazing has not worked well because the goals of management have often focused on maximizing commodity production and maximizing use. These goals inevitably lead to continued deterioration of the ranges, since when one works within this paradigm, things that reduce grazing damage will always be seen as added costs that cannot be afforded in hard economic times.

Where is the Forest Service in this debate? On the one hand, its researchers are willing partners in setting different goals for the future: "desired future conditions" rather than outputs are supposed to drive management. But commodities and efficient maximum utilization are still the principal criteria for management. For example, the 1990 Umatilla National Forest Plan—by far the most environmentally focused of the three Blues forest plans—argues that grazing can be tripled with the help of science. The plan states that in fifty years, with intensive management, the Forest Service can increase grazing from 109,000 AUMs (animal unit months—one cow and her calf on the ground for one month) to 274,000 AUMs.[7] This statement comes after thirty pages detailing the damages done by cattle to riparian zones, meadows, plant communities, salmon spawning habitat, in an area where 90 percent of the streams are—by the plan's own admission—in poor condition. Beef consumption is also down, cattle markets are not what they used to be, and the Forest Service is being sued right and left for fish habitat violations. But none of this seems to disturb the planners; they are still working within a paradigm of intensive management, where the goal is to maximize biological potentials.

But there are other ways of thinking about grazing; other goals that can motivate management. Jack Southworth, a cattle rancher in Seneca, Oregon, spoke about this:

For almost the first 100 years of the ranch, we never thought of the ecosystem. We did everything we could to simplify it to make it easier to understand, and therefore to manage. For example, in the 1950s, the Soil Conservation Service built a nifty plan to straighten the Silvies River where it runs through a couple of miles of our meadows. And we got rid of those obnoxious willows that got in our way during haying; those branches would break a mower section now and then. But, then we had to build rip-rap along the streambanks to stabilize them. . . . And the more we managed it, the worse it became. . . .

I used to give a class at Oregon State University about ranch management. I had a slide that showed some nice cross-bred cattle. I showed this slide for three years before I saw the creek. The creek banks were really eroded, and I didn't see it until someone in the class pointed it out to me. What's happening throughout our society is that we ranchers for all time didn't see the creek, and now we're starting to.[8]

Southworth is advocating a shift in the ways people envision the land: an altered paradigm that lets one see the creek and not just the fat cows. At the core of this is a set of goals focused not on producing maximum commodities, but on restoring biodiversity and complexity to the land—while also producing some commodities. Instead of focusing on beef production as the goal, Southworth argues: "Cattle are not an end or a goal in themselves; they're a tool. They're a tool we can use to make a living. It's a tool we can also use to get some benefits on the side." What then should be the goals, if not more fat cows? One way of setting new goals is to focus on what kind of land you want. Instead of just cows, the Southworths decided: "Our landscape goal for the ranch was to have a dense stand of perennial grasses with some shrubs. We wanted our forest areas to be healthy and uneven-aged in the stand. We wanted the creeks on the ranch to be winding and stocked with beaver and lined with willow." They changed their vision of a good life on a good land, and that changed the way they treat the land.

There is nothing correct or "natural" about any of these visions of the land; they are all products of human intervention. There is no way to work with the land and not end up changing it. If people decide to exclude timber harvests and grazing entirely from the Blues, the alternative will be tourism, which assumes a sentimentalized view of nature where the observer is an outsider, someone whose true work and true home is elsewhere. The preservation of the Blues as a park for recreationists and vacation homes is no more natural than the Forest Service's "desired future conditions" for the Blues. This goal depends on an idealized vision of nature, just as much as traditional Forest Service management did. The idealized visions differ, but they are all expressions of human desire.

There are ways of living on the land that pay attention to the land, and ways that do not. The land is full of information, and trying to attend to this information—trying to monitor the effects of human actions—is a task whose complexity has overwhelmed federal agencies and individuals alike. Many of the problems of the last century in the Blues have come from people trying to force the land to fit an idealized vision—of wild nature, of a productive regulated forest, of a grassland utilized to its full biological potential. The problem with these ideal visions is that they make it hard to pay attention to the land itself. But that does not mean if we do away with visions, we will see the true nature of a place. It doesn't exist. People will always look at the land through an idealized vision of what they want from the land. There are visions of nature which are more respectful than others; visions which allow information to go both ways. No one can restore the Blues back to their original state; however, we can restore the Blues to an inevitably altered, but not inevitably impoverished, biota—by giving up our ideals of maximum efficiency and commodity production, and substituting other ideals which allow for complexity, diversity, and uncertainty.

Notes

ABBREVIATIONS

MNF Malheur National Forest
RCF Forest Service Research Compilation Files, National Archives, Region VI, Entry 115, Boxes 135 to 139. Most of the Research Compilation Files for Region VI (Oregon and Washington) have been microfilmed and are available in the University of Washington microfilm library, file A1527.
UNF Umatilla National Forest
WWNF Wallowa Whitman National Forest

Place and Ecology

1. Wilson Price Hunt, "Journal," in *The Discovery of the Oregon Trail: Robert Stuart's Narrative of His Journey,* ed. Philip A. Rollins (New York, 1935), 285.

2. Information on climate and physical geography comes largely from the three forest plans: the *Umatilla National Forest Land and Resource Management Plan, Final Environmental Impact Statement* (USDA Forest Service, Washington, D.C., 1990), III-30; *Malheur National Forest Land and Resource Management Plan, Final Environmental Impact Statement* (USDA Forest Service, Washington, D.C., 1990); and the *Wallowa Whitman National Forest Land and Resource Management Plan, Final Environmental Impact Statement* (USDA Forest Service, Washington, D.C., 1990).

3. *Umatilla Plan,* III, passim; *Malheur Plan,* III, passim; *Wallowa Whitman Plan,* III, passim.

4. Lisa Graumlich, "Long-term Records of Temperature and Precipitation in the Pacific Northwest Derived from Tree Rings" (Ph.D. diss., University of Washington, College of Forest Resources, 1985).

5. D. W. Meinig, *The Great Columbia Plain: A Historical Geography, 1805–1910* (Seattle, 1968), 106.

6. For information on the Mount Mazama explosions, see Charles G. Johnson, Jr., et al., "Biotic and Abiotic Processes of Eastside Ecosystems," in vol. 3: *Assessment, Eastside Forest Ecosystem Health Assessment,* ed. Richard L. Everett (USDA Forest Service General Technical Report PNW-GTR-322, 1994, 1–20. For an overview of management impacts on different inland soils, see Alan E. Harvey, et al., "Biotic and Abiotic Processes in Eastside Ecosystems: The Effects of Management on Soil Properties, Processes, and Productivity," in vol. 3: *Assessment, Eastside Forest Ecosystem Health Assessment,* ed. Richard L. Everett (USDA Forest Service General Technical Report PNW-GTR-323, 1994), 25–45. Also see J. Michael Geist et al., "Assessing Physical Conditions of Some Pacific Northwest Volcanic Ash Soils after Forest Harvest," *Soil Science Society of America Journal* 53 (1989): 946–50.

7. Frederick C. Hall, "Historical and Present Conditions of the Blue Mountain Forests," *Natural Resource News* (March 1994), 1–2.

8. Jack Ward Thomas, ed., *Wildlife Habitats in Managed Forests, the Blue Mountains of Oregon and Washington* (USDA Forest Service, 1979), 20.

9. The Wallowas were north of where the biggest ponderosas grew in the Blues, so larger trees probably existed. These particular tree sizes were noted by R. M. Evans, "General Silvical Report Wallowa and Minam Forests, 1912," National Archives, Forest Service Research Compilation Files, Region VI, Entry 115, Box 135 (hereafter abbreviated as RCF). Most of the Research Compilation Files for Region VI (Oregon and Washington) were microfilmed and are in the University of Washington microfilm library, file A1527. Tree size averages from early and late 1900s are not directly comparable, for several reasons. First, it is hard to know exactly what the 1912 averages meant: did they include the young trees, or just mature ones? Second, the 1990 averages include only trees large enough to be harvested; if all age classes were included, the average size would be much smaller, since over 50 percent of the ponderosa is immature now on the forests. Age class distributions have changed enormously because of heavy logging, and this affects size averages. But even when only mature trees of harvestable size are included, the 1990 population of ponderosa is much smaller than the 1912 population. See the *Wallowa Whitman National Forest Plan* (1990).

10. Frederick Hall, "Ecology of Natural Underburning in the Blue Mountains of Oregon," USDA Forest Service Pacific Northwest Region Regional Guide 51–1 (August 1977), 5. For a recent synthesis of fire ecology, see James K. Agee, *Fire Ecology of Pacific Northwest Forest* (Washington, D.C., 1993), 113–150. For a very useful summary of fire ecology in the inland West, see M. F. Crane and William C. Fisher, *Fire Ecology of the Forest Habitat Types of Central Idaho* (USDA Forest Service General Technical Report INT-GTR-218, 1986).

11. Narcissa Whitman, "Diary and Letter," in Clifford Drury, ed., *First White Women over the Rockies: Diaries, Letters, and Biographical Sketches of the Six Women of the Oregon Mission Who Made the Overland Journey in 1836 and 1838,* 2 vols. (Glendale, Calif., 1963), 87, 88–93.

12. H. D. Foster, "Report on the Silvics of the Blue Mountains (E) National Forest" (1908), RCF 135.

13. Grand fir is sometimes seen as a separate species from white fir, sometimes as the same species. At the moment, consensus seems to be that they are one species, so when I write grand fir, I also include what used to be called white fir. Douglas-fir is not actually a fir; so grand fir and white fir are called the true firs. When I write true fir or grand fir, I am not including Douglas-fir.

14. Evans, "Wallowa and Minam Forests" (1912).

15. Ibid.

16. Ibid.

17. George Bright, "Umatilla Studies: Annual Silvical Report 2/23/11," RCF 137.

18. H. D. Foster, "Blue Mountains" (1908), 6.

19. Evans, "Wallowa and Minam Forests" (1912).

20. Daniel Mathews, *Cascade-Olympic Natural History* (Portland, 1988), 44.

21. Crane and Fisher, *Fire Ecology,* 7. Lodgepole seedlings also grow very quickly in the open sunlight, more quickly than its associates.

22. Ibid.

23. *Wallowa Whitman Forest Plan* (1990), III-45.

24. Hall, "Ecology of Natural Underburning" (1977), 1–13; Agee, *Fire Ecology* (1993), 320–38. Also see Kathleen Ryoko Maruoka, "Fire History of *Pseudotsuga menziesii* and *Abies grandis* Stands in the Blue Mountains of Oregon and Washington" (master's thesis, University of Washington, 1994), 21–33.

25. Frederick Hall was the first ecologist to argue this for the Blues, in "Ecology of Natural Underburning" (1977), 1–13. Since Hall, others such as Crane and Fisher (1986) and Agee (1993) have also developed this theme.

26. Hall (1977) argued this for the Blue Mountains, and Stephen Pyne developed the theme more generally in *Fire in America: A Cultural History of Wildland and Rural Fire* (Princeton, 1982).

27. John D. Guthrie, "Blame it on the Indians: Forester explodes myth that Red Men set fires to keep forests open," press release, 1933, Malheur National Forest, Supervisor's Office, John Day.

28. Hall, "Ecology of Natural Underburning" (1977), 5–7.

29. Ibid., 7–11; Crane and Fisher, *Fire Ecology* (1986), 8–12.

30. For an overview of the effects of fire on soil nutrients, see Agee, *Fire

Ecology (1993), 151–171. For debates on fire's effects on inland ecosystems, see the March 1994 issue of *Natural Resource News,* which was devoted to fire. Also see the chapters in John D. Walstad et al., eds., *Natural and Prescribed Fire in Pacific Northwest Forests* (Corvallis, Oregon, 1990). Harvey et al., "Biotic and Abiotic Processes" (1994), give a good summary of the effects of burning on inland soils (pp. 20–24).

31. Foster, "Report on the Silvics of the Wenaha Forest Reserve, 10/1/06," RCF 135. Evans, "Wallowa and Minam Forests" (1912) added that in mixed-conifer stands within the Wallowa forest, "crown fire in mature stands are extremely rare."

32. Arthur R. Tiedemann and James Klemmedson, "Prescribed Burning and Productivity: A Nutrient Management Perspective," *Natural Resource News* (March 1994), 6–9.

33. Ibid.

34. Harvey et al., "Biotic and Abiotic Processes" (1994), 20–23.

35. Tiedemann and Klemmedson, "Prescribed Burning and Productivity," 6–9.

36. See William Gast et al., *The Blue Mountains Forest Health Report* (Washington, D.C., 1991), II-12, II-24. For a review of insect ecology and forests, see David Perry, "Landscape Pattern and Forest Pests," *Northwest Environmental Journal* 4 (1988): 213–28; and particularly Karl J. Stoszek, "Forests under Stress and Insect Outbreaks," *Northwest Environmental Journal* 4 (1988): 247–61. Also see Timothy Schowalter's excellent article on pests and disease: "Forest Pest Management: A Synopsis," *Northwest Environmental Journal* 4 (1988): 313–18. This edition of the journal was devoted to forest pest management. The research notes at the end of the Winter 1990 edition of *Northwest Environmental Journal* (6:401–44) give a good overview of current research by forest entomologists. Boyd Wickman, formerly Forest Service research entomologist at the Forestry and Range Sciences Laboratory in La Grande, has published a useful review of insect and disease effects on Blue Mountains Forests: "Forest health in the Blue Mountains: The Influence of Insects and Diseases" (USDA Forest Service General Technical Report PNW-GTR-295, March 1992).

37. See Nancy Langston, "The General Riot of the Natural Forest: Landscape Change in the Blue Mountains," (Ph.D. diss., University of Washington, 1994; University Microfilms, 1994), 31–58.

38. Ibid.; also see Eastside Forests Scientific Society Panel (Dan Bottom, Sam Wright, Jim Bednarz, David Perry, Steven Beckwitt, Eric Beckwitt, James R. Karr, and Mark Henjum), *Interim Protection for Late-Successional Forests, Fisheries, and Watersheds: National Forests East of the Cascade Crest, Oregon and Washington: A Report to the United States Congress and the President,* ed. Ellen Chu and James R. Karr (Washington, D.C., 1994).

39. Johnson et al., "Biotic and Abiotic Processes" (1994), 1–22.

40. The wildlife biologist Lisa Lombardi suggested this example in a workshop at the 1994 Forest Reform Conference.

Before the Forest Service

1. William Cronon argued something similar for the New England forests in *Changes in the Land: Indians, Colonists, and the Ecology of New England* (New York, 1983). Richard White developed a similar argument for Whidbey Island, Washington, in *Land Use, Environment, and Social Change: The Shaping of Island County, Washington* (Seattle, 1980). Also see Stephen Pyne, *Fire in America: A Cultural History of Wildland and Rural Fire* (Princeton, 1982); and for an overview, see K. W. Butzer, "The Indian Legacy in the American Landscape," in *The Making of the American Landscape*, ed. Michael P. Conzen (Boston, 1990), 27–50. Douglas MacCleery has given an interesting example of how federal land managers might use such arguments in "Understanding the Role the Human Dimension Has Played in Shaping America's Forest and Grassland Landscapes," *Eco-Watch* (February 10, 1994), 1–12.

2. Carlos Schwantes, *The Pacific Northwest: An Interpretive History* (Lincoln, 1989), 19. Also see William G. Robbins and Donald W. Wolf, "Landscape and the Intermontane Northwest: An Environmental History," in vol. 3: *Assessment, Eastside Forest Ecosystem Health Assessment*, ed. Richard L. Everett (USDA Forest Service General Technical Report PNW-GTR-319, February 1994), 2.

3. Robbins and Wolf, "Landscape and the Intermontane Northwest," 2.

4. See D. W. Meinig, *The Great Columbia Plain: A Historical Geography, 1805–1910* (Seattle, 1968).

5. For example, Wilson Price Hunt wrote in his journal during the 1811 winter crossing of the Blues, after a day spent climbing over what seemed to him nearly impassable ridges: "On every side, were seen horse-trails used by the Indians in hunting deer, which must be very common because we have espied numerous bands of black-tail." Wilson Price Hunt, "Journal" in *The Discovery of the Oregon Trail: Robert Stuart's Narrative of His Journey*, ed. Philip A. Rollins (New York, 1935), 302.

6. Jerry Mosgrove, *The Malheur National Forest: A Ethnographic History* (USDA Forest Service, Pacific Northwest Region, 1980), 13.

7. Ibid., 29.

8. Robert T. Boyd, "The Introduction of Infectious Diseases among

the Indians of the Pacific Northwest, 1774–1874" (Ph.D. diss., University of Washington, 1985), 327.

9. James Clyman, *Journal of a Mountain Man* (Missoula, 1984), 121.

10. Washington Irving, *The Adventures of Captain Bonneville, U.S.A., in the Rocky Mountains and the Far West; Digested from His Journal, and Illustrated from Various Other Sources,* (New York, 1843), 271, 272.

11. J. M. Pomeroy, 1914 edition of the *East Washingtonian,* quoted in Gerald Tucker, "History of the Northern Blue Mountains," 1940, manuscript in Wallowa Whitman National Forest Supervisor's Office, Baker, Oregon, 51.

12. Peter Skene Ogden, *Snake Country Journals, 1826–1827,* ed. K. G. Davies and A. M. Johnson (London, 1961), 7, 9, 19, 118, 126–27; quoted in Robbins and Wolf, "Landscape and the Intermontane Northwest," 4–5.

13. Meriwether Lewis, *Original Journals of the Lewis and Clark Expedition, 1804–1806,* ed. Reuben Gold Thwaites (New York, 1959), 3: 286.

14. John Kirk Townsend, *Narrative of a Journey across the Rocky Mountains to the Columbia River* [1839] (Lincoln, 1978), 246; cited in Robbins and Wolf, "Landscape and the Intermontane Northwest," 5.

15. Ibid., 1–8; See also Pyne, *Fire in America,* for similar arguments about the Great Plains.

16. For example, see Thomas J. Farnham, "Travels in the Great Western Prairies, the Anahuac and Rocky Mountains, and in the Oregon Territory," in John W. Evans, ed., *Powerful Rockey: The Blue Mountains and the Oregon Trail* (La Grande, 1990), 63.

17. Hunt, "Journal," 301–2.

18. Very little is known about the ecological effects of horse introductions. Richard Mack, however, has done a great deal of research on changes in the inland Northwest grasslands; see his overview, "Invaders at Home on the Range," *Natural History* (February 1984), 40–46. For another region, see Richard White, *The Roots of Dependency: Subsistence, Environment, and Social Change among the Choctaws, Pawnees, and Navajos* (Lincoln, 1983), 100, 247–48.

19. Meinig, *Great Columbia Plain.*

20. Ibid., 134.

21. USDA Forest Service, "Fish and Game, Five Year Report, 1925," Umatilla National Forest Historical Files, Supervisor's Office, Pendleton.

22. For example, see Thomas T. Veblen and Diane C. Lorenz, *The Colorado Front Range: A Century of Ecological Change* (Salt Lake City, 1991). And see James Agee, "The Historical Role of Fire in Pacific Northwest Forests," in *Natural and Prescribed Fire in Pacific Northwest Forests,* ed. John D. Walstad et al. (Corvallis, 1990), 26–27.

23. Robbins and Wolf, "Landscape and the Intermontane Northwest," 12.

24. George Simpson, "Fur Trade and Empire," in *George Simpson's Journal*, ed. Frederick Merk (Cambridge, Mass., 1931), 46; see also Meinig, *Great Columbia Plain*.

25. See Roderick Nash, *Wilderness and the American Mind* (New Haven, 1977); H. Paul Sanmire, "Historical Dimensions of the American Crisis," in *Western Man and Environmental Ethics*, ed. Ian G. Barbour (Reading, Mass., 1973), 66–76; and Anne Farrar Hyde, *An American Vision: Far Western Landscape and National Culture, 1820–1920* (New York, 1990), 17.

26. Hunt, "Journal," 285.

27. Robert Stuart, *On the Oregon Trail: Robert Stuart's Journey of Discovery*, ed. Kenneth Spaulding (Norman, 1953), 70.

28. Ibid., 109.

29. Ibid., 115.

30. Irving, *Adventures of Captain Bonneville*, 3.

31. Ibid., 188.

32. John W. Evans, ed., *Powerful Rockey: The Blue Mountains and the Oregon Trail* (La Grande, 1990), 30.

33. Alexander Ross, *The Fur Hunters of the Far West*, ed. Kenneth Spaulding (Norman, 1956), 120.

34. Ibid., 177.

35. Ibid., 189.

36. An excellent overview of this work is in Robert J. Naiman, Carol A. Johnston, and James Kelley, "Alteration of North American Streams by Beaver," *BioScience* 38 (1988): 753–61.

37. R. J. Naiman, J. M. Melillo, and J. E. Hobbie, "Ecosystem Alteration of Boreal Forest Streams by Beaver (*Castor canadensis*)," *Ecology* 67 (1986): 1254–69.

38. Naiman et al., "Alterations of North American Streams."

39. Henry Spalding, letter, cited in Christopher L. Miller, *Prophetic Worlds: Indians and Whites of the Columbia Plateau* (New Brunswick, N.J., 1985), 87.

40. Ibid., 91; also see Clifford Drury, *Henry Harmon Spalding* (Caldwell, Idaho, 1936).

41. Patricia Nelson Limerick, *The Legacy of Conquest: The Unbroken Past of the American West* (New York, 1987), 37–41. Also see Miller, *Prophetic Worlds*, 87.

42. Henry Spalding, letter, in Miller, *Prophetic Worlds*, 91.

43. Why the missionaries came in the first place is not entirely clear. The Nez Percé and Flathead tribes had initially sent a delegation to St.

Louis requesting missionaries; however, since they lacked a good interpreter it is uncertain exactly what their intention was. The tribes had no
desire to become farmers, although they welcomed cattle; they probably
also had little intention of abandoning their own religions and converting
to Christianity. Christopher Miller (*Prophetic Worlds*, 23, 33, 35) argues that
a 300-year cold spell, along with overhunting induced by horses and guns,
had reduced food supplies. That, along with near-constant warfare with
the Bannocks, and epidemics brought by the Europeans and sweeping up
the Columbia River, had convinced the Plateau Indians that the world was
near its end. This millennial tradition had the misfortune to intersect with
the equally millennial tradition of the American Board of Missions, a Protestant sect with a deep faith in the coming doom of heathen souls. It is
not entirely clear that the Plateau tribes were in such trouble; tribal sources
record that although deer and elk were at a low ebb around 1800, populations had largely recovered by 1830, as reported in Gerald Tucker, "History
of the Northern Blue Mountains" manuscript in a Wallowa Whitman National Forest Supervisor's Office, Baker, 1940; Jerry Gildemeister, ed., "Bull
Trout, Walking Grouse, and Buffalo Bones: Oral Histories of Northeast Oregon Fish and Wildlife," Oregon Department of Fish and Wildlife, La
Grande (April 1992), 15–36. At any rate, settlement—for either themselves
or Americans—was not what the tribes had in mind.

44. Marcus Whitman, in Archer B. Hulbert and Dorothy P. Hulbert,
Marcus Whitman, Crusader: Part Three, 1843 to 1847, (Denver, 1941), 102.

45. Phoebe Judson, *A Pioneer's Search for an Ideal Home* (Lincoln, 1984),
146, 22, 15.

46. Narcissa Whitman, quoted in *First White Women over the Rockies:
Diaries, Letters, and Biographical Sketches of the Six Women of the Oregon Mis-
sion Who Made the Overland Journey in 1836 and 1838,* 2 vols, ed. Clifford
Drury (Glendale, Calif., 1963), 127.

47. Asa Smith, in *The Diaries and Letters of Henry H. Spalding and Asa
Bowen Smith,* ed. Clifford Drury (Glendale, Calif., 1958).

48. Whitman, In Drury, *White Women,* 127.

49. Asa Smith, letter to sister, in Drury, *White Women,* 111, 174.

50. Narcissa Whitman, letter of October 24, 1836, in Drury, *White
Women,* 109.

51. Meinig, *Great Columbia Plain,* 137.

52. Spalding, Letter of April 1, 1843, cited in Meinig, *Great Columbia
Plain,* 183.

53. Richard White, *"It's Your Misfortune and None of My Own": A History
of the American West* (Norman, 1991), 193.

54. John Charles Fremont, *Report of the Exploring Expedition to the Rocky*

Mountains in the Year 1842, and to Oregon and North California in the Years 1843–44 (Washington, D.C., 1845); White, *"It's Your Misfortune,"* 123.

55. Hyde, *American Vision,* 31.

56. Fremont, *Report,* 272, 274, 280.

57. Ibid., 283.

58. Ibid., 280.

59. Clyman, *Journal of a Mountain Man,* 148.

60. John Kerns, "Journal of Crossing the Plains to Oregon," in Evans, *Powerful Rockey,* 192.

61. Sarah Sutton, "A Travel 1854," in Evans, *Powerful Rockey,* 253–54.

62. Rebecca Ketcham, "From Ithaca to Clatsop Plains: Miss Ketcham's Journals of Travel," in Evans, *Powerful Rockey,* 237.

63. James W. Nesmith, "Diary of the Emigration of 1843," in Evans, *Powerful Rockey,* 101.

64. Cecelia Adams and Parthenia Blank, "Twin Sisters on the Oregon Trail," in Kenneth L. Holmes, ed., *Covered Wagon Women: Diaries and Letters from the Western Trails, 1840–1890* (Glendale, Calif., 1986), 5:298–304.

65. Ketcham, in Evans, *Powerful Rockey,* 238.

66. W. T. Newby, "William T. Newby's Diary of the Emigration of 1843," in Evans, *Powerful Rockey,* 107.

67. John G. Glenn, "Journal, 1852," in Evans, *Powerful Rockey,* 202.

68. Harriet A. Loughary, "Travels and Incidents," in Holmes, *Covered Wagon Women,* 8:155.

69. Armeda Jane Parker, "Diary of Armeda Jane Parker," in Evans, *Powerful Rockey,* 339.

70. Robbins and Wolf, "Landscape and the Intermontane Northwest," 14.

71. Mosgrove, *Malheur National Forest* (1980), 35–41.

72. Nancy C. Glenn, letter, in Holmes, *Covered Wagon Women,* 8:14–26.

73. General James F. Rusling, *Across America: Or, the Great West and the Pacific Coast* (New York, 1874), 232–33.

74. John David Unruh, *The Plains Across: The Overland Emigrants and the Trans-Mississippi West,* 1840–1860 (Urbana, 1982); White, *"It's Your Misfortune,"* 185–86.

75. John G. Leiberg's 1899 survey of the southern Cascades mentioned that fires increased in frequency after white settlement. Settlers set fires that "devastated much larger areas" than Indians fires ever had. John B. Leiberg, "Cascade Range and Ashland Forest Reserves and Adjacent Regions," in *Twenty-first Annual Report of the United States Geological Survey to the Secretary of the Interior, 1899–1900, Part V, Forest Reserves* (Washington,

D.C., 1900), 277–78, 288. Quoted in Robbins and Wolf, "Landscape and the Intermontane Northwest," 10–11. Frederick V. Coville agreed that settlers created worse fires, usually as a result of road building and logging: in "Forest Growth and Sheep Grazing in the Cascade Mountains of Oregon," USDA Division of Forestry, Bulletin 15 (1898), 19–20, 29–30, and 33. Quoted in Robbins and Wolf, 11.

76. M. L. Erickson, "Report on the Proposed Chesnimnus Reserve, 1907," RCF 135.

77. Carl Ewing, Forest Supervisor on the Umatilla National Forest, letter to Regional Forester in Portland, May 12, 1938, UNF Historical Files, Supervisor's Office, Pendleton.

78. Jon Skovlin, *Fifty Years of Research Progress: A Historical Document on the Starkey Experimental Forest and Range.* (USDA Forest Service General Technical Report PNW-GTR-266, May 1991), 5–6.

79. Ibid., 7.

80. Lawrence Rakestraw, *A History of Forest Conservation in the Pacific Northwest, 1891–1913* (New York, 1979), 100.

81. Skovlin, *Fifty Years,* 7.

82. USDA Forest Service, "Historical Information, Malheur Studies, February 5, 1940, on file in the MNF Historical Files, Supervisor's Office, John Day.

83. H. D. Langille, "A Report on the Proposed Blue Mountain Reserve," RCF 139.

84. USDA Forest Service, "Historical Information, Malheur Studies" (1940).

85. Ibid.

86. USDA Forest Service, "Studies, Malheur, Historical Information, Long Creek District" (1940), on file in the MNF Historical Files, Supervisor's Office, John Day.

87. USDA Forest Service, "Historical Information, Malheur Studies" (1940).

88. Skovlin, *Fifty Years,* 5–9.

89. USDA Forest Service, "Historical Information, Malheur Studies" (1940).

90. William D. Rowley, *U.S. Forest Service Grazing and Rangelands: A History* (College Station, Texas, 1985), 25–35.

91. E. H. Libby, President, Lewiston-Clarkston Irrigation Company, Letter to J. M. Schmitz, Forest Ranger in Charge, Wenaha Reserve, January 31, 1906.

92. H. D. Langille, "Report on the Proposed Heppner Forest Reserve," RCF 135 (1903).

93. Gerald Tucker, "Historical Sketches of Wallowa National Forest," manuscript on file in Wallowa Whitman National Forest Supervisor's Office, Baker (1970).

94. The zooarcheologist Jack Broughton suggested this to me; his archeological research in the Sacramento Valley strongly suggests that the same thing happened there. See Jack Broughton, "Late Holocene Resource Intensification in the Sacramento Valley, California: The Vertebrate Evidence," *Journal of Archaeological Science* 21 (1994): 501–14.

95. Loren Powers, "Pioneer Memories, Powers Family, Lostine Oregon," typed manuscript, no date. Quoted in Grace Bartlett, *The Wallowa Country, 1867–1877* (Fairfield, Washington, 1984), 27.

96. Tucker, "Historical Sketches," 266.

97. Langille, "Report on the Proposed Heppner Reserve," (1903).

98. Overton Price, Associate Forester District 6, to Supervisor O'Brien, 1906, UNF Historical Files, Supervisor's Office, Pendleton.

99. Gildemeister, "Bull Trout" (1992), Howard Fisk speaking, 24; Roland Huff speaking, 23.

100. H. D. Foster, "Report on the Silvics of the Blue Mountains (E) National Forest Oregon, 1908," RCF 139.

101. Skovlin, *Fifty Years,* 11.

102. M. L. Erickson, "Timber Sales, Wallowa Forest Reserve, 10/3/06," RCF 135.

103. Erickson, "Forest Conditions Blue Mountains National Forest (now Whitman)," RCF 136 (1906).

104. W. H. B. Kent, "Examination and Report on the Proposed Wenaha Forest Reserve, Washington and Oregon," RCF 135 (1904).

105. Thomas R. Cox, ed., *This Well-Wooded Land: Americans and Their Forests from Colonial Times to the Present* (Lincoln, 1985), 138.

106. Langille, "Proposed Blue Mountain Reserve" (1906).

107. Foster, "Blue Mountains" (1908).

108. David A. Clary, *Timber and the Forest Service* (Lawrence, 1986), 13.

The Feds in the Forests

1. Lawrence Rakestraw, *A History of Forest Conservation in the Pacific Northwest, 1891–1913* (New York, 1979), 160–161.

2. Richard White, *"It's Your Misfortune and None of My Own": A History of the American West* (Norman, 1991), 140–50; H. D. Langille, "A Report on the Proposed Blue Mountain Reserve," RCF 139 (1906).

3. Henry Brown, a reporter for the *Oregonian,* finally ended up accus-

ing Binger Hermann, head of the General Land Office, of nepotism and carelessness but not fraud; Senator Williamsby and Superintendent Ormsby of fraud; and the U.S. Geological Survey and the Bureau of Forestry of careless work. Rakestraw, *Forest Conservation,* 87–90.

4. Ibid., 161.

5. Langille to Secretary of Agriculture Wilson, 1907, National Archives, Department of the Interior, National Forests, Blue Mountains, Box 17; quoted in Rakestraw, *Forest Conservation,* 160.

6. See Samuel P. Hays, *Conservation and the Gospel of Efficiency: The Progressive Conservation Movement, 1890–1920* (Cambridge, Mass., 1959).

7. Rakestraw, *Forest Conservation,* 69.

8. Ibid., 77.

9. Smith Ripley, "Memoir," 1912, typed manuscript, UNF Historical Files, Supervisor's Office, Pendleton.

10. Ibid., 7, 13.

11. Ibid., 5.

12. Quoted in Hays, *Conservation,* 124.

13. Umatilla National Forest, Press release, September 12, 1906, UNF Historical Files, Supervisor's Office, Pendleton.

14. David A. Clary, *Timber and the Forest Service* (Lawrence, 1986), 16.

15. For example, Roderick Nash, *Wilderness and the American Mind* (New Haven, 1977), 134–38; Thomas R. Cox, ed., *This Well-Wooded Land: Americans and Their Forests from Colonial Times to the Present* (Lincoln, 1985); Clary, *Timber.*

16. For the best accounts of colonists' attitudes toward nature, see William Cronon, *Changes in the Land: Indians, Colonists, and the Ecology of New England* (New York, 1983), and John R. Stilgoe, *Common Landscape of America, 1580–1845* (New Haven, 1982); also see Michael Pollan, *Second Nature: A Gardener's Education* (New York, 1991), 160–68.

17. Cox, *Well-Wooded Land;* Pollan, *Second Nature,* 165–68.

18. George Perkins Marsh, *Man and Nature* [1864], ed. David Lowenthal (Cambridge Mass., 1965), quoted in Cox, *Well-Wooded Land,* 145.

19. Marsh, *Man and Nature,* 204.

20. K. P. Davis, *Forest Management* (New York, 1966); quoted in B. Thomas Parry, Henry J. Vaux, and Nicholas Dennis, "Changing Conceptions of Sustained-yield Policy on the National Forests," *Journal of Forestry* (March 1983), 150–54.

21. Clary, *Timber,* 6–7.

22. Bernard Fernow, "What Is Forestry?" USDA Forestry Bulletin 5 (1891).

23. Susan Flader, *Thinking Like a Mountain: Aldo Leopold and the Evolu-*

tion of an Ecological Attitude Toward Deer, Wolves, and Forests (Columbia, Missouri, 1974), 141.

24. Rakestraw, *Forest Conservation,* 18.

25. Gifford Pinchot, *Breaking New Ground* (New York, 1947), 50–79.

26. Ibid., 152.

27. C. S. Judd, "Lectures on Timber Sales at the University of Washington, February 1911," RCF 136.

28. District Forester F. E. Ames, "Addresses given at the 1910 joint supervisors' meeting for the Northwest region (Oregon and Washington)," RCF 136.

29. Henry Graves, *Annual Report of the Forester 1911,* USDA Forest Service (Washington, D.C., 1912), 33.

30. Henry Graves, *Annual Report of the Forester 1912,* USDA Forest Service (Washington, D.C., 1913), 16.

31. Thorton T. Munger, "Basic Considerations in the Management of Ponderosa Pine Forests by the Maturity Selection System, 1936," and letter by C. J. Buck, Regional Forester, to Blues supervisors, September 15, 1936; UNF Historical Files, Supervisor's Office, Pendleton.

32. H. D. Foster, "Report of the Silvics of the Wenaha Forest Reserve, 10/1/06," RCF 135.

33. George Bright, "The Relative Merits of Western Larch and Douglas-fir in the Blue Mountains, Oregon," RCF 135 (1913).

Making Sense of Strangeness: Silvics in the Blues

1. G. H. Cecil to Gifford Pinchot, March 16, 1909, RCF 136.

2. Ibid.

3. Lawrence Rakestraw, *A History of Forest Conservation in the Pacific Northwest, 1891–1913* (New York, 1979), 253.

4. M. L. Erickson, "Timber Sales, Wallowa Forest Reserve, 10/3/06," RCF 135.

5. Erickson, "Report on the Chesnimnus Reserve," RCF 135 (1907); W. H. B. Kent, "Examination and Report on the Proposed Wenaha Forest Reserve," RCF 135 (1904); also see W. H. B. Kent, "Inspection Report on The Chesnimnus Reserve," RCF 136 (July 1907).

6. H. D. Foster, "Report of the Silvics of the Wenaha Forest Reserve, 10/1/06," RCF 135.

7. M. L. Erickson, "Report on Blue Mountains West, 12/29/06: Silvics: Strawberry Mt. Reserve, " RCF 135.

8. Ibid.

9. See, for example, Michel Foucault, *Power/knowledge: Selected Interviews and Other Writings, 1972–1977,* ed. and trans. C. Gordon (New York, 1980).

10. H. D. Foster, "Report on the Silvics of the Blue Mountains East National Forest Oregon," RCF 139 (1908).

11. George Vancouver, *A Voyage of Discovery to the North Pacific Ocean and Round the World, 1791–1795,* ed. W. Kaye Lamb (London, 1984).

12. Steve Fletcher, Forest Health Coordinator for the Wallowa-Whitman National Forest, interview with author, August 1992.

13. R. M. Evans, "General Silvical Report Wallowa and Minam Forests," RCF 135 (1912).

14. Henry David Thoreau, "Natural History of Massachusetts" and "Succession of Forest Trees," in *Selected Works,* ed. Walter Harding (Boston, 1975).

15. For histories of ecology see Robert E. Ricklefs, *Ecology,* 2d. edition (New York, 1979), 717ff.; Donald Worster, *Nature's Economy: The Roots of Ecology* (San Francisco, 1977); Robert P. McIntosh, *The Background of Ecology: Concept and Theory* (Cambridge and New York, 1985); R. Tobey, *Saving the Prairies: The Life Cycle of the Founding School of American Plant Ecology, 1895–1955* (Berkeley, 1981); and Frank N. Egerton, ed., *History of American Ecology* (Salem, 1984).

16. Other ecologists quickly argued that the contingencies of place and history had more effect on forests than the monoclimax theory of succession implied. Herbert Gleason, for example, argued in 1926 that superficially similar plant associations differed from place to place—thus pointing to an important role of the specific site. Given enough knowledge about the particular site, ecologists still thought they had enough information to know exactly where history would take a forest. A few years later, in 1935, Arthur G. Tansley proposed the concept of the ecosystem, a complex system consisting of "the whole complex of physical factors forming what we call the environment." In effect, this was a recognition of interconnections and of indirect effects. But chance events of history still were not seen as very important until, in 1953, the ecologist R. H. Whittaker argued that there was no absolute climax for any area. Although these ideas about ecosystems, changing climaxes, and the possible confusions of history were enormously important within academic ecology, they had little influence on how foresters thought about managing forests. Herbert Gleason, "The Individualistic Concept of the Plant Association," *Bulletin of the Torrey Botanical Club* 53 (1926): 7–26; reprinted in Edward J. Kormondy, ed., *Readings in Ecology* (Englewood Cliffs, 1965); Arthur G. Tansley, "The Use and Abuse of Vegetational Concepts and Terms," *Ecology* 16 (1935):

284–307; R. H. Whittaker, "A Consideration of Climax Theory: The Climax as a Population and Pattern," *Ecological Monographs* 23 (1953): 41–78.

17. George Bright, "Umatilla Studies: Annual Silvical Report 2/23/11," RCF 137.

18. Bernard Fernow, "What Is Forestry?" USDA Forestry Bulletin 5, 1891.

19. The word "black" was crossed out in the typescript and "lodgepole" was written over it.

20. H. D. Foster, "Blue Mountains East National Forest, report for July-September 1907," RCF 139.

21. M. L. Erickson, "Forest Conditions Blue Mountains National Forest (now Whitman)," RCF 136 (1906).

22. George Bright, "The Relative Merits of Western Larch and Douglas-fir in the Blue Mountains, Oregon," RCF 135 (1913).

23. Erickson, "The Wallowa Forest Reserve: Silvics: The Forest, 10/3/1906," RCF 135.

24. Foster, "Wenaha," 1907.

25. John D. Guthrie, "Blame it on the Indians: Forester explodes myth that Red Men set fires to keep forests open," press release 1933, Malheur National Forest, Supervisor's Office, John Day.

26. Frederick E. Ames, letter to forest officers 2/3/09, about a circular letter of May 20, 1907, entitled "Record of Cut-over Areas," RCF 136.

27. Kan Smith, "Windfall Damage on Cutover Areas, February 1915," RCF 139, 8, 49.

28. Ibid.

29. Frederick E. Ames, letter to supervisors introducing Smith's windfall studies, RCF 139 (1915).

30. Thomas R. Cox, ed., *This Well-Wooded Land: Americans and Their Forests from Colonial Times to the Present* (Lincoln, 1985), 18.

31. Richard White, *"It's Your Misfortune and None of My Own": A History of the American West* (Norman, 1991), 406. Many of the Blues inspection reports support this conclusion. For example, see H. D. Langille, "A Report on the Proposed Blue Mountain Reserve," RCF 139 (1906). Yet there was often a great deal of local anger at the irrigation interests. Many people perceived irrigators as investors who were merely using ecological arguments to steal land for their own financial benefit, "using the preservation of the timber only as a guise," as the *Blue Mountain Eagle* charged June 27, 1902: "The large irrigation companies of Harney County . . . are desirous of having all of the territory created into a forest reserve, in hopes that by stopping the settlement of that part of the country, the water supply of the streams leading to Harney and Malheur Lakes would be increased thereby." In other words, all they wanted was profit, and because there were no rail-

roads into the forest at the moment, their best profit would come from preserving the forest.

32. USDA Forest Service, *Malheur National Forest Land and Resource Management Plan, Final Environmental Impact Statement* (Washington, D.C., 1990), III-58. Within 50 meters (164 feet) of a 3 kilometer (1.86 mile) stretch of Catherine Creek in the Wallowa Whitman Forest, researchers found 420 plant species and 80 bird species.

33. John Minto, *Special Report on the History of Present Condition of the Sheep Industry of the United States* (U.S. Bureau of Plant Industry, Washington, D.C., 1892).

34. For example, see Cox, *Well-Wooded Land,* as well as Michael Williams, *Americans and Their Forests: A Historical Geography* (Cambridge, 1989).

35. D. M. Windsor, "Climate and Moisture Variability in a Tropical Forest: Long-term Records from Barro Colorado Island, Panama," *Smithsonian Contribution to the Earth Sciences* 29-1-146 (1990). Windsor argues that a 14 percent decline in annual precipitation over seventy years at Barro Colorado Island was caused by progressive large-scale deforestation on either side of the Panama Canal zone. Cited in Richard Condit, Stephen P. Hubbell, and Robin B. Foster, "Short-term Dynamics of a Neotropical Forest: Change within Limits," *BioScience* 42 (1992): 824–28.

36. For example, see Minto, *Special Report.* Similar sentiments are still expressed; see, for example, USDA Forest Service, *Malheur Plan,* III (1990).

37. T. E. Dawson, "Hydraulic Lift and Water Use by Plants: Implications for Water Balance, Performance, and Plant-Plant Interactions," *Oecologia* 95 (1993): 565–74; for a discussion, see Carol Kaesuk Yoon, "Plants Share Precious Water with Neighbors," *New York Times,* October 26, 1993.

38. Robert M. May, "An Overview: Real and Apparent Patterns in Community Structure," in Donald R. Strong, Jr., Daniel Simberloff, Lawrence G. Abele, and Anne Thistle, eds., *Ecological Communities: Conceptual Issues and the Evidence* (Princeton, 1982), 3–13.

39. This was not a localized argument: even in the 1991 forest plans, managers still argued that clearcuts were necessary in order to increase water flow. USDA Forest Service, *Umatilla National Forest Land and Resource Management Plan, Final Environmental Impact Statement* (Washington, D.C., 1990), III. Even in all three 1990 forest plans, foresters wrote approvingly that clearcutting was good because it "increases annual water yields, by decreasing evapotranspiration and by increasing runoff." USDA Forest Service, *Umatilla Plan,* III-63.

40. Herbert J. Miles, "Silvics: Annual Report for the Malheur National Forest," RCF 136 (1911).

41. Bright, "Umatilla Studies"; Evans "Wallowa and Minam."

42. Erickson, "Wallowa: Silvics: The Forest."

43. Evie Bull, "Habitat Utilization of the Pileated Woodpecker, Blue Mountains, Oregon" (master's thesis, Oregon State University, Corvallis, 1975); Jack Ward Thomas, *Wildlife Habitats in Managed Forests, the Blue Mountains of Oregon and Washington,* USDA Forest Service Agricultural Handbook 553 (1979), 137–139. Pileated woodpeckers in the Blues require dead trees that are at least 16 inches in diameter at breast height where the cavity is excavated, which is usually at least 31 feet above the ground; so nest trees must be at least 21 dbh. They prefer to nest in two-storied stands, with a crown closure of at least 70 percent. Their primary food source is carpenter ants and larvae, which are usually found in trees and logs with heart rot, which in turn develop in old stands.

44. Karl J. Stoszek, "Forests under Stress and Insect Outbreaks," *Northwest Environmental Journal* 4 (1988): 247–61.

45. Ibid.

46. Boyd Wickman, "Old-growth forests and history of insect outbreaks," *Northwest Environmental Journal* 6 (1990): 401–403. Also, as Stoszek pointed out, "repeated stunting of the terminal shoots of fast-growing pinés by the western pine-shoot borer changes the narrow, fine branched conical crown and slender form of ponderosa pine to a wide, bushy, and limby crown and a strongly tapered stem. The former is essential for the shade-intolerant pine to maintain competitive dominance on fertile sites supporting other shade-intolerant tree species. The shoot borer-modified form is not impaired in photosynthetic efficiency, and may be more effective in suppressing the development of other trees and shrubs. Increased canopy breadth on dry sites probably increases the ability of the pines to protect soil and soil moisture conditions."

47. Torolf Torgersen, Entomologist, Forestry and Range Sciences Laboratory, La Grande, pers. comm. August 1992.

48. For a recent example of attempts to define a healthy forest as one with a small ratio of mortality to growth, see Jay O'Laughlin, James G. MacCracken, David L. Adams, Stephen C. Bunting, Keith A. Blatner, and Charles E. Keegan III, *Forest Health Conditions in Idaho,* Idaho Forest, Wildlife and Range Policy Analysis Group Report 11 (December 1993), 135–63.

49. A. R. Moldenke, "Denizens of the Soil: Small, but Critical," *Natural Resource News* (August 1993), 3–5.

50. T. D. Schowalter, "Invertebrate Diversity in Old-growth versus Regenerating Forest Canopies," *Northwest Environmental Journal* 6 (1990): 403–4; A. R. Moldenke and J. D. Lattin, "Dispersal Characteristics of Old-growth Soil Arthropods: The Potential for Loss of Diversity and Biological

Function," *Northwest Environmental Journal* 6 (1990): 408–9; and J. D. McIver, A. R. Moldenke, and G. L. Parsons, "Litter Spiders as Bio-indicators of Recovery after Clearcutting in a Western Coniferous Forest," *Northwest Environmental Journal* 6 (1990): 409–12.

51. Torolf Torgersen, "The Forest Immune System—Its Role in Insect Pest Regulation," *Natural Resource News* (August 1993), 6–7.

52. Bright, "Relative merits of Douglas Fir and Larch" (1913).

Liquidating the Pines

1. David Clary, *Timber and the Forest Service* (Lawrence, 1986), 12–48.

2. Quoted ibid., 12.

3. Gifford Pinchot, *A Primer of Forestry,* USDA Farmer's Bulletin 358 (Washington, D.C., 1901), 12.

4. Henry Graves, *Annual Report of the Forester,* USDA Forest Service (Washington, D.C., 1911 and 1912).

5. For discussions of the Forest Service's attempts to sell timber before World War I, see Thomas R. Cox, ed., *This Well-Wooded Land: Americans and Their Forests from Colonial Times to the Present* (Lincoln, 1985); Clary, *Timber;* Thomas B. Parry, Henry J. Vaux, and Nicholas Dennis, "Changing Conceptions of Sustained-yield Policy on the National Forests," *Journal of Forestry* (March 1983), 150–154; William Robbins, *American Forestry: A History of National, State, and Private Cooperation* (Lincoln, 1985); and Graves 1911, *Annual Report.*

6. R. M. Evans, "General Silvical Report Wallowa and Minam Forests," RCF 135 (1912).

7. Foster, "Report of the Silvics of the Wenaha Forest Reserve, 10/1/ 06," RCF 135 (1906).

8. Clary, *Timber,* 68.

9. Gerald Tucker, "Historical Sketches of Wallowa National Forest" manuscript on file in Wallowa Whitman National Forest Supervisor's Office (Baker, 1970), 191–2.

10. H. D. Langille, "A Report on the Proposed Blue Mountain Reserve," RCF 139 (1906).

11. USDA Forest Service, "Malheur River Working Circle Plan," no date, but internal evidence sets the date after 1926 and before 1929. MNF Historical Files, Supervisor's Office, John Day; USDA Forest Service, "Umatilla Hilgard Project Report" (1926), National Archives, Forest Service Files. Record Group 115, Region 6, S-Timber Surveys D-6.

12. Frederick E. Ames, District Forester, "Addresses given at the 1910

joint supervisors' meeting for the Northwest region (Oregon and Washington)," RCF 136. Attempts to estimate allowable cuts set into motion the forest reconnaissances of 1908 to 1910. These reconnaissances were on-site surveys of tree species, reproduction, damage, soil types, and undergrowth. The General Land Office and the Geological Survey had intended to survey and inventory the land when they established the reserves, but mapping had only just begun and the data on forest resources were little more than guesses. The reconnaissances were the first step toward regulating land, and they were also the first records of what was present before the Forest Service started altering it.

13. USDA Forest Service, "Management Plans, Middle Fork of the John Day Working Circle," MNF Historical Files, Supervisor's Office, John Day (1930).

14. USDA Forest Service, "Memorandum: The Sustained Yield of the Burns Working Circle, February 23, 1923," MNF Historical Files, Supervisor's Office, John Day (1923).

15. USDA Forest Service, *The Use Book*, Administrative edition (Washington, 1907).

16. George Bright, "An Extensive Reconnaissance of the Wenaha National Forest in 1913," ed. David C. Powell, USDA Forest Service Publication F14-SO-08-94, Umatilla National Forest (Pendleton, 1994), 6.

17. E. J. Hanzlik, "The Growth and Yield of Douglas Fir on Various Sites in Western Washington and Oregon," S-Studies, 1912, R-6, 54-A-111/59859, National Archives Record Services, Seattle; quoted by Clary, *Timber*, 44.

18. Clary, *Timber*, 44.

19. USDA Forest Service, "Timber Sales Policy, District 5, 1908"; quoted by Clary, *Timber*, 34.

20. USDA Forest Service, "Sustained Yield of the Burns Working Circle" (1923).

21. Hanzlik, "Growth and Yield of Douglas Fir" (1912).

22. Kan Smith, "Windfall Damage on Cutover Areas, February 1915," RCF 139.

23. USDA Forest Service, "Malheur River Working Circle Plan" (no date).

24. USDA Forest Service, "Timber Sale Policy of the Forest Service" (Washington, D.C., 1920), quoted in Parry et al., "Changing Conceptions," 151.

25. The Hanzlik formula:

$Y = I + V/r$ where

Y = annual yield: or the amount to be cut during the first cycle

V = merchantable timber volume above rotation age: or the excess old growth to be liquidated

r = rotation age: which was set at 180 years for ponderosa pine, since the mills preferred large diameter pine at least 19" wide.

So V/r = the liquidation of old growth and mature timber, a one time only offer

and I = mean annual increment of the immature timber for the rotation (the growth rate of young trees)—which meant the sustained-yield capacity of the regulated forest; this was the amount that they could cut forever, or so they hoped. (Parry et al., "Changing Conceptions.")

26. Smith, "Windfall Damage" (1915).

27. Graves, *Annual Report* (1911).

28. M. L. Erickson, "Timber Sales, Wallowa Forest Reserve, 10/3/06," RCF 135.

29. USDA Forest Service, "Sale Prospectus: 124,000,000 feet western yellow pine and other species: Lower Middle Fork John Day River Unit Whitman National Forest, Oregon, July 1916," MNF Historical Files, Supervisor's Office, John Day (1916).

30. USDA Forest Service, "Management Plans, Middle Fork of the John Day" (1930). I could not find out if this was the same as the East Oregon Lumber Company that cut north of Enterprise.

31. Kevin Scribner, pers. comm., Blue Mountains Native Forest Alliance, Walla Walla, August 1994.

32. USDA Forest Service, "Sale Prospectus: Bear Valley Unit, 1922," Malheur National Forest Historical Files, Supervisor's Office, John Day.

33. Jerry Mosgrove, *The Malheur National Forest: An Ethnographic History,* USDA Forest Service, Pacific Northwest Region (1980), 183.

34. USDA Forest Service, "Planning Report, Sales, Bear Valley Unit, Malheur National Forest 6/30/22," MNF Historical Files, Supervisor's Office, John Day.

35. Assistant Forester's letter of August 8, 1922; cited in letter of C. M. Granger, the District Forester, to Acting Forester Mr. Sherman, concerning the Baker Working Circle plan, 1927, WWNF Historical Files, Supervisor's Office, Baker.

36. E. A. Sherman, Acting Forester, Letter to C. M. Granger, District Forester, and John Kuhns, Whitman Forest Supervisor, March 8, 1927, concerning the Baker Working Circle Plan submitted 2/14/27. WWNF Forest Historical Files, Supervisor's Office, Baker.

37. Mosgrove, *Malheur National Forest,* 183–95.

38. USDA Forest Service, "Sustained Yield of the Burns Working Circle" (1923).

39. USDA Forest Service, "Malheur River Working Circle Plan" (no date).

40. Ibid.

41. Ibid.

42. Ibid.

43. E. J. Hanzlik, "Memorandum for FM, re Management Plans, Umatilla, La Grande Working Circle, 1927," UNF Historical Files, Supervisor's Office, Pendleton.

44. USDA Forest Service, "Hilgard Project" (1926) (emphasis added).

45. USDA Forest Service, "Malheur River Working Circle Plan" (no date).

46. Ibid.

47. E. A. Sherman, Acting Forester, to C. M. Granger, District Forester, and John Kuhns, Whitman Forest Supervisor, March 8, 1927, and reply by planner concerning the Baker Working Circle Plan submitted 2/14/27, WWNF Historical Files, Supervisor's Office, Baker.

48. Cox, *Well-Wooded Land*, 219.

49. Clary, *Timber*, 81.

50. Parry et al., "Changing Conceptions," 152. Also see William G. Robbins, "Lumber Production and Community Stability: A View from the Pacific Northwest," *Journal of Forest History* (October 1987), 187–196.

51. Robert Stuart, *Annual Report of the Forester 1928*, USDA Forest Service (Washington, D.C., 1928).

52. USDA Forest Service, "Management Plans, Middle Fork of the John Day" (1930).

53. Hanzlik, "Memorandum for FM" (1927).

54. J. Kier, "La Grande Working Circle Policy Statement," UNF Historical Files, Supervisor's Office, Pendleton (1938).

55. Thornton T. Munger, "Basic Considerations in the Management of Ponderosa Pine Forests by the Maturity Selection System, 1936," UNF Historical Files, Supervisor's Office, Pendleton.

Animals: Domestic and Wild Nature

1. Meriwether Lewis, *Original Journals of the Lewis and Clark Expedition, 1804–1806*, ed. Reuben Gold Thwaites (New York, 1959), 3: 286.

2. Richard Mack, "Invaders at Home on the Range," *Natural History* (February 1984), 40–46.

3. Aldo Leopold, *A Sand Country Almanac* (New York, 1968), "Cheat Takes Over," 155.

4. John G. Clouston, "Some Thoughts on the Last Thirty-five Years," 2/18/57, on file in the UNF Historical Files, Supervisor's Office, Pendleton;

and James Iler, Malheur National Forest Supervisor, to R. E. Brooke, County Agricultural Agent, Canyon City, Oregon, March 7, 1940, letter on file in the MNF Historical Files, Supervisor's Office, John Day.

5. USDA, *Yearbook of the United States Department of Agriculture* (Washington, D.C., 1914), 16–17; cited in William D. Rowley, *U.S. Forest Service Grazing and Rangelands: A History* (College Station, Texas, 1985), 93.

6. USDA Forest Service, *Annual Report, 1909* (Washington, D.C., 1910), 381.

7. Karl Hess Jr., *Visions Upon the Land: Man and Nature on the Western Range* (Washington, D.C., 1992), 125–29; for detail on regulations and fees, also see Rowley, *Grazing and Rangelands* (1985).

8. Rowley, *Grazing and Rangelands,* 59.

9. USDA Forest Service, "Historical Information, Malheur Studies, February 5, 1940," MNF Historical Files, Supervisor's Office, John Day.

10. A. W. Wirch? (signature difficult to read), District Ranger, "Range Management Plan, Long Creek Ranger District, 1958," on file in the MNF Historical Files, Supervisor's Office, John Day.

11. Letters exchanged in December 1905 and January 1906 between E. H. Libby, President of the Lewiston-Clarkston Irrigation Company, and L. Hall, the Acting Head Forester in the Washington D.C. Office; between L. Hall and James Wilson, the Secretary of the Interior; between L. Hall and Senator Henry Cabot Lodge; between L. Hall and John M. Schmitz, the Forest Ranger in Charge. On file in the UNF Historical Files, Supervisor's Office, Pendleton.

12. Grazing letters 1905–1906, Umatilla.

13. [Wirch?], "Range Management Plan, Long Creek Ranger District, 1958," MNF Historical Files, Supervisor's Office, John Day; also see Thomas G. Alexander, *The Rise of Multiple Use Management in the Intermountain West: A History of Region 4 of the Forest Service,* USDA Forest Service Report-399 (1988), 44, for an Idaho example of the same thing.

14. [Wirch?], "Range Management Plan" (1958).

15. Alexander, *Rise of Multiple Use Management* (1988), 71, 90.

16. Rowley, *Grazing and Rangelands* (1985), 105.

17. For two excellent studies describing much of this early research, see Gerald S. Strickler and Wade B. Hall, "The Standley Allotment: A History of Range Recovery," USDA Forest Service Research Paper PNW-278 (1980); and Jon Skovlin, *Fifty Years of Research Progress:* (USDA Forest Service General Technical Report PNW-GTR-266, 1991).

18. For the research that established the value of bedding out, deferred grazing, and rotations, see Arthur Sampson, "The Revegetation of Overgrazed Areas: Preliminary report," USDA Forest Service Circular 158 (1908);

Arthur Sampson, "Natural Revegetation of Depleted Mountain Grazing Lands," USDA Forest Service Circular 169 (1909); Arthur Sampson, "Range Improvement by Deferred and Rotation Grazing," USDA Bulletin 34 (1913).

For an excellent review of ecological changes in the heavily grazed sub-alpine grasslands, see Strickler and Hall, "The Standley Allotment" (1980). Strickler and Hall revisited the places where Sampson had established coordinates and photographed range damage in 1907, and in 1955 and 1976 they rephotographed these specific sites. They found that some green fescue communities had made a partial recovery of vegetation cover, but this cover was only about 40 percent of expected. After almost seventy years, secondary species (rather than members of climax plant communities) dominated, while the green fescue (the climax species) was only starting to reestablish. In many other areas, continued overgrazing and frost heaving had prevented the establishment of *any* grass cover. No communities showed complete recovery to a green fescue climax. In areas where Sampson had reseeded with introduced grasses, the native communities seemed to be doing better—a surprising result. The nonnative grasses had not interfered with the restoration of the native community, probably because the introduced grasses (particularly timothy) did not survive more than three to five years in the high elevation mountains. This seemed to be long enough to provide an environment suitable for speedier reestablishment of native species, but short enough not to interfere with the native grasses. Yet overall, the heavy grazing at the turn of the century did enough damage that seventy years later, even after intensive restoration work, the communities were still struggling. As Strickler and Hall wrote, "Although recovery since 1907 was apparent, the early depletion of vegetation and soil erosion essentially modified the grassland habitats and regulated the rate and amount of recovery."

19. Alexander, *Rise of Multiple Use Management* (1988), 132.

20. Sampson, "Range Improvement" (1913).

21. John G. Clouston, "Some Thoughts on the Last Thirty-five Years," UNF Historical Files, Supervisor's Office, Pendleton (1957).

22. F. Horton, "Report on Extensive Grazing Reconnaissance, Camas and Hideaway Cattle and Horse Ranges, Umatilla, 1917," UNF Historical Files, Supervisor's Office, Pendleton.

23. F. Horton, "Starkey Cattle and Horse Division, Studies, Extensive, 1918," UNF Historical Files, Supervisor's Office, Pendleton.

24. Mr. Aldous, Grazing Examiner, "Memo. Office Report of Trip on Umatilla Forest Sept. 15 to 18, inc. [1914]," 1915, UNF Historical Files, Supervisor's Office, Pendleton.

25. Will Barnes, Acting Assistant Forester District 6 (Portland); letter introducing Mr. Aldous' grazing report, to Umatilla Forest Supervisor (unnamed), February 1, 1915, UNF Historical Files, Supervisor's Office, Pendleton.

26. See W. B. Greeley, *Report of the Forester, 1919,* USDA Forest Service (Washington, D.C., 1920).

27. Rowley, *Grazing and Rangelands* (1985), 116; Alexander, *Rise of Multiple Use Management* (1988), 88.

28. Rowley, *Grazing and Rangelands* (1985), 130.

29. The fee and permit situation is covered in great detail in Rowley (ibid., 135).

30. James Iler, Malheur National Forest Supervisor, to R. E. Brooke, County Agricultural Agent, Canyon City, Oregon, March, 7, 1940, letter in MNF Historical Files, Supervisor's Office, John Day.

31. Ibid. Also see Mollin, Secretary of the American National Livestock Association in "If and When It Rains . . ."; quoted in Rowley, *Grazing and Rangelands* (1985), 157.

32. Carl Ewing, Supervisor on the Umatilla National Forest, to Regional Forester in Portland, May 12, 1938, letter in UNF Historical Files, Supervisor's Office, Pendleton.

33. See Iler letter (1940).

34. See Ewing letter (1938).

35. U.S. Senate Document 199, *Report on the Western Range* (1936); nicknamed the Green Book, this was supervised by Associate Forester Earle Clapp, so the Forest Service had a great deal of influence over its message, a fact which irritated ranchers.

36. USDA Forest Service, "Planning Report, Sales, Bear Valley Unit, Malheur National Forest, 6/30/22," MNF Historical Files, Supervisor's Office, John Day.

37. Dana Berghuis, "Progress Report: 1938 Range Survey, Bear Valley Ranger District, Malheur National Forest, December 9, 1938," MNF Historical Files, Supervisor's Office, John Day.

38. Chapman, "Report on the Silvics of the Wallowa Forest Reserve," RCF 135 (1907).

39. Horton, "Starkey Cattle and Horse Division" (1918).

40. USDA Forest Service, "Studies, Malheur, Historical Information, Long Creek District." MNF Historical Files, Supervisor's Office, John Day (1940).

41. Berghuis, "Progress Report" (1938).

42. Rowley, *Grazing and Rangelands,* 173.

43. C. H. Adams, Inspector, to Cy. Bingham, Forest Supervisor, Malheur

National Forest, October 19, 1908, letter in MNF Historical Files, Supervisor's Office, John Day.

44. Horton, "Starkey Cattle and Horse Division" (1918).

45. Aldous, "Memo" (1915).

46. Berghuis, "Progress Report" (1938).

47. Iler letter (1940).

48. USDA Forest Service, "Chart Prepared at Supervisor's Meeting, Pendleton, May 4–8, 1938," UNF Historical Files, Supervisor's Office, Pendleton.

49. Berghuis, "Progress Report" (1938).

50. Ewing letter (1938).

51. [Wirch?], "Range Management Plan" (1958).

52. USDA Forest Service, "Fish and Game Five Year Report" (1925), UNF Historical Files, Supervisor's Office, Pendleton.

53. Gerald Tucker, "History of the Northern Blue Mountains" manuscript in Wallowa Whitman National Forest Supervisor's Office, Baker (1940).

54. Loren Powers, typed manuscript, no date. "Pioneer Memories, Powers Family, Lostine Oregon." Quoted in Grace Bartlett, *The Wallowa Country, 1867–1877* (Fairfield, Wash., 1984), 27.

55. USDA Forest Service, "Fish and Game" (1925).

56. Jerry Gildemeister, ed., "Bull Trout, Walking Grouse, and Buffalo Bones: Oral Histories of Northeast Oregon Fish and Wildlife," Oregon Department of Fish and Wildlife, La Grande (April 1992), Roland Huff speaking, 23.

57. Ibid., Ned Foye speaking, 27.

58. In 1912, the Forest Service put fifteen elk into a fenced pasture at Billy Meadows. In 1918, the Washington State Game Commission planted fifty more elk, and thirty more in 1930. These increased rapidly enough so that by 1933 elk were once more hunted on the Wenaha, and by the late 1930s, elk were hunted throughout the Blues. See Tucker, "History" (1940), 116.

59. Gildemeister, "Bull Trout" (1992), Earl and Charlene Papineau speaking, 29.

60. Ibid., 56.

61. Tucker, "History" (1940), 118.

62. R. D. Guthrie, "The Extinct Wapati of Alaska and Yukon Territory," *Canadian Journal of Zoology* 44 (1966): 47–57.

63. Susan Flader, *Thinking Like a Mountain: Aldo Leopold and the Evolution of an Ecological Attitude Toward Deer, Wolves, and Forests* (Columbia, Missouri, 1974), 55.

64. Ibid., 54, 31.

65. Ibid., 120.

66. Ibid., 60.

67. Ibid., 77.

68. Gildemeister, "Bull Trout" (1992), Howard Fisk speaking, 33.

69. Berghuis, "Progress Report" (1938).

70. USDA Forest Service, "Fish and Game" (1925).

71. Flader, *Thinking Like a Mountain*, 159.

72. Gildemeister, "Bull Trout," (1992), Gildemeister speaking, 15.

73. Ibid., Will Brown, Lloyd Crossland, Howard Fisk speaking, 44–45.

74. Ibid., Harry Huffman speaking, 16.

Fire

1. Stephen Pyne, *Fire in America: A Cultural History of Wildland and Rural Fire* (Princeton, 1982).

2. This analysis follows Pyne (ibid.), 263 ff.; see also Ashley L. Schiff, *Fire and Water: Scientific Heresy in the Forest Service* (Cambridge, Mass., 1962).

3. Pyne, *Fire in America*, 274.

4. Ibid., 102.

5. Ibid., 110.

6. Ibid., 270.

7. Ibid., 104.

8. Ibid., 274.

9. Ibid., 107.

10. Quoted in Pyne, 165. For more on fire debates, also see Thomas R. Cox, ed., *This Well-Wooded Land: Americans and Their Forests from Colonial Times to the Present* (Lincoln, 1985).

11. R. M. Evans, "General Silvical Report Wallowa and Minam Forests," 1912 RCF 135.

12. W. H. B. Kent, "Inspection Report on the Chesnimnus Reserve," RCF 136 (July 1907).

13. USDA Forest Service, "Forest Users' Map of the Umatilla National Forest 1931," 8 pages of information on the back of the map, Umatilla National Forest, Supervisor's Office, Pendleton.

14. J. H. Allen, County Judge, to Senator Rufus C. Holman, May 1, 1940; this letter contained a copy of Allen's testimony to a congressional hearing in the winter of 1939. Senator Rufus C. Holman to E. W. Loveridge, Acting Chief of Forest Service, May 8, 1940. E. W. Loveridge to Lyle F.

Watts, the Regional Forester in Portland, May 23, 1940. Lyle F. Watts, the Regional Forester, to Senator Rufus C. Holman, June 1, 1940. MNF Historical Files, Supervisor's Office, John Day.

15. Allen to Holman, May 1, 1940. (Subsequent quotations in the text are from this letter.)

16. Watts to Holman, June 1, 1940.

17. John D. Guthrie, "Blame it on the Indians: Forester explodes myth that Red Men set fires to keep forests open," press release, 1933, Malheur National Forest, Supervisor's Office, John Day.

18. See James K. Agee, "Fire and Weather Disturbances in Terrestrial Ecosystems of the Eastern Cascades," in vol. 3: *Assessment, Eastside Forest Ecosystem Health Assessment,* ed. Richard L. Everett (USDA Forest Service General Technical Report PNW-GTR-320, 1994), 37.

19. For debates on fire effects on inland ecosystems, see the March 1994 issue of *Natural Resource News,* which was devoted to fire. Also see the chapters in John D. Walstad et al., eds., *Natural and Prescribed Fire in Pacific Northwest Forests* (Corvallis, 1990). See also Judy Johnson, "Wildlife and Prescribed Fire—Impact and Improvement for Wildlife," typescript, 1994, National Audubon Society, 209 N. Clinton, Walla Walla, WA 99362.

20. Diedre Dether, fire ecologist at Baker Ranger District, WWNF, pers. comm., August 1992; see also M. F. Crane and William C. Fisher, *Fire Ecology of the Forest Habitat Types of Central Idaho* (USDA Forest Service General Technical Report INT-GTR, December 1986; Agee, "Fire and Weather Disturbances" (1994); James K. Agee, *Fire Ecology of Pacific Northwest Forests* (Washington, D.C., 1993), 250–300; and Kathleen Ryoko Maruoka, "Fire History of *Pseudotsuga menziesii* and *Abies grandis* Stands in the Blue Mountains of Oregon and Washington" (master's thesis, University of Washington, 1994).

21. Arthur Tiedemann and James Klemmedson, "Prescribed Burning and Productivity: A Nutrient Management Perspective," *Natural Resources News* (March 1994), 6–9.

22. J. D. Landsburg, "Response of Ponderosa Pine Forests in Central Oregon to Prescribed Underburning" (Ph.D. diss., Oregon State University, Corvallis, 1992).

23. P. H. Cochran and W. E. Hopkins, "Does Fire Exclusion Increase Productivity of Ponderosa Pine?" in *Proceedings, Management and Productivity of Western-Montane Forest Soils,* ed. A. E. Harvey and L. F. Neuenschwander (USDA Forest Service General Technical Report INT-GTR-280, 1991), 224–28.

24. M. G. Harrington and S. S. Sackett, "Past and Present Fire Influences

on Southwestern Ponderosa Pine Old Growth: Old Growth Forests in the Southwest and Rocky Mountain Regions, Proceedings of a Workshop" (USDA Forest Service General Technical Report RM-GTR-213, 1992).

25. Stephen S. Sackett and Sally M. Haase, "Soil and Cambium Temperatures Associated with Prescribed Burning," *Natural Resource News* (March 1994), 5.

Restoring the Inland West

1. USDA Forest Service, "Determination of Allowable Timber Cut on Forty-two Western National Forests" (Washington, D.C., 1962), quoted in Thomas B. Parry, Henry J. Vaux, and Nicholas Dennis, "Changing Conceptions of Sustained-yield Policy on the National Forests," *Journal of Forestry* (March 1983), 153.

2. Charles F. Wilkinson, *Crossing the Next Meridian: Land, Water, and the Future of the West* (Washington, D.C., 1992).

3. William Gast et al., *The Blue Mountains Forest Health Report* (Washington, D.C., 1991).

4. Torolf Torgersen, "The Forest Immune System—Its Role in Insect Pest Regulation," *Natural Resource News* (August 1993), 6–7.

5. USDA Forest Service, *Willamette National Forest Land and Resource Management Plan,* (Washington, D.C., 1965), quoted in David A. Clary, *Timber and the Forest Service* (Lawrence, 1986), 172.

6. Frederick Hall and Jack Ward Thomas, "Silvicultural Options," in Jack Ward Thomas, ed., *Wildlife Habitats in Managed Forests: The Blue Mountains of Oregon and Washington* (USDA Forest Service, 1979), 142. Frederick Hall was the fire ecologist who first argued that fires were essential to mixed-conifer and Douglas-fir communities in the Blues; Jack Ward Thomas is the wildlife biologist who in 1993 became Chief of the Forest Service—the first time a biologist, rather than a member of the timber program, has headed the Forest Service.

7. USDA Forest Service, *Umatilla National Forest Land and Resource Management Plan, Final Environmental Impact Statement* (Washington, D.C., 1990), III-25.

8. Ibid.

9. Steve Mealey, quoted in Eric Pryne, "Summer Forest Fires Spark Debate over Timber Policy," *Seattle Times,* September 9, 1994.

10. Larry LaRocco, quoted in article by Eric Pryne, "Unease over Logging to Control Fire," *Seattle Times,* September 10, 1994.

11. Dominic DellaSala, David Olson, and Saundra Crane, "Ecosystem

Management and Biodiversity Conservation: Applications to Inland Pacific Northwest Forests," in *Proceedings of a Workshop on Ecosystem Management in Western Interior Forests,* ed. D. Baumgartner and R. Everett, Washington State University Cooperative Extension Unit (Pullman, Washington, in press).

12. President Clinton, quoted in Jack Ward Thomas and Jim Baca, "Eastside Ecosystem Management Project Charter," January 21, 1994, in Eastside Ecosystem Management Project, Scientific Integration Team, "Framework for Ecosystem Management in the Interior Columbia River Basin, Working Draft—Version 1" (Walla Walla, May 1994).

13. Eastside Ecosystem Management Project, Scientific Integration Team, "Draft Framework" (1994), 5.

14. For example, see Jay O'Laughlin, James G. MacCracken, David L. Adams, Stephen C. Bunting, Keith A. Blatner, and Charles E. Keegan III, *Forest Health Conditions in Idaho,* Idaho Forest, Wildlife and Range Policy Analysis Group Report 11 (December 1993), Executive Summary, 5-25, especially p. 6.

15. R. Edward Grumbine argues this beautifully in *Ghost Bears: Exploring the Biodiversity Crisis* (Washington, D.C., 1992), 229–40.

16. See Jay O'Laughlin, James G. MacCracken, David L. Adams, Stephen C. Bunting, Keith A. Blatner, and Charles E. Keegan III, *Forest Health Conditions in Idaho,* Idaho Forest, Wildlife and Range Policy Analysis Group Report 11 (December 1993), 6–12, 24–40.

17. Eastside Ecosystem Management Project, Scientific Integration Team, "Draft Framework"; (1994) James K. Agee and D. R. Johnson, eds., *Ecosystem Management for Parks and Wilderness* (Seattle, 1988), 7–10; see also R. Edward Grumbine, "What Is Ecosystem Management?" *Conservation Biology* 8 (1994): 27–38.

18. Russell T. Graham, "Can Silviculture Replace the Role of Fire?" *Natural Resource News* (March 1994), 12–13.

19. Merrill R. Kaufmann, Russell T. Graham, Douglas A. Boyce, Jr., William H. Moir, Lee Perry, Richard T. Reynolds, Richard L. Bassett, Patricia Mehlhop, Carleton B. Edminster, William M. Block, and Paul Stephen Corn, *An Ecological Basis for Ecosystem Management* (USDA Forest Service General Technical Report RM 246, Fort Collins, 1994).

20. O'Laughlin et al., *Forest Health* (1993), Report, 43.

21. Daniel B. Botkin, *Discordant Harmonies: A New Ecology for the Twenty-first Century* (New York, 1990).

22. Henry Alden, "Watersheds, Landscapes, Biodiversity, Fire and Forest Management," The S. J. Hall Lectureship in Industrial Forestry, University of California (Berkeley, 1992), 10.

23. For an overview of controversies over the meanings of stability and balance in nature, see S. T. A. Pickett and P. S. White, *The Ecology of Natural Disturbance and Patch Dynamics* (Orlando, 1985); Stuart Pimm, "The Complexity and Stability of Ecosystems," *Nature* 307 (1984): 321–26; Stuart Pimm, *The Balance of Nature? Ecological Issues in the Conservation of Species and Communities* (Chicago, 1991); R. J. Vogl, "The Ecological Factors that Promote Perturbation-dependent Ecosystems," in *The Recovery Process in Damaged Ecosystems,* ed. John Cairns, Jr. (Ann Arbor, Michigan, 1980); Botkin, *Discordant Harmonies;* Stephen Woodley, James Kay, and George Francis, eds., *Ecological Integrity and the Management of Ecosystems* (Delray Beach, Fla., 1993).

24. J. W. Byler and S. Zimmer-Grove, "A Forest Health Perspective on Interior Douglas-fir Management," in *Proceedings, Interior Douglas-fir and Its Management,* ed. D. M. Baumgartner and J. V. Lotan (Washington State Cooperative Extension, Pullman, 1991), 103–8.

25. David Perry, "Landscape Pattern and Forest Pests," *Northwest Environmental Journal* 4 (1988): 213–28.

26. USDA Forest Service, "Forest Health through Silviculture and Integrated Pest Management: A Strategic Plan" (Washington, D.C., 1988); quoted in O'Laughlin et al., *Forest Health* (1993), Report, 57.

27. Ibid., Executive Summary, 6.

28. Ibid., 17, following the definition of forest health recommended by the Society of American Foresters in L. A. Norris, H. Cortner, M. R. Cutler, S. G. Haines, J. E. Hubbard, M. A. Kerrick, W. B. Kessler, J. C. Nelson, R. Stone, and J. M. Sweeney. "Sustaining Long-term Forest Health and Productivity," Task force report, Society of American Foresters, Bethesda, 1993.

29. Gast et al. (1991); also see DellaSala et al. (in press), Kaufmann et al. (1994).

30. James R. Karr has developed the concept of ecosystem integrity for aquatic communities; see his "Measuring Biological Integrity: Lessons from Streams," in Woodley et al., *Ecological Integrity* (1993). Also see James R. Karr, "Biological Integrity and the Goal of Environmental Legislation: Lessons for Conservation Biology," *Conservation Biology* 4 (1990): 244–50.

31. M. Sagoff, "Has Nature a Good of Its Own? in Robert Costanza et al., *Ecosystem Health: New Goals for Environmental Management* (Washington, D.C., 1992), 55–71.

32. Michael Pollan, *Second Nature: A Gardener's Education* (New York, 1991), 62.

33. Alexander Pope, quoted ibid., 190.

34. R. Edward Grumbine, "What Is Ecosystem Management?" *Conser-*

vation Biology 8 (1994): 27–38; R. Edward Grumbine, "Wildness, Wise Use, and Sustainability," *Environmental Ethics* 16 (1994): 227–50; Gary Snyder, *The Practice of the Wild* (San Francisco, 1990).

35. Pollan, *Second Nature,* 194, 192.

36. Ibid., 194.

37. DellaSala et al. (in press).

38. Pryne, *Seattle Times,* September 10, 1994.

39. USDA Forest Service, "Regional Forester's Eastside Forest Plans Amendment No. 1., Alternative 3, as Adopted" (Portland, Oregon, 1993).

40. For a more detailed argument about how I feel we should use information about presettlement forests, see Nancy Langston, "How Should We Interpret Historic Ranges of Variability in Restoring Public Lands?" submitted to *Conservation Biology.* For an attempt to use aerial photographs from the 1930s to the 1950s to derive estimates of presettlement forest composition, see John F. Lehmkul, Paul F. Hessburg, Richard L. Everett, Mark H. Huff, and Roger D. Ottmer, "Historical and Current Forest Landscapes of Eastern Oregon and Washington; Part 1: Vegetation Pattern and Insect and Disease Hazards," in vol. 3: *Assessment, Eastside Forest Ecosystem Health Assessment,* ed. Richard L. Everett (USDA Forest Service General Technical Report PNW-GTR-328, April 1994), 1–88. For an overview of this effort, see R. Everett, P. Hessburg, J. Lehmkuhl, M. Jensen, and P. Bourgeron, "Old Forests in Dynamic Landscapes, Dry-site Forests of Eastern Oregon and Washington," *Journal of Forestry* (January 1994), 22–25. For the first attempt to establish some sense of Blues presettlement forests see David Caraher, John Henshaw, Fred Hall, Walter H. Knapp, Bruce P. McCammon, John Nesbitt, Richard J. Pedersen, Iral Regenovitch, and Chuck Tietz, "Restoring Ecosystems in the Blue Mountains: A Report to the Regional Forester and the Forest Supervisors of the Blue Mountain Forests," USDA Forest Service Pacific Northwest Region Report (July 1992). For an idea of how managers interpret (and often misinterpret) these presettlement forests, see Douglas MacCleery, "Understanding the Role the Human Dimension Has Played in Shaping America's Forest and Grassland Landscapes," *Eco-Watch,* February 10, 1994.

41. Caraher, et al., "Restoring Ecosystems" (1992).

42. See Nancy Langston, "The General Riot of the Natural Forest: Landscape Change in the Blue Mountains" (Ph.D. diss., University of Washington, 1994; University Microfilms, Ann Arbor), 31–58.

43. Arthur R. Tiedemann and H. W. Berndt, "Vegetation and Soils of a 30-year Deer and Elk Exclosure in Central Washington," *Northwest Science* 46 (1972): 59–66; Paul J. Edgerton, "Influence of Ungulates on the Devel-

opment of the Shrub Understory of an Upper Slope Mixed Conifer Forest," in *Proceedings—Symposium on Plant-Herbivore Interactions* (USDA Forest Service General Technical Report INT-222, 1987).

44. Chris Maser, *The Redesigned Forest* (San Pedro, Calif., 1988), 3–58.

45. USDA Forest Service, *Malheur National Forest Land and Resource Management Plan, Final Environmental Impact Statement* (Washington, D.C., 1990), III-35.

Conclusion: Living with Complexity

1. William Kittredge, *Owning It All: Essays* (St. Paul, 1987), 60–61, 64.

2. William Gast et al., *Blue Mountains Forest Health Report,* USDA Forest Service Report (1991), 1–3.

3. Edward of Norwich, the Second Duke of York, *The Master of Game* (1407), ed. W. A. and F. Baille-Grohman, with an introduction by Theodore Roosevelt (London, 1909). My translation from the Middle English.

4. Wallace Stegner, *The American West as Living Space* (Ann Arbor, 1987), 3.

5. Ibid., 24.

6. Ibid., 21, 22.

7. USDA Forest Service, *Umatilla National Forest Land and Resource Management Plan, Final Environmental Impact Statement* (Washington, D.C., 1990), III.

8. Jack Southworth, "Ranching and Riparians," talk given in May 1993 at the Blue Mountains Natural Resources Institute, text reprinted in *Natural Resource News* (August 1993), 12–13.

Selected Bibliography

Government Documents and Publications

ABBREVIATIONS

MNF   Malheur National Forest

RCF   Forest Service Research Compilation Files, National Archives, Region VI, Entry 115, Boxes 135 to 139. Most of the Research Compilation Files for Region VI (Oregon and Washington) have been microfilmed and are available in the University of Washington microfilm library, file A1527.

UNF   Umatilla National Forest

WWNF   Wallowa Whitman National Forest

Adams, C. H. Letter to Cy. Bingham, Forest Supervisor, MNF, October 19, 1908. On file at the MNF Supervisor's Office, John Day.

Agee, James K. "Fire and Weather Disturbances in Terrestrial Ecosystems of the Eastern Cascades." In Vol. 3: *Assessment, Eastside Forest Ecosystem Health Assessment,* edited by Richard L. Everett (1994). USDA Forest Service General Technical Report PNW-GTR-320.

Aldous. "Memo. Office Report of Trip on Umatilla Forest, Sept. 15 to 18, inc. [1914]" (1915). UNF Historical Files, Supervisor's Office, Pendleton.

Alexander, Thomas G. *The Rise of Multiple Use Management in the Intermountain West: A History of Region 4 of the Forest Service* (1989). USDA Forest Service Report-399.

Allen, J. H., County Judge. Letter to Senator Rufus C. Holman, May 1, 1940; this letter contained a copy of his testimony to a Congressional Hearing in the winter of 1939. MNF Historical Files, Supervisor's Office, John Day.

Ames, Frederick E. Letter to forest officers 2/3/09, about a circular letter of May 29, 1907, entitled "Record of Cut-over Areas." RCF 136.

————. "Addresses given at the 1910 joint supervisors' meeting for the Northwest region (Oregon and Washington)." RCF 136.

————. Letter to Blues supervisors introducing Smith's windfall studies (1915). RCF 139.

Assistant Forester. Letter of August 8, 1922; cited in letter of C. M. Granger, the District Forester, to Acting Forester Mr. Sherman, concerning the Baker Working Circle plan, 1927. WWNF Historical Files, Supervisor's Office, Baker.

Barnes, Will. Letter introducing Mr. Aldous' grazing report, to Umatilla Forest Supervisor (unnamed), February 1, 1915. UNF Historical Files, Supervisor's Office, Pendleton.

Berghuis, Dana. "Progress Report: 1938 Range Survey, Bear Valley Ranger District, MNF." MNF Historical Files, Supervisor's Office, John Day.

Bright, George. "Umatilla Studies: Annual Silvical Report 2/23/11." RCF 137.

————. "The Relative Merits of Western Larch and Douglas Fir in the Blue Mountains, Oregon" (1913). RCF 135.

————. "An Extensive Reconnaissance of the Wenaha National Forest in 1913," edited by David C. Powell (1994). USDA Forest Service Publication F14-SO-08–94. Umatilla National Forest, Pendleton.

Buck, C. J. Letter to Blues supervisors, September 15, 1936. UNF Historical Files, Supervisor's Office, Pendleton.

Byler, J. W., and S. Zimmer-Grove. "A Forest Health Perspective on Interior Douglas-fir Management." In *Proceedings, Interior Douglas-fir and Its Management,* edited by D. M. Baumgartner and J. V. Lotan, Washington State Cooperative Extension, Pullman, 1991.

Caraher, David, John Henshaw, Fred Hall, Walter H. Knapp, Bruce P. McCammon, John Nesbitt, Richard J. Pedersen, Iral Regenovitch, and Chuck Tietz. "Restoring Ecosystems in the Blue Mountains, A Report to the Regional Forester and the Forest Supervisors of the Blue Mountain Forests." USDA Forest Service Pacific Northwest Region Report. Portland, 1992.

Cecil, G. H. Letter to Gifford Pinchot, March 16, 1909. RCF 136.

Chapman. "Report on the Silvics of the Wallowa Forest Reserve" (1907). RCF 135.

Clouston, John G. "Some Thoughts on the Last Thirty-five Years" (1957). UNF Historical Files, Supervisor's Office, Pendleton.

Cochran, P. H., and W. E. Hopkins. "Does Fire Exclusion Increase Productivity of Ponderosa Pine?" In *Proceedings, Management and Productivity of Western-Montane Forest Soils,* edited by A. E. Harvey and L. F.

Neuenschwander (1991). USDA Forest Service General Technical Report INT-GTR-280.

Colville, Frederick V. "Forest Growth and Sheep Grazing in the Cascade Mountains of Oregon." USDA Division of Forestry, Bulletin 15. Washington, D.C., 1898.

Cowlin, R. W., P. A. Briegleb, and F. L. Moravets. "Forest Resources of the Pondersoa Pine Region." USDA Miscellaneous Publication 490. Washington, D.C., 1942.

Crane, M. F., and William C. Fisher. *Fire Ecology of the Forest Habitat Types of Central Idaho* (1986). USDA Forest Service General Technical Report INT-GTR-218.

DellaSala, Dominic, David Olson, and Saundra Crane. "Ecosystem Management and Biodiversity Conservation: Applications to Inland Pacific Northwest forests." In *Proceedings of a Workshop on Ecosystem Management in Western Interior Forests,* edited by D. Baumgartner and R. Everett. Washington State University Cooperative Extension Unit, Pullman, 1995.

Eastside Ecosystem Management Project, Scientific Integration Team. "Framework for Ecosystem Management in the Interior Columbia River Basin, Working Draft—Version 1." Walla Walla, 1994.

Eastside Forests Scientific Society Panel (Dan Bottom, Sam Wright, Jim Bednarz, David Perry, Steve Beckwitt, Eric Beckwitt, James R. Karr, and Mark Henjum). *Interim Protection for Late-Successional Forests, Fisheries, and Watersheds: National Forests East of the Cascade Crest, Oregon and Washington: A Report to the United States Congress and the President,* edited by Ellen Chu and James R. Karr. Washington, D.C., 1994.

Edgerton, Paul J. "Influence of Ungulates on the Development of the Shrub Understory of an Upper Slope Mixed Conifer Forest." In *Proceedings— Symposium on Plant-Herbivore Interactions* (1987). USDA Forest Service General Technical Report INT-222.

Erickson, M. L. "Forest Conditions Blue Mountains National Forest (now Whitman)" (1906). RCF 136.

——. "Report on Blue Mountains West, 12/29/06: Silvics: Strawberry Mt. Reserve." RCF 135.

——. "Timber Sales, Wallowa Forest Reserve, 10/3/06." RCF 135.

——. "The Wallowa Forest Reserve: Silvics: The Forest, 10/3/1906." RCF 135.

——. "Report on the Chesnimnus Reserve" (1907). RCF 135.

Ewing, Carl. Letter to Regional Forester in Portland, May 12, 1938. UNF Historical Files, Supervisor's Office, Pendleton.

Evans, R. M. "General Silvical Report Wallowa and Minam Forests," 1912. RCF 135.

Fernow, Bernard. "What Is Forestry?" (1891). USDA Forestry Bulletin 5.

Fields, Benjamin F. Letter to Commissioner of the General Land Office, Asotin 2/20/03. National Archives, General Land Office, Record Group 49, Box 173.

Flory, Charles. "Addresses read at Supervisors' meeting, Portland" (1910). RCF 135.

Foster, H. D. "The Forest: Wenaha Reserve (1905). RCF 135.

———. "Report on the Silvics of the Wenaha Forest Reserve," 10/1/06. RCF 135.

———. "Blue Mountains East National Forest, report for July-September 1907." RCF 139.

———. "Report on the Silvics of the Blue Mountains (E) National Forest Oregon," 1908. RCF 139.

Gast, William, et al. *Blue Mountains Forest Health Report* (1991). USDA Forest Service Report.

Geist, J. Michael, John W. Hazard, and Kenneth W. Seidel. "Assessing Physical Conditions of Some Pacific Northwest Volcanic Ash Soils after Forest Harvest." *Soil Science Society of America Journal* 53 (1989): 946–950.

Gildemeister, Jerry, ed. "Bull Trout, Walking Grouse, and Buffalo Bones: Oral Histories of Northeast Oregon Fish and Wildlife." Oregon Department of Fish and Wildlife Paper. La Grande, 1992.

Graves, Henry. *Annual Report of the Forester 1912.* USDA Forest Service, Washington, D.C.

———. *Annual Report of the Forester 1913.* USDA Forest Service, Washington, D.C.

———. *Report of the Forester, 1919* (1920). USDA Forest Service, Washington, D.C.

Guthrie, John D. "Blame It on the Indians: Forester explodes myth that Red Men set fires to keep forests open" (1933). Press release, Malheur National Forest, Supervisor's Office, John Day.

Hall, Frederick. "Ecology of Natural Underburning in the Blue Mountains of Oregon." USDA Forest Service Pacific Northwest Region Regional Guide 51-1 (August 1977).

———. "Historical and Present Conditions of the Blue Mountain Forests." *Natural Resource News,* March 1994.

Hall, Frederick, and Jack Ward Thomas. "Silvicultural Options." In Jack Ward Thomas, ed., *Wildlife Habitats in Managed Forests: The Blue Moun-*

tains of Oregon and Washington. USDA Forest Service Agricultural Handbook 553. Washington, D.C., 1979.

Hanzlik, E. J. "The Growth and Yield of Douglas Fir on Various Sites in Western Washington and Oregon." S-Studies, 1912, R-6, 54-A-111/ 59859, National Archives Record Services, Seattle.

———. "Memorandum for FM, re Management Plans, Umatilla, La Grande Working Circle" (1927). UNF Historical Files, Supervisor's Office, Pendleton.

Harrington, M. G., and S. S. Sackett. "Past and Present Fire Influences on Southwestern Ponderosa Pine Old Growth: Old Growth Forests in the Southwest and Rocky Mountain Regions. Proceedings of a Workshop" (1992). USDA Forest Service General Technical Report GTR-RM-213.

Harvey, Alan E., J. Michael Geist, Gerald I. McDonald, Martin F. Jurgensen, Patrick H. Cochran, Darlene Zabowski, and Robert T. Meurisse. "Biotic and Abiotic Processes in Eastside Ecosystems: The Effects of Management on Soil Properties, Processes, and Productivity." In Vol. 3: *Assessment, Eastside Forest Ecosystem Health Assessment,* edited by Richard L. Everett (1994). USDA Forest Service General Technical Report PNW-GTR-323.

Holman, Senator Rufus C. Letter to E. W. Loveridge, Acting Chief of Forest Service, May 8, 1940. MNF Historical Files, Supervisor's Office, John Day.

Horton, F. "Report on Extensive Grazing Reconnaissance, Camas and Hideaway Cattle and Horse Ranges, Umatilla" (1917). UNF Historical Files, Supervisor's Office, Pendleton.

———. "Starkey Cattle and Horse Division, Studies, Extensive, 1918." UNF Historical Files, Supervisor's Office, Pendleton.

Iler, James. Letter to R. E. Brooke, County Agricultural Agent, Canyon City, Oregon, March 7, 1940. MNF Historical Files, Supervisor's Office, John Day.

Johnson, Charles G. Jr., Roderick R. Clausnitzer, Peter J. Mehringer, and Chadwick D. Oliver. "Biotic and Abiotic Processes of Eastside Ecosystems." In Vol. 3: *Assessment, Eastside Forest Ecosystem Health Assessment,* edited by Richard L. Everett (1994). USDA Forest Service General Technical Report PNW-GTR-322.

Judd, C. S. "Lectures on Timber Sales at the University of Washington, February 1911." RCF 136.

Kaufmann, Merrill R., Russell T. Graham, Douglas A. Boyce, Jr., William H. Moir, Lee Perry, Richard T. Reynolds, Richard L. Bassett, Patricia Mehlhop, Carleton B. Edminster, William M. Block, and Paul Stephen

Corn. "An Ecological Basis for Ecosystem Management" (1994). USDA Forest Service General Technical Report GTR-RM-246.

Kent, W. H. B. "Examination and Report on the Proposed Wenaha Forest Reserve, Washington and Oregon" (1904). RCF 135.

———. "Inspection Report on the Chesnimnus Reserve" (July 1907), RCF 136.

Kier, J. A. "La Grande Working Circle Policy Statement" (1938). UNF Historical Files, Supervisor's Office, Pendleton.

Langille, H. D. "Report on the Proposed Heppner Reserve" (1903). RCF 135.

———. "Supplemental Report on the Proposed Chesnimnus Reserve" (1904). RCF 135.

———. "A Report on the Proposed Blue Mountain Reserve" (1906). RCF 139.

———. Letter to Secretary of Agriculture Wilson (1907). National Archives, Department of the Interior, National Forests, Blue Mountains, Box 17.

Lehmkul, John F., Paul F. Hessburg, Richard L. Everett, Mark H. Huff, and Roger D. Ottmer. "Historical and Current Forest Landscapes of Eastern Oregon and Washington; Part 1: Vegetation Pattern and Insect and Disease Hazards." In Vol. 3: *Assessment, Eastside Forest Ecosystem Health Assessment,* edited by Richard L. Everett (1994). USDA Forest Service General Technical Report PNW-GTR-328.

Leiberg, John B. "Cascade Range and Ashland Forest Reserves and Adjacent Regions." In *Twenty-first Annual Report of the United States Geological Survey to the Secretary of the Interior, 1899–1900, Part V, Forest Reserves* (1900).

Libby, E. H. President of the Lewiston-Clarkston Irrigation Company, letter to L. Hall, the Acting Head Forester in the Washington, D.C., Office (1906). UNF Historical Files, Supervisor's Office, Pendleton.

Loveridge, E. W. Letter to Lyle F. Watts, the Regional Forester in Portland, May 23, 1940. MNF Historical Files, Supervisor's office, John Day.

MacCleery, Douglas. "Understanding the Role the Human Dimension has Played in Shaping America's Forest and Grassland Landscapes." *Eco-Watch,* February 10, 1994.

Miles, Herbert J. "Silvics: Annual Report for the MNF" (1911). RCF 136.

Minto, John. *Special Report on the History and Present Condition of the Sheep Industry of the United States.* U.S. Bureau of Plant Industry, Washington, D.C., 1892.

Mosgrove, Jerry. *The Malheur National Forest: An Ethnographic History.* USDA Forest Service, Pacific Northwest Region, 1980.

Munger, Thornton T. "Basic Considerations in the Management of Ponderosa Pine Forests by the Maturity Selection System." (1936). UNF Historical Files, Supervisor's Office, Pendleton.

Northwest Regional Council. *Economic Atlas of the Pacific Northwest, with Descriptive Text.* 2d edition. Portland, Oregon, 1942.

Norris, L. A., H. Cortner, M. R. Cutler, S. G. Haines, J. E. Hubbard, M. A. Kerrick, W. B. Kessler, J. C. Nelson, R. Stone, and J. M. Sweeney. "Sustaining Long-term Forest Health and Productivity." Task Force Report, Society of American Foresters, Bethesda, 1992.

O'Laughlin, Jay, James G. MacCracken, David L. Adams, Stephen C. Bunting, Keith A. Blatner, and Charles E. Keegan III. *Forest Health Conditions in Idaho.* Idaho Forest, Wildlife and Range Policy Analysis Group Report 11. Moscow, Idaho, 1993.

Pinchot, Gifford. *A Primer of Forestry.* USDA Farmer's Bulletin 358. Washington, D.C., 1901.

Price, Overton. Letter to Supervisor O'Brien, 1906. UNF Historical Files, Supervisor's Office, Pendleton.

Ripley, Smith. "Memoir" (1912). UNF Historical Files, Supervisor's Office, Pendleton.

Robbins, William G., and Donald W. Wolf. "Landscape and the Intermontane Northwest: An Environmental History." In Vol. 3: *Assessment, Eastside Forest Ecosystem Health Assessment,* edited by Richard L. Everett (1994). USDA Forest Service General Technical Report PNW-GTR-319.

Sampson, Arthur. "The Revegetation of Overgrazed Areas: Preliminary Report" (1908). USDA Forest Service Circular 158.

———. "National Revegetation of Depleted Mountain Grazing Lands" (1909). USDA Forest Service Circular 169.

———. "Range Improvement by Deferred and Rotation Grazing" (1913). USDA Bulletin 34.

Sherman, E. A. Letter to C. M. Granger, District Forester, and John Kuhns, Whitman Forest Supervisor, March 8, 1927. WWNF Historical Files, Supervisor's Office, Baker.

Skovlin, Jon. *Fifty Years of Research Progress: A Historical Document on the Starkey Experimental Forest and Range* (May 1991). USDA Forest Service General Technical Report PNW-GTR-266.

Smith, Kan. "Windfall Damage on Cutover Areas, February 1915." RCF 139.

Strickler, Gerald S., and Wade B. Hall. "The Standley Allotment: A History of Range Recovery" (1980). USDA Forest Service Research Paper PNW-278.

Stuart, Robert. *Annual Report of the Forester.* USDA Forest Service, Washington, D.C., 1928.

Sudworth, George. *Forest Atlas, Geographic Description of North American Trees, Part 1—Pines.* USDA Forest Service, Washington, D.C., 1913.

Taplin, Gary P. Letter to Commissioner of the General Land Office, 2/24/09. National Archives, General Land Office, Record Group 49, Box 173.

Thomas, Jack Ward, ed. *Wildlife Habitats in Managed Forests: The Blue Mountains of Oregon and Washington.* USDA Forest Service Agricultural Handbook 553. Washington, D.C., 1979.

Thomas, Jack Ward. "Ecosystem Management." Speech given to Forest Service public affairs personnel in Portland Oregon, April 11, 1993, and reprinted in *Natural Resource News,* Blue Mountain Natural Resources Institute.

Thomas, Jack Ward, and Jim Baca. "Eastside Ecosystem Management Project Charter." In Eastside Ecosystem Management Project, Scientific Integration Team, "Framework for Ecosystem Management in the Interior Columbia River Basin, Working Draft—Version 1." Walla Walla, 1994.

Tucker, Gerald. "History of the Northern Blue Mountains" (1940). WWNF Supervisor's Office, Baker.

———. "Historical Sketches of Wallowa National Forest" (1970). WWNF Supervisor's Office, Baker.

Umatilla National Forest. Press release, September 12, 1906. UNF Historical Files, Supervisor's Office, Pendleton.

USDA Forest Service. 1907. *The Use Book.* Administrative edition. Washington, D.C.

———. 1910. *Forest Service Annual Report, 1909.* Washington, D.C.

———. 1916. "Sale Prospectus: 124,000,000 feet Western Yellow Pine and Other Species: Lower Middle Fork John Day River Unit Whitman National Forest, Oregon, July 1916." MNF Historical Files, Supervisor's Office, John Day.

———. 1917. "Powder River Timber Survey." UNF Historical Files, S-Timber Surveys, Supervisor's Office, Pendleton.

———. 1920. "Timber Sale Policy of the Forest Service." Washington, D.C.

———. 1922. "La Grande Working Circle." UNF Historical Files, S-Timber Surveys, Supervisor's Office, Pendleton.

———. 1922. "Planning Report, Sales, Bear Valley Unit, Malheur National Forest, 6/30/22." MNF Historical Files, Supervisor's Office, John Day.

———. 1922. "Report on Sales in the Bear Valley Unit." MNF Historical Files, Supervisor's Office, John Day.

———. 1922. "Sale Prospectus: Bear Valley Unit." MNF Historical Files, Supervisor's Office, John Day.

———. 1923. "Memorandum: the Sustained Yield of the Burns Working Circle, February 23, 1923." MNF Historical Files, Supervisor's Office, John Day.

———. 1925. "Fish and Game Five Year Report." UNF Historical Files, Supervisor's Office, Pendleton.

———. 1926. "Umatilla Hilgard Project Report." National Archives, Forest Service Files, Record Group 115, Region 6, S-Timber Surveys D-6.

———. 1930. "Camas Creek Project." UNF Historical Files, S-Timber Surveys, Supervisor's Office, Pendleton.

———. 1930. "Management Plans, Middle Fork of the John Day Working Circle." MNF Historical Files, Supervisor's Office, John Day.

———. 1931. "Forest Users' Map of the Umatilla National Forest." UNF Historical Files, Supervisor's Office, Pendleton.

———. 1933. "Draft of Malheur National Forest Management Plan." MNF Historical Files, Supervisor's Office, John Day.

———. 1938. "Chart Prepared at Supervisors' Meeting, Pendleton, May 4–8, 1938." UNF Historical Files, Supervisor's Office, Pendleton.

———. 1940. "Historical Information, Malheur Studies, February 5, 1940." MNF Historical Files, Supervisor's Office, John Day.

———. 1940. "Studies, Malheur, Historical Information, Long Creek District." MNF Historical Files, Supervisor's Office, John Day.

———. 1962. "Determination of Allowable Timber Cut on Forty-two Western National Forests." Washington, D.C.

———. 1965. *Willamette National Forest Land and Resource Management Plan.* Washington, D.C.

———. 1988. "Forest Health through Silviculture and Integrated Pest Management: A Strategic Plan." Washington, D.C.

———. 1990. *Malheur National Forest Land and Resource Management Plan, Final Environmental Impact Statement.* Washington, D.C.

———. 1990. *Umatilla National Forest Land and Resource Management Plan, Final Environmental Impact Statement.* Washington, D.C.

———. 1990. *Wallowa Whitman National Forest Land and Resource Management Plan, Final Environmental Impact Statement.* Washington, D.C.

———. 1993. "Regional Forester's Eastside Forest Plans Amendment No. 1, Alternative 3, as Adopted." Portland, Oregon.

———. No date. "Malheur River Working Circle Plan." Internal evidence sets the date after 1926 and before 1929. MNF Historical Files, Supervisor's Office, John Day.

U.S. Department of Agriculture. *Yearbook of the United States Department of Agriculture.* Washington, D.C., 1914.

U.S. Department of the Interior. *Rules and Regulations Governing Forest Reserves.* Washington, D.C., 1897.

U.S. Senate. *Report on the Western Range.* Senate Document 199. Washington, D.C., 1936.

Watts, Lyle F. Letter to Senator Rufus C. Holman, June 1, 1940. MNF Historical Files, Supervisor's Office, John Day.

Wickman, Boyd. "Forest Health in the Blue Mountains: The Influence of Insects and Diseases" (1992). USDA Forest Service, General Technical Report PNW-GTR-295.

[Wirch? A. W.] "Range Management Plan, Long Creek Ranger District" (1958). MNF Historical Files, Supervisor's Office, John Day.

Other Works

Adams, Cecelia, and Parthenia Blank. "Twin Sisters on the Oregon Trail." In *Covered Wagon Women: Diaries and Letters from the Western Trails, 1840–1890,* vol. 5, edited by Kenneth L. Holmes. Glendale, Calif.: A. H. Clarke Co., 1986.

Agee, James K. *Fire Ecology of Pacific Northwest Forests.* Washington, D.C.: Island Press, 1993.

———. "The Historical Role of Fire in Pacific Northwest Forests." In *Natural and Prescribed Fire in Pacific Northwest Forests,* edited by John D. Walstad, Steven R. Radosevich, and David V. Sandberg. Corvallis: Oregon State University Press, 1990.

Agee, James K., and Darryll R. Johnson, eds. *Ecosystem Management for Parks and Wilderness.* Seattle: University of Washington Press, 1988.

Alden, Henry. "Watersheds, Landscapes, Biodiversity, Fire and Forest Management." The S. J. Hall Lectureship in Industrial Forestry, University of California, Berkeley, 1992.

Baker, F. A. "The Influence of Forest Management on Pathogens." *Northwest Environmental Journal* 4 (1988): 229–46.

Bartlett, Grace. *The Wallowa Country, 1867–1877.* Fairfield, Wash.: Ye Galleon Press, 1984.

Beebe, Spencer. "Relationships between Insectivorous Hole-nesting Birds and Forest Management." Yale University School of Forestry and Environmental Studies Publications, 1–49, 1974.

Botkin, Daniel B. *Discordant Harmonies: A New Ecology for the Twenty-first Century.* New York: Oxford University Press, 1990.

Boyd, Robert T. "The Introduction of Infectious Diseases Among the Indians of the Pacific Northwest, 1774–1874." Ph.D. dissertation, University of Washington, 1985.

Broughton, Jack. "Late Holocene Resource Intensification in the Sacramento Valley, California: The Vertebrate Evidence." *Journal of Archaeological Science* 21 (1994): 501–14.

Bull, Evie. "Habitat Utilization of the Pileated Woodpecker, Blue Mountains, Oregon." Master's thesis, Oregon State University, Corvallis, 1975.

Butzer, K. W. "The Indian Legacy in the American Landscape." In *The Making of the American Landscape,* edited by Michael P. Conzen. Boston: Unwin Hyman, 1990.

Clary, David A. *Timber and the Forest Service.* Lawrence: University Press of Kansas, 1986.

Clyman, James. *Journal of a Mountain Man.* Missoula: Mountain Press, 1984.

Condit, Richard, Stephen P. Hubbell, and Robin B. Foster. "Short-term Dynamics of a Neotropical Forest: Change within Limits." *BioScience* 42 (1992): 824–28.

Conzen, Michael P., ed. *The Making of the American Landscape.* Boston: Unwin Hyman, 1990.

Cox, Thomas R., ed. *This Well-Wooded Land: Americans and Their Forests from Colonial Times to the Present.* Lincoln: University of Nebraska Press, 1985.

Cronon, William. *Changes in the Land: Indians, Colonists, and the Ecology of New England.* New York: Hill and Wang, 1983.

Davis, Kenneth P. *Forest Management.* New York: McGraw-Hill, 1966.

Dawson, T. E. "Hydraulic Lift and Water Use by Plants: Implications for Water Balance, Performance, and Plant-Plant Interactions." *Oecologia* 95 (1993): 565–74.

Dick, Louis, ed. "A History of the Confederated Tribes of the Umatilla, Compiled from Tribal Elders." Unpublished manuscript on file in the Umatilla National Forest Supervisor's Office, Pendleton Oregon, undated, compiled in 1978 and 1979.

Drury, Clifford, ed. *The Diaries and Letters of Henry H. Spalding and Asa Bowen Smith Relating to the Nez Perce Mission 1838–1842.* Glendale, Calif.: A. H. Clark Co., 1958.

———. *First White Women over the Rockies: Diaries, Letters, and Biographical Sketches of the Six Women of the Oregon Mission Who Made the Overland Journey in 1836 and 1838.* 2 vols. Glendale, Calif.: A. H. Clark Co., 1963.

———. *Henry Harmon Spalding.* Caldwell, Idaho: Caxton Printers, 1936.

Edward of Norwich, the Second Duke of York. *The Master of Game,* edited by W. A. and F. Baille-Grohman, with an introduction by Theodore Roosevelt. London [1407], 1909.

Egerton, Frank N., ed. *History of American Ecology.* Salem, New Hampshire: Ayer, 1984.

Evans, John W., ed. *Powerful Rockey: The Blue Mountains and the Oregon Trail, 1811–1883*. La Grande: Eastern Oregon State College, 1990.

Everett, R., P. Hessburg, J. Lehmkuhl, M. Jensen, and P. Bourgeron. "Old Forests in Dynamic Landscapes, Dry-site Forests of Eastern Oregon and Washington. *Journal of Forestry,* January 1994, 22–25.

Farnham, Thomas J. *Travels in the Great Western Prairies, the Anahuac and Rocky Mountains, and in the Oregon Territory.* In *Early Western Travels 1748–1846,* edited by Reuben Thwaites. Cleveland, 1906.

Flader, Susan. *Thinking Like a Mountain: Aldo Leopold and the Evolution of an Ecological Attitude Toward Deer, Wolves, and Forests.* Columbia: University of Missouri Press, 1974.

Foucault, Michel. *Power/Knowledge: Selected Interviews and Other Writings, 1972–1977,* edited and translated by Colin Gordon. New York: Pantheon, 1980.

Fremont, John Charles. *Report of the Exploring Expedition to the Rocky Mountains in the Year 1842, and to Oregon and North California in the Years 1843–44.* Washington, D.C., 1845.

Gleason, Herbert. "The Individualistic Concept of the Plant Association." *Bulletin of the Torrey Botanical Club* 53 (1926): 7–26; reprinted in *Readings in Ecology,* edited by Edward J. Kormondy. Englewood Cliffs, N.J.: Prentice-Hall, 1965.

Glenn, John G. "Journal, 1852." In *Powerful Rockey: The Blue Mountains and the Oregon Trail,* edited by John W. Evans. La Grande: Eastern Oregon State College, 1990.

Graham, Russell T. "Can Silviculture Replace the Role of Fire?" *Natural Resource News,* March 1994, 12–13.

Graves, Henry. *Practical Forestry in the Adirondacks.* New York, 1899.

Graumlich, Lisa. "Long-term Records of Temperature and Precipitation in the Pacific Northwest Derived from Tree Rings." Ph.D. dissertation, University of Washington, College of Forest Resources, Seattle, 1985.

Grumbine, R. Edward. *Ghost Bears: Exploring the Biodiversity Crisis.* Washington, D.C.: Island Press, 1992.

———. "What Is Ecosystem Management?" *Conservation Biology* 8 (1994): 27–38.

———. "Wildness, Wise Use, and Sustainability." *Environmental Ethics* 16 (1994): 227–50.

Guthrie, R. D. "The Extinct Wapati of Alaska and Yukon Territory." *Canadian Journal of Zoology* 44 (1966): 47–57.

Hansen, Henry P. "A Pollen Study of a Subalpine Bog in the Blue Mountains of Northeastern Oregon." *Ecology* 24 (1943): 70–78.

Harden, Absalom. "Journal." In *Powerful Rockey: The Blue Mountains and the Oregon Trail,* edited by John W. Evans. La Grande: Eastern Oregon State College, 1990.

Hastings, Loren. "Diary of Loren B. Hastings, a Pioneer of 1847." In *Powerful Rockey: The Blue Mountains and the Oregon Trail,* edited by John W. Evans. La Grande: Eastern Oregon State College, 1990.

Hays, Samuel P. *Conservation and the Gospel of Efficiency: The Progressive Conservation Movement, 1890–1920.* Cambridge: Harvard University Press, 1959.

Hess, Karl, Jr. *Visions Upon the Land: Man and Nature on the Western Range.* Washington, D.C.: Island Press, 1992.

Hulbert, Archer B., and Dorothy P. Hulbert. *Marcus Whitman, Crusader: Part Three, 1843 to 1847.* Denver, 1941.

Hulbert, Archer. *Where Rolls the Oregon.* New York, 1933.

Hunt, Wilson Price. "Journal." In *The Discovery of the Oregon Trail: Robert Stuart's Narrative of His Journey,* edited by Philip A. Rollins. New York, 1935.

Hyde, Anne Farrar. *An American Vision: Far Western Landscape and National Culture, 1820–1920.* New York: New York University Press, 1990.

Irving, Washington. *The Adventures of Captain Bonneville, U.S.A., in the Rocky Mountains and the Far West; Digested from His Journal, and Illustrated from Various Other Sources.* New York, 1843.

Johnson, Judy. "Wildlife and Prescribed Fire—Impact and Improvement for Wildlife." Typescript, 1994, National Audubon Society, 209 N. Clinton, Walla Walla, WA 99362.

Josephy, Alvin M., Jr. *The Nez Perce Indians and the Opening of the North West.* New Haven: Yale University Press, 1965.

Judson, Phoebe Goodell. *A Pioneer's Search for an Ideal Home.* Lincoln: University of Nebraska Press, 1984.

Karr, James R. "Biological Integrity and the Goal of Environmental Legislation: Lessons for Conservation Biology." *Conservation Biology* 4 (1990): 244–50.

———. "Measuring Biological Integrity: Lessons from Streams." In *Ecological Integrity and the Management of Ecosystems,* edited by Stephen Woodley, James Kay, and George Francis. Delray Beach, Fla.: St. Lucie Press, 1993.

Kerns, John. "Journal of Crossing the Plains to Oregon." In *Powerful Rockey: The Blue Mountains and the Oregon Trail,* edited by John W. Evans. La Grande: Eastern Oregon State College, 1990.

Ketcham, Rebecca. "From Ithaca to Clatsop Plains: Miss Ketcham's Journals of Travel." In *Powerful Rockey,* edited by John Evans. La Grande, 1990.

Kimerling, A. Jon, and Philip L. Jackson, eds. *Atlas of the Pacific Northwest.* 7th edition. Corvallis: Oregon State University Press, 1985.

Kittredge, William. *Owning It All: Essays.* St. Paul: Graywolf Press, 1987.

Kormondy, Edward J., ed. *Readings in Ecology.* Englewood Cliffs: Prentice-Hall, 1965.

Küchler, A. W. "Manual to Accompany the Map, Potential Natural Vegetation of the Conterminous United States." *American Geographical Society Special Publication* 36 (1964).

Landsburg, J. D. "Response of Ponderosa Pine Forests in Central Oregon to Prescribed Underburning." Ph.D. dissertation, Oregon State University, Corvallis, 1992.

Langston, Nancy. "The General Riot of the Natural Forest: Landscape Change in the Blue Mountains." Ph.D. dissertation, University of Washington, 1994. University Microfilms, Ann Arbor.

——. "How Should We Interpret Historic Ranges of Variability in Restoring Public Lands?" Submitted to *Conservation Biology.*

Leopold, Aldo. *A Sand Country Almanac.* New York: Oxford University Press, 1968.

Lewis, Meriwether. *Original Journals of the Lewis and Clark Expedition, 1804–1806,* edited by Reuben Gold Thwaites. New York, 1959.

Limerick, Patricia Nelson. *The Legacy of Conquest: The Unbroken Past of the American West.* New York: W. W. Norton, 1987.

Loehr, R. *Forests for the Future.* St. Paul: Minnesota Historical Society, 1952.

Loughary, Harriet A. "Travels and Incidents." In *Covered Wagon Women: Diaries and Letters from the Western Trails, 1840–1890,* vol. 8, edited by Kenneth L. Holmes. Glendale, Calif.: A. H. Clark Co., 1986.

Mack, Richard. "Invaders at Home on the Range." *Natural History* (February 1984): 40–46.

Maser, Chris. *The Redesigned Forest.* San Pedro, Calif.: R. and E. Miles, 1988.

Marsh, George Perkins. *Man and Nature* [1864], edited by David Lowenthal. Cambridge, Mass., 1965.

Maruoka, Kathleen Ryoko. "Fire History of *Pseudotsuga menziesii* and *Abies grandis* Stands in the Blue Mountains of Oregon and Washington." Master's thesis, University of Washington, Seattle, 1994.

Mathews, Daniel. *Cascade-Olympic Natural History.* Portland, Oregon: Raven Editions in conjunction with the Audubon Society, 1988.

May, Robert M. "An Overview: Real and Apparent Patterns in Community Structure." In *Ecological Communities: Conceptual Issues and the Evidence,* edited by Donald R. Strong, Jr., Daniel Simberloff, Lawrence G. Abele, and Anne Thistle. Princeton: Princeton University Press, 1982.

McIntosh, Robert P. *The Background of Ecology: Concept and Theory.* Cambridge and New York: Cambridge University Press, 1985.

McIver, J. D., A. R. Moldenke, and G. L. Parsons. "Litter Spiders as Bioindicators of Recovery after Clearcutting in a Western Coniferous Forest." *Northwest Environmental Journal* 6 (1990): 409.

Meinig, D. W. *The Great Columbia Plain: A Historical Geography, 1805–1910.* Seattle: University of Washington Press, 1968.

Miller, Christopher L. *Prophetic Worlds: Indians and Whites of the Columbia Plateau.* New Brunswick, N.J.: Rutgers University Press, 1985.

Moldenke, A. R. "Denizens of the Soil: Small, but Critical." *Natural Resource News,* August 1993.

Moldenke, A. R. and J. D. Lattin. "Dispersal Charcteristics of Old-growth Soil Arthropods: The Potential for Loss of Diversity and Biological Function." *Northwest Environmental Journal* (1990): 408–9.

Munford, J. Kenneth. "Historical Background: Discovery and Early Settlement." In *Atlas of the Pacific Northwest,* edited by A. Jon Kimerling and Philip L. Jackson. Corvallis: Oregon State University Press, 1985.

Naiman, Robert J., J. M. Melillo, and J. E. Hobbie. "Ecosystem Alteration of Boreal Forest Streams by Beaver (*Castor canadensis*)." *Ecology* 67 (1986): 1254–69.

Naiman, Robert J., Carol A. Johnston, and James Kelley. "Alteration of North American Streams by Beaver." *BioScience* 38 (1988): 753–61.

Nash, Roderick. *Wilderness and the American Mind.* New Haven: Yale University Press, 1977.

Nesmith, James. "Diary of the Emigration of 1843." In *Powerful Rockey: The Blue Mountains and the Oregon Trail,* edited by John W. Evans. La Grande: Eastern Oregon State College, 1990.

Newby, W. T. "William T. Newby's Diary of the Emigration of 1843." In *Powerful Rockey,* edited by John W. Evans. La Grande, 1990.

Odell, W. H. "Original Field Notes, September 16 1866, Wallowa County Clerk's Office, Enterprise Oregon." Quoted in Grace Bartlett, *The Wallowa Country, 1867–1877.* Fairfield, Wash.: Ye Galleon Press, 1984.

Ogden, Peter Skene. *Snake Country Journals, 1826–1827,* edited by K. G. Davies and A. M. Johnson. London: Hudson's Bay Record Society, 1961.

Olson, Sherry H. *The Depletion Myth: A History of Railroad Use of Timber.* Cambridge: Harvard University Press, 1971.

Parker, A. J. 1990. "Diary of Armeda Jane Parker." In *Powerful Rockey: The Blue Mountains and the Oregon Trail,* edited by John W. Evans. La Grande: Eastern Oregon State College, 1990.

Parry, Thomas B., Henry J. Vaux, and Nicholas Dennis. "Changing Conceptions of Sustained-yield Policy on the National Forests." *Journal of Forestry* (March 1983): 150–54.

Perry, David. "Landscape Pattern and Forest Pests." *Northwest Environmental Journal* 4 (1988): 213–28.

Pickett, S. T. A., and P. S. White. *The Ecology of Natural Disturbance and Patch Dynamics.* Orlando, Fla.: Academic Press, 1985.

Pimm, Stuart. "The Complexity and Stability of Ecosystems." *Nature* 307 (1984): 321–26.

——. *The Balance of Nature? Ecological Issues in the Conservation of Species and Communities.* Chicago: University of Chicago Press, 1991.

Pinchot, Gifford. *Breaking New Ground.* New York: Harcourt, Brace, 1947.

Pollan, Michael. *Second Nature: A Gardener's Education.* New York: Dell, 1991.

Pryne, Eric. "Summer Forest Fires Spark Debate over Timber Policy." *Seattle Times,* September 9, 1994.

——. "Unease Over Logging to Control Fire." *Seattle Times,* September 10, 1994.

Pyne, Stephen. *Fire in America: A Cultural History of Wildland and Rural Fire.* Princeton: Princeton University Press, 1982.

Rakestraw, Lawrence. *A History of Forest Conservation in the Pacific Northwest, 1891–1913.* New York: Arno Press, 1979.

Ricklefs, Robert E. *Ecology.* 2d edition. New York: Chiron Press, 1979.

Robbins, William G. *American Forestry: A History of National, State, and Private Cooperation.* Lincoln: University of Nebraska Press, 1985.

——. "Lumber Production and Community Stability: A View from the Pacific Northwest." *Journal of Forest History* (1987): 187–96.

Ross, Alexander. *The Fur Hunters of the Far West,* edited by Kenneth Spaulding. Norman: University of Oklahoma Press, 1956.

Rowley, William D. *U.S. Forest Service Grazing and Rangelands: A History.* College Station: Texas A & M University Press, 1985.

Rusling, James F. *Across America: Or, the Great West and the Pacific Coast.* New York, 1874.

Sackett, Stephen S., and Sally M. Haase. "Soil and Cambium Temperatures Associated with Prescribed Burning." *Natural Resource News,* March 1994.

Sagoff, M. "Has Nature a Good of Its Own?" In *Ecosystem Health: New Goals for Environmental Management,* edited by Robert Costanza, Bryan G. Norton, and Benjamin D. Haskell. Washington, D.C.: Island Press, 1992.

Schiff, Ashley L. *Fire and Water: Scientific Heresy in the Forest Service.* Cambridge: Harvard University Press, 1962.

Schlich, Sir William. *Manual of Forestry.* 4th edition. London, 1910.

Schowalter, Timothy. "Forest Pest Management: A Synopsis." *Northwest Environmental Journal* 4 (1988): 313–18.

———. "Invertebrate Diversity in Old-growth versus Regenerating Forest Canopies." *Northwest Environmental Journal* 6 (1990): 403–404.

Schwantes, Carlos. *The Pacific Northwest: An Interpretive History.* Lincoln: University of Nebraska Press, 1989.

Simpson, George. "Fur Trade and Empire." In *George Simpson's Journal,* edited by Frederick Merk. Cambridge: Harvard University Press, 1931.

Snyder, Gary. *The Practice of the Wild: Essays.* San Francisco: North Point Press, 1990.

Southworth, Jack. "Ranching and Riparians." Talk given in May 1993 at the Blue Mountains Natural Resources Institute, text reprinted in *Natural Resource News,* August 1993, 12–13.

Steen, Harold K. *The U.S. Forest Service: A History.* Seattle: University of Washington Press, 1976.

Stegner, Wallace. *The American West as Living Space.* Ann Arbor: University of Michigan Press, 1987.

Stilgoe, John R. *Common Landscape of America, 1580–1845.* New Haven: Yale University Press, 1982.

Stoszek, Karl J. "Forests under Stress and Insect Outbreaks." *Northwest Environmental Journal* 4 (1988): 247–61.

Strong, Donald R., Jr., Daniel Simberloff, Lawrence G. Abele, and Anne Thistle, eds. *Ecological Communities: Conceptual Issues and the Evidence.* Princeton: Princeton University Press, 1982.

Stuart, Robert. *On the Oregon Trail: Robert Stuart's Journey of Discovery,* edited by Kenneth Spaulding. Norman: University of Oklahoma Press, 1953.

Sutton, Sarah. "A Travel 1854." In *Powerful Rockey: The Blue Mountains and the Oregon Trail,* edited by John W. Evans. La Grande: Eastern Oregon State College, 1990.

Tansley, Arthur G. "The Use and Abuse of Vegetational Concepts and Terms." *Ecology* 16 (1935): 284–307.

Thoreau, Henry David. "Natural History of Massachusetts" and "Succession of Forest Trees." In *Selected Works,* edited by Walter Harding. Boston: Houghton Mifflin, 1975.

Tiedemann, Arthur R., and H. W. Berndt. "Vegetation and Soils of a 30-year Deer and Elk Exclosure in Central Washington." *Northwest Science* 46 (1972): 59–66.

Tiedemann, Arthur R., and James Klemmedson. "Prescribed Burning and Productivity: A Nutrient Management Perspective." *Natural Resource News,* March 1994.

Tobey, R. *Saving the Prairies: The Life Cycle of the Founding School of American Plant Ecology, 1895–1955.* Berkeley: University of California Press, 1981.

Torgersen, Torolf. "The Forest Immune System—Its Role in Insect Pest Regulation." *Natural Resource News,* August 1993, 6–7.

Townsend, John Kirk. *Narrative of a Journey across the Rocky Mountains to the Columbia River* [1839]. Lincoln: University of Nebraska Press, 1978.

Unruh, John David, Jr. *The Plains Across: The Overland Emigrants and the Trans-Mississippi West, 1840–1860.* Urbana: University of Illinois Press, 1982.

Vancouver, George. *A Voyage of Discovery to the North Pacific Ocean and round the World, 1791–1795,* edited by W. Kaye Lamb. London: Hakluyt Society, 1984.

Veblen, Thomas T., and Diane C. Lorenz. *The Colorado Front Range: A Century of Ecological Change.* Salt Lake City: University of Utah Press, 1991.

Vogl, R. J. "The ecological factors that promote perturbation-dependent ecosystems." In *The Recovery Process in Damaged Ecosystems,* edited by John Cairns, Jr. Ann Arbor: Ann Arbor Science Publishers, 1980.

Walstad, John D., Steven R. Radosevich, and David V. Sandberg, eds. *Natural and Prescribed Fire in Pacific Northwest Forests.* Corvallis: Oregon State University Press, 1990.

Warming, Eugenius. *Oecology of Plants: An Introduction to the Study of Plant Communities.* Translated by Percey Groom and Isaac Balfour. London: Oxford University Press, 1909.

White, Richard. *Land Use, Environment, and Social Change: The Shaping of Island County, Washington.* Seattle: University of Washington Press, 1980.

———. *The Roots of Dependency: Subsistence, Environment, and Social Change among the Choctaws, Pawnees, and Navajos.* Lincoln: University of Nebraska Press, 1983.

———. *"It's Your Misfortune and None of My Own": A History of the American West.* Norman: University of Oklahoma Press, 1991.

Whitman, Narcissa. "Diary and Letter." In *First White Women over the Rockies: Diaries, Letters, and Biographical Sketches of the Six Women of the Oregon Mission Who Made the Overland Journey in 1836 and 1838,* edited by Clifford Drury. 2 vols. Glendale, Calif.: A. H. Clark Co., 1963.

Whittaker, R. H. "A Consideration of Climax Theory: The Climax as a Population and Pattern." *Ecological Monographs* 23 (1953): 41–78.

Wickman, Boyd. "Old-growth Forests and History of Insect Outbreaks." *Northwest Environmental Journal* 6 (1990): 401–3.

Wilkinson, Charles F. *Crossing the Next Meridian: Land, Water, and the Future of the West.* Washington, D.C.: Island Press, 1992.

Williams, Michael. *Americans and Their Forests: A Historical Geography.* Cambridge: Cambridge University Press, 1989.

Windsor, D. M. "Climate and Moisture Variability in a Tropical Forest: Long-term Records from Barro Colorado Island, Panama." *Smithsonian Contribution to the Earth Sciences* 29-1-146 (1990).

Woodley, Stephen, James Kay, and George Francis, eds. *Ecological Integrity and the Management of Ecosystems.* Proceedings of a conference held in April 1991 at the University of Waterloo, Ontario. Delray Beach, Fla.: St. Lucie Press, 1993.

Worster, Donald. *Nature's Economy: The Roots of Ecology.* San Francisco: Sierra Club Books, 1977.

Yoon, Carol Kaesuk. "Plants Share Precious Water with Neighbors." *New York Times,* October 26, 1993.

Index